MW01296821

Praise for The Traditional Mass

"Motivated by profound respect for and love of the *usus antiquior* of the Roman rite, and drawing on an impressive range of valuable sources, Michael Fiedrowicz's appreciation of the history, form, and theology of the older form of the Mass as it has developed in tradition underlines the value of its more widespread celebration in our day. Readers will find here much with which to grow in their appreciation of Pope Benedict XVI's insistence that, in respect of the older liturgy: 'What earlier generations held as sacred, remains sacred and great for us too, and it cannot be all of a sudden entirely forbidden or even considered harmful. It behooves all of us to preserve the riches which have developed in the Church's faith and prayer, and to give them their proper place' (July 7, 2007). The publication of this English translation, which deserves careful study, marks another important step towards achieving that goal."
—**DOM ALCUIN REID**, Founding Prior, Monastère Saint-Benoît

"This historically rigorous and theologically informed book is indispensable for anyone who cares about Pope Benedict XVI's liturgical vision. I am delighted that this outstanding introduction to the traditional form of the Roman Mass is now available to Anglophone readers."
—**FR. UWE MICHAEL LANG**, Cong. Orat., St. Mary's University

"Michael Fiedrowicz here accomplishes something well-nigh miraculous: a comprehensive introduction to the elaborate history, complex structure, and sublime theology of the traditional Latin Mass—supported by abundant scholarship—all within the scope of a single highly readable volume. His treatment of organic development, Latin, Gregorian chant, the orations, the Offertory, the Roman Canon, eastward orientation, and the benefits of fixed ritual are among the best I have ever seen. His respectful but incisive critique of defects in last century's liturgical reform runs like a countermelody against the principal theme. Quite simply, this is the best one-volume work on the classical Roman Mass published since the Second Vatican Council."
—**PETER A. KWASNIEWSKI**, author of *Noble Beauty, Transcendent Holiness*

"This multifaceted and comprehensive study of the traditional Roman rite of the Mass is meticulously footnoted and features an extensive, up-to-date bibliography. Each of its three major parts could stand on its own, which makes it all the more valuable as a reference work. I am pleased that Angelico Press has made available in English translation Prof. Fiedrowicz's substantive achievement — the fruit of careful research, orthodox faith, and reverence for the riches handed on in tradition."

—**FR. THOMAS KOCIK**, Society for Catholic Liturgy, contributor to the *New Liturgical Movement*

"The Roman Church has been rendered a great service with the publication of Prof. Michael Fiedrowicz's *The Traditional Mass*. This monumental and much needed work presents the history, form, and theology of the Roman Mass in a manner both comprehensive and yet succinct enough to be accessible to every Catholic, scholar or neophyte! Whereas previous tomes on the Roman Liturgy have often been too technical to appeal to the average Catholic, Fiedrowicz's style — simple, informative, yet profound — grips and guides the reader from the outset. A further advantage of his work is that, in contrast to the traditional Roman Mass, he educates the reader about the liturgical issues of the *Novus Ordo Missae*, masterfully integrating these significant lessons in a subtle, unpolemical fashion. I heartily recommend this masterpiece to all Catholics who desire to better understand and appreciate the traditional Roman Mass, and thereby increase their devotion to this venerable rite of the Holy Sacrifice."

—**LOUIS J. TOFARI**, Romanitas Press

The Traditional Mass

THE TRADITIONAL
MASS

*History, Form, & Theology
of the Classical Roman Rite*

MICHAEL FIEDROWICZ

Translated by Rose Pfeifer

 Angelico Press

It is a fact without doubt that the Roman Missal represents in its entirety the loftiest and most important work in ecclesiastical literature, being that which shows forth with the greatest fidelity the life-history of the Church, that sacred poem in the making of which *ha posto mano e cielo e terra.*[1]

---

1   I. Schuster, *The Sacramentary (Liber Sacramentorum). Historical and Liturgical Notes on the Roman Missal*, trans. by A. Levelis-Marke (London: Burns & Oates, 1924), vol. I, part 1, v. Quotation: Dante, *Paradiso* xxv, 2 ("heaven and earth have set their hand" [trans. Longfellow]).

CONTENTS

Contents

INTRODUCTION

WITH THE APOSTOLIC LETTER *SUMMORUM PONTIFI-cum* of July 7, 2007, Pope Benedict XVI made the richness of the traditional Mass newly accessible to the entire Church. It states: "The Roman Missal promulgated by St Pius V and reissued by Bl. John XXIII . . . must be given due honor for its venerable and ancient usage" (*ob venerabilem et antiquum eius usum debito gaudeat honore*).[2]

In view of the continually growing interest in the traditional form of the Roman rite of Mass, an introduction to its history, form, and theology is more than ever desirable, particularly given the ever increasing open-mindedness toward the inherited liturgy in the younger generation of priests, seminarians, and laity, who to date have been introduced only to the modernized form. In contrast to conventional explanations of the Mass, which explicate the steps in the celebration of the Holy Eucharist, the present work will treat many further aspects requisite for a deeper understanding of the traditional rite: the historical development of the Ordinary of the Mass, the liturgical year, sacred language, orientation of celebration, rituality, and sacrality, as well as theological principles (e.g., prayers, readings, Offertory, and Canon; *lex orandi, lex credendi*). Footnotes quote extensively from worthwhile authors and works that go beyond the scope of this book; such materials have been rare or difficult to access until recently.

The following portrayal of the traditional Roman Mass is bound to the basic hermeneutical principles of St Augustine. According to him, one must not "look to discover their [i.e., the Scriptures'] meaning from those who, for whatever compelling reason, have declared bitter war on their authors and publishers." The bishop of Hippo demanded instead a

---

2 Benedict XVI, Apostolic Letter *Summorum Pontificum*, July 7, 2007, art. 1. Cf. Pontificial Commission *Ecclesia Dei*, Instruction *Universae Ecclesiae*, May 13, 2011, on the Application of the Apostolic Letter *Summorum Pontificum* of His Holiness Pope Benedict XVI (April 30, 2011), no. 6: "On account of its venerable and ancient use, the *forma extraordinaria* is to be maintained with appropriate honor" (*Propter venerabilem et antiquum usum forma extraordinaria debito honore est servanda*).

hermeneutic of agreement: an adequate understanding of a challenging work requires fundamental readiness to study the subject with love.[3] This principle applies equally to Holy Scripture and to the traditional liturgy of the Church.

Since Pope Benedict XVI intended with his Apostolic Letter *Summorum Pontificum* to "[offer] to all the faithful the Roman liturgy...as a precious treasure to be preserved,"[4] the following presentation wishes to contribute to this goal by revealing the preciousness and beauty of the traditional liturgy of the Church, so as to bring about a new appreciation and "the appropriate honor."

---

3   Augustine, *De utilitate credendi* 13 (FC 9, 115–19 / Augustine, *On Christian Belief*, trans. by M. O'Connell, *The Works of St Augustine* I/8 [Hyde Park, NY: New City Press, 2005], 126).

4   Pontifical Commission *Ecclesia Dei*, Instruction *Universae Ecclesiae*, no. 8a: "*Ipsae Litterae intendunt: a) Liturgiam Romanam in Antiquiori Usu, prout pretiosum thesaurum servandum, omnibus largire (recte: largiri) fidelibus.*"

PART I

History

1

Phases of Development

THE BEGINNINGS
(SECOND AND THIRD CENTURIES)

On the eve of the Passion, the Apostles received from the Lord the directive and authority to celebrate the sacrifice of the New Covenant. In accordance with the word of Christ, "Do *this* in memory of me," the Apostles were to repeat that which was done by Christ Himself in the cenacle. At the same time, however, the continuation of that duty required that the plain repetition of the gestures and words of Christ be further developed, and that the Eucharistic "remembrance" be enclosed in a wreath of prayers, hymns, and rites, in order to keep pure the inner nucleus established by Christ, while at the same time unfurling, as much as possible, the double meaning of the Greek word λειτουργία (*leiturgia*), that is, "a work of God for mankind" and "a work of mankind for God."

Although the celebration of the Mass exhibited a few peculiarities in the various groups of rites of the fourth century, its possession of a principally structural unity makes it clear that the Eucharist received its basic uniform structure in the circle of the Apostles, even before they dispersed throughout the entire world to proclaim the Gospel.[1] That few of the liturgies (even the far distant Eastern rite) diverged is demonstrated by an example of the mid-second century, when, in 154, Pope Anicetus invited Bishop Polycarp of Smyrna, who was visiting Rome, to celebrate the Eucharist; without this unity, a larger deviation in ritual execution would have been expected.[2] The unity of the liturgy of the first three centuries was one of type, not of

---

1 Cf. B. Capelle, "Précis d'histoire de la Messe": idem, *Travaux liturgiques de doctrine et d'histoire*. II: Histoire. La Messe (Louvain: Centre Liturgique, Abbaye du Mont César, 1962), 9–30, 12f.

2 Eusebius, *Historia ecclesiastica* 5,24,17 (SCh 41, 71 / Eusebius Pamphili, *Ecclesiastical History*. Books 1–5, trans. by R. J. Deferrari, *The Fathers of the Church* 19 [New York: Fathers of the Church, Inc., 1953], 338).

details. The latter were thoroughly diverse and varying. As many details gradually developed into customs and were preserved as traditions, while other parts of the common type in the individual churches experienced extensions or condensations, the differing groups of rites originated, as they are recognized from the beginning of the fourth century.[3]

From the earliest time, it became particularly significant for further development that the instruction "Do this" was not taken as referring to the Last Supper in its entirety, originally enclosed in a Jewish Passover meal, in such a way that the meal would be regarded as the basic structure of the Eucharist.[4] In the New Testament, the expression "the Lord's Supper" (*Dominicam coenam*; in German, *Herrenmahl*) appears only once, in 1 Corinthians 11:20. In the sixteenth century, it was Luther who first introduced a different way of speaking of the Lord's Supper (*Abendmahl*, the Lord's Supper — literally "evening meal"[5]). This shift in terminology signaled a break with the tradition of one and a half millennia. The early Christian community did not repeat Christ's Last Supper as such, but only its intrinsic Eucharistic action, that is, the consecration of bread and wine. In contrast to the Last Supper, which followed the sequence of the rite of the Jewish Passover meal — the breaking and distribution of the bread before the main meal, followed by the passing of the blessed cup or chalice (cf. Lk 22:20: "After he had supped") — only the words of consecration over the bread and wine were included, combined in a unified action and inserted into a prayer of thanksgiving (*eucharistia*), in which the remembrance (*anamnesis*) of the work of Redemption immediately follows the double consecration, as is suggested in the words of the Apostle Paul, "For as

---

3 Cf. J. A. Jungmann, *Missarum sollemnia* I (Freiburg i. Br.: Verlag Herder, ⁵1962), 42; in English, *The Mass of the Roman Rite: Its Origins and Development* [trans. by F. A. Brunner] (New York, NY: Benziger, 1951), vol. I, 32; A. Fortescue, *The Mass. A Study of the Roman Liturgy* (London: Longmans & Green, ²1937), 51–53; F. Probst, *Liturgie des 4. Jh. und deren Reform* (Münster: Aschendorff Verlag, 1893), 319–54; A. Baumstark, *Vom geschichtlichen Werden der Liturgie* [EcOra 10] (Freiburg i. Br.: Verlag Herder, 1923), 29–36 (i.e., ch. 5: "multiplicity and uniformity").

4 Cf. J. Ratzinger, "Form and Content in the Eucharistic Celebration," idem, *The Feast of Faith. Approaches to a Theology of the Liturgy*, trans. by G. Harrison (San Francisco: Ignatius Press, 1986), 33–60 (= idem, *Theology of the Liturgy* [Collected Works 11] [San Francisco: Ignatius Press, 2014], 299–318).

5 Cf. J. A. Jungmann, "'Abendmahl' als Name der Eucharistie," ZKTh 93 (1971): 91–94.

often as you shall eat this bread, and drink the chalice, you shall show the death of the Lord" (cf. 1 Cor 11:26). Broken off from the Jewish Passover meal, the celebration could be performed not only once during the year, but weekly. The "Lord's Day" (cf. Rev 1:10) formed the new context of the Eucharist from that time onward. The Prayer of Thanksgiving (*eucharistia*), spoken over the gifts, had already become an identifier of the liturgy of the Mass itself by the beginning of the second century.[6]

As this Prayer of Thanksgiving had originally been bound with a preceding nourishing meal, as in the Pauline portrayal (1 Cor 11:17–34), certain abuses of the Christian celebration of *agape* would soon necessitate a division between the nourishing meal and the Eucharist (cf. 1 Cor 11:22). The first evidence of this new form is an exchange of letters from the second century (ca. 111/113) between the Roman governor Pliny and the Emperor Trajan, in which a morning celebration of the Eucharist for the Province of Bithynia in Asia Minor is indicated.[7]

Half a century later, the apologist Justin offered the first detailed account, describing the practice of weekly Sunday Eucharistic celebrations in the mid-second century in Rome.[8] The most important components of these Eucharistic celebrations are a scriptural service (consisting of readings from the Old and New Testaments, a sermon, and prayers of intercession) and a subsequent Eucharistic prayer of blessing over the bread and wine mixed with water, of which those present partake. The account documents how the Eucharistic celebration, removed from a meal of nourishment, had in the meantime combined itself with a Christian scriptural service, after the

---

6 Cf. Ignatius of Antioch, *Epistula ad Ephesios* 31,1; *Ep. ad Philadelphios* 4; *Ep. ad Smyrnaeos* 7,1; 8,1 (Fischer 152.196.208.210 / *The Epistles of St Clement of Rome and St Ignatius of Antioch*, trans. by J. A. Kleist, *Ancient Christian Writers* 1 [Westminster, MD: The Newman Press / London: Longmans Green, 1961], 65.86.92f.). Cf. Jungmann, *Missarum sollemnia* I, 20, 27f.; idem, *The Mass of the Roman Rite* I, 15, 21f.; idem, *The Early Liturgy: To the Time of Gregory the Great*, trans. by F. A. Brunner (Notre Dame, IN: University of Notre Dame Press, 1959), 44–49; idem, "Von der 'Eucharistia' zur 'Messe,'" ZKTh 89 (1967): 29–40.

7 Cf. Jungmann, *Missarum sollemnia* I, 23f.; idem, *The Mass of the Roman Rite* I, 18. Cf. Pliny, *ep.* X 96 and 97.

8 Justin, *1 Apologia* 67,3–8 (SCh 507, 308–12 / St Justin, *The First and Second Apologies*, trans. by L. W. Barnard, *Ancient Christian Writers* 56 [New York / Mahwah, NJ: Paulist Press, 1997], 71f.); for the Eucharistic celebration in the context of a baptismal liturgy cf. *1 Apologia* 65, 1–5 (SCh 507, 302–4 / *The First and Second Apologies*, 70). Cf. Jungmann, *The Early Liturgy*, 40–44.

final separation from the Synagogue, where the first Christians initially had still taken part in the Jewish readings and prayers. The Eucharistic celebration, as described by Justin, already reveals the essential elements that will be preserved in the large groups of liturgies of the following centuries, including the Roman rite of Mass. At the same time the Apologist bears witness, with all desirable clarity, to the belief in the Real Presence, when he emphasizes:

> For we do not receive these things as common bread nor common drink; but in like manner as Jesus Christ our Savior having been incarnate by God's *logos* took both flesh and blood for our salvation, so also we have been taught that the food eucharistized through the word of prayer that is from Him, from which our blood and flesh are nourished by transformation, is the flesh and blood of that Jesus who became incarnate.[9]

Difficult to classify is the evidence of the *Apostolic Tradition*,[10] which passes down the complete text of a Eucharistic prayer. Whether this Eucharistic prayer can be considered as representative for the Sunday worship service of the Roman Church at the beginning of the third century is admittedly uncertain. The anaphora is quoted as a sample formulary in connection with an episcopal consecration, not as the Eucharistic prayer of a Sunday celebration of the Eucharist. The text of the prayer possesses the following structure: In the first place, God's work of Redemption is proclaimed and praised in Jesus Christ, who as the *Logos* effected creation and at the same time, as man, effected Redemption. The thanksgiving for the work of redemption merges organically into the account of the Last

---

9 Justin, *1 Apologia* 66,2 (SCh 502, 306 / *The First and Second Apologies*, 70).

10 *Traditio Apostolica* 4 (FC 1, 220–26 / Ἀποστολικὴ παράδοσις. *The Treatise on the Apostolic Tradition of St Hippolytos of Rome, Bishop and Martyr*, eds. G. Dix / H. Chadwick [London: SPCK, ²1968], 6–9); cf. J.M. Hanssens, *La liturgie d'Hippolyte. Ses documents, son titulaire, ses origines et son charactère* [Orientalia Christiana analecta 155] (Rome: Pontificium Institutum Orientalium Studiorum, 1965); H.-L. Barth, *Die Mär vom antiken Kanon des Hippolytos. Untersuchungen zur Liturgiereform* (Cologne: Una Voce, 1999), 169–71; M. Smyth, "L'anaphore de la prétendue 'Tradition Apostolique' et la prière eucharistique romaine," RevSR 81 (2007): 95–118; Jungmann, *The Early Liturgy*, 64–73.

Supper's institution with the consecration of bread and wine. The second section ties in with Christ's order to repeat this and gratefully contemplates what takes place in the sacred action. Directly after the anamnesis follows an expression of offering: "*Memores igitur mortis et resurrectionis eius offerimus tibi panem et calicem.*" In both concepts (*memores . . . offerimus*) is manifested the theological understanding of the Eucharist as commemoration and offering, or rather, sacrifice. Thus the notion of sacrifice is found to be clearly expressed already in the oldest tradition. The differences with the later Roman Canon, as it is attested to since the end of the fourth century, are indeed so meaningful that the Eucharistic prayer of the *Traditio Apostolica* cannot be seen as the forerunner of the Canon, which was later considered to be *the* Eucharistic prayer of the Church of Rome.[11]

The template of a model text in the *Apostolic Tradition* is an important indication of an initial codifying, or rather, textualization of the prayer. Justin's aforementioned practice, of freely formulating the Eucharistic prayer,[12] gradually yielded to the use of strict formulae or texts, which initially could be passed down verbatim, by oral tradition, but were also later recorded for reuse.[13] Especially successful texts, or those from well-respected figures, were thus preserved and made repeatable. The decline of free formulations of liturgical prayers was an unambiguous symbol that those early times were gradually ending, of which it is said, "The words of the Roman liturgy, besides that they are the expression of the vows of the Church, which is holy, are also the words of saints, of men capable of

---

11   According to Smyth, "L'anaphore de la prétendue 'Tradition Apostolique,'" the anaphora originated in western Syria and received its final redaction in the first half of the fourth century. Despite a Latin translation of the *Traditio Apostolica* in the fifth century, this anaphora had no influence on the Western liturgy.

12   Cf. Justin, *1 Apologia* 67, 5 (SCh 507, 310 / *The First and Second Apologies*, 71); *Didache* 10,7 (FC 1, 126 / *The Didache*, trans. by J. A. Kleist, *Ancient Christian Writers* 6 [New York, NY / Mahwah, NJ: Newman Press, 1997], 71); *Traditio Apostolica* 9 (FC 1, 238 / *Treatise on the Apostolic Tradition*, 19).

13   Cf. R. P. C. Hanson, "The Liberty of the Bishop to Improvise Prayer in the Eucharist," *Vigiliae Christianae* 15 (1961): 173–76; Jungmann, *Missarum sollemnia* I, 39–43, 79f., 478f.; idem, *The Mass of the Roman Rite* I, 30–33, 61f., 373; A. Bouley, *From Freedom to Formula: The Evolution of the Eucharistic Prayer from Oral Improvisation to Written Texts* [Studies in Christian Antiquity 21] (Washington, DC: Catholic University of America Press, 1981).

finishing the hymn begun by angels."[14] The adherence to that which was established and approved, the unity with the metropolitan Church, and finally the defense against heresy, were important motives in the gradual but irreversible replacement of an original freedom of form that was subject only to the criterion of orthodoxy.[15] At the turn of the fourth to the fifth century, the initial North African councils had promoted textual regulation and ecclesiastical approbation of important liturgical prayers. This practice soon became common in other regions as well.

Given that accounts as detailed as those provided by Justin's *Apologia* or the *Traditio Apostolica* are lacking for the third and fourth centuries, the further development of the old Roman liturgy of the Mass cannot be traced with certainty. Attempts at reconstruction on the basis of later sources frequently remain hypothetical.[16]

FURTHER DEVELOPMENTS DURING ANTIQUITY

Under Emperor Constantine (313–337), the bishop of Rome had maintained a permanent residence, as well as his own church, at the Lateran.[17] The bishop's liturgy celebrated here, as well as later in the station churches, differed from the divine service celebrated by the Roman priests in the titular churches of the city. Due to a lack of sources, one cannot obtain a clear picture of the fourth century. Toward the end of the fourth century, however, the Roman Canon with changing Prefaces can be identified. At the beginning of the fifth century, the section of the Canon between the Sanctus and the consecration had already largely received its current form. The basic shape of the celebration of the Mass, as described by Justin, meanwhile has been commonly expanded through three priestly prayers — at the beginning, over the offerings, and after Communion. Chants taken

---

14   H. Kenelm Digby, *Mores Catholici: or, Ages of Faith*, vol. II, book V (New York / Cincinnati / Chicago: Benziger Brothers, 1905), 61.

15   Cf. *Traditio Apostolica* 9 [10] (FC 1, 240f. / *Treatise on the Apostolic Tradition*, 19): "Only let his prayer be correct and right [in doctrine]." Cf. E. Dekkers, "Créativité et orthodoxie dans la *lex orandi*," MD 111 (1972): 20–30.

16   Thus, for example K. Gamber, *Missa Romensis. Beiträge zur frühen römischen Liturgie und zu den Anfängen des Missale Romanum* [SPLi 3] (Regensburg: Verlag Friedrich Pustet, 1970).

17   For the rich interior, cf. P. Batiffol, *La paix constantinienne et le catholicisme* (Paris: Librairie Lecoffre, [4]1929), 352f.

from the psalms have been inserted between the readings. Corresponding to the Communion of the faithful, a presentation of the gifts on the part of the people was developed. Shortly before the end of the fourth century it became common to accompany both processions with a psalm sung by a schola. Soon the clergy's entrance was also framed by the singing of the Introit. Justin's aforementioned prayer of all believers between the sermon and the presentation of the gifts[18] existed at the end of the fifth century as a common prayer of the Church, whose form would have corresponded to the contemporary *orationes sollemnes* of Good Friday. Under Pope Gelasius I (492–496), who is remembered for his liturgical creations, this prayer was replaced with a Kyrie litany based on an oriental model (*Deprecatio Gelasii*), which shortly afterward received a new place, being combined with the oration at the close of the initial part of the Mass. The original alternating prayer changed and shortened at this point to a repeated Kyrie call, since important concerns had already found expression in the intercessions of the Canon. With the Eastern Church as a model, the Sanctus was introduced into the Eucharistic prayer at the beginning of the fifth century. As far as the priest's central prayers and the chants embellishing this *Ordo Missae* were concerned, the liturgy of the Mass was already complete in its basic structure at the turn of the fourth to the fifth century. Since the fourth century, the liturgy had been richly embellished for many reasons: the number of believers increased when the time of persecutions ended, Sunday had become a national day of rest allowing more time to be taken up by the worship service, the building of grand basilicas made possible the expansion of solemn ceremonies, the liturgical chant received special attention, and the liturgical year developed from the new feast days (Christmas, Epiphany) and days commemorating the saints.[19]

While a time of increased hardship came with the Goth and Lombard invasions of Rome during the fifth and sixth centuries, Roman divine

---

18 Cf. Justin, *1 Apologia* 67,5 (SCh 507, 310 / *The First and Second Apologies*, 71).

19 Cf. E. Cattaneo, *Il culto cristiano in Occidente. Note storiche* [BEL.S 13] (Rome: Edizioni Liturgiche, ²1984), 79–96; E. Dassmann, *Kirchengeschichte* II/2 (Stuttgart: Kohlhammer Verlag, 1999), 124–40; J. Quasten, *Music and Worship in Pagan and Christian Antiquity* (Washington, DC: National Association of Pastoral Musicians, 1983); H. Brakmann, "Jahr (kultisches)," RAC 16 (1994): 1106–18.

worship, in contrast, found expression in still greater splendor, as the papacy became the last foothold and single glory for the population of the afflicted city. In the papal liturgy the presence of St Peter's successor gained its most tangible expression for the Roman people. In particular, the stational liturgy,[20] which the pope would celebrate in a particular church together with members of the papal court and citizens of all parts of the city, formed the brilliant high point of the Roman liturgy of the Mass in the seventh and eighth centuries.[21] This liturgy was regulated through an ever richer and more detailed ritual, which provided for a multitude of liturgical offices (acolytes, lectors, subdeacons, deacons, archdeacons, and schola singers), made use of a heightened language of prayer, and utilized both grand vestments (chasuble and dalmatic) and multiple insignia (stole, maniple, staff, miter, pontifical shoes, and pallium).[22] This glorious form of celebration was influenced in many regards by ceremonies of the imperial court.

The Roman stational liturgy developed into an important point of origin for the further development of the celebration of the Mass. By virtue of its being anchored in writing, the episcopal liturgy could be employed as a model, or *Missa Normativa*, wherever the Roman liturgy should be adopted, even outside of Rome. This decisive significance received expression in the persistence of the basic structure of each celebration, even in completely different contexts, be it a small rural parish or a Low Mass.[23] This basic form contained the following parts and elements:[24]

---

20   Cf. J.P. Kirsch, "L'origine des stations liturgiques du missel romain," EL 41 (1927): 137–50; idem, *Die Stationskirchen des Missale Romanum* [EcOra 19] (Freiburg i. Br.: Verlag Herder, 1926); U. Nersinger, *Liturgien und Zeremonien am Päpstlichen Hof* I (Bonn: Nova & Vetera, 2010), 345–68.

21   Description by Jungmann, *Missarum sollemnia* I, 88–98; idem, *The Mass of the Roman Rite* I, 67–74; H.B. Meyer, *Eucharistie — Geschichte, Theologie, Pastoral*; zum Gedenken an den 100. Geburtstag von Josef Andreas Jungmann SJ am 16. Nov. 1989 [GdK 4] (Regensburg: Verlag Friedrich Pustet, 1989), 196–99; P. Batiffol, *Leçons sur la messe* (Paris: Librairie Lecoffre J. Gabalda, ⁹1941), 65–99; A.A. King, *Liturgy of the Roman Church* (London / New York / Toronto: Longmans & Green, 1957), 397–401.

22   Cf. Th. Klauser, "Der Ursprung der bischöflichen Insignien und Ehrenrechte": idem, *Gesammelte Arbeiten zur Liturgiegeschichte, Kirchengeschichte und christlichen Archäologie*, ed. by E. Dassmann [JAC.E 3] (Münster: Aschendorff Verlag, 1974), 195–211.

23   Cf. Batiffol, *Leçons sur la messe*, 98f.

24   Cf. Meyer, *Eucharistie*, 196–98; F. Cabrol, *The Mass of the Western Rites*, trans. by C.M. Antony (London: Sands, 1934), 44–89; Batiffol, *Leçons sur la messe*, 65–99; B. Luykx,

The "classical Roman liturgy of the Mass"
(The classical Roman Rite) of the Mass)

Phases of Development

I. Opening
    a. Introit antiphon
    b. Prayers at the foot of the altar (still without prescribed texts)
    c. Kyrie litany
    d. Gloria (only in episcopal Masses)
    e. Greeting (_Dominus vobiscum_ / Bishop: _Pax vobis_)
    f. Oration

II. Scriptural Service
    a. Epistle
    b. Interlectional chant(s)
    c. Gospel
    d. Homily (when applicable)

III. Eucharist
    a. Greeting (_Dominus vobiscum_ / Bishop: _Pax vobis_)
    b. Invitation to prayer: _Oremus_ without oration
    c. Presentation of the gifts with the singing of the Offertory antiphon
    d. Prayer over the offerings
    e. Preface
    f. Sanctus
    g. Canon
    h. _Pater Noster_
    i. Greeting and kiss of peace
    j. Breaking of the species and commingling
    k. Agnus Dei
    l. Communion with Communion chant and prayer

IV. Conclusion
    a. Dismissal: _Ite missa est_
    b. Exit with blessing: _Benedicat vos Dominus_ ("The Lord bless you")

"Der Ursprung der gleichbleibenden Teile der Messe (Ordinarium Missae)": Th. Bogler (ed.), _Priestertum und Mönchtum. Gesammelte Aufsätze_ [LuM 29] (Maria Laach: Ars Liturgica Buch- und Kunstverlag, 1961), 72–119, 75–77.

These basic traits characterize the classical Roman rite down to the present day. In later times, this structure of the Roman-Latin liturgy of the Mass has seen only slight changes. All further modifications were incorporated into the existing structure in such a way that its most important parts remained undisturbed. Since the time of Pope Gregory the Great (590–604), the text, in particular the Canon, as well as the *Ordo Missae*, survive as a holy tradition that, with the exception of insignificant details, none dared to touch.[25] In this respect, the classical celebration of the Mass can be rightfully referred to as the Rite of St Gregory.

THE SACRAMENTARIES

This pope's name is also found in the title of one of the most meaningful liturgical books of ancient times, the *Sacramentarium Gregorianum*.[26] After the texts of prayers, in particular the priest's orations for liturgical use on certain feasts and occasions, were compiled into so-called *libelli* during the fifth century, the codifying of the liturgy for the city of Rome was reflected in various sacramentaries, which, in contrast to the early medieval *Ordines Romani*, were not an extended description of the divine worship in the sense of later rubrical books, but rather contained only the texts of the prayers themselves, as well as the prayers and Prefaces that vary from feast to feast, which were spoken during the celebration of the Mass. The sacramentaries were associated with the names of important popes, and estimates vary as to how great a part each had in the collection of texts named after him.

The *Leonianum*, named after Leo I (440–461), also known as the *Veronense* after the unique manuscript from Verona's Capitolare library, is an informal collection of *libelli*, or rather, set formularies for the Mass (most of them with opening prayer, prayer over the gifts, Preface, closing prayer, and prayer of blessing) for individual feasts of Our Lord and the saints as

---

25 Cf. Fortescue, *The Mass*, 173.

26 For the liturgical books of the Roman Mass cf. Jungmann, *Missarum sollemnia* I, 77–87; idem, *The Mass of the Roman Rite* I, 60–66; Meyer, *Eucharistie*, 189–94; M. Klöckener, "Sacramentary": S. Döpp / W. Geerlings (eds.), *Dictionary of Early Christian Literature*, trans. by M. O'Connell (New York: Crossroad, 2000), 519–21; C. Folsom, "Liturgical Books of the Roman Rite": A. Chupungco (ed.), *Handbook for Liturgical Studies* I. Introduction to the Liturgy (Collegeville, MN: The Liturgical Press, 1997), 245–314, 245–54.

well as other occasions, but without regard to solemn liturgical times. Many texts date back to the fifth century. Various passages may be the wording of Leo I.[27] In addition, texts composed by later popes (Gelasius I, Vigilius [537–555]) have found their way into the collection. These were included by the popes in the Lateran in the second half of the sixth century, and also by Roman priests of other churches who adapted them for their own uses. Multiple texts of the *Leonianum* (ca. 246 formulas) are found in the *Missale Romanum* (1962). Three of these prayers are contained in the daily *Ordo Missae* (*Aufer a nobis*; *Deus, qui humanae substantiae*; *Quod ore sumpsimus*).

A definite enhancement in content and composition is demonstrated in the *Gelasianum* (Gelasian Sacramentary or rather Old Gelasian Sacramentary), an eighth-century manuscript named after Pope Gelasius I (492–496). It follows the liturgical year, beginning with the Vigil of Christmas, and mirrors the liturgy as it would have been celebrated by a priest in a Roman titular church in the seventh century. The standard Mass formularies include two opening prayers, Secret, Postcommunion, and prayer of blessing *ad populum*, as well as occasional Prefaces and varying insertions into the Canon.

The texts of the papal festal liturgy and stational liturgy are again provided by the *Gregorianum*, whose original version probably developed in Rome around 630 under Honorius I (625–638). Here an older collection of texts was incorporated and completed, being most likely brought together by Gregory the Great (590–604). It contains old Roman prayer compositions next to texts by this pope himself, from which quite a few have been retained in the *Missale Romanum* (1962).[28] By means of further additions,

27 Cf. A.P. Lang, *Leo der Große und die Texte des Altgelasianums* (Steyl: Steyler Verlags-Buchhandlung, 1957), 465–77.

28 For example, the Christmas Preface, the Collect for Epiphany, the Preface for Easter and the Ascension, as well as countless Sunday Collects. Cf. Gamber, *Missa Romensis*, 116–21; B. Capelle, "La main de S. Grégoire dans le sacramentaire grégorien": idem, *Travaux liturgiques* II, 161–75; H. Ashworth, "The Liturgical Prayers of St Gregory the Great," *Traditio* 15 (1959): 107–61; A.G. Martimort, *L'église en prière* I (Paris: Desclée de Brouwer, 1983), 61; J. Deshusses, *Le sacramentaire grégorien. Ses principales formes d'après les plus anciens manuscrits* I [SpicFri 16] (Fribourg/Switzerland: Academic Press, ²1979), 50–53; idem, "Grégoire et le sacramentaire grégorien": *Grégoire le Grand*: Chantilly, centre culturel Les Fontaines, 15–19 Sept. 1982 [Colloques internationaux du Centre National de la recherche scientifique] (Paris: Éditions du Centre National de la recherche scientifique, 1986), 637–43; additional bibliography in Jungmann,

at the turn of the seventh to the eighth century, a complete sacramentary for the papal liturgy developed (containing, among others, an *Ordo Missae*, Canon, solemn liturgy of ordination, Masses for particular occasions, and benedictions). The *Gregorianum* became the foundation of the later Missal of Pius V, which ultimately was merely a further development of the Gregorian Sacramentary.

The first complete description of the Roman liturgy of the Mass comes from the end of the seventh/beginning of the eighth century. The so-called *Ordo Romanus Primus* portrays how the pope, surrounded by bishops as well as higher and lower clergy, performed the Easter Mass with great solemnity.[29] This description of a pontifical ceremony in the city of Rome was the point of origin for all further developments. Many of the Collects and Prefaces contained in this formulary are preserved to this day in the wealth of prayers of the classical Roman Missal.

All of the aforementioned sacramentaries and *Ordines* impressively document the distinct interest that the Roman Church had in the liturgy between the fifth and eighth centuries. No other Church could produce liturgical texts of similar importance on this scale.

The liturgy of the city of Rome of late antiquity was certainly in no way uniform in scale: besides the papal stational liturgy there was the liturgy celebrated by the priests in the titular churches. Furthermore, special customs existed for individual churches. Nevertheless, the Roman liturgy, by reason of its various characteristics, possessed an unmistakable shape: the prayers always directed themselves through Christ to the Father, unlike in the Eastern liturgy; they displayed dogmatic precision, succinct brevity, and stylistic perfection of form. The ceremony was simple and unemotional, practical and sensible. Discipline, gravity, and dignity were the specific attributes of the old Roman liturgy.[30]

Missarum sollemnia I, 81n17; idem, *The Mass of the Roman Rite* I, 63n17.

29   Text: M. Andrieu, *Les Ordines Romani du haut moyen âge* II. Les textes (Ordines I–XIII) [SSL Études et Documents 23] (Louvain: Spicilegium sacrum Lovaniense, 1971), 74–108. Cf. J. Nebel, "Die 'ordentliche' und die 'ausserordentliche' Form des römischen Messritus," FKTh 25 (2009): 173–203, 176–78.

30   Cf. E. Bishop, "The Genius of the Roman Rite": idem, *Liturgica Historica: Papers on the Liturgy and Religious Life of the Western Church* (Oxford: Clarendon Press, 1962 [repr. of the first ed. 1918]), 1–19, 6–13.

In contrast to the Eastern rites, which have invariable but sometimes multiple anaphoras, the Roman liturgy possesses a multitude of varying orations relating to the feast or occasion, yet only a single main Eucharistic prayer, though there are various Prefaces as well as different insertions on particular solemn feasts. Until the ninth century, the ancestral liturgy in Rome remained virtually free from foreign elements. The Kyrie and Gloria, which come from the East, belong to the few borrowings from other sources.

THE ROMAN RITE WITHIN THE RITES OF LATE ANTIQUITY

Since the fourth century, various groups of rites developed in the East and West, which corresponded to different basic types of celebration of the Eucharist.[31] The patriarchal seats of Rome, Alexandria, and Antioch became notable as crystallization centers of liturgical tradition. It was these places of apostolic activity that kept the connection between the liturgy and its origins alive. Shortly after the Council of Nicaea (325), Byzantium/Constantinople became a further center of rite development. The rites of these centers of liturgical tradition were the sources from which further rites derived. The West Syrian rites (Malankara, Malabar, and Maronite) and the East Syrian rites (Chaldean and Syro-Malabar) have their foundations in Antioch. From the region of Alexandria come the Coptic and Ethiopic rites. Byzantium initially borrowed Antioch's tradition, but opened itself to influences from Asia Minor and Jerusalem before the Byzantine liturgy found acceptance in the Greek-speaking world (Turkey, Greece, Cyprus) and later especially in the Slavic regions (Russia, Serbia, Ukraine, Bulgaria). Just as the majority of Eastern rites in their final form were heavily influenced by the Byzantine liturgy, for the West Rome became the definitive power that shaped and unified the liturgies of its area of influence.

In the West, in addition to the Roman liturgy, which presumably influenced the liturgy of its neighbor North Africa, there was in Italy the Milanese

---

31 Cf. Meyer, *Eucharistie*, 130–64, 135 (scheme); H.-J. Feulner, "Liturgy": Döpp / Geerlings (eds.), *Dictionary of Early Christian Literature*, 384–88 (scheme); A. Heinz, "Liturgie": LThK[3] 6, 979f. (scheme); Jungmann, *The Early Liturgy*, 200–37; idem, *Missarum sollemnia* I, 43–63; idem, *The Mass of the Roman Rite*, I, 33–49; G. Kretschmar, "Abendmahlsfeier I. Alte Kirche," *Theologische Realenzyklopädie* 1 (1977): 229–78, 250–69; A. Fortescue, "Rites," *The Catholic Encyclopedia* XIII (New York: Robert Appleton Company, 1911): 64–72.

liturgy (Ambrosian rite) as well as various liturgies in the churches in Ravenna, Aquileia, and Benevento. Furthermore, there was the old Gallican liturgy (*Missale Gothicum, Missale Gallicanum Vetus*), which experienced its greatest development in the sixth and seventh centuries and was initially the most widespread rite of the Occident (Gaul, parts of Italy), as well as the Old Spanish, or rather, Mozarabic liturgy, which experienced its zenith in the seventh century in the kingdom of the Visigoths and remains in Toledo until the present. Finally, from variegated currents of influence there emerged the Celtic rite (Ireland: Stowe Missal). Under the name "Gallican" liturgy, the aforementioned rites are occasionally contrasted with the Roman-North African rites: compared to the conservative and unemotional Roman liturgy, the Gallican liturgy had opened itself up to oriental influences,[32] and exhibited a great diversity of many local special customs, but possessed a fundamental unity in style and structure.

Even though the non-Roman liturgy of the West, with few exceptions, disappeared, and the Roman rite stepped into its place, it was not primarily the result of a papally-forced unification of the liturgy, though certain popes, such as Gregory VII, Innocent III, and Paul V wished for and worked for the standardization of the liturgies of the Church in the West. Crucial for the triumph of the Roman rite were the prestige of Rome and the dignified, exemplary character of its liturgy, which was greatly admired.

Originally, however, the Roman rite was only the local rite for the city of Rome itself. The Patriarchs of the East significantly formed the liturgy of their areas of influence; in contrast, although the bishop of Rome was indeed the patriarch of the Occident, the greater part of the Latin Church of the West did not initially follow the Roman rite, but rather the various forms of the so-called Gallican rites. Over many centuries, the bishop of Rome was the sole Patriarch whose own rite had prevalence only in the seat of his patriarchate, not in the remaining area of his patriarchy. The gradual expansion of the Roman rite over Rome's surrounding areas is due less to the initiative of the popes than to that of the bishops or rulers of other regions, who sought to align themselves with the liturgical customs of the Roman Church.

---

32   Cf. J. Quasten, "Oriental Influence in the Gallican Liturgy," *Traditio* 1 (1943): 55–78.

Early on, the Roman rite became regulatory beyond the city of Rome for the central Italian dioceses, which belonged to the bishop of Rome's area of jurisdiction.[33] The local churches situated outside of the Roman metropolitan district selectively adopted some elements of the Roman liturgy, as indicated by the *Canon Missae* of the Milanese Church at the time of Ambrose, or let themselves be formed by the style of prayer of the Roman bishops, whose texts were collected and distributed in *libelli*.

THE ROMAN MASS IN THE MIDDLE AGES

The celebration of the Eucharist according to the Roman rite, as it was first celebrated in the city of Rome, and later also in central Italy, underwent a considerable change in two aspects between late antiquity and the Middle Ages. For one, the territory of the Roman liturgy increased, in that it was now adopted by the countries north of the Alps and in the Frankish-Germanic regions. Secondly, its form changed, in that it absorbed elements of non-Roman liturgical traditions. The texts of the old Roman celebration of the Mass remained largely untouched, but were expanded through texts of Gallican and Frankish tradition, supplemented by private prayers of the priest, and finally embellished with elements of rich ceremonial gestures.

As the Roman rite, due to individual travelers to Rome—bishops, clerics, monks, pilgrims—had already gained fame and prestige in the kingdom of the Franks from the middle of the seventh century, Charlemagne (768–814) especially promoted the "Romanization" of the liturgy in his kingdom, in order to set the clear order of the Roman rite against the low level of an ancestral Gallican liturgy, the diversity of which had become unmanageable, and to strengthen the unity of the new Carolingian kingdom by means of unity in religious worship.[34] As a metaphor attributed to Charlemagne states, Rome is the pure fountain to which man must always return.[35]

---

33   Cf. DH 212, 215f.; Innocent I (402–417), *Epistula ad Decentium* (Cabié 20–23).

34   Only in Spain, where the Moors ruled, as well as in a few regions of Northern Italy (amongst others Aquileia) and in the Duchy of Benevento did the original rites remain for a while longer; in Milan and Toledo these have been preserved to the present day.

35   Cf. H. Schneider, "Karolingische Kirchen- und Liturgiereform—Ein konservativer Neuaufbruch": C. Stiegemann / M. Wemhoff (eds.), *799: Kunst und Kultur der Karolingerzeit*.

Thus the emperor requested from Pope Hadrian an authentic copy of the Gregorian Sacramentary (Old Gregorian), which reached Charlemagne in Aachen between 785 and 786 under the name *Hadrianum*, and was used as a model for transcriptions in the palace library.[36] The sacramentary sent from Rome to Aachen was certainly one of the showpieces of the Papal Registry, but not one of the most current, as, owing to the decline of the Roman scriptoria, there was not time to make a representative exemplar for the Emperor that conformed to the newest liturgical development. The incomplete aspect of the *Hadrianum* had to do with the liturgical year — it lacked the Sundays after both Pentecost and Christmas; moreover it concentrated on the stational liturgy celebrated by the pope himself. In order to comply with the requirements of the Frankish Church, the sacramentary was further supplemented with prayer texts, mostly coming from Gallico-Frankish tradition (e.g., the *Gelasianum* from the eighth century), which were initially included as a supplement to the book, but later, for practical reasons, found their place inside the sacramentary itself.

The legacy of the papal liturgy of late antiquity, with its solemn rituals, could not however be transmitted unchanged into the new setting, as it was given to the bishops' sees and monasteries, centers of the Carolingian liturgical reform. A certain simplification was required, which nevertheless sought to follow the traditional order wherever possible, occasionally down to the last detail. Thus the feasts of all of the Roman martyrs, regardless of the many unfamiliar names, were carried over into the Frankish sacramentary. Even the specification of the Roman stational churches was included. The instructions from the *Ordo Romanus Primus* relating to the Roman papal liturgy were reverently copied in full and taken as the basis for the local practice. Gradually at first, from the turn of the ninth century, a flexible adaptation and enhancement of the Roman *Ordines* took place.[37]

Karl der Große und Papst Leo III. in Paderborn II (Mainz: Verlag Philipp von Zabern, 1999), 771–81, 773.

36 Cf. H. Lietzmann, *Das Sacramentarium Gregorianum nach dem Aachener Urexemplar* [Liturgiegeschichtliche Quellen 3] (Münster: Aschendorff Verlag, 1921).

37 Cf. J. Nebel, *Die Entwicklung des römischen Messritus im ersten Jahrtausend anhand der Ordines Romani. Eine synoptische Darstellung* (Rome: Pontificium Athenaeum S. Anselmi de Urbe, 2000); idem, "Il rito della messa romana nella luce dell'origine della sua identità," RivLi 89 (2002): 716–29.

Thus, from the middle of the ninth century, there entered the Roman collection of texts a wealth of prayers intended for the silent, private recitation of the celebrant; these were added to the *Ordo*, at first reluctantly, then finally finding their way into the rite itself, where they became fixed components. Not a single detail of the ceremonies should be lacking its corresponding prayer. The vesting, the entrance, the kissing of the altar, the incensing, the elevating of the bread and wine during the Offertory, and the washing of hands, for example, were all accompanied by such personal prayers of the celebrant. A portion of these prayers corresponds to the texts used today, either in entirety or approximately (*Orate fratres*; *Domine Jesu Christe, Fili Dei vivi*; *Placeat*). All of these prayers were not, at the core, transformations or superficial alterations, but a ripening of the Roman rite, a synthesis of the externally ceremonial and internally spiritual dimensions of the liturgy of the Mass.[38] A few of these prayers were to accompany certain gestures that were performed in silence in the original papal liturgy. In this way, the piety of the celebrant would be protected against automatism and the prayer would give a spiritual meaning to the gestures. Other prayers were used to evoke in the celebrant the sentiments of recollection that he should have as he approached the altar, performed the offering of the gifts, prepared himself for Communion, or received it.[39] These prayers conformed harmoniously to the places that were left open for the personal prayers of the priest in the traditional *Ordo Missae* at the arrival at the altar, at moments in the Offertory and Communion rites, and finally at the end of the Mass.

A striking development on a completely different level was the dramatic arrangement of the ceremonies. Changing positions of the candlestick bearer accompanying the bishop, multiple incensations of the altar, the solemn proclamation of the Gospel with procession, incense, candles,

---

38 Cf. Nebel, "Die 'ordentliche' und die 'ausserordentliche' Form," 178f., 182; B. Luykx, "Der Ursprung der gleichbleibenden Teile der Messe," 79–91; E. Lodi, "Les prières privées dans le déroulement de la messe romaine," A. M. Triacca / A. Pistoia (eds.), *L'eucharistie: célébrations, rites, piétés*. Conférences Saint-Serge XLIe semaine d'études liturgiques, Paris, 28 June–1 July [BEL.S 79] (Rome: C.L.V.-Edizioni Liturgiche, 1995), 235–57.

39 Cf. Batiffol, *Leçons sur la messe*, 29.

acclamation (*Gloria tibi, Domine*), and the kissing of the evangelistary as well as the concluding kiss of the altar with its accompanying prayer (*Placeat*), all belonged to the new provisions that developed the *Ordo Romanus Primus* further in the Frankish lands. The Canon, which was meanwhile being prayed in silence, was embellished by means of many gestures, bows, and signs of the Cross, to become a vivid action of the priest (*actio*).[40] Furthermore, the liturgies of Palm Sunday, Holy Week, and the Easter Vigil received dramatic elements. The Palm Sunday procession, the washing of the feet on Holy Thursday, the adoration of the Cross on Good Friday, the blessing of fire, Paschal candle, and baptismal water — such were the new, concrete, and moving ceremonies with which the Celtic and Germanic clergy, who served within the Carolingian kingdom, had enriched the formerly unemotional and rather laconic Roman rite. Thus was established the so-called Romano-Gallican mixed liturgy, which, in the aftermath, profoundly determined the spirituality and worship practices of the Roman and Germanic peoples.[41]

Decisive for further development was the ritual form that the Romano-Gallican Mass had found around the turn of the millennium in the so-called Rhenish *Ordo Missae*, which originated in the Rhineland area and spread outwards (St Gallen, Reichenau, St Alban/Mainz), and was initially intended for episcopal celebration, based on the papal liturgy of the Mass from the seventh and eighth centuries (*Ordo Romanus* I) and its Frankish adaptation (*Ordo Romanus* V, second half of the ninth century) and containing from them many elements that still belong to the *Ordinarium* of the Roman rite of the Mass today.[42] Already soon after its rise, this *Ordo Missae* reached Italy, where it determined the further development.

---

40 By the expression *actio*, the Canon itself is also meant. Cf. Jungmann, *Missarum sollemnia* I, 229; II, 129; idem, *The Mass of the Roman Rite* I, 172f.; II, 102f.

41 Cf. Th. Klauser, "Die liturgischen Austauschbeziehungen zwischen der römischen und fränkischen Kirche vom 8. bis zum 11. Jh.": idem, *Gesammelte Arbeiten zur Liturgiegeschichte*, 139–54. C. Vogel, *Les échanges liturgiques entre Rome et les pays francs jusqu'à l'époque de Charlemagne: Le chiese nei regni dell'Europa occidentale e i loro rapporti con Roma sino all'800*, I. [Settimana di Studio del Centro Italiano di Studi sull'Alto Medioevo 7] (Spoleto: [s.n.], 1960), 185–295.

42 For structure, see Meyer, *Eucharistie*, 207f.; furthermore Luykx, "Ursprung," 91–119.

RETURN TO ROME

In the meantime, from the end of the ninth century, Rome's cultural-religious life had reached an all-time low. The liturgy was in a state of decay. The clergy and laity alike neglected divine worship. Liturgical books were no longer produced. Like a ray of light in that *saeculum obscurum*, at the end of the tenth century, liturgical texts appeared in Italy and Rome itself that replaced the native form of the old Roman liturgy with the type of the Roman rite that had meanwhile further developed north of the Alps. In addition to the Roman Cluniac monasteries, which maintained the divine worship according to the traditional form of the Order's Frankish homeland and consequently provided a reputation for it in Rome, during the tenth century it was above all the Hohenstaufen monarchs Otto I and Otto II who exerted their sovereignty over Rome in the service of a liturgical reform in the Eternal City. Through the donation of liturgical books, as they were artistically rendered in the scriptoriums north of the Alps, the life of divine worship in the city was fundamentally revived, so that now, soon after the turn of the millennium, those traits were included that originally had been particular to the liturgy of the Frankish-Germanic peoples.

Thus these peoples contributed in their own manner to the preservation of the Roman liturgy for Rome itself and for medieval Christendom during a critical phase of its history and to the re-establishment of the unity of the liturgy in the Occident, as the Roman tradition, with a few additions, was received back in its place of origin. In unexpected ways, Rome retrieved the liturgical treasure that had initially been bequeathed to the Gallo-Frankish peoples, then to the other Germans. The rites had become richer in the meantime, but were also burdened with some elements foreign to the Roman spirit. Upon the return of this further-developed Roman liturgy (eleventh to thirteenth centuries), many prayers that did not appear temperate or sober enough were therefore omitted or replaced with shorter and more concise prayers in conformity with the Roman mentality. Thus, the prayers at the foot of the altar were adopted almost in full, the prayers accompanying the Offertory partially, while from the multiple private "apologia prayers" of the celebrant, originating from the penitential spirit of monasticism, only the *Suscipe, sancta Trinitas* remained. It can, however, be said that the rite of the Mass itself experienced scarcely any substantial changes, except for minimal details, since the time of late antiquity.[43] This appears especially in the fact that, when the priest celebrates a private Mass, he now performs by himself all the parts that, in the original form of the Mass, are divided among the bishop, deacon, and subdeacon as specific tasks. The characteristic processions of the originally Roman Pontifical liturgy themselves were maintained, at least rudimentarily, in the different turns of the priest's body at the altar from the one side to the other. Each private Mass is thus, ultimately, the Papal Mass reduced to its simplest expression.[44]

With Gregory VII (1073–1085), the popes once again assumed leadership in the area of the Roman liturgy. The "Gregorian reform" aimed for the standardization of the liturgy in the occidental dioceses and especially strove for an adaptation of the Roman practice in places with their own liturgical rite, as in Milan and Spain.

In Rome itself, since the High Middle Ages, the so-called *usus Romanae curiae* had developed, the liturgical use of the Roman Curia.[45] More and more during the eleventh and twelfth centuries, the papal liturgy was concentrated in the Lateran palace's house chapel, which can still be seen today above the "holy stairs" (*scala sancta*). A remembrance of the rich treasure of relics that lends the chapel its name, "*Sancta Sanctorum*," lingers on in the prayer *Aufer a nobis* following the Confiteor, when the priest, stepping up to the altar, speaks of approaching *ad Sancta sanctorum*.[46] After Pope Innocent III (1198–1216) had already had an *Ordinarium* made specifically

---

43 Cf. Nebel, "Die 'ordentliche' und die 'ausserordentliche' Form," 179.

44 Cf. Batiffol, *Leçons sur la messe*, 99.

45 Text: S. Van Dijk, *The Ordinal of the Papal Court from Innocent III to Boniface VIII and Related Documents* [SpicFri 22] (Fribourg/Switzerland: Academic Press, 1975), 494–526; cf. S. Van Dijk and J. Hazelden Walker, *The Origins of the Modern Roman Liturgy: The Liturgy of the Papal Court and the Franciscan Order in the Thirteenth Century* (Westminster, MD: Newman Press, 1960).

46 Cf. A. Baumstark, *Missale Romanum. Seine Entwicklung, ihre wichtigsten Urkunden und Probleme* (Eindhoven / Nimwegen: Wilhelm van Eupen, Verlagsbuchhandlung, 1929), 145. The biblical expression *Sancta sanctorum* was, however, already used for the House of God; cf. Jerome, *In Ezechielem* 13,44,17/21 (CCL 75, 657 / St Jerome, *Commentary on Ezechiel*, trans. by Th.P. Scheck, *Ancient Christian Writers* 71 [New York / Mahwah, NJ: The Newman Press, 2017], 524).

for the papal chapel, the Papal Curia under Honorius III (1216–1227) received its own missal, corresponding to its requirements of combining the older texts of the papal chapel with that of the Lateran cloister. This missal clearly differed from the liturgical services of the Roman city churches; it was tailored for the frequent travels of the Curia and marked by a strong simplification compared to the numerous prayer texts of the new missals spread about in the northern lands.

That this order of the celebration of the Mass *secundum usum Romanae curiae* spread from the city of Rome to the entire Catholic Church during the course of the thirteenth century is especially owing to the Franciscan Order.[17] The great mobility of the new mendicant order confronted them with the fact that a friar who traveled across Europe discovered in every place a Roman rite that had entwined itself, in particular places or in particular monasteries, with all kinds of local traditions of their own, so that a unified form could in no way be recognized. There was neither a uniform Missal nor a Roman Congregation to control and guarantee the uniformity of the rite. In view of the uncontrollable variety of liturgical customs that posed a certain consequential danger to the continuity and stability of the spiritual life of the itinerant mendicant, the Franciscan Order decided, in loyalty to the pope, to obligate their own friars to the *usus Romanae curiae*. The Roman Curia's Order of the Mass was revised in 1243 by the Franciscan Minister General, Haymo of Faversham, in such a way that it was appropriate for both solemn offices of the convent and private Masses in the churches of the Order.[48] For the first time in this context, the ceremonial actions — genuflections, bows, signs of the Cross, and other gestures — were written down[49] and became a firm element of the Roman rite through such exact recording, later continued (1498; 1502)

47 The title of this missal is: *Incipit ordo Missalis secundum consuetudinem Romanae Curiae* (sometimes: *Romanae Ecclesiae*).

48 From then on the Franciscan Missal bore the title: *Incipit ordo Missalis Fratrum Minorum secundum consuetudinem Romanae Curiae* (also sometimes: *Romanae Ecclesiae*). Text: *Missale Franciscanum Regulae* codicis VI.G.38 Bibl. Nat. Neapol. A cura di M. Przeczewski [Monumenta Studia Instrumenta Liturgica 31] (Vatican City: Libreria Editrice Vaticana, 2003).

49 Text: S. Van Dijk (ed.), *Sources of the Modern Roman Liturgy: The Ordinals by Haymo of Faversham and Related Documents (1243–1307)*, vol. 2: Texts (Leiden: Brill Academic Publishers, 1963), 2–14.

by the papal Master of Ceremonies Johann Burchard of Strassburg with minute arrangement of even the smallest gestures.[50] The esteem enjoyed by the Franciscan books of the liturgy in Rome is demonstrated by the fact that already in 1240, Pope Gregory IX planned to make the Franciscan Breviary and Missal binding for the entire Church. In 1277, Nicholas III introduced their liturgical books to the Roman basilicas. The first printing (*editio princeps*) of the *Missale Romanum*, that is, the Roman Curia's Missal of 1474,[51] still bears unmistakable traces of the monastic-Franciscan provenance when a "hebdomadary" or a "convent Mass" is mentioned in the rubrics. Thus, thanks to the Franciscans, the liturgical practices of the Roman Curia spread throughout the entire Occident and in this way gradually became the universal form of the Roman celebration of the Mass.

THE REFORMS OF THE COUNCIL OF TRENT
Cause and purpose

Even though the Franciscans' use of the Roman Missal had blazed the trail for a certain standardization of the liturgy in Europe, the celebration of the Mass was still marked by stark differences in the late Middle Ages. The Roman liturgy may have possessed exclusive prestige, but it was altered according to preference in each diocese and adjusted according to local conditions. Liturgical legislation still lay in the hands of the bishops. New feasts and Mass formularies, along with a wealth of Sequences and votive Masses, easily found their way into the Roman liturgy. Many, especially in the missals produced by hand, were of purely private origin, without approbation from the Church authorities. The invention of the printing press increased this variety, since individual printers or their employers selected and arranged the texts differently, and printed Missals were used alongside the customary ones or underwent the handwritten

---

50 Text: J. W. Legg (ed.), *Tracts on the Mass* [Henry Bradshaw Society 27] (London: Harrison and Sons, 1904), 121–87. Cf. C. Braga, *La genesi storica delle rubriche* (Liturgica 1): E. Cattaneo / A. G. Martimort [i.a.] (eds.), Introduzione agli studi liturgici (Rome: Centro di Azione Liturgica, 1962), 39–66.

51 Text: *Missalis Romani editio princeps Mediolani anno 1474 prelis mandata*. Reimpressio vaticani exemplaris introductione aliisque elementis aucta curantibus A. Ward / C. Johnson [BEL. S 84; Instrumenta Liturgica Quarreriensia. Supplementa 3] (Rome: C. L. V.-Edizioni Liturgiche, 1996).

insertion of local texts. Between the *editio princeps* of the Roman Curia's Missal (1474) and the *Missale Romanum* of 1570, an excess of 300 printed Missals appeared.

Meanwhile, dissatisfaction with the chaotic conditions of the practice of divine worship and the deteriorating situation of liturgical books was widespread. Along with that came concern over the serious abuses of the celebration of Mass, which was often combined with superstitious beliefs arising from popular piety. Futile past attempts at reform had shown that individual bishops and provincial synods were unable to cope with the pending problems. But the attacks of the Protestant reformers, who questioned both the Catholic understanding of the Mass (the sacrificial concept) and the concrete practice of divine worship, made a comprehensive reform of the liturgy inevitable, which, according to the opinion of that time, could only be initiated by an ecumenical council. If the Reformation had taken place not least by way of liturgical "reforms," so that the difference between Catholicism and Protestantism had often become difficult to recognize in practice, then dogmatic clarifications and boundaries were just as necessary as a reorganization of liturgical life and the underlying liturgical books. The Council of Trent (1545–1563) attended to these pending issues in its various sessions.[52]

With the decree on the sacrament of the Eucharist (Real Presence, transubstantiation, veneration: DH 1635–61), teachings on the sacrifice of

---

52 Cf. U. M. Lang, "The Tridentine Liturgical Reform in Historical Perspective," idem (ed.), *Authentic Liturgical Renewal in Contemporary Perspective* (London / New York [i.a.]: Bloomsbury T&T Clark, 2017), 109–24; H. Jedin, "Das Konzil von Trient und die Reform des Römischen Messbuches," *Liturgisches Leben* 6 (1939): 30–66; idem, "Das Konzil von Trient und die Reform der liturgischen Bücher," EL 59 (1945): 5–38 (= idem, *Kirche des Glaubens. Kirche der Geschichte. Ausgewählte Aufsätze und Vorträge* II [Freiburg i. Br.: Verlag Herder, 1966], 499–525); R. Theisen, *Mass Liturgy and the Council of Trent* (Collegeville, MN: St John's University Press, 1965); W. Haunerland, "Einheitlichkeit als Weg der Erneuerung — Das Konzil von Trient und die nachtridentinische Reform der Liturgie," M. Klöckener / B. Kranemann (eds.), *Liturgiereformen. Historische Studien zu einem bleibenden Grundzug des christlichen Gottesdienstes* [Teil I] (Münster: Aschendorff Verlag, 2002), 436–65; R. Knittel, *"Deformata Reformare* — Liturgische Missbräuche und Reformanliegen in den Trienter Reformdekreten," FKTh 12 (1996): 247–260; J. A. Jungmann, "Das Konzil von Trient und die Erneuerung der Liturgie," in G. Schreiber (ed.), *Das Weltkonzil von Trient* I (Freiburg i. Br.: Verlag Herder, 1951), 325–36; B. Deneke, "Konzil von Trient und heilige Messe," *Dominus vobiscum* 8 (2014): 4–11.

the Mass (character of propitiation, honor of the saints, Canon, approval of the exclusive Communion of the priest, rejection of the vernacular: DH 1738–60), and a further decree primarily on disciplinary and ceremonial questions concerning the nature of the Mass (*Decretum de observandis et evitandis in celebratione missae*: COD 3, 736f.), the Council reinforced the Catholic understanding of the Faith against the Reformation's attacks, while at the same time creating the doctrinal foundations and practical principles for a prospective reform of the liturgy of the Mass. It states:

> The sacrifice (*res sacra*) should be performed everywhere and by all people according to the same rite, so that the Church of God may have but one voice and that we allow no difference (*dissentio*) whatsoever to be found among us, even in the slightest thing. In order to achieve this goal, the following efforts must be taken: after all Missals with superstitious or apocryphal prayers have been purged, they should be rendered perfectly pure (*pura*), splendid (*nitida*), faultless (*integra*) to all people; they should be identical, at least among secular priests, save for legitimate and non-abusive customs of the people that may be preserved. Some strict (*certae*) rubrics for the ceremonies should be stipulated, which the celebrants must uniformly respect, so that the people may not be alienated by new or different rites or take offense.

In summary, it states: "The missals should be restored according to the use and the old practice of the Holy Roman Catholic Church."[53] The will of the Council called for the standardization of the missal, its purging of all faults, the restoration of the Roman rite in its original form, its binding force for the entire Church, and respect for legitimate customs.

The Fathers of the Council placed these duties in the hands of the pope. In this way, the tendency of centralizing the liturgical legislation in Rome, emerging already since Gregory VII (1073–1085), found its conclusion.[54]

---

53 *Acta Concilii Tridentini*, ed. by Görresgesellschaft (Freiburg i. Br.: Verlag Herder, 1919), VIII, pars 5a: no. 420, 421, p. 917, 921.

54 Cf. J.M. Pommarès, *Trente et le missel. L'évolution de la question de l'autorité compétente en matière de missels* [BEL.S 94] (Rome: C.L.V.-Edizioni Liturgiche, 1997); idem, "L'autorité

The bishops' previous autonomy in liturgical questions was over; the principle of liturgical decentralization had increasingly proved unsuitable for meeting new challenges, by reason of the want of authority and the lack of consequent action by members of the episcopate.

The Missale Romanum *of 1570*

The commission established by Pope Pius IV in 1564 and extended by Pope Pius V for the implementation of the Council's mandated reforms worked all the more efficiently, and it included as a member, among others, the high-ranking scholar, Cardinal G. Sirleto, custodian of the Vatican Library. Already in 1570, just a few years after the close of the Council, the *Missale Romanum ex decreto sacrosancti concilii Tridentini restitutum, Pii V. Pont. Max. iussu editum* appeared.[55] Through the bull of promulgation, *Quo Primum*, of July 14, 1570, this Missal, with certain qualifications, was established as binding for the entire Church.[56] Thus was realized the wish for a unified Missal for the entire Church based on Roman tradition, as articulated by Bishop Tommaso Campeggio at the opening of the Council.

The contents and structure of the *Missale*[57] largely correspond to the order developed over the course of the centuries by the Roman Curia, which, as a result of the wider distribution through the Franciscan Order, already enjoyed acceptance by a considerable portion of the universal Church. The Bull of Introduction, placed at the beginning, and the Imprimatur are

---

légitime en matière de liturgie": *Foi et liturgie*. Actes du septième colloque d'études historiques, théologiques et canoniques sur le rite romain [Versailles, Novembre 2001] (Versailles: CIEL, 2002), 91–113.

55 Text: *Missale Romanum. Editio princeps (1570)*. Edizione anastatica, introduzione e appendice a cura di M. Sodi / A.M. Triacca [Monumenta Liturgica Concilii Tridentini 2] (Vatican City: Libreria Editrice Vaticana, 1998).

56 Cf. M. Klöckener, "Die Bulle *Quo Primum* Papst Pius V. vom 14. Juli 1570 zur Promulgation des nachtridentinischen *Missale Romanum*" (Liturgische Quellentexte lateinisch-deutsch 2), *Archiv für Liturgiewissenschaft* 48 (2006): 41–51; R. Dulac, "La bulle de saint Pie V promulgant le Missel Romain restauré," *Itinéraires* 162 (1972), 13–47 (trans.: M. Davies, *Pope Paul's New Mass*, Liturgical Revolution III [Dickinson, TX: Angelus Press, 1980], 571–80).

57 Cf. A.J. Chadwick, "The Roman Missal of the Council of Trent": A. Reid (ed.), *T & T Clark Companion to Liturgy* (New York [i.a.]: Bloomsbury T&T Clark, 2016), 107–31; J. Baudot, *Le Missel Romain. Ses origines, son histoire* II (Paris: Bloud & Cie., 1912), 114–24; M. Sodi, "Il *Missale Romanum* tra l'edizione del 1474 e quella del 1962," RivLi 95/1 (2008) = *Celebrare con il Messale di San Pio V* (Monografie di Rivista liturgica), 55–77, 63–67.

followed by the general rubrics and the special rubrics (*ritus servandus*), which in each case were borrowed with slight changes from the great papal Master of Ceremonies of the fifteenth century, Johann Burchard. The recourse to his Order of the Mass "*sine cantu et ministris*" signified a far-reaching decision that the private Mass of the priest should provide the basic form for the renewed liturgy of the Mass. For the solemn form, the appropriate amendments were added. With that, the *Missale Romanum* sanctioned the order of the private Mass, which, already long before Johann Burchard,[58] had been developed into its own Ordo at the Roman Curia from the beginning of the thirteenth century, but which, as a practice, dates far back into the early Middle Ages, having its roots in the individual celebrations of the monastic priests in the cloisters.[59] The rubrics of the *Missale Romanum* are followed by the prayers of preparation and thanksgiving, references for the calculation (*computus*) of feasts, a calendar, and an index of feasts. For practical but also theological reasons, the Order of Mass was inserted into the *temporale* or Proper of the season, which begins with the First Sunday of Advent, in the middle of the book, between the Easter Vigil and Easter Sunday. Following the second section of the *temporale* are the *sanctorale* or Proper of the saints, from the Vigil of the Apostle Andrew (November 29) until the Feast of St Catherine of Alexandria (November 25), and the Common of the saints, as well as votive and Requiem Masses. Various blessings form the conclusion of the Missal, the order of which remained basically identical from that point onward.

Important achievements of the labor of reform appeared firstly in the calendar, for, unlike earlier editions of the *Missale*, which contained hardly any days without feasts, it now offered about 160 such days, and with that, conferred upon Sundays, as well as weekdays of the Lenten season, especially, their fitting status.[60] The general rubrics required that the celebration of

---

58 Cf. Meyer, *Eucharistie*, 214f.

59 Cf. A. Häussling, *Mönchskonvent und Eucharistiefeier. Eine Studie über die Messe in der abendländischen Klosterliturgie des frühen Mittelalters und zur Geschichte der Messhäufigkeit* [LQF 58] (Münster: Aschendorff Verlag, 1973); O. Nussbaum, *Kloster, Priestermönch und Privatmesse* [Theoph. 14] (Bonn: Peter Hanstein Verlag, 1961); Jungmann, *Missarum sollemnia* I, 279–306; idem, *The Mass of the Roman Rite* I, 212–33; Meyer, *Eucharistie*, 240f.

60 Cf. E. Focke / H. Heinrichs, "Das Kalendarium des Missale Pianum vom Jahr 1570 und seine Tendenzen," *Theologische Quartalschrift* 120 (1939): 383–400, 461–69.

the Mass be fundamentally consistent with the *Breviarium Romanum* (1568) published shortly before, to which the Collect and Gospel of the Missal were precisely matched. Sundays and feast days, as well as specific times of the liturgical year, were protected from substitution by votive Masses. The number of Prefaces was reduced to those eleven that had already been approved in the Roman liturgy since the end of the eleventh century, and aside from special Prefaces of certain orders and dioceses, no new Prefaces were added until the beginning of the twentieth century (for the Mass of the Dead and for St Joseph, 1919; for the feast of Christ the King, 1925; for the Mass of the Sacred Heart, 1928). From the wealth of Sequences, which numbered over 100 in some older Missals, only those of Easter (*Victimae paschali laudes*), Pentecost (*Veni Sancte Spiritus*), Corpus Christi (*Lauda Sion Salvatorem*), and the Requiem Mass (*Dies irae*) remained.[61] A practical improvement was effected in the Common of the saints, which now contained forms of the Mass for individual categories of saints, instead of the manifold selection of texts in previous Missals, as well as a Mass for the Dedication of a Church.

As Pope Pius V emphasized in the bull of promulgation *Quo Primum*, the achievement of the Commission's work consisted in returning the Missal to the original norm and rite of the holy Fathers (*ad pristinam Missale sanctorum Patrum normam ac ritum restituerunt*).[62] For this purpose, old codices that were found in the Vatican Library or elsewhere were painstakingly compared. Likewise, writings and testimonials of old, respected authors were consulted. The aim of this task of textual criticism was to return to authentic tradition, that is, to trace the variants in the Missals commonly in use back to the unity and purity of the original. It was, therefore, technically speaking, neither a reform, in the modern sense, nor a sort of archeological reconstruction to restore a supposed original

---

61 The *Stabat Mater* was not introduced to the whole Church until 1727.

62 This was confirmed by his successor, Clement VIII, with the document, "Cum sanctissimum eucharistiae documentum" (likewise printed in the *Missale Romanum*): *Pius Papa V Missale romanum ex decreto sacri Concilii Tridentini ad veterem et emendatiorem normam restitui, Romaeque imprimi curavit* ("Pope Pius V, in accordance with a decree of the sacred Council of Trent, took care that the Roman Missal be restored according to the old and more correct pattern, and printed in Rome").

state as imagined in later times. The Missal's title (*Missale Romanum ex decreto... restitutum*) as well as the bull of promulgation (*Missale... restituerunt*) speak similarly of a restoration.[63] The "original norm and rite of the holy Fathers" was named as a criterion for the restoration.[64] The intention of taking bearings from the great liturgical tradition of the Roman Church was evident during the Council when a Vatican manuscript of the *Sacramentarium Gregorianum* was specifically sent from Rome to Trent in 1563.[65] The goal of a return to the liturgy of the city of Rome was in the minds of the reform commission as well. As is especially demonstrated by the adaptation of the calendar and the selection of the Prefaces, it was largely the time of Gregory VII that presented an important point of reference for the revision of the liturgical books. That pope of the eleventh century was clearly considered by the Tridentine era as an advocate and champion of authentic Roman tradition. The *usus Romanae curiae* took on fundamental importance as it had developed over the course of the centuries since the time of Innocent III (1198–1216). Insofar as the Missal of the Roman Curia largely remained free of the numerous errors that arose from frequent transcriptions and printings, but especially as it was unaffected by late medieval proliferations that found their way into the liturgical books in the form of apocryphal Prefaces, feasts of saints of only local significance, questionable votive Masses, and popular Sequences, the Missal used in Rome itself could become the basis of the uniform missal that would be prescribed for the universal Church.

A comparison of the *Missale Romanum* of 1570 to the first printed edition of the Roman Missal in 1474 shows to what a small degree that edition presented something new, and how strong, in fact, the continuity was with the previous liturgical tradition of the Church in Rome. Aside from the Last Gospel, which is absent in the first edition, but which was not an innovation of the Trent Missal, as it is already found in other Missals of the thirteenth century, there are, at most, minimal differences.[66]

---

63   Cf. Dulac, "La bulle," 14, 28.

64   This is more fully expounded in the bull *Quod a Nobis* for the promulgation of the *Breviarium Romanum* (1568).

65   Cf. J. Deshusses, "Le sacramentaire grégorien de Trente," RBen 78 (1968): 261–81.

66   Cf. Batiffol, *Leçons sur la messe*, 3f.

After the Gospel, the *Per evangelica dicta deleantur nostra delicta* was inserted, which in turn did not represent an invention of the Tridentine Missal, but is witnessed in analogous forms already in the twelfth and thirteenth centuries. In the Offertory prayer *Offerimus* of 1474, it states: *pro nostra et pro totius mundi salute* (for the salvation of us and of the whole world), while the text of 1570 does not have the second *pro*. The phrase *Orate pro me fratres* (1474) was replaced with *Orate fratres* (1570). The final blessing no longer took place before, but after the silent prayer of the priest (*Placeat tibi, sancta Trinitas*). So minor are the changes Pius V ordered to be made to the previous Missal that they are conspicuous only to an expert. It is precisely the insignificance of the differences that demonstrates the indisputable continuity that exists between the two Missals, separated by nearly a century. This continuity was recently validated by the *Institutio generalis* of the *Novus Ordo Missae* (2000): "In fact, the Missal of 1570 differs very little from the first printed edition of 1474, which in turn faithfully takes up again the Missal used in the time of Pope Innocent III."[67] These examples likewise demonstrate that that which was new in the *Missale Romanum* of 1570 with respect to the *editio princeps* of 1474 was in no way created for the first time for the Tridentine Missal, but was rather already common in other liturgical traditions. The "new" prayers and ceremonies were not owed to the plans of a papal liturgical commission, but were the result of a codifying of that which had developed over the course of the centuries. The liturgical legislation did not initiate any new practices, but rather incorporated certain elements of older traditions into the Roman rite of 1570.

As more recent appraisals frequently emphasize, the Tridentine reform commission would scarcely have been capable of reconstructing the ancient Roman form of the celebration of the Mass in so short a time, based on the

---

67 *Missalis Romani Institutio generalis.* Ex editione typica tertia cura et studio Congregationis de Cultu Divino et Disciplina Sacramentorum excerpta (Vatican City: Libreria Editrice Vaticana, 2002), Nr. 7, p. 8: *Re quidem vera Missale illud anni 1570 paululum admodum distat a primo omnium anno 1474 typis edito Missali, quod vicissim fideliter quidem repetit Missale temporis Innocentii PP. III.* The same text may be found in the *Institutio Generalis* (1970), Procemium, no. 7.

state of knowledge at the time;[68] the opinion that they did such a thing (or intended to do such a thing) arises from liturgical archaeologism, which sees the ideal in a return to the earliest stages of development and considers all later forms as obscurations or deviations to be overcome. Neither the Council Fathers of Trent nor Pope Pius V would have embraced such a perception. The reform commission had freed the liturgy from many later embellishments, though they retained the elements that lent a poetic touch to the severe Roman rite. The plethora of longer Sequences was eliminated, but the four of greatest quality were preserved. Processions and extensive ceremonies were reduced, though their most expressive forms, such as the consecration of the Paschal candle, ashes applied in the form of a cross, the procession with palms, and the impressive Holy Week rites were retained.[69]

When reference is made to the "Tridentine Mass" or the "missal of Pius V," the impression occasionally arises that that Council "enacted" a specific form of the liturgy, or that that pope "created" a particular Missal. Consequently, then, over the course of history, new councils and new popes for their part could enact a new form of the liturgy and create a new missal. Historical findings contradict this assumed logic. Pope Pius V in fact initiated only a gentle revision of the Missal commonly used in the Roman Church, and made the rite of the pope and the city of Rome binding for the universal Church of the Latin tradition. The Missal promulgated in 1570 by the bull *Quo Primum* was no legal mandate for how the Mass was to be celebrated from now on, but rather it sanctioned the way in which the Mass had been celebrated until then in Rome.[70] Such a codification had become necessary in order to lead the liturgy out of the state of uncertainty, disorder, and arbitrariness to which it had yielded through the concurrence of various factors. The lack of uniform legislation in liturgical matters up to this point; the medieval diversity in this area, with its exuberant forms of expression; and finally, the intrusion of heretical elements into many

---

68   Cf. Jungmann, *Missarum sollemnia* I, 181; idem, *The Mass of the Roman Rite* I, 137; Meyer, *Eucharistie*, 171; Haunerland, "Einheitlichkeit," 446f.

69   Cf. Fortescue, *The Mass*, 208.

70   Cf. M. Davies, *Pope Paul's New Mass*, 3f.; idem, *Cranmer's Godly Order—The Destruction of Catholicism through Liturgical Change* [Liturgical Revolution I] (Ft. Collins, CO: Roman Catholic Books, ²1995), 115.

local rites during the Reformation period and, as a consequence, arbitrary modifications of the Mass — omission of the Canon, suppression of the saints named there, discontinuation of important texts (Introit, Gradual, and Offertory), and insertion of unauthorized prayers[71] — had brought the liturgy to a crisis, which Pius V, taking up the reforming impulse of the Council of Trent, effectively counteracted, in that he made the *Missale Romanum* of 1570 the stable foundation for a comprehensive renewal of the liturgical life of the Church.[72] He decreed that the Mass, "from now on and for all times," was not allowed to be celebrated in any form other than that of the Missal issued by him.[73]

Pius V certainly recognized the limits of papal power and respected the rights of tradition when he conceded the continuation of those liturgies that were at least 200 years old, as for example, the rites of Milan, Toledo, Braga, Lyon, Liège, Cologne, and Trier, as well as the Dominican and Carthusian rites. That just such a period of time was stipulated may be associated with the emergence of the precursors of the Reformation and their heretical movements (Wycliffe, Hussites).[74] Distinct liturgical traditions already in existence before that time were considered indubitably Catholic and so did not need to be replaced by the Roman Missal.

With the creation of a Missal that guaranteed a unified rite, clear rubrics, and orthodox prayers, without introducing anything new, but rather restoring the classical order according to the standard liturgical tradition developed by the Roman Curia, in order to suppress abuses and free the rite from religious subjectivism as well as other interferences, the intention of the Council of Trent was met to the fullest. No imaginary "Spirit of Trent" must be summoned to declare the Missal to be a suitable implementation of the wishes of the Council Fathers. Unity of the rite of Mass and "restoration of the original, venerable, ancient character and thereby the *Romanitas* of the

71   Cf. Jedin, *Reform des römischen Messbuchs*, 44.

72   Cf. the Collect for the feast of this Saint; cf. also M. Fiedrowicz, "Liturgiereform wider den Zeitgeist. Papst Pius V. — Erneuerung aus Überlieferung," *Dominus vobiscum* 5 (2012): 4–16.

73   Bull *Quo Primum*: . . . *ne in posterum perpetuis futuris temporibus . . . alias quam iuxta Missalis a Nobis editi formulam decantetur aut recitetur.*

74   Cf. Cattaneo, *Il culto cristiano in Occidente*, 318; G. Oury, *La Messe de S. Pie V à Paul VI* (Solesmes: Abbaye Saint-Pierre, 1975), 155f.

liturgy of the Mass" were the two most important desires of the reform.[75] The *Missale Romanum* of 1570 corresponded to longstanding demands for a unified standard for the Roman-Latin rite. It was an impressive conclusion of the Catholic reform movement of the sixteenth century, which found its most tangible and forward-looking expression in the Council of Trent.

Despite some exceptions in the older orders (Carthusians, Dominicans, and Premonstratensians) and individual dioceses (Lyon, Toledo, Milan, and Braga),[76] despite initial hesitations in compliance and temporary countermovements (Neo-Gallican liturgy: France, seventeenth/nineteenth centuries),[77] or the abandonment of diocesan liturgies effected only much later (Münster, Cologne, and Trier, end of the nineteenth century),[78] the *Missale Romanum* found a prompt reception in the universal Church, all things considered. For succeeding centuries, it was *the* Missal of the Roman Catholic Church.

Notwithstanding certain special traditions, the unity of the Church found its most concrete expression in the unity of the rite of the Mass: "Thanks to this masterpiece of religious wisdom, the Catholic was a stranger in no land. Wherever he travelled, he heard the children of the Church singing the same holy chants of Rome—the mother and mistress of Christians."[79] Conversely, the newly-unified liturgy stabilized the unity of the Church against all centrifugal tendencies.

The Sacred Congregation of Rites, created by Pope Sixtus V in 1588, served liturgical unity by supervising adherence to liturgical orders and, in case of doubt, deciding on the correct interpretation of the rubrics.[80]

---

75 Jedin, *Reform des römischen Messbuchs*, 52.

76 Cf. A. A. King, *Liturgies of the Primatial Sees* (London: Longmans, Green, 1957 [repr. Bonn: Nova & Vetera, 2005]).

77 Cf. P. Guéranger, *Institutions liturgiques* II (Paris [i.a.]: Sociéte générale de librairie catholique, ²1880); Meyer, *Eucharistie*, 270f.

78 Cf. A. Heinz, "Im Banne der römischen Einheitsliturgie. Die Romanisierung der Trierer Bistumsliturgie in der zweiten Hälfte des 19. Jahrhunderts," *Römische Quartalschrift für Christliche Altertumskunde und Kirchengeschichte* 79 (1984): 37–92 (= idem, *Liturgie und Frömmigkeit—Beiträge zur Gottesdienst- und Frömmigkeitsgeschichte des (Erz-)Bistums Trier und Luxemburgs zwischen Tridentinum und Vatikanum II* [Trier: Kliomedia, 2008], 243–81).

79 Digby, *Mores Catholici*, 35.

80 Cf. F. R. McManus, *The Congregation of Sacred Rites: A Dissertation* [Canon Law Studies 352] (Washington, DC: The Catholic University of America Press, 1954); R. Naz, "Rites, S.

In this way, it would prevent the newly-unified liturgy from gradually dissolving back into countless variations and returning to the chaotic condition of earlier times. The Congregation was not authorized to change the rubrics or texts of prayers. If necessary, it should indeed restore the liturgical books (*Pontificale*, *Rituale*, and *Caeremoniale*), but it was not created as an organ of further liturgical development. As the description of their members states, "for the protection of the holy rites appointed by the fathers" (*patres sacris tuendis ritibus praepositi*): the Congregation primarily served the preservation of the existing rites.

The question of immutability and enduring force of validity

In the aftermath, it became of special importance that the pope commanded not only the unity and perpetual force of validity but also the immutability of the *Missale Romanum*. The bull of promulgation, *Quo Primum*, requires "that nothing be added to Our newly published Missal, nothing omitted therefrom, and nothing whatsoever altered therein."[81]

This prohibition of changing the Missal applied to each and every individual in the Church, apart from later popes. In so far as it was not a question of a dogmatic regulation, but rather of a disciplinary nature, the principle of *"par in parem potestatem non habet"* — "a peer has no power over his peer" — applies. Indeed, a pope cannot repeal a dogma defined by one of his predecessors. In disciplinary questions, however, no pope may bind his successors to his own decrees. The stipulation maintained in *Quo Primum* can be found in other documents of papal legislation that were indeed changed or abolished by later successors. A distinction must be made, however, between the pope's possession of a *legal* right and his possession of a *moral* right.[82] If a pope possesses authority to release what another pope by virtue of the same authority has bound, then only on the gravest grounds may this practice be undertaken. They must be reasons that would have moved the predecessor in the same situation to abolish

---

Congrégation des," DDC 7 (1958/65): 691–94; Jungmann, *Missarum sollemnia* I, 183f.; idem, *The Mass of the Roman Rite* I, 139. Henceforth in the notes, "SCR" = Sacred Congregation of Rites.

81   For argumentation with this statement after the liturgical reform of Vatican II, cf. Oury, *La Messe*, 27–38.

82   Cf. Davies, *Pope Paul's New Mass*, 14f.

his own law, otherwise the highest authority would suffer from continually contradictory instructions.[83] Even the highest authority of the Church may not change at will the ancient and venerable liturgy of the Church.[84] This signifies an abuse of power (*abusus potestatis*). The authority of the bull of promulgation *Quo Primum* is especially grounded in the fact that here a pope regulated the liturgy in the exercise of the fullness of his papal power and in complete consensus with the vote of an ecumenical council, and in addition, he found himself in accordance with the unbroken tradition of the Roman Church, as well as — regarding the fundamental parts of the Missal — in accordance with the universal Church.[85] Above all, the fact that the *Missale Romanum* of 1570 was intended to be the most perfect liturgical expression of the Catholic teaching on the Eucharist, as the Council of Trent had defined it for all times over against Protestant errors, is a significant argument that the Missal itself, as well as the dogmatic definition of Trent, should remain substantially unchanged for all time.[86] In view of all of these factors, a revocation of the bull *Quo Primum*

---

83 Cf. Dulac, "La bulle," 43; J. Ratzinger, *Salt of the Earth. The Church at the End of the Millennium*, trans. by A. Walker (San Francisco: Ignatius Press, 1997), 176f.: "A community is calling its very being into question when it suddenly declares that what until now was its holiest and highest possession is strictly forbidden and when it makes the longing for it seem downright indecent. Can it be trusted any more about anything else? Won't it proscribe again tomorrow what it prescribes today?" T.M. Kocik, *The Reform of the Reform? A Liturgical Debate: Reform or Return* (San Francisco: Ignatius Press, 2003), Appendix V: J.P. Parsons, "A Reform of the Reform?," 226f.: "The symbolic repudiation of the tradition of Christendom, as Cardinal Ratzinger has stated, has contributed very greatly to an undermining of confidence in the Church in general. While it may be possible *logically* to believe in a Church that is an infallible guide in doctrines of faith and morals but that, for most of the time since her foundation, has promoted, in Archbishop Bugnini's striking phrase, 'lack of understanding, ignorance, and dark night' in the worship of God, it is not possible *psychologically* to carry out a mental juggling act of this sort for very long or on a scale that involves any great number of people. If the *lex orandi* could be so profoundly misguided for so many centuries, what confidence can be placed in the *lex credendi* upheld through these long centuries by the same misguided papacy and ecclesiastical authorities? Here again the adage *lex orandi, lex credendi* rules, but with a new and destructive twist. Either the *damnatio memoriae* of the traditional liturgy must be clearly and publicly revoked, or confidence in the Church's authority will never be recovered."

84 Cf. *Catechism of the Catholic Church* (1992), no. 1125: "Even the supreme authority in the Church may not change the liturgy arbitrarily, but only in the obedience of faith and with religious respect for the mystery of the liturgy."

85 Cf. Dulac, "La bulle," 44.

86 Cf. Davies, *Pope Paul's New Mass*, 16, 590.

remains, legally considered, a possibility, but it could hardly happen with moral justice without seriously calling the *depositum fidei* into question.[87] When Pius V granted and allowed the use of the Missal he promulgated with the power of his apostolic authority "for now and for all times" (*etiam perpetuo*), subsequent history showed that this use could indeed be limited, but was never entirely forbidden.[88] Although Pope Paul VI promulgated a new Order of the Mass (NOM) such that it would "take the place of the old one" (*ut in locum veteris substitueretur*),[89] the Apostolic Constitution *Missale Romanum* (April 3, 1969), in spite of the pressure exerted on the pope, did not employ any condition that explicitly and absolutely abrogated, that is, explicitly and entirely annulled, the Missal used up to that point.[90] The Constitution certainly intended the *Missale Romanum* (1962) to be replaced by a new Missal, but did not, however, intend to suppress the former categorically.[91] Benedict XVI confirmed this in his motu proprio *Summorum Pontificum* of July 7, 2007 (Art. 1), in which he speaks of the "never-abrogated *editio typica* of the Roman Missal."[92]

87 Cf. Dulac, "La bulle," 44.

88 The continued validity of the MRom (1962) alongside the NOM is argued for with, among others, the right of reasonable custom (*consuetudo centenaria aut immemorabilis*): CIC (1983), can. 28: "But unless the law makes express mention of them, it does not revoke centennial or immemorial customs, nor does a universal law revoke particular customs"; likewise CIC (1917), can. 30. Cf. Davies, *Pope Paul's New Mass*, 10, 581–83; H.-L. Barth, *"Die Liebe Christi drängt uns"—Aufsätze zur Kirchenkrise und ihrer Überwindung* (Ruppichteroth: Canisius-Werk, 2003), 125f.; Dulac, "La bulle," 44.

89 Paul VI, Allocution at Consistory, May 24, 1976, in R. Kaczynski (ed.), *Enchiridion Documentorum Instaurationis Liturgicae* II (Rome: C.L.V.-Edizioni Liturgiche, 1988), 117, no. 3477.

90 Cf. G. Weishaupt, *Päpstliche Weichenstellungen. Ein kirchenrechtlicher Kommentar und Überlegungen zur "Reform der Reform"* (Bonn: Verlag für Kultur und Wissenschaft, 2010), 32f.

91 Cf. Weishaupt, *Päpstliche Weichenstellungen*, 33; E.M. De Saventhem, "Die Weitergeltung des 'alten' Missale," UVK 23 (1993): 171–82.

92 Cf. likewise the Letter to the Bishops that accompanies the Apostolic Letter *Summorum Pontificum* on the Roman liturgy prior to the reform of 1970 (July 7, 2007): "As for the use of the 1962 Missal as a *Forma extraordinaria* of the liturgy of the Mass, I wish to draw attention to the fact that this Missal was never juridically abrogated and, consequently, in principle was always permitted" (AAS 99 [2007]: 795; original text in Italian). Cf. Weishaupt, *Päpstliche Weichenstellungen*, 28–35; W.F. Rothe, *Liturgische Versöhnung. Ein kirchenrechtlicher Kommentar zum Motu proprio "Summorum Pontificum" für Studium und Praxis* (Augsburg: Dominus-Verlag, 2009), 59; A.S. Sánchez-Gil, "Gli innovativi profili canonici del Motu proprio *Summorum Pontificum* sull'uso della Liturgia romana anteriore alla riforma del 1970," *Ius Ecclesiae* 19 (2007): 689–707, 697–705; N. Lüdecke, "Kanonistische Anmerkungen zum Motu

Later revised editions of the Missale Romanum *until 1962*

How the instruction of Pius V that the Missal must not be changed was simultaneously respected and received in a differentiated way[93] already became apparent under Pope Clement VIII (1592–1605). In some printings of the *Missale Romanum*, without authorization, the Old Latin renderings (*Vetus Latina*) of the biblical hymn texts (Introit, etc.) had been replaced with the Vulgate version, the lectionary had been changed in places, and other "corrections" had been carried out; in response, the pope had the Roman Missal restored to its original textual form by a commission (Baronius, Bellarmine, and Gavanti). At the same time, he determined certain improvements (clearer distinction between priestly and episcopal final blessings),[94] clarified certain parts of the rubrics,[95] and increased the number of feast days.[96] The revised Missal was promulgated with the bull *Cum Sanctissimum* on July 7, 1604.

A second revised edition of the Missal appeared in 1634 under Urban VIII (1623–1644), who linguistically improved the rubrics and, still poetically

---

proprio *Summorum pontificum,*" LJ 58 (2008): 3–34, 8–14; M. Rehak, *Der ausserordentliche Gebrauch der alten Form des Römischen Ritus. Kirchenrechtliche Skizzen zum Motu proprio Summorum Pontificum vom 07.07. 2007* [MThS.K 64] (St Ottilien: Eos Verlag, 2009), 36–55.

93   Cf. F. Cabrol, "Missel Romain," DACL 11/2 (1934): 1468–94, 1487–90; M. Noirot, "Livres liturgiques de l'Église Romaine," DDC 6 (1957): 595–606; Meyer, *Eucharistie*, 268–72; Jungmann, *Missarum sollemnia* I, 185f.; idem, *The Mass of the Roman Rite* I, 140; P. Jounel, "L'évolution du Missel Romain de Pie IX à Jean XXIII (1846–1962)," *Notitiae* 14 (1978): 246–58; Barth, *Die Liebe Christi*, 118: "If Pius V warned in *Quo Primum* against changes, this can only mean the preservation of the Missal promulgated by him *in toto*, i.e., as a whole liturgical work, not an immutability *in omnibus*, i.e., in all and everything down to the last detail, as the practice of the following centuries showed."

94   According to MRom 1570, the priest should make three Signs of the Cross at the Last Blessing.

95   Clemens VIII, *Cum Sanctissimum: Verum in eo munere peragendo factum est, ut non-nulla ex diligenti librorum antiquorum collatione in meliorem formam redacta, et in regulis et rubricis aliqua uberius et clarius expressa sint, quae tamen ex illorum principiis et fundamentis quasi deducta, illorum sensum imitari potius, et supplere, quam aliquid novi afferre videantur* [In accomplishing this task, some texts were rendered by careful collation of the old books into a more appropriate form and some elements of the instructions as well as rubrics were expressed more fully and clearly, all of which were in the manner of deductions from their principles and foundations, so that they appear to imitate and complete their meaning rather than introduce something new].

96   Cf. J. O'Connell, "A sixteenth century Missal," EL 62 (1948): 102–4.

active even as pope, had two Missal hymns, in addition to the Breviary hymns, revised in the direction of classical meter and Latinity.[97]

How little later popes saw themselves as authorized to make *greater* changes to the traditional Missal is shown in the example of Benedict XIV (1740–1758), who, for all his commitment to liturgical reform, nevertheless did not revise the Missal. Along with the numerous feasts of saints that have been continually incorporated into the Missal since Pius V, as well as slight changes regarding questions of rubrics, a more important innovation in later times consisted in the appointment, under Pope Clement XIII in 1759, of the Preface of the Holy Trinity for green Sundays, taking the place of the *Praefatio Communis* hitherto employed. A revision of Leo XIII (1884) confined itself to the rubrics, accommodating the decisions enacted in the meantime by the Congregation of Rites, and to a revised form of the *sanctorale*, based on the built-up enrichment of the calendar of the saints.

A new *editio typica* was first prepared under Pope Pius X (1903–1914) and promulgated by a decree of the Congregation of Rites on July 25, 1920 under Benedict XV (1914–1922). Again the changes were confined to the rubrics (limitations of the votive Masses and Masses for the Dead), a reduction of the *Missae propriae pro aliquibus locis* from over 200 to 62, the readmission of the old forms of the hymn texts, and the acceptance of two new Prefaces (St Joseph, Requiem Mass).[98] Thus the actual Order of the Mass had not been changed by the popes since the Council of Trent.

The Missal experienced what was undoubtedly the most profound change since 1570 with the renovation of the liturgy of the Easter Vigil (1951) and Holy Week (1956) under Pope Pius XII (1939–1958).[99] After a simplified

---

97 It was the texts of *Gloria laus et honor* (Palm Sunday) and *Pange lingua gloriosi lauream certaminis* (Good Friday). Cf. Baumstark, *Missale Romanum*, 153. Cf. C. Barthold, "Papae poetae — Päpste als Dichter": H.-L. Barth (ed.), *Wahrheit und Schönheit. Christliche Literatur als Einklang von Glaube und Kunst* (Mülheim/Mosel: Carthusianus Verlag, ²2012), 35–125, 103f.

98 Cf. F. Brehm, *Die Neuerungen im Missale* (Regensburg: Verlag Friedrich Pustet, 1920); A. Fortescue, *La Messe. Étude sur la liturgie Romaine*, trans. by A. Boudinhon, Appendice III. La récente édition du Missel (Paris: P. Lethielleux, libraire-éditeur, 1921), 537–39; Cabrol, "Missel Romain," 1489f.; J. Shaw (ed.), *The Case for Liturgical Restoration* (Brooklyn, NY: Angelico Press, 2019), "Prefaces," 113f.

99 Cf. H. J. Auf der Maur, *Feiern im Rhythmus der Zeit* I. Herrenfeste in Woche und Jahr [GdK 5] (Regensburg: Verlag Friedrich Pustet, 1983), 130–32.

version of the rubrics (with the observance of many feasts of the saints, vigils, and octaves either no longer obligatory or abrogated) was already established by the decree of the Congregation of Rites, *Cum Nostra Hac Aetate*[100] on March 23, 1955, Pope John XXIII (1958–1963), by the motu proprio *Rubricarum Instructum* of July 26, 1960, replaced the General Rubrics of the *Missale Romanum* (1570) as well as the later *Additiones et Variationes* of Pius X with the *Codex Rubricarum*, which entered the 1962 Missal with a modified version of the *Ritus Servandus* and the section *De Defectibus*.[101] This Missal also still contained the bull *Quo Primum* in its first pages and emphasized the continuity with the Missal of Pius V. The Missal of Paul VI less than a decade later is the first that no longer contains the Tridentine Missal's bull of promulgation.

The restructuring of the rubrics of 1960 was the first change since 1570 that concerned the Order of the Mass itself. Psalm 42 (*Judica Me*) and the Last Gospel are omitted on certain occasions, and the Confiteor and absolution of the people before Communion were removed, even though they belong to the *Rituale* rather than the Missal. The changes did not have any dogmatic bearing, though they constituted a certain precedent, in so far as now the *Ordo Missae* itself had, for the first time in 400 years, been subject to interference. Subsequently, the Canon did not remain unchanged either. In December of 1962, the name of St Joseph was introduced into the first list of saints.

In reviewing the various editions of the *Missale Romanum*, it becomes apparent that in most respects it remained unaltered in substance over a period of nearly 400 years (1570–1962). The only changes carried out

---

100 Cf. A. Bugnini / I. Bellocchio, *De rubricis ad simpliciorem formam redigendis. Commentarium ad Decretum S. R. C. diei 23 martii 1955* [BEL.P 7] (Rome: C.L.V.-Edizioni Liturgiche, 1955).

101 *Codex Rubricarum* (1960), in AAS 52 (1960): 593–740. Cf. *Ritus servandus in celebratione Missae et De defectibus in celebratione Missae occurrentibus, calendarium, ordo incensationis altaris, praecipua corrigenda in veteribus editionibus* (Vatican City: Typis Polyglottis Vaticanis, 1962); "Ordinationes ad librorum liturgicorum editores circa novas ... Missalis editiones," EL 75 (1961): 401–47 (excerpts of more important passages); F. Kruse, *Die Reform der Rubriken in Brevier und Messfeier* (Cologne: Verlag Wort und Werk, 1960). For the structure of this edition of the missal in general cf. Sodi, "Il *Missale Romanum* tra l'edizione del 1474 e quella del 1962," 69–74. Cf. M. Reinecke, "50 Jahre *Missale Romanum* 1962," *Dominus vobiscum* 5 (2012): 19–25.

were in the area of the rubrics, the introduction of new feasts of saints and Prefaces, and Holy Week. In most respects, the Missal of John XXIII remained in continuity with the Missal of Pius V. One may even maintain that under similar circumstances, the Dominican pope himself would have initiated the changes later carried out, as they ever cautiously took place.

2

Terminology

THE ROMAN RITE OF THE MASS, WHOSE HISTORY HAS
been traced, has received manifold names since the introduction of the
Novus Ordo Missae, each with its own validity, but also possessing certain
limitations. Frequently the "old Mass" is spoken of. The short and neat
wording is correct, in so far as this form of the celebration of the Mass
is of a venerable age and in its core constituents—Canon, orations, pericopes—dates back to Christian antiquity. In the current usage, however,
where new is considered to be better *a priori*, the phrase can easily give
the impression of something antiquated and no longer up to date. The
"old Mass" then easily appears as "the Mass of yesterday," or rather, as "the
outdated Mass." That the "old Mass," however, is no matter of aestheticiz-
ing nostalgia but rather the main concern of an "avant-garde of tradition"
(Mosebach), which seeks to reclaim the importance of the forms of the
past for the present, and which, in view of tradition and that which is
worth protecting, can act as a spiritual cutting edge, is shown in the bold
saying: "the Mass of tomorrow."[1]

This future sustainability is founded not least on the fact that the names
of saints who have significantly shaped this rite are indissolubly linked
with this Mass. As Pope Gregory the Great (590–604) lent the Roman
Canon its definite design, later only slightly altered, set the *Pater Noster*
in its present place, and created various prayers that are still preserved in
today's *Missale Romanum* (1962), one can justifiably speak of the "Gregorian rite," or rather, "the Mass of St Gregory."[2] By the same token, "the

---

1   Cf. G. Rodheudt, "Nostalgie oder Avantgarde?," *Vatican-Magazin* 12 (2008): 39–47,
47: "The 'Old Mass' is necessary for the Church's recovery from sickness. All that it needs is
a vanguard to put it back on the candlestick. It is the Mass of tomorrow, because without it
there will be no tomorrow."

2   Cf. M. Mosebach, *The Heresy of Formlessness. The Roman Liturgy and Its Enemy*, rev.
ed., trans. by G. Harrison (Brooklyn, NY: Angelico Press, 2018), 43–44: "It should really be

Missal of St Pius V" can be spoken of, provided we remain aware that this pope could as little create a new Missal as any other Successor of Peter; rather, he only promulgated a uniform missal for the Latin Church with the *Missale Romanum* of 1570, which was rooted in the centuries-old tradition of the Roman rite and at the same time could give proof of its theological-spiritual quality, as it already at that time went back over 400 years without great alterations. As this Missal was the fruit of the Council of Trent, we can indeed speak of the "Tridentine Mass,"[3] in so far as the Missal of 1570 is the adequate expression of the Catholic theology of the sacrifice of the Mass solemnly defined at this council.[4]

Recognizing that the Missal of Trent, according to the words of the bull of promulgation *Quo Primum*, is in no way a new creation or substantial change of the Missal used at that time, but rather a restoration according to the "original norm and rite of the holy Fathers," the rite that was codified there can be referred to as the "traditional Mass," by reason of the unbroken continuity of tradition.[5] This applies to the past preceding the Tridentine Council as well as the aftermath, since that rite has been faithfully passed down with only minimal changes up to the present time. The expression "the traditional Mass" also identifies the corresponding rite

---

called the Mass of Saint Gregory the Great, just as the Orthodox speak of the Liturgy of Saint John Chrysostom." Cf. Antonio Cardinal Cañizares, "Préface de l'édition espagnole": N. Bux, *La réforme de Benoît XVI. La liturgie entre innovation et tradition* [Annexe 2] (Perpignan: Édition Tempora, 2009), 201: "the Byzantine rite already knows a liturgy of St Gregory, pope of Rome: that of the presanctified used during Lent."

3   In the last official communiqué: Congregation for Divine Worship and the Discipline of the Sacraments, *Quattuor Abhinc Annos* / Letter to the presidents of episcopal conferences, Oct. 3, 1984 (AAS 76 [1984]: 1088f.) / trans.: *Osservatore Romano*. English edition Oct. 22, 1984: "so-called 'Tridentine rite.'"

4   Cf. Rodheudt, "Nostalgie oder Avantgarde?," 44: "The Council of Trent...does not invent anything new. But it newly catalogs and rearranges the liturgical treasuries to make them unassailable against the disturbances of the time."

5   Cf. J. Bona, *Rerum liturgicarum libri II*, 1,6,3: *Opera omnia* (Antwerp: H. & C. Verdussen / B. Foppens / J.B. Verdussen, 1694), 209: *Debet igitur unaquaque Ecclesia custodire ritus suos, sed receptos a Maioribus, longoque usu praescriptos, et legitima auctoritate approbatos. Si quid vero innovatum, si quid perperam immutatum, id expungendum et corrigendum est* [Each Church shall preserve her own rites, but they must be received from the forefathers and established by longstanding use and given approbation by legitimate authority. However, if something new is introduced, if it is falsely changed, it has to be expunged and corrected].

as the inalienable component of the *depositum fidei*. The early Christian theorist of the Catholic principle of tradition, St Vincent of Lérins, defined the character of authentic transmission, when he timelessly and effectively explained the apostolic instruction *depositum custodi* ("keep that which has been committed to thy trust," 1 Tim 6:20):

> What is "committed"? It is that which has been entrusted to you, not that which you have invented; what you have received, not what you have devised; not a matter of ingenuity, but of doctrine; not of private acquisition, but of public tradition; a matter brought to you, not created by you, a matter you are not the author of, but the keeper of; not the teacher, but the learner; not the leader, but the follower. This deposit, he says, guard. Preserve the "talent" (Mt 25:15) of the Catholic faith unviolated and unimpaired. What has been entrusted to you may remain with you and may be handed down by you. You received gold; hand it down as gold. I do not want you to substitute one thing for another; I do not want you shamelessly to put lead in the place of gold, or, deceitfully, copper. I do not want something that resembles gold, but real gold.[6]

Applied to the classical Roman rite of the Mass, these statements demonstrate how even here the principles formulated by Vincent were always truly observed. Already the Apostle Paul, otherwise so theologically creative, understood that in the core area of the Faith, the mystery of the Holy Eucharist, he was only a reliable transmitter of that which he had himself received: "For I have received of the Lord that which also I delivered unto you, that the Lord Jesus, in the same night in which he was betrayed, took bread, and giving thanks, broke and said: Take ye and eat: This is my body, which shall be delivered for you" (1 Cor 11:23f.). In a similar way, the Apostles' successors, popes and bishops, as well as priests, monks, theologians, and masters of ceremonies, have always considered the rite

---

6 Vincent of Lérins, *Commonitorium* 22,3–5 (CCL 64, 177 / Vincent of Lérins, *Commonitories*, trans. by R.E. Morris, *The Fathers of the Church* 7 [New York: Fathers of the Church, Inc., 1949], 308).

of the Mass as an entrusted *depositum* that they must faithfully transmit, without replacing what they have received with something entirely new and different. The term "the traditional Mass" embodies this fundamental non-disposable character and pre-givenness of the liturgical rite, which cannot be invented, imagined, and originated by anyone, but rather is received from tradition and passed on by means of tradition. It was especially this distinctive loyalty to tradition that allowed the Roman liturgy to maintain its identity for centuries, while only allowing alterations where "the good of the Church genuinely and certainly requires them,"[7] and, in contrast, to resist all those efforts for reform that would have frivolously relinquished the treasures collected in the past in sacramentaries, antiphonaries, and lectionaries.[8] The lovely expression "the Mass of all times" (or "the Mass of ages") emphasizes this unique continuity of tradition. In its continual development this rite of Mass has included the wealth of all epochs within itself and in unchanged identity shows itself to the peoples of all times.[9]

---

7   Second Vatican Council, SC 23. Cf. M. Davies: "Examine the changes that have been made, and find one, just one, that the good of the Church *genuinely and certainly required*. You will search in vain. Find one—just one—that has made us better and more spiritual Catholics. You will search in vain. Find one that has contributed to the unity of the Church. You will search in vain. Find one that has grown organically from forms already existing. You will search in vain. Did the *Judica me* really have to go? Was the beautiful double *Confiteor* truly a cause of spiritual atrophy? Did kneeling at the *Incarnatus* cause great harm to the cause of doctrinal orthodoxy? Were those sublime Offertory prayers alienating young Catholics from the faith? Did the good of the Church genuinely and certainly require that the inspired word of the Last Gospel no longer be read at the conclusion of every Mass?" ("The New Mass. An Ecumenical Compromise," *The Latin Mass* [January–February 1993]: 39).

8   Cf. A. Croegaert, *Les rites et prières du Saint Sacrifice de la Messe* I (Malines: [s.n.], 1954), 519: "The basic law of the Roman Church's discipline of worship . . . is indeed the maintenance of tradition, the religious respect for antiquity; this instinct of immutability protects it against the spirit of novelty and maintains it similar to herself—not that she condemns without mercy all change and progress, but she knows that it is easier to innovate than to maintain. The more liturgical studies advance, the more we see all the gratitude we owe to the Roman Church, which has constantly resisted the enterprises instigated by this fever of innovations and has faithfully kept the centuries-old treasures of her piety, so patiently accumulated in her lectionaries, her sacramentaries, her antiphonaries, her liturgical books by her great popes: Leo, Gelasius, and Gregory. One wonders what would have become of our liturgy if it had been abandoned to the anti-traditional whims of so many of our contemporaries, who are animated by a zeal more pious than enlightened."

9   Cf. Mosebach, *Heresy of Formlessness*, 52: "The miracle of Catholicism was a rite that spoke to mankind's most elevated minds and to unlettered goat-herds, to Chinese and

The expression introduced with the motu proprio *Summorum Pontificum* (July 7, 2007), "extraordinary form (*forma extraordinaria*) of the Roman rite,"[10] is, if anything, a formulation of liturgical discipline,[11] while the term "older use/custom" (*usus antiquior*), used simultaneously in this context, remains purely on the chronological level.[12] Both terms may ecclesiastically fulfill their purpose for the moment, but in the long run will hardly be capable of revealing to all believers that "the Roman liturgy in the *usus antiquior* [is] a precious treasure to be preserved."[13]

If the "older use" does not merely look back over the fifty years in which it has been celebrated, but rather represents a work of art of the first rank, cultivated over the course of many centuries, then the title "classical rite of the Mass" may unquestionably be awarded, pertaining to the classical character of the perfected form, which gives adequate expression to the substance, notions, and ideas, harmoniously unifies truth and beauty, contains both depth and fullness, proves to be exemplary, and remains timelessly significant.

Where and when throughout the centuries was this exact Mass not celebrated: in the great cathedrals of Europe, by bishops and cardinals in

---

Africans, Crusader knights and atomic physicists." R. de Mattei, *La Liturgia della Chiesa nell'epoca della secolarizzazione* (Chieti: Edizioni Solfanelli, 2009), 74f.: "The Mass of the Apostles opened and closed all the twenty-one ecumenical councils of the Church, from Nicaea to Vatican II. It was celebrated beneath the magnificent vaults of St Peter's as well as in the most humble and remote chapels at the ends of the earth, wherever the zeal of the missionaries arrived. It was at the center of the liturgy of all religious orders founded in history; it was celebrated on the fields of the Crusades, on the papal galleys, before the battles of Lepanto and of Kahlenberg, just before the liberation of Vienna; the splendor of Cluny and the liturgical revival of Dom Guéranger wrapped it in majesty and splendor. The martyrs of the faith in the twentieth century, from Mexico to Spain, to communist Russia, drew strength from it to resist their torturers. The same words, the same gestures, the same rite, the same creed, nourished the Church and the Christian society over the centuries."

10 To what extent *one* rite with *two* forms of expression can be spoken of is critically discussed by A. Hocquemiller / L.-M. de Blignières, "Zur Frage der 'zwei Ausdrucksformen' des Römischen Ritus," UVK 39 (2009): 195–217, 209–11.

11 Cf. J. Nebel, "Die 'ordentliche' und die 'ausserordentliche' Form," 174.

12 Cf. Card. Cañizares, "Préface de l'édition espagnole," Bux, *Réforme* (Annexe 2), 201: "'extraordinary form'... is a characterization far too extrinsic. *Usus antiquior* has the defect of being a purely chronological reference."

13 Instruction *Universae Ecclesiae* of the Pontifical Commission Ecclesia Dei (May 13, 2011), no. 8a, in AAS 103 (2011): 413–20, 415.

grand vestments, accompanied by choruses and orchestras, but also in the remotest mission stations in the jungle with the poorest of provisions; in time-honored abbey churches as well as on the front lines of the theaters of war; in the pope's private chapel as well as in concentration camp barracks; at the coronation of emperors as well as in a hermit's cell; at the discovery of new continents as well as in the sickrooms of medieval infirmaries — always and everywhere it was the same Mass!

Who has not celebrated this exact Mass for centuries past, prayed with these exact words, heard the same Gospel on exactly the same day of the year: Thomas More, Teresa of Avila, Ignatius of Loyola, Peter Canisius, the Curé of Ars, Cardinal John Henry Newman, Pope Pius X, and count-less other saints. How many faithful have not taken upon themselves the greatest sacrifice for the sake of this Mass?[14] How many have not become martyrs for the sake of this Mass?[15] How many conversions has it not given, provoked by an encounter with exactly this rite?[16]

14 Cf. M. Davies, *Cranmer's Godly Order*, 295–96: "But this despised remnant had a treasure denied to those who looked upon them with such contempt, the Mass of St. Pius V, described by Father Frederick Faber as 'the most beautiful thing this side of heaven.' This was the pearl of great price for which they were prepared to pay all that they had — and pay it they did, priest and layman, butcher's wife and schoolmaster. The victors had the churches and cathedrals built for the celebration of the traditional Latin Mass, the vanquished had the Mass, and it was the Mass that mattered."

15 Cf. Alcuin Reid (ed.), *A Bitter Trial. Evelyn Waugh and John Carmel Cardinal Heenan on the Liturgical Changes*, rev. ed. (San Francisco: Ignatius Press, 2011), 35: "As the service pro-ceeded in its familiar way, I wondered how many of us wanted to see any change. The church is rather dark. The priest stood rather far away. His voice was not clear and the language he spoke was not that of everyday use. This was the Mass for whose restoration the Elizabethan martyrs had gone to the scaffold."

16 Cf. F. Lelotte, *Heimkehr zur Kirche. Konvertiten des 20. Jahrhunderts* 3 (Lucerne: Rex-Verlag, 1958), 208f.: "The symbolism of the liturgy charmed him (*sc.*, Robert Hugh Ben-son, 1871–1914), as it has always captured the artists. The depth and breadth of the content and the importance of the Catholic liturgy he could only suspect, at most, but the touching and devout way in which the Catholic liturgy was celebrated spontaneously came to him." K. Brem, *Konvertit und Kirche* (Nürnberg: Glock und Lutz, 1960), 241: "Incidentally, I (*sc.*, K.L.W. Pahl, born 1818) often went to Catholic churches, and, although I did not know the faith, my mind was soon deeply moved by the solemnity of the service, the silence and devotion of the kneeling faithful crowd, and involuntarily I was struck with wonder and awe at visiting a church into which I had previously considered it a sin against the Almighty to step." Reid (ed.), *Bitter Trial*, 41: "I (*sc.*, E. Waugh) was not at all attracted by the splendour of her great ceremonies — which the Protestants could well counterfeit. Of the extraneous attractions of

What works of art have not been created to serve exactly this rite? In the realm of music one thinks of the unique sound of Gregorian chant, the grand compositions of Palestrina and de Victoria; in the realm of architecture one thinks of the Gothic cathedrals or the imposing works of Bramante and Michelangelo.[17] In painting, Raphael's so-called *Disputà* shows the triumph of the Holy Eucharist that binds Heaven and earth, and all who have celebrated the sacrifice of the Mass in its traditional form gather there around the monstrance. Finally, in literature one finds, in different forms, positive reminiscences of the old liturgy, in no way only by Catholic authors, but even by those outside the Church.[18]

The classical rite can identify itself by the power of forming saints, obtaining conversions, and inspiring artists.

---

the Church [the one] which most drew me was the spectacle of the priest and his server at low Mass, stumping up to the altar without a glance to discover how many or how few he had in his congregation.... That is the Mass I have grown to know and to love." V. Neumann, *Die Theologie des Renouveau catholique* [Regensburger Studien zur Theologie 65] (Frankfurt a. M.: Peter Lang Verlag, 2007), 107, 126, 140.

17 Cf. K. Lechler, *Die Confessionen in ihrem Verhältnisse zu Christus* (Heilbronn: Verlag Gebr. Henninger, 1877), 166f.: "Out of the Mass, among other things, the most profound splendor and ingenious fullness of the Catholic Church's architectural style has grown.... Only on account of this worship can the proud majesty of a Gothic cathedral be understood.... But Romanesque architecture, too, has its necessary requirement in the service of the Mass.... Without the High Mass, no master builder of the spirited Middle Ages would have developed the basilica to this sublime, serious, and magnificent style. Without the Catholic service, neither Raphael nor Fra Angelico, Hubert van Eyck nor the younger Holbein, nor Lorenzo Ghiberti, Veit Stoss, and Peter Vischer would have brought to light the wonders of their brush and chisel, and adorned the Church of God on earth with a wealth of holy beauty that will remain a gem for all ages." M. Brillant (ed.), *Eucharistia. Encyclopédie populaire sur l'eucharistie* (Paris: Bloud et Gay, 1941), 829–912.

18 Cf. Mosebach, *Heresy of Formlessness*, 79: "Here we sense the liturgy's immense cultural and creative power. Even its opponents could not avoid being in its shadow; they actually depended for nourishment on its aesthetic substance." Cf. B. Matteucci, "L'eucaristia nella letteratura," A. Piolanti (ed.), *Eucaristia. Il mistero dell'altare nel pensiero e nella vita della chiesa* (Rome [i.a.]: Desclée de Brouwer, 1957), 1171–88.

3

Organic Development and Continuity

IN 1845, JOHN HENRY NEWMAN WROTE ABOUT TWO
great Church Fathers of the fourth century, Athanasius, representing the
Eastern Church, and Ambrose, representative of the Western Church, in
his work, *An Essay on the Development of Christian Doctrine*:

> May we not add, that were those same saints who once sojourned,
> one in exile, one on embassy, at Treves, to come more northward
> still, and to travel until they reached another fair city, seated among
> groves, green meadows, and calm streams, the holy brothers would
> turn from many a high aisle and solemn cloister which they found
> there, and ask the way to some small chapel where Mass was said
> in the populous alley or forlorn suburb?[1]

Newman is asking: if both of those great witnesses of the Faith of the
early Church were to come into our times, to enter English lands, to reach
Oxford, what situation would they discover there, where could they turn to
celebrate the Holy Mass? The Anglicans — as Newman has in mind — possess the grand houses of God. One thinks of the awesome cathedrals of
Canterbury, Winchester, Salisbury, York, and Durham. The Catholics, on
the other hand, have preserved the Faith as the Apostles handed it down
to them, despite their marginal existence in society at that time.[2] "[They
would] ask the way to some small chapel where Mass was said," wrote

---

1   J. H. Newman, *An Essay on the Development of Christian Doctrine* (Westminster, MD:
Christian Classics, 1968), 98.

2   The antithesis "they have the churches, we the faith" is already found analogously in
the Arian controversy in the middle of the 4th century: cf. Athanasius, *Epist. filiis suis* (PG
26, 1189) and Gregory Nazianzen, *Oratio* 33,15 (SCh 318, 188f. / Cyril of Jerusalem, *Catechetical
Lectures*, Gregory Nazianzen, *Select Orations*, trans. by C. G. Browne / J. E. Swallow, *A Select
Library of the Nicene and Post-Nicene Fathers of the Christian Church*, 2nd series, 7 [New York:
The Christian Literature Company / Oxford: James Parker, 1894; repr. 1976], 333).

Newman. In other words: they looked for a place, remote and unimposing as it may be, where they would find the Holy Mass celebrated in the same way in which they had celebrated it. And, Newman asserts further, they would find this place where the Catholic Missal lay on the altar, and not the Anglican *Book of Common Prayer* (1549).[3]

The objection can be raised, however: is not this view an anachronism? How could a Christian from the fourth century recognize the liturgical forms of late antiquity in the so-called Tridentine Missal and consider the Missal promulgated by Pope Pius V in 1570 as an adequate expression of the early Christian spirit of prayer? Yet even for a fourth-century Christian, the Tridentine Missal clearly deserves precedence over the *Book of Common Prayer*, the official liturgical book of the Anglican denomination, as that Anglican confessional document broke "with essential early Christian traditions, especially in Eucharistic theology,"[4] and already in the second modified edition of 1552 no longer used the word "Mass." The Anglican worship service was stripped of all references to sacrifice, it was celebrated on a table facing the people, and all of the prayers were audibly recited in English, that is, in the mother tongue, for the congregation. Communion was distributed under both species, with the host put into the hand.[5]

Newman's thought quoted above, whereby each of those two representatives from the early time of the Faith discovered and sensed with unmistakable intuition that the Holy Mass, celebrated around 1845 in a small chapel with the so-called Tridentine Missal, was their own, still leads to the question: was there truly a noticeable continuity between a fourth-century celebration of the Eucharist and the 1570 codified rite of the Mass, which is at the basis of the 1962 Missal, and therefore at the basis of that form of the rite of Mass for which Pope Benedict XVI once

---

3 B. Fischer, "Book of Common Prayer," *Lexikon für Theologie und Kirche* 2 (²1958): 603f.

4 Fischer, "Book of Common Prayer," 603; cf. M. Davies, "Die Zerstörung des englischen Katholizismus durch die anglikanische Liturgiereform," UVK 32 (2002): 89–112; idem, *Cranmer's Godly Order — The Destruction of Catholicism through Liturgical Change* [Liturgical Revolution I] (Ft. Collins, CO: Roman Catholic Books, ²1995).

5 Cf. Davies, "Zerstörung," 110; Ph. Hughes, *The Reformation in England* III (London: Hollis & Carter, 1954), 88–91.

again, with the motu proprio *Summorum Pontificum* on 7/7/07, provided a right of residence in the Church? Has not liturgical historical research demonstrated by now how many elements that are considered to be characteristic of the "old Mass" came to be included relatively recently, and in no way therefore belonged to the Roman rite in its earliest stage? Let us name only a few: the prayers at the foot of the altar belong to the younger texts of the classical rite of the Mass. The Confiteor was first observed in the tenth century, the psalm *Judica me* appeared in the ninth or tenth century. The Offertory prayers, recited silently by the priest at the Offertory (*Offerimus / In spiritu humilitatis / Suscipe, sancta Trinitas*), as well as the *Orate fratres*, are first discovered in the sacramentaries of the ninth/tenth century and reached the Missal of the Papal Curia only in the thirteenth century. The silent Canon began to prevail from the middle of the eighth century. The priest's preparatory prayers before Holy Communion are discovered in the Missals of the eleventh century. The Last Gospel — the prologue of the Gospel of John — was first added to the Dominican Missal in the thirteenth century, and was made obligatory for the entire church by the Dominican Pope Pius V in 1570.

All of these, however, were additions or enhancements that did not alter the liturgy of the Mass.[6] Instead, these prayers and gestures were intended

6 Cf. M. Mosebach, *Häresie der Formlosigkeit. Die römische Liturgie und ihr Feind* (Munich: Carl Hanser Verlag, 2007), 222f.: "The enemies of the traditional rite never forget to point out with triumph that talk of an 'unaltered liturgy' is a myth. In truth, there has never been any reluctance to intervene in the rite. There has by no means been merely that unconscious, unnoticed, organic development and unfolding of the rite, of which the defenders of the ritual tradition speak, but many extremely conscious measures ordered from above. What reader of the great work of Josef Jungmann, for example, would contradict this assertion? It appears, if one reads such scholarly accounts, that there has in fact been ceaseless movement in the succession of liturgical functions. This psalm has been inserted here and that one left out there. This sequence was used here and that one was deleted there. Intercessions and processions came and went. The blessing was given from the altar or when the bishop leaves the altar. The liturgical colors multiplied. Special liturgical vessels came into use and disappeared again. Some prayers were heard aloud in one century, softly in another, then again prayed aloud; others were first prayed in the sacristy, and later in the church. Anyone who wants to get lost in this jungle may do so — but a confirmation of the thesis that the liturgy was never felt to be inviolable, he will *not* find there. I would like to hear the following concession from the lips of one of the friends of reform: namely, that, in the history of the Church until Pope Paul VI, no one ever dared to question the following main features of the traditional liturgy: the sacral

only to express more clearly and deeply the mystery of the Mass.[7] In a certain way, this amplification of the liturgy resembles the process of the development of dogma. The monastic priest of southern Gaul, Vincent of Lérins (434), once compared the function of theologians in the Church with that of the Old Testament figure of Bezalel, who, "filled with the spirit of God, with wisdom and understanding, and knowledge in all manner of work" (Ex 31:2f.), completed the tabernacle of the Ark of the Covenant not according to his own plans, but by the Wisdom of God:

> O priest, O interpreter, O doctor, if a gift of heaven has prepared you by mental power, experience, and knowledge, to be the Bezalel of the spiritual Tabernacle, to cut the precious gems of divine dogma (*pretiosas divini dogmatis gemmas exsculpe*), to put them together faithfully (*fideliter coapta*), to adorn them judiciously (*adorna sapienter*), to add glamor, grace, and loveliness (*adice splendorem, gratiam, venustatem*) . . . [8]

The description easily lends itself to the shaping of the Roman rite of the Mass. This further decoration was indubitably a process of growth, yet characterized by a great continuity on the level of texts and ceremonies, as a comparison of the *Missale Romanum* (1962) with the oldest source document of the Roman rite, the *Ordo Romanus Primus* (end of the seventh, beginning of the eighth century) will show.[9] Of this Missal it

---

language; the celebration of the liturgy *versus orientem*, with priests and congregation together aligned toward the risen Christ; finally, the most important: the character of the liturgy as a sacrificial rite. These elements of the liturgy were always sacrosanct and beyond discussion, and of course the Second Vatican Council submitted to this tradition. It is amazing how well a biased liturgical science has managed to keep these simple facts carefully hidden under a raft of detailed knowledge." (This appendix, *De liturgia recuperanda*, is not contained in the English translation of this book.)

7 Cf. M. Davies, *Pope John's Council* [Liturgical Revolution II] (Kansas City, MO: Angelus Press, [2]2008), 345f.

8 Vincent of Lérins, *Commonitorium* 22,6 (CCL 64, 177 / Vincent of Lérins, *Commonitories*, 308).

9 Cf. S. Conrad, "Ein Ritus in zwei Formen? Über die Frage der Einheit des Römischen Ritus," *Theologisches* 40 (2010), 239–60, 251, where the ritual continuity is demonstrated using the example of the beginning of the Mass.

can be said with justice that it is the only "Missal that has grown continuously throughout the centuries, starting with the sacramentaries of the ancient Church."[10]

This process of continual development was accompanied from time to time by an effort to purify the existing form, in which many elements incorporated over the course of history but ultimately foreign to the Roman spirit were rejected and removed (e.g., the number of the private prayers of the priest, the so-called apologiae, or the abundance of Sequences).[11] Such purifying acts were always carried out in a cautious and restrained manner, in reverence for tradition. The historically perfected form of the Roman rite was never discarded as unsuitable for the requirements of the present age in order to be replaced by newly fabricated products, as for example the French liturgists of the eighteenth century demanded should be done in order to introduce the so-called Neo-Gallican reformed liturgy.[12] In a similar way, the introduction of the so-called Quiñones

10   J. Ratzinger, *Milestones: Memoirs 1927–1977*, trans. by E. Leiva-Merikakis (San Francisco: Ignatius Press, 1998), 147f. Cf. M. Righetti, *Manuale di storia liturgica* III: L'eucaristia (Milan: Àncora Editrice, 1949), 154: "The Tridentine Missal was the final outcome of a long evolution, which, through its main phases, is affiliated essentially with the oldest tradition of the Roman Church, transmitted in the Sacramentaries and the *Ordines*. The fundamental elements that make up the plan of the *Ordo Missae* are Roman: and if, in some of their areas, with the passing of the centuries, there were inserted formulas and peculiarities of foreign origin, they have not altered the essential structure; indeed, they have made the ancient austere beauty stand out. If, in short, we can say that our Mass is substantially the same as it was for St Gregory, St Gelasius, St Leo, St Hippolytus, St Justin, it reunites us even with the Mass of the Apostles and with the *Coena Dominica*."

11   Cf. pp. 21 and 30.

12   Cf. P. Guéranger, *Institutions liturgiques* II, 225f.: "Here are some men who wish to persuade the Catholic Church, in one of her greatest and most illustrious provinces, that she lacks a liturgy in conformity with her needs, that she knows less about the things of prayer than some doctors of the Sorbonne, that her faith lacks a suitable expression—because the liturgy is the expression of the faith of the Church. Moreover, these presumptuous men who have weighed the Church, who have probed her needs, do not merely pronounce that her liturgy errs in some details by defect or by excess, but present her to the people as devoid of a suitable system in all of her worship. They begin to draw up a new scheme for the offices—new as to the general and the specific lines. Here they are at work: the books of St Pius V, which are nothing else than those of St Gregory, are not even worth naming anymore.... A complete system must be hatched from a particular brain and printed." Idem, "Considérations sur la liturgie catholique," *Mémorial catholique* 28 (February 1830), 51, 54: "Any liturgy that we will have seen newly introduced, which would therefore not be that of our fathers, cannot deserve

Breviary (1534), which consisted almost exclusively of texts from Sacred Scripture, proved a failure, as did the reform plans of the Synod of Pistoia (1786), which were affected by the Enlightenment.[13] As a glance at the historical development shows, the liturgical rites, ceremonies, and prayers were never drafted by committees of experts. In general, all of the development is in fact due to the liturgical practice itself, whose usages and customs were first collected and codified in the rubrics only after they had been proven in practice.[14] A few, such as the Roman Canon, have belonged to the unchangeable, sacrosanct core of the Mass from earliest times. Many ceremonies have their source in practical requirements, such as the Gradual chant, which filled the time between the Epistle and the proclamation of the Gospel while the procession made its way to the ambo. Others found their way in later, as they grew from the piety of medieval Christians and gradually became fixed components of the Mass, such as the reading of the Last Gospel. It is accurately said: "Liturgies are not made, they grow in the devotion of centuries."[15] The

---

this name. A people did not arrive at the seventeenth century of its existence without having had a language sufficient to its thought.... There are churches in France that, next year, with the help of printers, will be able to date from 1831 the liturgies that their luminaries fabricate from top to bottom in the silence of their study!" Quoted from: Dom Guéranger, *Abbé de Solesmes, par un moine bénédictin* I (Paris: Éditions Plon [i.a.], 1909), 56f.

13 Cf. L. Dobszay, *The Restoration and Organic Development of the Roman Rite*, with an introduction and ed. by L.P. Hemming (London / New York: T & T Clark, 2010), 6f.: "The three characteristic features of these reform-rites may be summed up as follows: (a) They were the expression of individual, voluntaristic ideas.... (b) They were not rites that evolved over long periods and developed through an ongoing process of minor changes, but were the result of hasty work at a writing desk. (c) They exuded a detectable odour of insensitivity or downright contempt for the tradition. They could not properly appreciate the importance of tradition in liturgical life. Even if the authors did not declare it (as their descendants did at the end of the twentieth century), they were convinced that the liturgy ought not to preserve the past, but rather was to serve the requirements of their own age, and they behaved as if the two were mutually exclusive."

14 Cf. Davies, *Cranmer's Godly Order*, 115f.: "It would be impossible to find evidence of some form of liturgical commission being set up in the early Church which decided, for example, that it would be fitting for the priest to kiss the altar from time to time, deciding upon the most appropriate moments for this to be done, and then composing rubrics to ensure that priests acted upon their instructions in future. What happened was that the priest kissed the altar at certain times as a result of customs which had grown up naturally, and eventually this gesture was formally codified as a rubric."

15 O. Chadwick, *The Reformation* (Harmondsworth: Penguin Books, 1981), 119.

traditional Mass is a form of prayer perfected over the centuries, owing to a living process of organic growth and development.

Even though the rite of the Mass indisputably changed in the course of the centuries, there were never numerous changes of a drastic kind in a short time;[16] rather, there were often imperceptible changes that resembled gradual structural change in nature.[17] It was ever evident that the new forms "in some way grew organically from forms already existing."[18] The development of the classical Roman rite of the Mass perfectly corresponds to the criteria that Vincent of Lérins formulated for the authentic development of ecclesiastical doctrine:

> In the same way, the dogma of the Christian religion ought to follow
> these laws of progress, so that it may be consolidated in the course
> of years, developed in the sequence of time, and sublimated by
> age — yet remain incorrupt and unimpaired, complete and perfect
> in all the proportions of its parts and in all its essentials (let us
> call them members and senses), so that it does not allow of any
> change, or any loss of its specific character, or any variation of its
> inherent form. . . . Whatever has been planted in the husbandry
> of God's Church by the faith of the fathers should, therefore, be
> cultivated and guarded by the zeal of their children; it should
> flourish and ripen; it should develop and become perfect. For it
> is right that those ancient dogmas of heavenly philosophy should
> in the course of time be thoroughly cared for, filed, and polished;
> but it is sinful to change them, sinful to behead them or mutilate

16 Cf. Dobszay, *Restoration*, 5f.: "There were theoreticians in the field of the Roman rite as early as the Middle Ages who were discontented with what they experienced in their environment; they proposed modifications, sometimes even significant modifications. . . . These reformers differed, however, from 'modern' ones in three respects: they never laid hands on the essential elements of the rite; their proposals were — in comparison with the entirety of the rite — few in number; and in most cases they did not want to 'improve' the rite, but rather to effect a 'return' from 'disturbed' or 'corrupted' forms to the 'pristine' practice of Rome."

17 Cf. Mosebach, *Heresy of Formlessness*, 9: "Such changes as occurred took place organically, unconsciously, unintentionally, and without a theological plan. They grew out of the practice of liturgy, just as a landscape is altered over centuries by wind and water." Cf. ibid., 17f.

18 Cf. Second Vatican Council, SC 23.

them. They may take on more evidence, clarity, and distinctness, but it is absolutely necessary that they retain their plenitude, integrity, and basic character. . . . The Church of Christ, zealous and cautious guardian of the dogmas deposited with it, never changes any phase of them. It does not diminish them or add to them; it neither trims what seems necessary nor grafts things superfluous; it neither gives up its own nor usurps what does not belong to it. But it devotes all its diligence to one aim: to treat tradition faithfully and wisely; to nurse and polish what from old times may have remained unshaped and unfinished; to consolidate and to strengthen what already was clear and plain; and to guard what already was confirmed and defined.[19]

The organic, homogenous unfolding of the traditional rite of the Mass can similarly be illustrated on the basis of the seven criteria identified by John Henry Newman in his work *Essay on the Development of Christian Doctrine* (1845) in order to show how the changes witnessed in the form of the Roman Catholic Church over the course of centuries are the expression of a continuous and seamless development.[20] The first criterion is the "Preservation of Type," which deals with the protection of the original form and proportions. With all of the changes to the outward form, the Eucharist's sacrificial character in the traditional rite of the

---

19 Vincent of Lérins, *Commonitorium* 23,9.12f.16f. (CCL 64, 178–80 / Vincent of Lérins, *Commonitories*, 310–12). Cf. A. Reid, *The Organic Development of the Liturgy* (San Francisco: Ignatius Press, ²2005), 308: "Organic development holds openness to growth (prompted by pastoral needs) and continuity with Tradition in due proportion. It listens to scholarly *desiderata* and considers anew the value of practices lost in the passage of time, drawing upon them to improve liturgical Tradition gradually, only if and when this is truly necessary. Ecclesiastical authority supervises this growth, at times making prudential judgments about what is appropriate in the light of the needs of different ages, but always taking care that liturgical Tradition is never impoverished, and that what is handed on is truly that precious heritage received from our fathers, perhaps judiciously pruned and carefully augmented (but not wholly reconstructed), according to the circumstances of the Church in each age, ensuring continuity of belief and of practice." Similarly L. Bouyer, *The Liturgy Revived: A Doctrinal Commentary of the Conciliar Constitution on the Liturgy* (London: Darton, Longman & Todd, 1965), 54; P. Guéranger, *Institutions liturgiques* I (Paris [i.a.]: Sociéte générale de librairie catholique, ²1878), 154f.

20 Cf. Newman, *Development of Christian Doctrine*, 169–206.

Mass remained decisive, while the meal aspect of the action of the sacrifice is subordinate and secondary.[21] The second criterion is "Continuity of Principles." Theocentrism and never anthropocentrism has been part of the inner basic policy of the classical rite, which manifests itself in the outward form. The traditional form of the liturgy does not consider itself as a parish assembly, but rather as the performance of worship with two dimensions, the glory of God (latreutic goal) and the sanctification of the people (sacramental-soteriological goal). "Power of Assimilation" constitutes the third criterion of organic development, which derives its vitality from the adoption of outside and foreign elements, without losing its own identity. A concrete example of this is the so-called Roman-Frankish mixed liturgy, in which the original form of the Pontifical High Mass incorporated elements of monastic piety — such as private prayers of the priest — and was embellished through rich ceremonial forms and gestures. The fourth criterion, "Logical Sequence," consists in recognizing, in retrospect, an inner coherence between the earlier and later stages of development. In this sense, the later silent prayers of the priest come up as the spiritual interpretation of the liturgical action that was already previously done without accompanying prayers (e.g., oblation, incensing, and washing of the hands). In the same way, the prayers at the foot of the altar are only the later organic development of the earlier acts of preparation (silent pauses or prostrations before the altar, apologia, and the praying of psalms belonging to the entrance ritual). The fifth criterion, "Anticipation of Its Future," demands that later occurrences be not completely new; rather, future developments must already be suggestively present in some form. Thus, for instance, Communion in the mouth, accepted during the Middle Ages, was already anticipated in earliest times in those original gestures of Communion that manifested veneration (e.g., obeisance, veiled hands, and genuflection). "Conservative Action on Its Past" demands, as the sixth criterion, that previous achievements may not be overturned and abandoned by further developments. An indication of organic development

---

21 Cf. Pius XII, Encyclical Letter *Mediator Dei* (AAS 39 [1947]: 562 / trans.: R. Kevin Seasoltz [ed.], *The New Liturgy: A Documentation, 1903 to 1965* [New York, NY: Herder and Herder, 1966], 137).

is continuity, not breaking with the past.[22] The classical rite of Mass perfectly satisfies this criterion, when, for example, elements of the original pontifical liturgy, such as processions, have been preserved in principle, even in the simple private Mass, although in a reduced form, such as a turning of the celebrant's body or a change from one side of the altar to the other. The seventh and last criterion is "Chronic Vigor." In contrast to many ideas and innovations that, after a sensational beginning, quickly grew old or completely vanished, genuine development can be identified by permanence and unspent vitality. The classical Roman rite organically and continually evolved from its core components over the course of 1,500 years. Its chronic vigor is apparent not least in the fact that on the eve of Vatican II, neither the laity, nor the parish clergy, nor the bishops were demanding profound changes to the liturgy.[23] Its chronic vigor is

---

22 Cf. the declaration of English Catholic Bishops against the Anglican interference with the rite: the Cardinal Archbishop and Bishops of the Province of Westminster, *A Vindication of the Bull 'Apostolicae Curae'* (London: Longmans Green, 1898), 42: "They (*sc.*, national or local churches) must not omit or reform anything in those forms which immemorial tradition has bequeathed to us. For such an immemorial usage, whether or not it has in the course of ages incorporated superfluous accretions, must, in the estimation of those who believe in a divinely guarded visible Church, at least have retained whatever is necessary; so that in adhering rigidly to the rite handed down to us we can always feel secure: whereas, if we omit or change anything, we may perhaps be abandoning just that element which is essential. And this sound method is that which the Catholic Church has always followed. ... That in earlier times local churches were permitted to *add* new prayers and ceremonies is acknowledged. ... But that they were permitted to *subtract* prayers and ceremonies in previous use, and even to remodel the existing rites in the most drastic manner, is a proposition for which we know of no historical foundation, and which appears to us absolutely incredible." Quoted from: Davies, *Cranmer's Godly Order*, 109; cf. 140. Cf. P. Guéranger, *Institutions liturgiques* III (Paris [i.a.]: Sociéte générale de librairie catholique, ²1883), 494f.: "It seems to me that in no matter, but least of all in matters of religion, does progress have the right to present itself in the form of destruction and upheaval. ... Progress for the liturgy must consist rather in enrichment by the acquisition of new forms than in the violent loss of the old ones."

23 Cf. Ratzinger, *Milestones*, 122: "The reform of the liturgy in the spirit of the liturgical movement was not a priority for the majority of the Fathers, and for many not even a consideration." Reid, *Organic Development*, 298: "In the light of the only moderate calls for liturgical reform made in response to the antepreparatory consultation of the worldwide episcopate in 1959, and in the light of the scope and importance of the liturgical books published up to 1962, it is fair to say that on the eve of the Council neither John XXIII, the dicasteries of the Holy See, the Pian commission, the worldwide episcopate, nor the publishers of liturgical books envisaged that a root and branch liturgical reform was imminent." Idem, "On the Council Floor: The Council Fathers' Debate of the Schema on the Sacred Liturgy," U. M. Lang (ed.),

also further demonstrated by the fact that it is just those monasteries, communities, and seminaries that have preserved the traditional rite,[24] or at least have cultivated it alongside the newer form of the liturgy, that have attracted growing attention and increasing numbers of entrants in recent decades and years.[25] *Succisa virescit*—having been cut down, it flourishes: this motto of the Benedictine Abbey of Monte Cassino, which after afflictions and destructions was invariably rebuilt, can also be applied to the classical rite of the Mass, which despite exterior adversity over the course of history has proven and will continue to prove its chronic vigor.

Insofar as the evolution of the traditional Roman rite of the Mass corresponds to this organic, homogeneous development, there existed no doubt for John Henry Newman that both of the fourth-century witnesses of the Faith, Athanasius and Ambrose, would recognize, in the sacrifice of the Mass celebrated according to the *Missale Romanum* promulgated by Pope Pius V in 1570, the form of the Eucharist familiar to them.

Liturgies grow, as the great old houses of worship grew, over centuries. In fact, the traditional Mass resembles many of the great old churches in the

---

Authentic Liturgical Renewal, 125–43, 138: "A revolution in the liturgical life of the Church was simply not on the agenda. Indeed ... concerns were expressed lest this occur and do real damage to the spiritual life of the faithful and to the sound aims of the council itself." Davies, *Pope Paul's New Mass*, 83, 85: "There was definitely no widespread desire for liturgical change in English-speaking countries before Vatican II among the laity, the parish clergy, or the bishops. Even when desire for change did exist, it rarely envisaged more than a greater use of the vernacular. Those who advocated change were looked upon as cranks by most of the faithful.... Not the least account was ever taken of whether or not laity wanted change. Clerical bureaucrats had evolved a theory of what the liturgy ought to be like and this was what it was going to be like, even if it emptied the churches.... Dom Gregory Murray typified the attitude of these bureaucrats perfectly when ... he insisted that it is 'not a question of what people want; it is a question of what is good for them.'"

24 Cf. Th. Grimaux, *Venez et voyez. Les communautés traditionnelles en France* (Feucherolles: La Nef, 2007). Cf. Pope Benedict XVI, Letter to the Bishops that accompanies the Apostolic Letter *Summorum Pontificum* (AAS 99 [2007]: 796): "Immediately after the Second Vatican Council it was presumed that requests for the use of the 1962 Missal would be limited to the older generation which had grown up with it, but in the meantime it has clearly been demonstrated that young people too have discovered this liturgical form, felt its attraction and found in it a form of encounter with the Mystery of the Most Holy Eucharist particularly suited to them."

25 Thus, for instance, the Brompton Oratory in London and the major seminary of the French diocese of Fréjus-Toulon.

process of its origination. Such monuments were not constructed within a short amount of time like modern buildings, but rather they grew up over the course of centuries under the hands of generations who were working for eternity.[26] They were endowed with the works of stonemasons, sculptors, carpenters, and painters; each of them provided his own contribution, but all were filled with the single purpose of worthily fashioning the House of God. Just as virtually every part of St Mark's Basilica in Venice from the floor to the roof was added in one century or another from various foreign countries, the Christian liturgy was formed from the treasures of Jerusalem, Rome, and Byzantium. Bricks from various cultural groups and time periods were brought together and used for its construction. Elements from the Jewish synagogue service (readings), the ancient Roman style of prayer (Canon),[27] oriental Christianity (Kyrie eleison),[28] monastic spirituality (silent prayers), and others converged here. As elements from diverse origins were assumed into the Roman Mass, its form attained its unique universality.[29]

The traditional Mass in the Roman rite is an ancient building, stamped with many centuries and styles, often amended and further embellished, sometimes restored here and there, a building in which one can trace, part

26 Cf. B. Frost, *The Meaning of the Mass* (London: Mowbray, [2]1935), 74f.

27 Cf. A. Baumstark, "Antik-römischer Gebetsstil im Messkanon": *Miscellanea liturgica in honorem L. Cuniberti Mohlberg* (Vatican City: Edizioni Liturgiche, 1948), vol. I, 300–31.

28 Cf. I. Schuster, *The Sacramentary (Liber Sacramentorum)*, trans. by A. Levelis-Marke (London: Burns & Oates, 1927), vol. III, part 5, 3–13; A. A. King, *Liturgy of the Roman Church* (London / New York / Toronto: Longmans & Green, 1957), 444–51.

29 Cf. J. Brinktrine, *Die heilige Messe in ihrem Werden und Wesen* (Paderborn: Verlag Ferdinand Schöningh, [3]1950), 128: "The stones of this monumental structure were borrowed from the most diverse cultures: the Jewish-Oriental, the Greek-Hellenistic, the Roman-Latin, the Germanic-medieval culture, and yet all the pieces are joined together to create a building of harmony and beauty before our minds. The liturgies of the great Churches of the East as well as the Occident have contributed to enriching and embellishing the Order of the Mass of Rome: in the liturgy of the Mother of all Churches they find each other in harmony. Hardly anywhere in religious literature can one find such a variety and richness in the individual parts and such consistency and unity in the whole. Other intellectual products, including religious ones, are national in character and reflect a certain national culture; the Roman liturgy, which in its first part has harmoniously united elements of different cultures, old and new, is transnational. It is a symbol of universality within the Church of Christ, which embraces the peoples and nations of all ages separated by race and custom, language and culture, and gathers them together 'in the unity of the Faith.'"

by part, the century of its origin, but only in the rarest of cases identify the artist who designed this or that element and added it to the whole.[30] In contrast to modern architecture, where the name of the architect is permanently connected with the buildings he constructed, the creators of the great cathedrals of the Middle Ages remain mostly anonymous. They completely withdraw behind the works they created. In a similar way, the traditional Mass has no author; one can hardly ever say who created a particular prayer or introduced a certain ceremony. It is precisely in this anonymity that the greatness of the traditional Mass lies: "Since Holy Mass had no author..., everyone was free to believe and feel that it was something eternal, not made by human hands."[31]

The comparison between the liturgy and the construction of a church building, between the worship service and the house of worship, can be applied on yet another level. It is not only in the gradual growth of form and shape that the genesis of the liturgy of the Mass resembles the construction of a church. The effect that the created and designed space produces in those praying there is similar in many ways to that which the liturgy's traditional form of prayer is capable of bringing about.

Merely entering into a House of God deserving of the name can com-municate what it is about. Whoever enters such a place intuitively senses that this is a *sacred* place, separated from the restlessness and activity of the streets, withdrawn from the goals of commerce and consumption — a place sanctified, initially by its consecration but also by the many praying worshipers who have lingered here, asking, thanking, lamenting, praising. Sanctified by the countless baptisms, numberless confessions, marriages, confirmations, sanctified by missions, devotions, processions, private Masses, and solemn ceremonies. Whoever enters such a place senses how the stones and pictures have, as it were, absorbed all of these prayers

---

30 Cf. A. Baumstark, *Vom geschichtlichen Werden der Liturgie* [EcOra 19] (Freiburg i. Br.: Verlag Herder, 1923), 71: "All seemingly impersonal development, after all, is only the result produced by numerous actions of individuals who remain in secrecy. Every particular idiom of liturgical discourse must first be used by a very particular individual, each particular cultic gesture first performed by individuals. But these individuals, whose words or gestures, solidified in formulas, lived on for many centuries, step behind their creations, like the traveling poets behind the real folk epic."

31 M. Mosebach, *Heresy of Formlessness*, 18.

over decades and centuries and likewise radiate forth an atmosphere of prayer. Whoever enters such a place senses: I do not stand alone before God; an immeasurable crowd of praying men before me has already stood and knelt before God; I am entering a place of prayer that has been built before my time, which encloses and surrounds me, supporting and accompanying my personal prayers. It is just the same with the traditional form of the Holy Mass. Whoever celebrates it enters into a spiritual space, in an atmosphere suffused with prayer, which receives and permeates his own personal prayers.[32]

The church building does not just pour forth an atmosphere of prayer; the architecture also *directs* prayer: portal and atrium, nave and side aisles, columns, arches and steps, light and darkness, the glint of gold and play of the colors, ornament and symbol, the dome and the high altar, all direct the gaze, guide the senses, and lead the praying soul. In the same way, the traditional Mass possesses its own architectonics that differ from those of the revised form, and it is exactly in these differences that the particular "charism" of the classical rite emerges.

The rite of entrance with the prayers at the foot of the altar and the double *Confiteor* of the priest and the acolyte, the direction of the prayer toward the altar, the richness of the diversely arranged gestures — signs of the Cross, genuflections, bows, and changing from the left to the right side — the silent Canon, the form of receiving Communion, the Last Gospel: all these are diverse elements that, like the architectonic form of the church building, lead the praying soul, prepare it, allow it to pause, to continue, and to rise up.

With the classical Mass, it is as with entering an old house of worship: whoever has ascended a few steps and opened the heavy entrance doors, that is, whoever has searched for an entrance, in spite of opposition, reservations, or other difficulties, will find himself in a sacred space, where

---

32 I. F. Görres, *Die leibhaftige Kirche* (Frankfurt a.M.: Verlag Knecht-Carolusdruckerei, 1950), 44: "We know...the unspeakable sense of simultaneity with hundreds of generations when the Exsultet is heard on Holy Saturday, or the Te Deum at some feasts: the Ambrosian hymn of praise, the Athanasian or Nicaean Creed — to the knowing and feeling, these are not dead names, but a lively call and pulse through the centuries, a hand grip backward through the ebb and flow of cultures."

the symmetry of its proportions, with the preciousness of its materials and with the central placement of the high altar and tabernacle, leads the praying worshiper in a prescribed order, lends support, leads him out of the sphere of the profane and banal to allow him to feel the closeness of the sacred, and finally centers his gaze on Him toward Whom all liturgies are ultimately directed—on God, as He reveals Himself in His Son's sacrifice upon the Cross and remains with us in the Sacrament of the Altar.

PART II

Form

4

Gradations of Ritual

THE CLASSICAL ROMAN RITE OF THE MASS RECOG-
nizes various grades of solemnity. Three main types can be distinguished:
the Solemn High Mass with deacon and subdeacon (*Missa Solemnis*);
the simple, sung service (*Missa Cantata*), celebrated by the priest with
at least two acolytes and the congregation, though often done with MC,
thurifer, acolytes, and torchbearers; Low Mass (*Missa Lecta*) without
singing, celebrated with one or two acolytes, and the congregation may
be in attendance.

The Pontifical Mass of the bishop of Rome, as it was first described
in the *Ordo Romanus Primus* (seventh/eighth century), constituted the
basic form from which the others developed.[1] With the further spread
of the Roman rite into northern countries, that first Roman *Ordo*
was adapted for ordinary episcopal services, and later formed the basis for
the priest's Mass. In many cases it is only in view of this origin that
one can understand the meaning and function of individual elements
of the Roman rite of the Mass, which has preserved that basic structure
even in simpler degrees of solemnity; even in the simplest form of a
private Mass, the priest fulfills everything that was originally allocated
to various agents of the liturgical action (bishop, deacon, subdeacon,

---

1   Cf. M. Andrieu, *Les Ordines Romani du haut moyen âge* II [SSL 23] (Louvain: Spicilegium sacrum Lovaniense, 1960), 65–108. Cf. Conrad, "Ein Ritus in zwei Formen?," 254:
"The old Gregorian rite consistently thinks from top to bottom according to its logic. The
norms of the liturgy are the papal chapel and — already in a gradated form — the pontifical
Mass of the bishop. All other celebrations are in principle reduced forms of these ideal
celebrations." The liturgical reform of Vatican II completed a shift in paradigm, insofar
as now the congregation's Mass celebrated by the priest has become the *Missa normativa*,
while all other forms were its enhancement or reduction; cf. A. Bugnini, *The Reform of
the Liturgy 1948–1975*, trans. by M.J. O'Connell (Collegeville, MN: Liturgical Press, 1990),
340. Concerning this point, see Conrad, "Ein Ritus in zwei Formen?," 254: "With this
principle, one departs from the tradition inherited from the old sources of the Roman rite."

and schola).[2] Consequently, the complete liturgy is contained *in nuce* in each Low Mass.

The Solemn Pontifical Mass is a Pontifical Mass arranged with special ceremonies, preserving some of the rites of the earliest times of the Roman Church.[3] The Pontifical Mass still bears in its rich ceremonial clear traces of the ancient Papal Mass, and sets alive before our eyes, if only in an understated way, the liturgy of the early medieval *Ordines Romani*. The Pontifical Mass, which specially expresses the episcopal privileges and insignia, was regulated after the Council of Trent in the *Caeremoniale Episcoporum* (1600) prescribed for the Universal Church.[4] The bishop celebrates it with two Mass Levites (deacon and subdeacon), an assistant priest in a cope, two assistant deacons in dalmatics, a master of ceremonies, assistants to carry the staff, miter, and gremial,[5] two ministers for the book and bugia,[6] two acolytes, a thurifer, and four torch-bearers. The ceremonial putting on of the pontifical vestments that lie on the altar precedes the Mass and takes place during the singing of Terce. On the Gospel side, a throne with a canopy stands ready for the bishop, where he takes his place during the scriptural part of the service.[7]

The solemn High Mass celebrated by a priest is also designed after the pattern of the episcopal Levitical Mass.[8] It can be traced back to the

---

2 Cf. Batiffol, *Leçons sur la messe*, 307: "The private Mass is a reduction of the High Mass, and . . . the High Mass is an adaptation of the papal Mass of the eighth century."

3 Cf. the description by J. Pinsk / C. J. Perl, *Das Hochamt. Sinn und Gestalt der Hohen Messe* (Salzburg / Leipzig: Verlag Friedrich Pustet, 1938), 186–91; J. Brinktrine, *Die feierliche Papstmesse und die Zeremonien bei Heilig- und Seligsprechungen* (Freiburg i. Br.: Verlag Herder, 1925); U. Nersinger, *Liturgien und Zeremonien*, 371–425.

4 Cf. *Caeremoniale episcoporum, editio princeps (1600)*. Edizione anastatica, introduzione e appendice a cura di A. M. Triacca [Monumenta Liturgica Concilii Tridentini 4] (Vatican City: Libreria Editrice Vaticana, 2000).

5 A cloth on which the bishop places his hands when sitting, designed to protect his vestments during the application of unctions, among other things.

6 A wax candle in a candlestick, which is brought to the throne for readings and prayers, originally for practical reasons, and which is a symbol that the prayers can only be rightly understood and recited in the light of Faith.

7 Cf. the description by Pinsk / Perl, *Hochamt*, 180–86.

8 Cf. the description by Pinsk / Perl, *Hochamt*, 162–80, for the richness of symbolism; cf. M. Mosebach, "Gedanken zum Levitenamt," *Rundbrief Pro Missa Tridentina* 10 (1996): 3–6; idem, *Heresy of Formlessness*, 105–16.

tenth/eleventh century. The subdeacon and deacon have various duties during the readings, where they proclaim the Epistle and Gospel, as well as during the Mass of the Faithful, where the subdeacon carries the chalice with a humeral veil from the credence table to the altar, afterward performs the preparations of the chalice with the deacon, and holds the paten with the humeral veil during the Canon, and the deacon assists the priest with the chalice ceremonies (covering it with the pall, and the elevation). At the distribution of Communion, the deacon accompanies the priest and holds the Communion paten. At the purification, the subdeacon assists the priest, taking the chalice to the credence table afterward. The final *Ite missa est* is sung by the deacon.

The form of Low Mass with one acolyte was the basis for the Mass's presentation in both the *Rubricae Generales* and the *Ritus Servandus* in the *Missale Romanum* of 1570 (as well as the *Missale Romanum* of 1962). It was by far the most frequently used form of the celebration of the Mass at that time, when the great majority of the then numerous clergy celebrated Mass daily. These rubrics were supplemented with additional notes for the *Missa Solemnis*. As an exception, rather, the form of a High Mass without deacon or subdeacon was mentioned,[9] which was otherwise referred to as a "Sung Mass" (*Missa Cantata, Missa in Cantu*).[10] This Sung Mass was recommended as the most excellent form of the Mass in the Instruction on Sacred Music (1958), as it "manifest[s] the grandeur of the divine mysteries and prompts the minds of those present to the pious contemplation of them."[11] The possibility of participation by the faithful (*circumstantes*) at Low Masses (*Missa Lecta*) with one acolyte was also anticipated by the rubrics (*Missale Romanum* 1570/1962).[12] The Instruction on Sacred

9   Cf. *Ritus servandus in celebratione Missae* VI, 8.

10   Here the priest sings all texts indicated in the rubrics as to be chanted by the celebrant (Intonation of the *Gloria* and *Credo*; *Dominus vobiscum*; Prayer; Preface; *Per omnia* at the end of the Canon; *Pater Noster*; end of the *Libera*; *Pax Domini*; Postcommunion; *Ite missa est*). Cf. SCR, *Instruction on Sacred Music and Sacred Liturgy* (*De Musica Sacra et Sacra Liturgia ad mentem litterarum encyclicarum Pii Papae XII "Musicae sacrae disciplina" et "Mediator Dei"*) (AAS 50 [1958]: 633 / Seasoltz, *Documentation*, 257); *Codex Rubricarum* (1960), no. 271.

11   Cf. SCR, *De Musica Sacra et Sacra Liturgia* (AAS 50:639 / Seasoltz, *Documentation*, 262).

12   According to the CIC (1917), can. 813 §1, one acolyte was required. Masses without an acolyte were tolerated only in exceptional cases. Cf. E. Weigl, "Die Alleinmesse (sine ministro

Music (1958) requires a loud recitation of the prayers in the presence of a large congregation.[13] Under the influence of the Liturgical Movement, the so-called *Missa Dialogata* (or *Recitata*), where the faithful speak, completely or in part, what is said by the minister or sung by the choir at a High Mass, had developed since the early part of the twentieth century. When no other faithful are present, the acolyte at a Low Mass represents all of the Catholic people.[14]

This form of the celebration of the Mass had become much more prevalent ever since the second half of the seventh century, after the number of priests in the monasteries had greatly increased, while secular priests practiced daily celebration, even when no congregation was present, and Mass stipends were increasingly given for the private concerns of the faithful, especially for the benefit of the dead.[15] The term often used in this

---

et sine populo)," MThZ 2 (1951): 46–51. According to the CIC (1983), can. 906, the celebration of the Mass without the participation of at least one person is allowed only for a just and reasonable cause. Cf. G. May, "Das Recht auf Einzelzelebration," UVK 27 (1997): 147–72, 163f.: "It is thus up to the individual priest to judge if the obligation to have at least one participant in his Mass is not applicable. It has been rightly said that such a just and rational reason always exists when otherwise either the celebration would be omitted or one would have to participate in a concelebration." Cf. Weishaupt, *Päpstliche Weichenstellungen*, 49: "Since it is a disciplinary norm, it is left to the priest, who celebrates the Mass according to the traditional *usus*, whether he applies the old or the new norms for the servers. Certain earlier disciplinary regulations need not be unconditionally taken into account when celebrating the extraordinary form of Mass. This means that the priest also in the traditional form of the 'private Mass,' if there is a reasonable cause, can apply the extensive determination of can. 905 (*sic! recte: 906*) of the current ecclesiastical code."

13 Cf. SCR, *De Musica Sacra et Sacra Liturgia* (AAS 50:634 / Seasoltz, *Documentation*, 266): "Where the rubrics prescribe the *clara voce*, the celebrant must recite the prayers loud enough so that the faithful can properly and conveniently follow the sacred rites. This must be given special attention in a large church, and before a large congregation."

14 Cf. Thomas Aquinas, *STh* III, 83, 5 ad 12, in *Summa Theologiae*, vol. 59 (3a. 79–83): Holy Communion, trans. by Th. Gilby (Oxford: Blackfriars Publications [i.a.], 1975), 175: "Nevertheless one server suffices in private Masses; he takes the place of the Catholic people, on whose behalf he answers the priest in plural." The first recorded instance of the Dialogue Mass was in 1908 in Belgium; a decree permitting it (under certain circumstances) was issued in 1922 by the Sacred Congregation of Rites.

15 Cf. J. Bona, *Rerum liturgicarum libri II*, 1,14,1: *Opera omnia*, 231: "*Semper viguit in Ecclesia privatae missae, uno saltem praesente et ministrante, laudabilis consuetudo, quam Haeretici Misoliturgi aliquando prohibitam fuisse nunquam poterunt demonstrare. Sive enim dicatur privata a loco, quia in privato aliquo Oratorio agitur: sive a tempore, quia non festis, sed privatis diebus fit: sive ab assistentibus, quia vel unus, vel pauci ei intersunt: sive ex eo*

context, *Missa Privata*, should not be mistaken to mean that this celebration of the Mass is not a public and communal act of worship of the Church.[16] Due to certain circles of the Liturgical Movement having rejected such celebrations of the Mass, Pope Pius XII expressly defended its legitimacy in his liturgical encyclical (1947).[17] To serve as a reminder that even this form of the Mass is a public act of the worship of God, done in the name of Christ and the Church, the Sacred Congregation of Rites in the Instruction on Sacred Music (1958) desired that the expression "private Mass" not be used in the future.[18] The Catechism of the Council of Trent had already rejected this usage for similar reasons.[19] Nevertheless, it should not be

---

quod solus Sacerdos in ea communicet: sive alia quacumque ex causa: semper eam licitam, semperque in usu fuisse, probatissimis veterum Patrum testimoniis et exemplis demonstrabo" [In the Church there has always existed the laudable practice of private Mass, if at least one server is present. Heretics hostile toward the liturgy tried in vain to prove that it was once prohibited. Whether it is now called 'private' according to the place, because it is said in some private oratory; or according to the time, because it is said not on feast days, but on 'private' days; or according to those present, because one or few participate; or because only the priest communicates in it; or for any other reason, I will deliver the proof by the testimonies and examples of the most acknowledged ancient Fathers that private Mass has always been legal and always been in practice].

16   Cf. J.H. Newman, "The Daily Service," Sermon 21 in *Parochial and Plain Sermons*, vol. III (Westminster, MD: Christian Classics, 1966), 316: "Who then will dare speak of loneliness and solitude, because in man's eyes there are few worshippers brought together in one place? or, who will urge it as a defect in our Service, even if that were the case? Who, moreover, will so speak, when even the Holy Angels are present when we pray, stand by us as guardians, sympathize in our need, and join us in our praises?"

17   Pius XII, *Mediator Dei* (AAS 39:556f. / Seasoltz, *Documentation*, 133): "Moreover, this sacrifice, necessarily and of its very nature, has always and everywhere the character of a public and social act, inasmuch as he who offers it acts in the name of Christ and of the faithful, whose Head is the divine Redeemer, while he offers it to God for the holy Catholic Church, and for the living and the dead. This is undoubtedly so, whether the faithful are present . . . or are not present, since it is in no wise required that the people ratify what the sacred minister has done." In the same sense CIC (1983), can. 904.

18   SCR, *De Musica Sacra et Sacra Liturgia* (AAS 50:633 / Seasoltz, *Documentation*, 257). Cf. *Codex rubricarum* (1960), no. 269.

19   Cf. *Catechismus ex decreto Concilii Tridentini* (Regensburg: Verlag Manz, 1865), Pars II, caput IV, LXXX: "*Nulla missa, ex communi usu ecclesiae celebrata, dicenda est privata. Ex quo facile perspicitur, omnes missas communes censendas esse, ut quae ad commune omnium fidelium utilitatem et salutem pertinent* (Conc. Trid. sess. 22. c. 6. can. 8)" [No Mass celebrated according to the common use of the Church should be called 'private'; hence it is easy to perceive that all Masses, as being conducive to the common benefit and salvation of all the faithful, are to be considered common to all].

forgotten that the so-called "private Mass" was never synonymous with the *Missa sine populo*, at which only an acolyte is present.[20] It is much more a question of a Mass that the priest celebrates from personal devotion or by reason of a private Mass stipend and that is not a public Mass (*Missa publica*), i.e., not a parish or convent Mass.[21]

20 The term is a new creation in the rubrics of the liturgical reform and does not have an adequate equivalent in the MRom 1962. On the use of the term in *Summorum Pontificum*, art. 2 (and art. 4), according to which a "Mass without the people" can be celebrated even in the presence of several faithful, cf. Weishaupt, *Päpstliche Weichenstellungen*, 57f.; M. Rehak, *Der ausserordentliche Gebrauch der alten Form*, 60–65.

21 Cf. W. Lurz, *Ritus und Rubriken der heiligen Messe* (Wurzburg: Echter-Verlag, ³1952), 527: "In the latter sense, a High Mass with deacon and subdeacon can be considered as a 'private Mass.'"

5

Structure and Components of the Celebration of the Mass

THE CLASSICAL RITE OF THE MASS INCLUDES TWO main parts, which further subdivide: the Foremass, or Mass of the Cat-echumens, since in the early Church the candidates for Baptism had to leave the divine worship afterward, and the Mass of the Faithful. The scriptural portion of the service and the Eucharistic sacrifice were placed as counterpoints to each other and related to each other just as the atrium, vestibule, and sanctuary were in an old Christian basilica.[1]

THE MASS OF THE CATECHUMENS
Opening
1. Prayers at the Foot of the Altar. The priest's entrance takes place in such a way that he first pauses with the acolyte at the foot of the altar and here — hence the name — recites "the prayers at the foot of the altar." These include a variety of individual prayers (Psalm 42, Confiteor, versicle, and prayers while approaching the altar), which should interiorly prepare the priest and the acolyte, the representative of the people, for the celebration of the sacrifice of the Mass, so that right from the beginning they call to mind the thought of sacrifice (*Introibo ad altare Dei*), their sinfulness and need for forgiveness (Confiteor), and the requisite purity of heart (*Aufer a nobis*), and allow for a final preparatory reflection on the sacred event that is about to begin.[2] The prayers at the foot of the altar emphasize the sacredness of the upcoming action, which requires of the priest and

---

1 A figurative arrangement of the course of the Mass is offered by Th. Schnitzler, *Die Messe in der Betrachtung* II (Freiburg i. Br.: Verlag Herder, 1957), 353–56; P. Parsch, *The Liturgy of the Mass*, trans. and adapted by H. E. Winstone (London / St Louis, MO: Herder, ³1961), 61; M. Gaudron, *Die Messe aller Zeiten* (Altötting: Sarto-Verlag, 2006), 34f.

2 Cf. J. Brinktrine, *Messe*, 57: "Psychologically, this is very subtle: everything great has to be prepared; you can ascend to the summit only slowly."

the faithful alike appropriate dispositions, awakened in various ways by the individual prayers. Since neither a personal greeting nor a free-form introduction begins the Mass, in the mutual look at God the theocentrism of the sacred action becomes manifest and in the pre-shaped formula the timeless prayer of the Church can be perceived.

The origin of the prayers at the foot of the altar is a concrete example of the organic development of the liturgy of the Mass. A praying pause, e.g., the pope or celebrant prostrating himself before the altar (seventh/eighth century), an acknowledgement of his own unworthiness with a plea for forgiveness (apologia prayers: ninth century), the common recitation of Psalm 42 — along with other psalms — on the way to the altar (ninth/tenth century), various psalm versicles (twelfth century), which transitioned from the act of repentance to the prayer *Aufer a nobis* (tenth century), all these things gradually grew together into the inventory of preparatory prayers that found its final form in the decree of Pope Pius V that Psalm 42 be prayed at the foot of the altar.[3]

Prayed alternately between the priest and acolyte, the psalm *Judica me* is predestined to accompany by prayer the approach to the altar and to emphasize the sacrificial character of the celebration of the Eucharist on account of the verse within it that serves as the antiphon: *Introibo ad altare Dei* (Ps 42:4). The very first words spoken by the priest after the sign of the Cross show how the Holy Mass is directed toward the altar, that is, toward the sacrifice, and therefore toward God. But also in its entirety this psalm — the prayer of someone who is afflicted, who is far from the sanctuary and confidently longs to be able to participate once more in the feasts of the Lord — is most suitable for becoming the voice of the Church, which, beset by the interior and exterior afflictions of this world, longs to come before God, to be led by Him, and joyously to give Him thanks in

---

3 M. Grégoire, "La confession devant l'Autel," in *La Préparation de l'Eucharistie. De l'introït à l'offertoire* [Cours et conférences des semaines liturgiques VI] (Louvain: Éditions de Abbaye du Mont César / Bruges: Desclée de Brouwer, 1928) [hereafter, *La Préparation de l'Eucharistie*], 17–33. H. Hoping, "Der *Introitus* und das Stufengebet als Schwellentexte der römischen Messe": St. Heid (ed.), *Operation am lebenden Objekt. Roms Liturgiereformen von Trient bis zum Vaticanum II* (Berlin: be.bra-wissenschaft-verlag, 2014), 305–15; M. Reinecke, "Das Stufengebet. Seine Entstehung und Entwicklung sowie seine Bedeutung und Funktion im Rahmen der Vormesse," *Dominus vobiscum* 10 (2015): 20–33.

praise of His faithfulness.[4] Moreover, the psalm reflects the basic structure and interior dynamic of the celebration of the Mass, insofar as here can be found again the classical teaching of the three states of the spiritual life — purgative, illuminative, and unitive.[5] Interior purification and the separation from the secular world necessary for this are emphatically expressed in the first verse: *Discerne causam meam de gente non sancta, ab homine iniquo et doloso erue me*, which corresponds to the act of repentance in the Confiteor. The plea of the third verse, *Emitte lucem tuam et veritatem tuam*, finds fulfillment especially in the Mass of Catechumens with the proclamation of the Epistle and Gospel. Unity with God is finally articulated in the fourth verse, *Introibo ad altare Dei*, which refers to the sacrificial action and Holy Communion in a special way.

The Confiteor follows after the close of the psalm. As a testimonial from the beginning of the second century already documents, the sacrifice of the Mass has always been preceded by a confession of sin.[6] According to the oldest testimonies of the Roman rite, the pope had bowed before the altar after approaching it, at first silently (seventh century), but soon a prayer for himself and for the sins of the people was included (eighth century). Later, various Confiteor formulae grew from this; the current form found its shape during the twelfth century in the Roman Church. The admission of guilt opens with the sign of the Cross and the psalm verse, *Adiutorium nostrum in nomine Domini, qui fecit caelum et terram* (Ps 123:8) — an expression of religious conviction that the ability to confess sins and, more importantly, forgiveness, are granted by God and obtained through the Cross. In the traditional rite of the Mass, praying the Confiteor is not optional, but obligatory, not standing upright, but in a deeply humble bow, recited not by the priest and people together, but as a dialogue.

---

4 Cf. R. Kaschewsky, "*Introibo ad altare Dei* — Psalm 42 in der Deutung Augustins und Thomas' von Aquin," UVK 31 (2001): 96–105. In the Masses of Passiontide, this psalm is omitted, as the Church interprets it here as the voice of Christ (cf. Introit of Passion Sunday) and in this prophetic sense does not wish to place next to it a prayer of the priest with the same words. The omission of Ps 42 was later extended to the Masses for the Dead. Cf. Grégoire, "La confession," 31–33.

5 Cf. M. Ramm, *Zum Altare Gottes will ich treten. Die Messe in ihren Riten erklärt* (Thalwil: Priesterbruderschaft St Petrus, ⁴2009), 48.

6 Cf. *Didache* 14,1 (FC 1, 132f. / *The Didache*, 23).

First the priest confesses his guilt before God and the Church, and asks the people, represented by the acolyte, for their intercession, whereupon the acolyte, again as a representative of the people, first carries out this intercession (*Misereatur tui*), and then himself speaks the Confiteor and on his part asks for the intercession of the priest, who subsequently complies (*Misereatur vestri*). The following prayer, accompanied by a sign of the Cross: *Indulgentiam, absolutionem, et remissionem peccatorum nostrorum tribuat nobis omnipotens et misericors Dominus*, was originally the common sacramental formula of absolution, but here, in that the priest includes himself (*tribuat nobis*), it has the character of a sacramental, a powerful intercession of the Church, which confers the forgiveness of venial sins when said with true sorrow. The terms *indulgentia, absolutio*, and *remissio* are synonyms that, with the stylistic device of a triad, express the complete forgiveness of sins. In its original form, the Confiteor features the invocation of various saints by name—the Blessed Virgin Mary, the Archangel Michael, John the Baptist, the Apostles Peter and Paul—who are particularly meaningful for the relationship between holiness and sin, between guilt and forgiveness, be it as Mary, the Mother of God unstained by original sin (*Immaculata*), the Refuge of Sinners (*refugium peccatorum*: Litany of Loreto) and advocate (*advocata nostra*: Salve Regina); be it as the warrior against the enemy of God (St Michael), or as admonisher for conversion (St John the Baptist); be it as the steward of the ecclesiastical power of loosing (St Peter), as converted sinner and herald of the Faith (St Paul), or principally as exemplar of holiness or intercessor for the people. The enumeration of saints resembles a glance into the open heavens, where the disorder of sin is opposed by godly order in the form of a "hierarchy of saints": "In these names heaven appears as a hierarchically articulated court: at the very top there are the 'Queen of Angels, Patriarchs and Prophets,' then the 'Prince of the heavenly host' and then 'the first of those born of woman' and finally the 'Apostle-princes.'"[7]

In its dialogue construction, the traditional form of the admission of guilt corresponds completely to the requirements of the Apostle James: "Confess therefore your sins one to another: and pray for one another, that

---

7   M. Mosebach, "On the *Confiteor* of the Old Rite," in *Heresy of Formlessness*, 102.

you may be saved" (Jas 5:16). The confession required by the Apostle and the subsequent intercession may only be deliberately completed by the priest and people as counterparts and in succession, insofar as the confession (*Confiteor*) requires a listener who is not speaking at the same time himself, while the intercession that follows (*Misereatur*) again implies the silence of the one confessing. Finally, in the divided recitation of the admission of guilt is made visible the special position of the priest, who is just as subject to weakness and guilt as the common faithful, and equally dependent on God's mercy, except that by virtue of his ordination his character remains distinct from that of the people. When, as is usual, the priest begins the Confiteor alone, it is — similar to the *Nobis quoque peccatoribus*, spoken aloud during the silent prayers of the Canon — a humble admission that the priest is the first who must accuse himself of his sins in order to be worthy of celebrating the sacred mysteries.

The general prayer for forgiveness, with a medium bow by the celebrant, follows a short litany between the priest and acolyte, consisting of various psalm versicles with responses (Ps 84:7f.; 101:2) that ask for God's attention with Advent-like longing (*Deus tu conversus vivificabis nos...*), His mercy, and His salvation — Christ Himself (*Ostende nobis misericordiam tuam et salutare tuum da nobis*), and they implore the answering of prayers (*Domine exaudi orationem meam...*). An exchange of greetings (*Dominus vobiscum — Et cum spiritu tuo*), followed by *Oremus*, introduces the conclusion to the prayers at the foot of the altar, which the priest speaks silently as he climbs the steps to the altar and kisses it. Here in the first prayer (*Aufer a nobis*) the priest prays once again to be allowed to approach the holy altar with a pure heart (*ut ad Sancta sanctorum puris mereamur mentibus introire*).[8] Having reached the altar, the priest speaks a final prayer for forgiveness, while he lays his hands on the altar and invokes the intercession of

---

8   The biblical expression *Sancta sanctorum* [Holy of Holies] has been used for the House of God from early on; cf. Jerome, *In Ezechielem* 13,44,17/21 (CCL 75, 657 / St Jerome, *Commentary on Ezechiel*, 524). For the designation of the altar cf. Eusebius, *Historia ecclesiastica* 10,4,68 (SCh 55, 102 / Eusebius Pamphili, *Ecclesiastical History. Books 6–10*, trans. by R.J. Deferrari, *The Fathers of the Church* 29 [New York: Fathers of the Church, Inc., 1955], 266): τὸ... ἁγίων ἅγιον (*to... hagiōn hágion*). It may also be a reminder of the papal house chapel in the Lateran Palace, which is identified as the *Sancta sanctorum* because of the numerous relics treasured there.

the saints (*Oramus te, Domine, per merita sanctorum tuorum . . . ut indulgere digneris omnia peccata mea*). The simultaneous kiss of the altar honors this place as a symbol of Christ, and assures the priest and also the community of the assistance of those saints especially whose relics are enshrined in the altar (*quorum reliquiae hic sunt*). During the course of the celebration of the Mass, the priest kisses the altar a total of eight times — and during the Pontifical High Mass the altar kiss is omitted before the Collect, since the pontiff is not standing at the altar but at the throne or faldstool, while an additional kiss is made before the sign of peace. In this way, the celebrant consistently seeks to symbolically renew his association with Christ, in whose Person he is acting, and to receive for himself from Christ what is granted to the people (*Dominus vobiscum*; *Pax* in Pontifical High Masses).

Since the approach to the altar is requested in increments, as it were, in the prayers at the foot of the altar, accompanied by continual prayers for cleansing, the rite insistently shows that an increasing nearness to God must be accompanied by an always greater desire to conform to His holiness.

2. Incensing the Altar. In Solemn High Masses, the incensing of the altar now follows. Observed as a practice since the eleventh century, the current form was determined by Pope Pius V. The liturgical use of incense impressively demonstrates how the Church thoughtfully regards the natural qualities of things in order to unfurl from them a wealth of spiritual applications.[9] The symbolic expressiveness of incense relies on the grains of incense dissolving in the live coals in order to be transformed into a sweet fragrance, which on the one hand travels upward, and on the other hand spreads through the sanctuary and church, pervading horizontally and vertically in equal measure. Ancient customs, instructions from Old Testament worship (cf. Lev 16:13), and New Testament allusions converge in the liturgical incensing to make a holy symbol from this gift of the Orient, whose first meaning — the honor of God (*honor thuris*) — is already pronounced in the prayer of blessing (*Ab illo benedicaris in cuius honore cremaberis. Amen* ✠) after the priest has inserted the incense. Applying

---

9 Cf. M. Pfeifer, *Der Weihrauch. Geschichte — Bedeutung — Verwendung* (Regensburg: Verlag Friedrich Pustet, ³2018); M. Mosebach, "Der Weihrauch": *Rundbrief Pro Missa Tridentina* 8 (1994): 11–13.

grains of incense to the glowing coals three times is likewise a reminder that this honor is given to the Triune God. After the product of nature is placed in the service of the supernatural order through the prayer of blessing, the priest incenses first the altar crucifix, then, if necessary, relics, statues, or other images of the saints, followed by the altar, with a precisely ordered sequence of double motions, visually explained in many Missals (*ordo incensationis altaris*), which inundates all of the parts of the altar in a cloud of incense that possesses the purifying (lustrative) and sanctifying effects of a sacramental, and furthermore contains a diverse symbolism. As the cloud was already a sign in the Old Testament for the special nearness and presence of God (cf. Lev 16:12f.; Ex 24:15–18; 40:32–36), so the incense is also (1) a symbol of prayers ascending to God (cf. Ps 141[140]:2; Rev 5:8) and of the disposition of sacrifice borne with burning love, (2) royal homage for the Son of God's coming to earth (cf. Mt 2:11), as well as (3) a splendid gesture of obeisance before the divine throne (Rev 8:3), thus resembling the ceremonial of heavenly divine worship imitated in the earthly liturgy. With the incensing, the altar is set apart and honored as the holy place of sacrifice and worship as well as the point of contact between heaven and earth. Finally, the priest is also incensed, since he stands at the altar as Christ's representative and offers the sacrifice of the Mass.

3. Introit. As the prayers at the foot of the altar, ever remaining the same, are more of a personal and private preparation of the priest and people for the mystery of the Mass in general, the Introit marks the actual beginning of the day's liturgy and is therefore prayed aloud by the priest with the sign of the Cross[10] at the Epistle side of the altar, each time with a changing text that agrees with the impending celebration and with the distinct mysteries of that feast.[11] The entrance chant therefore corresponds to the variety of characters that embody, according to the feast and time of year, joy (*Gaudete*;

---

10   At a Requiem this is done over the Missal, as the blessing of the sacrifice of the Mass should first and foremost be bestowed on the soul of the departed.

11   Cf. J.J. Kramp, *Introitus. Die Eingangspsalmen zu den Messen der Sonntage und Herrenfeste neu übersetzt und erklärt* (Münster: Regensbergsche Verlagsbuchhandlung, 1937); A. Fortescue, "Introit," *The Catholic Encyclopedia* VIII (New York: Robert Appleton Company, 1910): 81f.; E. Flicoteaux, "L'Introït de la Messe," in *La Préparation de l'Eucharistie*, 35–46; (Mme.) Flad, "L'Introït dans le cycle liturgique": ibid., 47–65.

Laetare), rejoicing (*Jubilate Deo*; *Alleluia*), thanksgiving (*Protexisti me*), lamentation (*Miserere mihi*), holy fear (*Terribilis est locus iste*) or petition (*Exsurge, Domine*; *Da pacem*; *Respice in me*). Originally, from approximately the fifth century, when the end of the time of persecution made possible a greater expansion of the liturgy, the introit accompanied the solemn entrance procession of the pope or bishop with the clergy. Until the celebrant reached the altar, the *Schola Cantorum*, divided into two choirs, sang a psalm with an antiphon (refrain) and the closing doxology (*Gloria Patri*).[12] The shortening or absence of the entrance procession as well as the introduction of the private Mass ushered in the current form of the introit, consisting of four parts—antiphon, core (first verse of the psalm), *Gloria Patri*, and the repeated antiphon. In this condensed form, the introit still reminds us today of the early days of the Church—of the solemn entrance processions of the ancient Roman liturgy; of the Christocentric piety that, in the songs of the Old Covenant, heard Christ speaking to the Father and the Church praying to or about her Lord;[13] and, finally, of the struggle for orthodoxy, whose victory is manifested in the implementation of the doxological formula *Gloria Patri et Filio et Spiritui Sancto*, which professed the consubstantiality of the three divine Persons against the contestation of Arianism in the 4th century and here found expression in the liturgy.[14] The concentration on the antiphon and on the first verse of the Psalm can often bring about a downright dramatic effect, for instance, at the Christmas Midnight Mass when the mystery of the Incarnation of the eternal Son of God, sung as the antiphon ("Thou art my son; this day have I begotten thee," Ps 2:7), is simultaneously confronted with the resistance of the world distanced from God ("Why have the Gentiles raged: and the people devised vain things?," Ps 2:1).[15]

---

12   The *Gloria Patri*, admittedly, is not found in the oldest times, so that it is also absent from Passion Week and Holy Week, where older liturgical traditions have been preserved. Later liturgical interpreters often explain this absence as an expression of sorrow, for which reason Requiem Masses also do not contain the *Gloria Patri*.

13   Cf. B. Fischer, *Die Psalmen als Stimme der Kirche. Gesammelte Studien zur christlichen Psalmenfrömmigkeit*, ed. by A. Heinz (Trier: Paulinus-Verlag, 1982); M. Fiedrowicz, *Psalmus vox totius Christi. Studien zu Augustins 'Enarrationes in psalmos'* (Freiburg i. Br.: Verlag Herder, 1997).

14   Cf. Jungmann, *Missarum sollemnia* I, 423; idem, *The Mass of the Roman Rite* I, 328.

15   The shorted introit in the NOM ("The Lord hath said to me: Thou art my son; this day have I begotten thee") does not reveal this drama.

The selection of psalms was determined either by a psalm's entire contents fitting the thought of the day or by an individual verse that clearly embodied the special character of the particular feast. Occasionally this main idea is not expressed in the first verse of the psalm, so that only a view of the entire psalm will reveal why it was originally chosen for the respective celebration of the Mass. For example, the psalm chosen for the feast of Epiphany (Ps 71) does not speak of the bringing of gifts and the kings of the earth rendering homage to the Messiah until verse 10f., while the first verse ("Give to the king Thy judgment, O God") does not contain a specific reference to the mystery of the feast. The antiphon is normally taken from the psalm (*Introitus regularis*), and a verse especially significant for the feast is selected in order to sound the mystery of the feast right from the beginning, often even with the first words (*Dominus dixit ad me: Filius meus es tu, ego hodie genui te*: Midnight Mass for Christmas; *Resurrexi, et adhuc tecum sum*: Easter Sunday). In addition, the antiphon can also be taken from another book of the Bible (*Introitus irregularis*), as for example the *Puer natus est nobis* from the Prophet Isaiah (9:6) of the Mass for Christmas during the day. Furthermore, non-biblical texts may be referred to. Thus the introit of many Marian Masses, *Salve, sancta parens*, dates back to the poet Sedulius (fifth century), and the text used for the feast of certain saints, *Gaudeamus omnes in Domino, diem festum celebrantes*, was likely composed by Pope Gregory the Great.[16] In contrast to the way in which the Introit antiphon of many feast days indicates the motive of the liturgical celebration, the texts for the Sundays after Pentecost originate from a continual passage through the Book of Psalms (from Ps 12 to Ps 118), whose suitable verses were also selected for the remaining chants — Alleluia, Offertory, and Communion.

Kyrie

Following the Introit, the Kyrie of the traditional Mass consists of *Kyrie eleison–Christe eleison–Kyrie eleison*, each repeated three times by the priest and the acolyte or people in alternation.[17] The *Kyrie eleison* was originally

---

16 Cf. Jungmann, *Missarum sollemnia* I, 425; idem, *The Mass of the Roman Rite* I, 329.

17 Cf. A. Fortescue, "Kyrie Eleison," *The Catholic Encyclopedia* VIII (New York: Robert Appleton Company, 1910): 714–16; M. Daras, "Le 'Kyrie eleison,'" in *La Préparation de l'Eucharistie*, 67–79.

the people's answer to the invocation of a litany of intercession recited by the deacon, which was adopted by the Roman liturgy from the Greek Church (fifth century),[18] and was at that time sung during the procession to the stational church, or rather between the Introit and the Collect at the beginning of the Mass. Soon the Kyrie detached itself from the invocations to form the introduction and conclusion of the litany. After this litany had lost its place in the Roman Mass, the liturgical acclamation of *Kyrie eleison* lived on as a chant with an independent meaning, and was enriched by the alternating *Christe eleison*[19] to receive finally its current form, having nine invocations (seventh century).[20] The survival of the Kyrie call (even in its Greek form, though detached from its original context), its development into an independent form, and its permanent placement at the beginning of the celebration of the Mass, are all due to the fact that in these words, the Kyrie unites brevity, intensity, and richness of content in a singular way.

Homage to God (*Kyrie*) and petition for salvation (*eleison*) combine here and demonstrate at the very beginning of the celebration of the Mass its cultic and worshiping dimension, as well as its redemptive and sanctifying dimension. Originally in all its parts an appeal only to Christ, as a powerful profession of His divinity (cf. Jn 20:28: "My Lord and my God"), the acclamation with the *Kyrie–Christe–Kyrie* exchange later (ninth century) acquired a Trinitarian meaning, in which the thrice-repeated invocation emphasizes the intensity of the plea and also testifies to the religious truth that wherever one divine Person is invoked, both of the other Persons are included at the same time, as these do not exist separate from one another, but rather reside together mutually (*perichoresis, circumincessio*). Thus the cry for help becomes a small doxology that leads over to the Great Doxology, the Gloria, whose acclamations take up and expand on the cries of the Kyrie. The Kyrie is also connected to this angelic song of praise (cf. Lk 2:14) through

---

18   According to Jungmann, *Missarum sollemnia* I, 433–35; idem, *The Mass of the Roman Rite* I, 336f., the old Roman Kyrie litany is preserved in the so-called *Deprecatio Gelasii*, a prayer of intercession for the universal Church similar to the great Good Friday Prayers of Intercession.

19   Already indicated by Gregory I, *Epistula* 9,26 (CCL 140A, 587).

20   The indication in the *Breviarium Romanum* (March 12) that Pope Gregory the Great determined the number of nine is by all means probable. Cf. Gregory I, *Epistula* 9,26 (CCL 140A, 586).

the nine appeals that were assigned early on to the nine choirs of angels, and thus interwove the earthly liturgy with heaven's hymn of praise. As a cry of mankind in need of redemption, the *Kyrie eleison* is deeply rooted in the prayers of the Old and New Testaments (cf. LXX Is 33:2; Bar 3:2; Ps 6:3; 40:5,11; Mt 15:22; 20:30; Mk 10:48; Lk 17:13), as it simultaneously captures ancient acclamations to kings and cultic invocations to Sol, god of the sun,[21] in order to render homage to Christ as the true King (cf. Jn 18:37) and as the "Sun of justice" (Mal 4:2). The Kyrie finally connects the Western Church with the Church of the East, whose Greek language of prayer resounds in the Latin liturgy as well. In this way, the Kyrie impressively places before our eyes the universality of the Church, in that it brings Eastern and Western Christianity together on a synchronous level, allows the prayers of the Old and New Covenant to flow into the liturgical prayer on a diachronic level, leads the ancient desire for a Savior to fulfillment, and finally allows the earthly liturgy to sound together with that of Heaven.

Gloria

Intoned by angels at the birth of Christ (cf. Lk 2:14), the *Hymnus Angelicus* was continued by the early Church and developed into a song of praise of the Triune God.[22] The Great Doxology originates from the Orient, where a text that largely conforms to today's version is already found in the fifth century. The final Latin form is first documented in the ninth century. Its acceptance into the Roman liturgy of the Mass had already taken place in the sixth century. The Gloria was initially sung only in the Christmas Mass at Midnight, but soon also on Sundays and feasts of the Martyrs. Originally the intonation of this hymn was reserved to the bishops, as in the early Church these were considered to be the "Angels of the Church" (cf. Rev 2:1–3:22). At first, priests were permitted to intone this hymn only on Easter, but beginning in the eleventh century, this was also allowed on the remaining feast days. In the classical rite of the Mass, the *Gloria*

---

21 Cf. Schnitzler, *Messe* I, 11f.; F. J. Dölger, *Sol Salutis. Gebet und Gesang im christlichen Altertum* [LQF 16/17] (Münster: Aschendorff Verlag, ³1972), 60–103.

22 Cf. A. Fortescue, "Gloria in Excelsis Deo," *The Catholic Encyclopedia* VI (New York: Robert Appleton Company, 1909): 583–85; (Abbé) Maranget, "Le 'Gloria in excelsis,'" in *La Préparation de l'Eucharistie*, 81–91.

is sung on all feasts, with the exception of the feast of the Holy Innocents (provided it is not a Sunday); on all Sundays, excepting the seasons of Advent, Septuagesima, and Lent;[23] on all ferial days during the Easter Season; and finally in all votive Masses of the Blessed Virgin on Saturday and votive Masses of the Holy Angels, in addition to the first through third class votive Masses not celebrated in violet.[24]

The Gloria is a continuation of the Kyrie, in that it allows the latter's doxological character to become an extensive praise of the Most Holy Trinity; simultaneously, on the one hand, it takes up the earlier cry for salvation (*miserere nobis*) while on the other hand answering with the thankful, joyful acknowledgement of having been redeemed. The singing of the *Hymnus Angelicus* directs the gaze toward the coming consecration that renews and continues the mystery of Christmas — the *Logos* becoming Flesh — as it is also retrospectively professed in the Last Gospel in the prologue of St John. In the Gloria, the fourfold intention of the sacrifice of the Mass (*sacrificium latreuticum, eucharisticum, propitiatorium, impetratorium*) is clearly expressed: adoration (*Gloria in excelsis Deo; laudamus te; quoniam tu solus sanctus*), thanksgiving (*gratias agimus tibi*), expiation (*qui tollis peccata mundi, miserere nobis*), and impetration (*suscipe deprecationem nostram*). The priest's closing sign of the Cross also demonstrates that the glorification of the Triune God is completed in the most perfect way in the sacrifice of the Cross and its unbloody renewal upon the altar.

---

23 Cf. Thomas Aquinas, *STh* III, 83,4, in *Summa Theologiae*, vol. 59, trans. by Th. Gilby, 157: "This (i.e., the *Gloria*) is sung on feast days and is omitted in those sorrowful offices which recall our unhappy state."

24 Cf. R. Kaschewsky, "Die Rubriken — ein endlich überwundenes Relikt?," UVK 36 (2006): 357–65, 360: "The rule that it (i.e., the *Gloria*) as a jubilant praise is omitted on mourning and fasting days and in the Masses for the dead, requires no justification. But why is it also omitted in the 'simple' votive Masses, which are permitted for any intentions on days without feasts, as well as whenever the Sunday Mass is repeated on weekdays? ... Here a more pedagogical concern can be observed: here, too, 'inflation' should be prevented, and the lesser solemnity of the day in question can be felt just by the omission of the *Gloria*. How cautiously the Church proceeds here, however, can be recognized by the exceptions: If the votive Mass is a Mass of the holy Angels or of a holy Angel, the *Gloria* is used anyway, even if it is just a 'simple' votive Mass — because the angels were indeed the first who sang this hymn over the crib in Bethlehem. And if a 'simple' votive Mass in honor of the Blessed Virgin Mary, which in itself should be celebrated without the *Gloria*, is held on a Saturday, it still has the *Gloria*, because Saturday is in a special way the day of honor of the Blessed Mother."

Oration

For the subsequent Oration (*oratio*), the priest turns to God as the advocate of those assembled, bringing a plea to Him. The Oration is also called the Collect (*collecta*), as it summarizes the prayers of the faithful in a few words that are adapted to express collectively the manifold requests in a form of "supraindividual piety."[25] So that both the individual prayer and the union with the prayer of the Church may succeed through God's assistance, the priest greets the faithful with *Dominus vobiscum* after kissing the altar; they respond with *Et cum spiritu tuo*, so that the priest may rightly pray by virtue of the Holy Ghost conferred on him in his ordination. This greeting occurs a total of seven times throughout the course of the Mass[26] in order to incorporate the faithful actively into the liturgical action[27] and in order to effect, through the exchanged greeting, that harmonious community promised by Christ: "For where two or three are gathered together in my name, there am I in the midst of them" (Mt 18:20). The subsequent call to prayer, *Oremus*, which precedes the Oration along with a bow to the altar crucifix, originally pertained to the silent personal prayers of the faithful that the following Collect then combined. The accompanying spreading and joining of hands demonstrates this inclusion and consolidation of the various intentions into a single prayer.

The core of the Orations developed between the fourth and seventh centuries. The structure of the Collects is largely unchanged. Two different types may be distinguished. The first and most likely older type limits itself to appeals and petitions.[28] The second type includes in addition a relative

---

25   J. Pascher, *Eucharistia. Gestalt und Vollzug* (Münster / Freiburg i. Br.: Aschendorff Verlag [i.a.], ²1953), 61.

26   Cf. Brinktrine, *Messe*, 89f.: "This seems to be a lot for modern feeling. But we must remember that the entire revelation virtually converges in this greeting, and that the salvation promised in the Old Covenant, and truly manifested in the New Covenant in the person of Emmanuel (God-with-us), is concentrated in it. Basically, everything is contained in this greeting and everything is said."

27   Cf. P. Parsch, *The Liturgy of the Mass*, 124: "All lovers of the liturgy have in these words (*sc.*, *Dominus vobiscum*) a comforting assurance that the Church not merely permits but indeed desires the active participation of people in the Mass."

28   For example, on Ash Wednesday: "*Praesta, Domine, fidelibus tuis: ut ieiuniorum veneranda solemnia, et congrua pietate suscipiant, et secura devotione percurrant*" [Grant, O Lord, to Thy faithful people that they may begin the venerable solemnities of fasting with

predication, which bases the request on the mystery of the feast or one of God's qualities.[29] Beside those, there are transitional forms between the two types. The Collects close, as do the Secret and Postcommunion, with a trinitarily-structured closing formula that emphasizes Christ's mediation.[30] In form, these prayers exhibit the height of rhetoric, and, in regard to content, they are a comprehensive testimony of the Catholic faith.[31]

While high-ranking feasts have only one Collect so that the particular thought for the day receives undiminished attention,[32] a maximum of two more Collects (and thus Secrets and Postcommunions as well) may, according to the current stipulations, be added as commemorations.[33] By way of example, on a ferial day after Passion Sunday (1st Collect), there are commemorations of St Justin, martyr (2nd Collect: April 14)

---

becoming piety, and may persevere to the end with steadfast devotion].

29 For example, on the feast of Pentecost: "*Deus, qui hodierna die corda fidelium Sancti Spiritus illustratione docuisti: da nobis in eodem Spiritu recta sapere, et de eius semper consolatione gaudere*" [O God, who on this day didst teach the hearts of Thy faithful by the light of the Holy Spirit, grant us in the same Spirit to be truly wise, and ever to rejoice in His consolation].

30 Cf. P. Bonhomme, "'Par Jésus-Christ Notre-Seigneur,'" in *La Préparation de l'Eucharistie*, 119–37.

31 See chapter 11 for full particulars.

32 Cf. Kaschewsky, "Die Rubriken," 362: "a matter that seems indeed somewhat complicated, but in which we can recognize the empathy and pedagogical care of the Church. First, the basic principle: the higher the rank of a feast, the less the 'co-mention'—that is the *commemoratio*—of another day is allowed. For example, if the feast of Corpus Christi or the Sacred Heart falls on the 5th of June, actually the feast of St Boniface, the latter is not mentioned,—not because this important saint of our fatherland would be detrimental to the mystery of the other feast, but to protect the worshipers' devout attention from dispersion. Only when two very or nearly equal celebrations fall on the same day, the 'repressed' feast is commemorated, i.e., his orations (Collect, Secret, and Postcommunion) are added to those of the feast day. If the Second Sunday of Advent falls on the 8th of December, the Mass will be taken from the feast of the Immaculate Conception of Mary—but the Sunday of Advent is so important that it will not be ignored, but its orations will be added to the feast, even if it is a High Mass."

33 At a High Mass such a commemoration is omitted in most cases. Cf. Kaschewsky, "Die Rubriken," 363: "The reason may be that High Mass is likely to involve a greater number of believers who are to be made familiar with just *one* feast's mystery; the festive style of the celebration is less compatible with the 'splitting up' into various subjects of devotion. On the other hand, in the Low Mass, which is often celebrated as a so-called private Mass, at least in a smaller circle, one usually deals with believers who are more familiar with the liturgy and are certainly able to include a second feast's mystery in their prayers."

as well as other martyrs (3rd Collect: Tiburtius, Valerian, and Maximus, † ca. 230 in Rome). The form of the commemorations allows many saints, even lesser known martyrs from the early centuries, to remain alive in the liturgical memory of the Church and not be abandoned through careless neglect.

Readings from Scripture

The scriptural portion of the service following the Collect consists of the Epistle, Gradual, and Gospel, which may be followed by a sermon.[34] In the Solemn High Mass, the Epistle is sung by the subdeacon and the Gospel by the deacon. While the subdeacon turns toward the altar, the deacon proclaims the Gospel toward the north, in eastern-oriented churches—a symbolic expression that the Gospel should drive out the powers of darkness and convert the pagans. At a Low Mass, changing from the Epistle to the Gospel side and the positioning of the missal facing somewhat north are remembrances of the practice in the early church of reciting the readings from two ambos situated in the north and south side.[35] The practice of directing the proclamation of the Gospel toward the north is a sign of the universal opening of the Church that does not limit the glad tidings to its own community.[36] In the current form, the reading of the Epistle and Gospel is not done facing the people, they are read in liturgical Latin, and the Gospel is accompanied by candles and incense, all of which express the latreutic character of the readings insofar as proclaiming the great deeds of God (*magnalia Dei*) does not simply fulfill a didactic function, but constitutes an act of glorifying God.[37]

---

34 Full particulars on the order and selection of the pericopes may be found in chapter 12.

35 The deacon initially proclaimed the Gospel from the northern ambo, toward the southern side where the men sat, but later turned toward the north, following the example of the priest, who, in Masses without a deacon, read the Gospel from the northern side of the altar.

36 Cf. T. Guillard, "Le missel romain, porteur du sacré": *Liturgie et sacré*. Actes du huitième colloque d'études historiques, théologiques et canoniques sur le rite catholique romain [Versailles, Novembre 2002] (Paris: CIEL, 2003), 351–60, 355: "The orientation of these readings is a sign of openness to the universality of the Church and not of retreat to the listening community."

37 Cf. Brinktrine, *Messe*, 114f. Concerning the ceremonies, cf. I. Van Houtryve, "L'Évangile," in *La Préparation de l'Eucharistie*, 157–69.

Before he proclaims the Gospel, the deacon asks a blessing from the bishop or priest (*Jube, domne, benedicere*). If the priest himself reads the Gospel, he bows deeply and recites two prayers at the middle of the altar (*Munda cor meum / Jube, Domine, benedicere*), the first of which recalls the inaugural vision of the Prophet Isaiah (cf. Is 6:5–7), asking to be cleansed from all sin to be worthy of proclaiming the words of Christ. At the reading of the Gospel, unlike the Epistle, the hands are not laid on the missal, but rather folded, as a sign of reverence for the words of the Lord that it contains.[38] After the proclamation of the Gospel the priest silently says *Per evangelica dicta deleantur nostra delicta* ("By the words of the Gospel may our sins be blotted out"). The proclamation of the Gospel has the power of a sacramental to remove venial sin with the appropriate disposition of the listener (cf. Jn 15:3).

Where appropriate, a sermon follows, during which the priest sometimes lays aside the chasuble or at least lays the maniple on the missal, as, according to the traditional rubrics, the homily does not intrinsically belong to the rite of the Mass.[39]

Interlectional chants

Between the Epistle and Gospel are various forms of interlectional chants, each corresponding with the liturgical season. Since the sixth century, today's shortened form of the Gradual—originally comprising an entire psalm and refrain and sung on the steps (*gradus*) of the ambo—consists of two psalm verses. A few Graduals originate from other books of the Bible and a few others are ecclesiastical compositions.[40] Often based on the reading,[41] the lyrical unfolding of the Gradual

---

38 The folded hands show that even the simple Mass seeks to preserve as much as possible the rite of the *Missa Sollemnis*, where the celebrant, with folded hands, listens to the deacon proclaim the Gospel. By the same token, the hands laid on the missal during the Epistle recall that the subdeacon holds the lectionary in his hands.

39 Cf. Mosebach, *Heresy of Formlessness*, 29f.

40 For example, *Benedicta et venerabilis* of Marian feasts (including Aug. 14); *Requiem aeternam* of the Masses for the Dead. Cf. A. Fortescue, "Gradual," *The Catholic Encyclopedia* VI (New York: Robert Appleton Company, 1909): 715–18.

41 For example, the Gradual on the feast of the Epiphany *Omnes de Saba venient, aurum et thus deferentes* ... (Is 60:6.1) is taken from the Reading (Is 60:1–6). On the feast of the

allows for a meditative contemplation of the Word and a reflection on the mysteries of the feast.

The subsequent Alleluia,[42] recited as a responsory, does not always frame a biblical verse, but often instead a thought formulated by the Church that sings the praise of the particular mystery of the feast and leads over to the Gospel.[43] During Eastertide there is a double Alleluia verse, the first replacing the Gradual. The joyful Alleluia is omitted in Masses of a sorrowful or penitential character (Septuagesima until Easter, Masses for the Dead, and ferial days in Advent). In these instances, the Alleluia is replaced with a Tract, which was originally sung "all at once" (equivalent to *tractim* or the Greek εἱρμός, *heirmos*: train, series, sequence). This hymn often corresponds to the Gospel.[44]

The Sequences—poetic commentaries on the overall celebration of the Mass—constitute a final form of interlectional chant, of which the *Missale Romanum* (1962) contains five, which contemplate the particular mystery of the feast in various ways, at times dramatic, at times interiorly mystical, at times confessional and dogmatic.[45]

Protomartyr Stephen (Dec. 26) the Reading (Acts 6:8–10; 7:54–59: persecution and death) corresponds to the Gradual *Sederunt principes, et adversum me loquebantur: et iniqui persecuti sunt me . . .* (Ps 118:23,86).

42   Cf. Rupert of Deutz, *De ecclesiasticis officiis* 1,35 (FC 33/1, 230): "*iubilamus magis quam canimus, unamque brevem digni sermonis syllabam in plures neumas vel neumarum distinctiones protrahimus, ut iucundo audito mens attonita repleatur et rapiatur illuc, ubi 'sancti exsultabunt in gloria, laetabuntur in cubilibus suis' (Ps 149:5)*" [we jubilate rather than sing, protracting one short syllable of the venerable text in several neumes or modulations of neumes, so that the mind is deeply touched and filled with the pleasant sound and is carried off to the place where "the saints exult in glory and rejoice in their chambers" (Ps 149:5)].

43   For example, on the feast of the Annunciation (March 25): "*Alleluia. Virga Jesse floruit: Virgo Deum et hominem genuit: pacem Deus reddidit, in se reconcilians ima summis. Alleluia*" [The rod of Jesse hath blossomed: a virgin hath brought forth God and man: God hath given peace, reconciling the lowest with the highest in Himself].

44   For example, on the First Sunday of Lent, where the long Tract (Ps 90:1–7, 11–16) corresponds to the Psalm quoted in the passage on temptation (Mt 4:1–11 with Ps 90:11f.).

45   *Victimae paschali laudes* (Easter); *Veni Sancte Spiritus* (Pentecost); *Lauda Sion* (Corpus Christi); *Stabat Mater* (feast of the Seven Sorrows of the Blessed Virgin Mary: Sep. 15 and Friday after the Sunday *Judica*); *Dies irae* (All Souls; Masses for the Dead). Cf. N. Gihr, *Die Sequenzen des römischen Messbuches dogmatisch und ascetisch erklärt* (Freiburg i. Br.: Verlag Herder, ²1900).

Credo

It is "meet and right at festive seasons to bring forth before our God every jewel of the Mysteries entrusted to us, to show that those of which He gave us we have lost none."[46] These words of Cardinal Newman may well be applied to the classical rite of the Mass, in which the Creed is prayed on all Sundays and high feast days following the Gospel or sermon.[47] The Credo first found entrance into the Roman Mass after it was initially used in the West in Spain in 589 as a proof of orthodoxy; later, around the year 800, it was also included in Frankish celebrations of the Mass. Confronted with Emperor Henry II's (1014) astonishment that the Roman Mass lacked a Credo, the clerics at that time answered that since the Roman Church would never be touched by heresy, it would not be necessary to sing the Creed more frequently.[48] Finally the Roman Church complied with the emperor's wishes, allowing the Roman pilgrims from all parts of the world to find the familiar Credo here in the center of the universal Church. The position of the Credo as the conclusion of the Mass of the Catechumens here expresses the agreement of the faithful with the Word of God that they have heard, rather than in the Spanish rite in which the Creed was

46 J.H. Newman, "The Gospel, a Trust Committed to Us," Sermon 22 in *Parochial and Plain Sermons*, vol. II (Westminster, MD: Christian Classics, 1966), 270.

47 The Credo is appointed for: all first class feasts and votive Masses, second class feasts of Our Lord and the Mother of God, all of the Masses for the octaves of Christmas, Easter, and Pentecost as well as the Masses of the main feasts of the Apostles and Evangelists, and finally the feast *Cathedra Petri* (Feb. 22). Cf. Kaschewsky, "Die Rubriken," 359: "In the Occidental Church, the rule has prevailed that there must be three special reasons for the *Credo*: *mysterium — doctrina — solemnitas. Mysterium* means that the content of the day is related to an article of the *Credo* — such as the birth and resurrection of the Lord, but also all Sundays, all of which have an Easter character. *Doctrina* means here that on the days of the apostles and evangelists, who have first proclaimed the faith, the *Credo* is to be prayed; in the past this was the case also at the feasts of the Doctors of the Church, since they explained, justified and passed on the faith — but since they were not the original 'creators' of the dogmas, the *Credo* was later omitted from their feasts. Finally, *solemnitas* means that the *Credo* lends a special shine to the day; so it is also spoken or sung at the feasts of patrons and at extraordinary votive Masses that have the rank of I Class, e.g., at a church consecration or a canonization. Behind this is the Church's wise concern that the indiscriminate daily recitation of the *Credo* does not lead to a kind of inflation, but that by hearing it, one becomes attentive and aware of the special content of the *Credo* and the reason for its recitation."

48 Cf. Berno of Reichenau, *De quibusdam rebus ad missae officium spectantibus* (PL 142, 1060f.).

intended as a proof of orthodoxy before Communion. Nevertheless, when used as a transition from the Mass of the Catechumens to the Mass of the Faithful, the Credo is the best means of preparing the faithful for Communion, as it devoutly professes the Incarnation of the eternal Son of God, allows the Eucharistic consecration to be recognized as a continuation of this mystery,[49] and helps the sacred character of Communion to be considered in the light of this mystery. The spiritual preparation that the recitation of the Creed allows was already emphasized by the Council of Toledo (589) at the admission of the Symbol [*symbolum*] into the Spanish rite of Mass: "It should be sung by the people in a loud voice so that the true Faith may have a clear testimony and so that the faithful, if they are there to receive the Body and the Blood of Christ, may purify their hearts through the Creed."[50]

In the traditional rite of the Mass, the shortened form of the Apostles' Creed (*Symbolum Apostolicum*) is not prayed, but rather the entire Niceno-Constantinopolitan Symbol, as it was formulated in 381 at the Council of Constantinople, which sought to end the Trinitarian theological controversy of the fourth century with a profession of faith that was also suited for liturgical use, primarily in the liturgy of baptism, and also later in the celebration of the Mass. The acceptance of this great profession of faith into the Mass was motivated by anti-Arianism in both Spain (sixth century) and France (ninth century), above all in order to defend Christ's true divinity unequivocally and dogmatically against all extenuations and reinterpretations, through the Creed's clear statements ("True God of true God, begotten, not made, consubstantial with the Father"). Accordingly, this Creed has an irreplaceable importance in the present day for opposing all neo-Arian tendencies that question the divinity of Christ and reduce His Person to that of an exemplary human being.[51] In so far as in the traditional rite of the Mass the Credo cannot be replaced by a song that lessens the precise

49   On the connection between the Incarnation and the sacrifice of the Mass, cf. the remarks on the Last Gospel further below in this chapter.

50   Mansi 9, 993.

51   Cf. R. Graber, "Die Aktualität des Konzils von Nicäa": H. Pfeil (ed.), *Unwandelbares im Wandel der Zeit* II (Aschaffenburg: Paul Pattloch Verlag, 1977), 225–41.

dogma, it is guaranteed that even today the Church can remain true to that affirmation of the divine consubstantiality of the Son (ὁμοούσιος τῷ Πατρί, *homoousios tō Patri, consubstantialis Patri*), a doctrine for the unswerving testimony of which a fourth-century confessor bishop like Athanasius of Alexandria was prepared to take upon himself exile for a total of seventeen years.[52]

Beyond the definite belief in Christ already contained in the wording, the genuflection at the words *Et incarnatus est* is an impressive sign of worship of the incarnate Son of God. Similarly, the bowing of the head at *simul adoratur* bears witness to the divinity of the Holy Ghost, which was staunchly defended at the same Council in 381 against the Pneumatomachian heretics who denied it. The priest's closing sign of the Cross primarily attests to the Cross being the path to eternal life (*Et vitam venturi saeculi*), but at the same time it is also a summary and manifest profession of faith in the Triune God of whom the Creed has spoken.

MASS OF THE FAITHFUL

Oblation

Offertory. The Mass of the Faithful begins with the Offertory, whose historical development and theology will be later discussed in detail. Just as he did at the Collect, the priest first kisses the altar before turning to the faithful for the liturgical greeting. The introductory *Dominus vobiscum* and *Oremus* are not related to the immediately following Offertory antiphon that originally accompanied the faithful's procession of the gifts with a longer psalmody (since the seventh century). Instead they belong to the

---

52 Cf. B. Capelle, "Le 'Credo,'" in *La Préparation de l'Eucharistie*, 171–84, 184: "This *Credo* must keep something of its anti-heretical character. Let it be a tribute of veneration and gratitude for our old Mother Church, the guardian of the Truth.... The Symbol proclaims her *one, holy, catholic* and *apostolic*. Certainly she is *one*—but her unity is so strong only because she is based on *una fides, unum baptisma*. She is *holy*—but she knows that, without dogma, this holiness would become piety that crumbles into a sentimentality destined to vanish. She is *catholic*—but the greater the multitude of believers, the more necessary is the clear profession of faith, which is their banner. That is why the great mark of the Church is to be *apostolic*—to pass through the centuries charged with her *Credo*, the divine burden received from the Apostles, to keep it valiantly and to carry it without fail to the ends of the earth and until the consummation of the ages."

Secret (*oratio secreta*) that, now separated from them with prayers of later origin, creates the conclusion of the Offertory and is spoken without the usual introduction to the Orations.[53] While in a Solemn High Mass the subdeacon brings the chalice to the altar and the deacon uncovers it and hands the paten to the priest, in the simple service it is the priest himself who uncovers the chalice and then lifts the host lying on the paten up to the crucifix and offers it with an accompanying prayer (*Suscipe, sancte Pater*). After the sign of the Cross is made with the paten over the corporal, manifesting the relationship of the sacrifice of the Mass to the sacrifice of the Cross, the host is laid on the corporal.[54] The paten is now put halfway under the corporal and later covered with the purificator. During the Solemn High Mass the subdeacon holds the paten for the praying of the Canon, cloaked with a humeral veil out of respect for the sacred vessel. Older forms of the Roman rite can be recognized here, where the paten was not yet used for the offering, but was first brought out at the beginning of the Canon by an acolyte (*patenarius*) and kept covered with a cloth, to be passed to the subdeacon and archdeacon at the Lord's Prayer. This practice is in turn based on the even older custom that in the Masses in the Roman titular churches the acolytes would hold a particle of the host consecrated in the Papal Mass on a reverently covered paten until this so-called *fermentum* was lowered into the chalice in order to express unity with the bishop of Rome. The preparation of the chalice by mixing water and wine, which is accompanied by an old Roman Christmas prayer (*Deus, qui humanae substantiae dignitatem*) — amplified by the indicator *per huius aquae et vini mysterium* — and carried out by the deacon and subdeacon in a Solemn High Mass, is followed by the offering of the chalice with the prayer *Offerimus tibi, Domine, calicem salutaris*. After the subsequent sign of the Cross with the chalice over the corporal, it is set upon the corporal, and covered with the protective pall. With that, in a bowed and humble attitude, the priest speaks a prayer of self-sacrifice

---

53   These words may have introduced the common prayer of the Church, that is, the intercessions, which once stood in this place and closed with a prayer which corresponds to the later Secret. Cf. Jungmann, *Missarum sollemnia* I, 618f.; idem, *The Mass of the Roman Rite* I, 483f.

54   As the name "corporal" already indicates, it is a symbol of the burial sheets which wrapped the body (*corpus*) of the Lord, sacrificed on the Cross.

that includes the faithful (*In spiritu humilitatis*). Then the priest lifts his eyes toward heaven, spreads his hands, blesses the offerings with the sign of the Cross, and prays with a kind of epiclesis, a prayer directed to the Holy Ghost (*Veni, Sanctificator*),[55] especially for the greatest blessing, consecration, to be bestowed on the oblations, as well as for the blessing of the sacrifice of the Mass for the entire Church.

Incensing. In the High Mass now follows the incensing of the sacrificial offerings, which became customary in Rome during the twelfth century, having originated in France (ninth/tenth century). On the one hand this is a symbol of prayer and sacrifice ascending to God, and on the other it is a rite of purification and sanctification. The preparatory blessing (*Incensum istud dignetur Dominus* ✠ *benedicere*), which asks especially the Archangel Michael's intercession as the protector of the Church (*Per intercessionem beati Michaelis archangeli*) and again links the earthly liturgy with the heavenly one (cf. Rev 8:3) (*stantis a dextris altaris incensi*), also gives the incense the power of a sacramental, as at the beginning of the Mass. Just as the incense is to purify the offerings from all impurities, it also envelops them in an atmosphere of sanctity. At the same time the incense symbolically expresses the ascending of the offered gifts and prayers. This is already indicated in the offering of the chalice (*Offerimus*), that it "may ascend before Thy divine Majesty as a sweet savor." Similarly it states later in the prayer at the incensing of the altar (*Dirigatur, Domine*): "Let my prayer, O Lord, be directed as incense in Thy sight: the lifting up of my hands as an evening sacrifice" (Ps 140:2). The ascending incense thus completes the rite of the lifting up of the offerings, whereby it abstracts them from their profane use and raises them up into God's sphere. The method of incensing (*ordo incensandi oblata*) emphasizes this, as the offerings are first incensed three times in the form of the Cross — a reinforced repetition of the *Veni, sanctificator... et benedic* ✠ *hoc sacrificium* — and then the censer is passed around circularly, twice from right to left and once from left to right — as a sign of segregation from everyday usage.[56]

---

55 Already witnessed since the beginning of the 9th century in the Irish Stowe Missal.

56 The number three is occasionally interpreted trinitarily, so that the two circles refer to the Father and the Holy Spirit while the individual circle is a symbol for the Son, who alone became man.

The accompanying prayer (*Incensum istud . . . ascendat ad te, Domine, et descendat super nos misericordia tua*) sees in the rising cloud of incense a prayer joining itself with Christ's sacrifice, and sees the fragrance flowing down as a symbol of the grace and mercy of God. The short prayer formula virtually contains a definition of sacrifice, as it describes the consummative exchange between heaven and earth and connects the ascending, cultic dimension of the sacrifice of the Mass with the descending, soteriological dimension. The subsequent incensing of the altar resembles the incensing at the beginning of the Mass, but is accompanied by a prayer (*Dirigatur, Domine*) that speaks of the evening sacrifice of incense (Ps 140:2) offered in the Temple of Jerusalem at its own altar, which stood in front of the altar of burnt offerings. In exact correspondence to the Old Testament worship in the temple, the offering of incense after the Offertory here precedes the great "burnt offering" that will be fulfilled on the altar in the renewal of the sacrifice of the Cross.[57] At the same time, the incensing of the altar becomes a manifest *Sursum corda*, which should awaken and deepen the attitude of prayer. The prayer that accompanies the handing over of the thurible (*Accendat in nobis Dominus ignem sui amoris, et flammam aeternae caritatis*) demonstrates the disposition necessary for the interior sacrifice by asking for a heart burning with love, as symbolized by the burning coals that consume the grains of incense and transform them into fragrance. The subsequent incensing of the celebrant, clergy, and people, with the sequence corresponding to their hierarchical arrangement,[58] is firstly a symbol for the way in which the blessings of the sacrifice of the Mass descend upon all the participants, but it also pays respect in a hierarchical way to the priest as Christ's representative and the remaining faithful as members of the mystical Body of Christ and as temples of the Holy Spirit.

---

57 Cf. Mosebach, "Weihrauch," 13: "By inserting the reenactment of Jesus' death into the sacrificial ritual of the Old Covenant, this memory of his death is unmistakably characterized as a sacrificial act. Thus the offering of incense supports the correct understanding of the holy Mass; the incense therefore has a catechetical significance which goes far beyond its solemn effect."

58 In a Solemn High Mass the deacon incenses the celebrant, those clergy who are present, and the subdeacon. The thurifer then incenses successively the deacon, the master of ceremonies, the acolytes and others servers, lastly the people (cf. *Ritus servandus in celebratione Missae* VII, 10).

Washing of the hands. The washing of the priest's hands, which was originally necessary for practical reasons at a time when he received the offerings from the hands of the faithful, later remained as a meaningful symbol of the need for spiritual purity. It is the manifest continuation of the prayer preceding the incensing *In spiritu humilitatis*. Only the tips of the thumbs and index fingers are purified, as these will touch the Body of the Lord. The accompanying prayer (Ps 25:6–12) expresses this symbolism in words (*Lavabo inter innocentes manus meas et circumdabo altare tuum*), just as it embodies the love of the House of God — consistent with the liturgical moment (*Dilexi decorem domus tuae et locum habitationis gloriae tuae*).

The prayer *Suscipe, sancta Trinitas*. Turning back from the Epistle side to the middle of the altar, the priest bows slightly, lays his folded hands on the altar, and reads the prayer *Suscipe, sancta Trinitas*, which summarizes the previous prayers of oblation and with new sentiments once more asks the Trinity to accept the sacrifice. The requested acceptance "in honor" (*in honorem*) of the saints would not and could not increase their heavenly glory, but rather can only obtain greater reverence for them on earth, as through the grace of the sacrifice of the Mass the faithful are capable of following the example of the saints and may experience the power of their intercession.[59]

The *Orate fratres* and the Secret. After kissing the altar, the priest turns to the people with the words *Orate fratres*, inviting them to join him in asking God to accept the sacrifice. Only the first two words of this prayer are spoken aloud, since the rest of the formula containing the intention (*ut meum ac vestrum sacrificium acceptabile fiat apud Deum Patrem omnipotentem*) was only included later. In a ceremonial remembrance of the time when the celebrant turned to the priests on his right and left sides, the priest at the *Orate fratres* turns in a complete half circle from right to left, as opposed to what is done at any *Dominus*

---

59 Cf. the explanation of this prayer by the Council of Trent, sess. XXII, cap. 3 (DH 1744): "And, although it is the custom of the Church to celebrate at times certain Masses in honor and in remembrance of the saints, she does not teach that sacrifice is offered to them, but to God alone who crowned them (cf. can. 5). Whence, the priest does not say: 'I offer the sacrifice to you, Peter and Paul (Aug., *Contra Faust.* XX,21 [CSEL 25, 562 / PL 42, 384]), but giving thanks to God for their victories, he implores their protection, 'that they may vouchsafe to intercede for us in heaven whose memory we celebrate on earth' (*Missale Romanum, Ordo Missae*, after the washing of hands)."

vobiscum, where he turns partway to the right and then turns back. This turning required the placing of the Missal on the altar to the celebrant's left, so that the next prayer could be read from it.

After a silent *Amen* and without an *Oremus*, the priest prays the Secret silently, which should explain the name of this prayer, called in older times the "prayer over the oblations" (*oratio super oblata*). In the Roman Missal, the texts of the Secrets are the same age as and have the same style as the Collects. The Secret's special characteristic is that it refers to the sacrifice offered upon the altar of God, in order to ask of God for those who offer it up a blessing that often relates to the mystery of the feast or the requests of the day.[60]

Preface

After the closing of the Secret is prayed aloud (*per omnia saecula saeculorum*), the prologue to the Canon, the Preface, opens with a solemn exchange of greetings, as is indicated in all Eastern and Western liturgies since the second and third centuries, which well supports an argument for Apostolic tradition. At the *Dominus vobiscum*, the priest does not turn to the people, as he has already entered into the Holy of Holies of the sacrifice and now only beholds God. He lays his hands on the altar, which represents Christ, in Whose name the priest is acting. The invitation to prayer is emphasized with corresponding gestures that manifestly express the lifting up of hearts (*Sursum corda*) with lifting up of the hands, and the reverent thanksgiving (*Gratias agamus Domino Deo nostro*) with the folding of the hands, a short glance upward, and an inclining of the head.

With regard to content, the Preface is a great prayer of thanks and praise, placed at the beginning of the Canon[61] and corresponding to the

---

60 So for example, on Pentecost: "*Munera, quaesumus Domine, oblata santifica: et corda nostra Sancti Spiritus illustratione emunda*" [Sanctify, we beseech Thee, O Lord, the gifts which we offer Thee, and cleanse our hearts by the enlightenment of the Holy Spirit]; on the feast of the Apostles Sts Peter and Paul: "*Hostias, Domine, quas nomini tuo sacrandas offerimus, apostolica prosequatur oratio: per quam nos expiari tribuas et defendi*" [May the prayer of Thine Apostles accompany the oblation we offer to be consecrated to Thy Name; and grant that by it we may be cleansed and defended]. Cf. A. Fortescue, "Secret," *The Catholic Encyclopedia* XIII (New York: Robert Appleton Company, 1912): 673f.

61 Cf. A. Fortescue, "Preface," *The Catholic Encyclopedia* XII (New York: Robert Appleton Company, 1911): 384–86; G. Lefebvre, "La Préface et ses rapports avec le Canon de la Messe," in *La Préparation de l'Eucharistie*, 135–47.

thanksgiving of Christ (*gratias agens*) that preceded the institution of the Sacrament of the Altar. As in oldest times the celebration of the Mass was referred to as *eucharistia*, this thanksgiving lives on especially in the Preface, while the Roman Canon is more strongly pervaded with the concept of sacrifice and intercession. The structure of the Preface commonly follows a three-tier basic pattern: (1) general praise of God; (2) particular reason for thanksgiving; (3) joining in with the angelic praise.

While in the early days of the Roman liturgy there was a multitude of Prefaces,[62] the number was gradually reduced,[63] so that the *Missale Romanum* possessed sixteen Prefaces as of 1962,[64] among them a core of very old Prefaces: Christmas, Epiphany, Lent, the Holy Cross, Mass of the Chrism,[65] Easter, Ascension, Pentecost, the Most Holy Trinity, the Blessed Virgin,[66] the Apostles, the common Preface. The Preface for the Mass of the Dead, which was created according to old patterns,[67] and the Preface for St Joseph, stylistically modeled on the Marian Preface, entered into the Missal under Pope Benedict XV in 1919. Pope Pius XI added the Preface of the Kingship of Our Lord (1925) and of the Sacred Heart (1928). In Masses that do not have their own Prefaces, the *Praefatio communis* is used, and for Sundays after Pentecost and during Advent, the Preface of the Most Holy Trinity is used, which took the place of the formerly used common Preface in 1759.[68] The

---

62   The *Leonianum* (sixth century) contains 267 Prefaces; the *Gelasianum* (seventh century) contains 54; the *Gregorianum / Hadrianum* (eighth century) contains 14, of which seven are contained in the *Missale Romanum* (1962): praefatio communis, Christmas, Epiphany, Easter, Ascension, Pentecost, feasts of the Apostles; later in Frankish regions, the Prefaces of the Holy Cross, Trinity, and Lent were added. See Shaw, *Liturgical Restoration*, 118–19.

63   Cf. J. Gassner, *The Canon of the Roman Mass: Its History, Theology, and Art* (Saint Louis, MO / London: Herder, 1950 [2nd impr.]), 116: "It was when the Gregorian Sacramentary took shape that the Canon remained definitely 'the unchangeable rule.' At the same time the number of Prefaces was restricted to ten in order to prevent too many changes in that prayer so closely connected with the Canon; to give to the introduction of the Canon something of the dignity of an unchangeable rule."

64   Cf. P. Bruylants, "Les Préfaces du Missel Romain," MD 87 (1966): 111–33.

65   Since the reform of Holy Week in 1956.

66   Already of an older date (ninth century, yet with slight variations), this Preface was prescribed under Urban II in 1095 at the Synod of Piacenza.

67   Cf. J. Brinktrine, "Die neue Präfation in den Totenmessen," ThGl 11 (1919): 242–45.

68   On the question of origin (Roman or Gallican liturgy, Spanish-Mozarabic sources) and stylistic as well as theological influences of Pope Leo I, cf. M. Drew, "The Doctrine of the Holy Trinity in the Traditional Roman Missal": *Theological and Historical Aspects of the*

decree *Quo Magis* of March 25, 2020 introduced an additional seven Prefaces for optional use (including three of the neo-Gallican Prefaces, now approved for all regions): the Preface of the Most Blessed Sacrament, of the Dedication of a Church, for All Saints and Holy Patrons, for the Holy Angels, for St John the Baptist, for Martyrs, and for weddings. Certain dioceses and religious orders continue to have permission to use other particular Prefaces.[69]

With their linguistically artistic form and poetic, hymn-like power of expression,[70] the Prefaces, as the entrance to the Eucharistic Prayer, resemble the richly decorated portals of Gothic cathedrals, in that they emphasize the special character of the feast or liturgical season and profess the faith of the Church in a thankful manner.[71] Through regular repetition the limited number of these Prefaces is especially suited for making a lasting impression on the memory of the faithful.

Sanctus

The Sanctus in the Western liturgy can be traced back to the first half of the fifth century,[72] while the Benedictus that follows was common in the Roman Missal since the seventh century at the latest.[73] Appropriately, both of these texts borrowed from the Bible stand at the beginning of the Canon,

---

Roman Missal: The Proceedings of the Fifth International Colloquium of Historical, Canonical and Theological Studies on the Roman Catholic Liturgy (Kingston & Surbiton: CIEL UK, 2000), 109–26, 118–20; J. A. Jungmann, "Um die Herkunft der Dreifaltigkeitspräfation," ZkTh 81 (1959): 461–65. For theology, cf. Dionysius Cartusianus, *Expositio Missae*, art. XVII [*Opera omnia* 35] (Tournai: Typis Cartusiae S. M. de Pratis, 1908), 350–52.

69   Cf. B. Opfermann, "Die heutigen liturgischen Sonderpräfationen," ThGl 46 (1956): 204–15; A. Zák, "Über die Präfationen," *Theologisch-praktische Quartalschrift* 58 (1905): 307–25.

70   Cf. J. Pascher, *Eucharistia*, 366–73; C. Mohrmann, *Liturgical Latin: Its Origins and Character* (London: Burns & Oates, 1959), 62–65.

71   Cf. E. Guillou, *Le livre de la messe. Mysterium fidei* (Paris: Société de production littéraire, 1975), 23: "Those which St Pius V in his wisdom has retained provide in detail, according to the circumstances, a magnificent *Credo* in Eucharistic form"; M. Lods, "Préface eucharistique et confession de foi. Aperçu sur les premiers textes liturgiques chrétiens," *Revue d'histoire et de philosophie religieuses* 59 (1979): 121–42.

72   As part of Christian prayers outside of the Eucharist, the Sanctus is witnessed at the turn of the first to second centuries by 1 *Clement* 34:6f. (FC 15, 146f. / *Epistles of St Clement*, 30).

73   Cf. A. Fortescue, "Sanctus," *The Catholic Encyclopedia* XIII (New York: Robert Appleton Company, 1911): 432f.; M. Grégoire, "Le 'Sanctus' et l'Agnus Dei,'" in *Le Canon de la Messe. De la préface à la communion* [Cours et conférences des semaines liturgiques VII] (Louvain: Éditions de Abbaye du Mont César / Bruges: Desclée de Brouwer et Cie,

because in it, through the consecration, will take place a theophany that the Church already anticipates as she joins in the singing of the angels, which the Prophet Isaiah saw before the Throne of God (cf. Is 6:1–3), as well as in the cry of joy at the coming Messiah with which the crowd of people greeted Christ's entrance into Jerusalem (cf. Mt 21:9). As the *Hosanna*, kept untranslated in the Gospel, is a cry of homage ("praise," "hail")[74] and is similar to the *Benedictus*,[75] the *Sanctus* expresses the unending dignity, majesty, and sanctity of God. The threefold repetition of the singular *Sanctus* was already understood in the fourth century as testimony of the three divine Persons and the simultaneous unity of Their being.[76] Both the Sanctus and Benedictus profess the central mysteries of the Faith, the Triune God and the coming of the Savior into the world.[77] As the praise of God by the angels (*Sanctus*) is followed by the people's song of praise (*Benedictus*) and the Church Militant on earth joins in with the hymns of the Church Triumphant, the earthly liturgy once again unites with the celestial liturgy ("Holy, holy, holy, Lord God Almighty": Rev 4:8), deriving its worth from being the echo and reflection of the latter. The priest's bent posture (*supplici confessione dicentes*: close of the Preface) is an expression of profound adoration, corresponding to the biblical description of the heavenly liturgy (cf. Rev 4:8; Is 6:2). At the joyful, triumphant hymn of the Benedictus, the priest rights himself again and crosses himself, since Christ comes to renew the sacrifice of the Cross on the altar in a sacramental form and to include the Church in this sacrifice.

The Canon

The Canon constitutes the center of the Holy Mass; its highpoint, the consecration, is surrounded with various prayers of offering and intercession.[78]

1929) [hereafter *Le Canon de la Messe*], 161–75.

74   In the Old Testament *Hosanna* means "help, save"; cf. Ps 117:25.

75   Cf. J.-B. Bossuet, *Explication de quelques difficultés sur les prières de la Messe* [*Œuvres* 4] (Paris: Librairie catholique Martin-Beaupré, 1868), 472: "On bénit Dieu lorsqu'on célèbre ses louanges."

76   Cf. Ambrose, *De Spiritu sancto* 3,16,110 (CSEL 79, 196f. / Ambrose, *Theological and Dogmatic Works*, trans. by R.J. Deferrari, *The Fathers of the Church* 44 [Washington, DC: Catholic University of America Press, 1963], 193).

77   According to a perfect or present meaning of *venit*, the *Benedictus* may refer to the accomplished Incarnation, or the upcoming Consecration.

78   On the history, theology, and ceremonies of the Canon, cf. chapter 14.

The priest begins the Canon (*Te igitur*) by emphasizing the first words with corresponding gestures of prayer—lifting the eyes and hands, bowing, kissing the altar[79]—and asking for acceptance as well as blessing (*uti accepta habeas et benedicas*)[80] of the offerings, which are offered up for the Catholic Church so that she may be granted peace, protection, unity, and guidance. As the sacrifice is offered up not only for the Church but also in her name,[81] the celebrant expresses his communion with the pope and local bishop as well as all orthodox believers of the Catholic and Apostolic Faith.

The universal petition for the Church as a whole is followed by the petition for the individuals who are remembered in this celebration of the Mass in a special way or for those who are present at it—the so-called *Memento* of the Living, which corresponds to the *Memento* of the Dead after the consecration.

The Commemoration leads into the invocation of the saints, in whose communion (*Communicantes et memoriam venerantes*) and through whose merits and intercession (*quorum meritis precibusque concedas*) individual prayers are given greater strength. The list of the saints named here (Mary, Joseph, twelve Apostles and twelve martyrs of the early Roman Church [first/fourth centuries][82]) has in turn an analogue after the consecration in a second Commemoration of the saints (*Nobis quoque*).

Before the consecration, a further prayer for the acceptance of the sacrifice is contained in the *Hanc igitur*, which condenses the multitude of human concerns into the possession of peace and eternal salvation. Following the Old Testament model (cf. Ex 29:15f.; Lev 16:21f.), the priest spreads his hands over the oblation to emphasize the Holy Mass's character of expiation.

The Canon's last strophe (*Quam oblationem*) before the consecration contains a request for transubstantiation that linguistically and stylistically leans on Roman legal terminology with its cumulative and partially synonymous expressions (*ratam, rationabilem, acceptabilemque facere digneris*)

---

79 For the exact description, see p. 207.
80 Simultaneously a pre-blessing and request for consecration.
81 The preposition *pro* also means "in the name of."
82 Enumerated in order of hierarchy: five popes, a bishop, a deacon, five laymen.

and presents an epiclesis, even though neither the Holy Ghost nor the *Logos* is expressly named.[83]

Conforming to the *actio Christi*, the gestures of the Lord at the Last Supper (*Qui pridie quam pateretur*), the priest speaks the words of consecration while bowing deeply, and adores the consecrated forms of bread and wine with a genuflection before and after the elevation (since the twelfth/thirteenth centuries for the host, fourteenth century for the chalice).[84]

The prayer following the consecration (*Unde et memores*) carries out Christ's mandate, "Do this in memory of me," and broadens the remembrance beyond the Passion to the Resurrection and Ascension of the Lord, which belong essentially to the sacrifice, in order to combine the liturgical remembrance with the sacrificial act of the Church (*offerimus*), who ultimately can offer up only that which has been given to her by God (*de tuis donis ac datis*).

With a further prayer for acceptance (*Supra quae*), the gaze is directed toward three sacrificial figures from the Old Testament — Abel, Abraham, and Melchisedech — whose sacrificial disposition the Church makes her own so that God may be well pleased with her offering.[85]

Once again the priest bows deeply and prays (*Supplices te rogamus*) for the acceptance of the sacrifice, but unites this request with a type of "Communion epiclesis," requesting heavenly grace and blessing on the partakers at the altar (*ex hac altaris participatione*).

As the fruit of the sacrifice of the Mass is not only meant to grant relief to the Church Militant on earth, but also to the Church Suffering in Purgatory, a *Memento* for the Dead follows that breathes the spirit of early Christendom in its figurative language.[86] The official prayer of the

83 Cf. Brinktrine, *Messe*, 197.

84 Cf. Brinktrine, *Messe*, 210: "The fact that the priest, having spoken the words of the Lord over the bread and the wine, immediately makes a genuflection and upholds the holy species to the people for worship, is quite a sure proof for the Catholic doctrine that transubstantiation is effected through the words of institution."

85 Cf. Thomas Aquinas, *STh* III, 83,4 ad 8, in *Summa Theologiae*, vol. 59, trans. by Th. Gilby, 163: "Though this sacrifice of itself ranks above the ancient sacrifices, yet these were acceptable to God on account of the devotion of men of old. Accordingly the priest asks that this sacrifice may be accepted by God, as the others were, because of the devotion of those who offer it."

86 Cf. (Abbé) Maranget, "La Grande Prière d'Intercession," in *Le Canon de la Messe*,

Church is here intended only for those who were baptized (*qui nos prae-cesserunt cum signo fidei*), who are deceased in peace with her (*et dormiunt in somno pacis*), as well as all those who rest in Christ (*omnibus in Christo quiescentibus*). At the closing *Per eundem Christum Dominum nostrum* the priest bows his head, which is elsewhere required at the mention of Jesus' name. This bowing of the head, however, also occurred in earlier ages in conclusions without the name of Jesus: this custom has been preserved uniquely here, and a symbolic meaning is attributed to it in the allegorical explanation of the Mass from the Middle Ages, which saw a remembrance of Christ, Who, when dying, bowed His head to free the righteous of the Old Covenant from the depths of the underworld.

Just as the bliss of Heaven is besought for the departed, subsequently in the second commemoration of the saints (*Nobis quoque*) the Church requests fellowship with them (*partem aliquam et societatem donare digne-ris*) for those faithful still on earth, who are aware of their own failures (as expressed in the prayer of the priest, who repentantly strikes his breast at the words *Nobis quoque peccatoribus*[87]) and who do not rely on their own merits but ask for everything through God's forgiveness (*non aestimator meriti, sed veniae, quaesumus, largitor, admitte*). Again the saints named here are martyrs of the early Church — after John the Baptist, seven men and seven women — who were highly venerated in Rome and are listed in order according to the date of their martyrdom.

Two praises of God form the close of the Canon, which above all empha-size Christ's position as mediator.[88] The first prayer, *Per quem haec omnia, Domine, semper bona creas, sancti✠ficas, vivi✠ficas, bene✠dicis et praestas*

177–91, 188: "The *Memento* of the deceased has an ancient flavor. It breathes the scent of the catacombs. Its very beautiful expressions return the distant echo of the inscriptions of underground Rome."

87   During the silence of the Canon, the priest raises his voice only at this place, as originally in the papal Pontifical High Mass the subdeacons remained in a humbly bowed position from the Sanctus on, and by means of the uplifted voice, received the signal to right themselves again and to fetch the paten for the breaking of the Host. Today, this breaking of the silence (in a slightly raised voice, per the rubrics for Solemn Mass) is used to signal the deacon to switch from the Gospel side of the celebrant to the Epistle side in readiness for removing the pall for the *Per ipsum* (minor elevation).

88   Cf. J. Kreps, "La doxologie du Canon (*Per quem haec omnia*)," in *Le Canon de la Messe*, 223–30.

nobis, looks at the Eucharistic gifts of bread and wine that God has created through His Son, has sanctified in the highest way through the consecration, has changed to life-giving food, and gives to the faithful in Holy Communion. It is a prayer of thanks for the consummated consecration and the Communion that follows.[89]

The Canon closes with a doxology (*Per ipsum*) and the minor elevation of the host and chalice. Before the appearance of the major elevation after the consecration during the Middle Ages, this was the only lifting up of the consecrated offerings, which are not shown here for the veneration of the people but are rather raised up for the glorification of God, as is similarly done at the prayers of offering during the Offertory. Five signs of the Cross, as ultimately determined by Pope Pius V, accompany the prayer and emphasize that finally it is the Cross through which "all honor and glory" (*omnis honor et gloria*) is offered to God. The first three signs of the Cross (*Per ✠ ipsum, et cum ✠ ipso, et in ✠ ipso*) are done with the Host over the chalice and recall the ancient Roman Mass (seventh century) where the deacon lifted up the chalice while the pope touched the rim of the chalice with the Host. As the separate consecration of Christ's Body and Blood symbolizes His violent, self-sacrificing death, the combination of the Host and chalice, that is, the unification of Christ's Body and Blood, is a symbol of the Resurrection. It is the Risen Christ who renders to God the most perfect honor and glory. The last two signs of the Cross (*tibi Deo Patri ✠ omnipotenti, in unitate Spiritus ✠ Sancti*) are done with the Host in front of the chalice to express the distinctness of these divine Persons from the Son, Who was sacrificed and rose again. A genuflection follows as a sign of adoration, and at the same time allows for a short pause before the closing formula in order to ponder the profundity of the words "all honor and glory." With the *Per omnia saecula saeculorum* spoken or chanted aloud, the priest departs from the silence of the Canon while the people for their part solemnly attest to and affirm the entire sacrifice with an *Amen*.

---

89 In earlier times (end of the fifth century) occasionally this prayer would be preceded by a blessing of natural produce, but that may not constitute the source of this prayer, which probably referred to the Eucharistic gifts from the beginning. Cf. Brinktrine, *Messe*, 224f.

The Communion

The Lord's Prayer. The Pater Noster, witnessed in the Latin Church since the fourth century,[90] is simultaneously the close of the Eucharistic Prayer and the preparation for Communion.[91] In a decree by Pope Gregory the Great (598), the Our Father, which before that time was most likely prayed directly before Communion, found its current place directly after the Canon, which it concluded,[92] being recognized as a prayer of blessing and sacrifice.[93] In relation to the Canon, the Pater Noster, as a solemn conclusion, corresponds to the Preface, which is the solemn prologue of the Eucharistic Prayer. The first petitions of the Our Father are a "sort of summary and recapitulation of the preceding Eucharistic prayer," formulated in short sentences, and they excellently apply to the sacrifice of the Mass.[94] As a prayer of sacrifice, the Pater Noster is reserved for the priest[95] who, after an introductory formula (*Oremus. Praeceptis salutaribus moniti…*), speaks it alone or sings it in one of the styles similar to the tone of the Preface, while he keeps his gaze directed toward the Host. The people respond with the last petition (*sed libera nos a malo*), which the priest answers with a silent *Amen*. The Our Father is suited for a prayer

90   Given the central placement of the Lord's Prayer in the life of the early Christian, who prayed it three times during the day, its use in the Church's highest act of worship may date back to Apostolic times, despite a lack of testimony. Cf. O. Rousseau, "Le 'Pater' dans la liturgie de la Messe," in *La Préparation de l'Eucharistie*, 231–41, 235; E. Vandeur, "Le 'Pater' et sa portée eucharistique," ibid., 243–49.

91   Cf. Vandeur, "Le 'Pater' et sa portée eucharistique," 249: "The *Pater* … placed at the center of the Mass, at the end of the Canon in its proper sense, when the sacrifice is accomplished, makes a magnificent link between this Sacrifice and the Sacrament which it introduces. It recalls the glory of God in its first requests; it implores the true peace of man in the last. As such, it really appears as a doctrinal synthesis of the Holy Mass."

92   J. Brinktrine, "Das Vaterunser in den Messliturgien," ThGl 13 (1921): 275–80, 279, emphasizes that "even after the transubstantiation has taken place, the Church can implore God to bless and accept the sacrifice, in so far as *she* is taken into account in the act of offering"; cf. idem, "Das Vaterunser als Konsekrationsgebet," ThGl 9 (1917): 152–54.

93   Cf. Gregory I, *Epistula* 9, 26 (CCL 140A, 587). Cf. Brinktrine, *Messe*, 247–49.

94   Cf. Jungmann, *Missarum sollemnia* II, 346; idem, *The Mass of the Roman Rite* II, 279: "The *sanctificetur* is a synopsis of the triple *Sanctus*; the *adveniat regnum tuum* is a kind of epitome of the two epiclesis prayers: *Quam oblationem* and *Supplices*; and the *fiat voluntas tua* sets forth the basic idea regarding obedience from which all sacrifice must proceed." Cf. Vandeur, "Le 'Pater' et sa portée eucharistique," 243–46.

95   Cf. Gregory I, *Epistula* 9,26 (CCL 140A, 587): *dicitur … a solo sacerdote.*

of preparation for the imminent Communion especially by reason of the request for bread, already interpreted in a Eucharistic sense by the early Church Fathers, but also because of the request for forgiveness of sins, which continues the Confiteor and the *Nobis quoque peccatoribus* of the Canon and can blot out venial sins as a sacramental, according to an early Christian understanding.[96]

The embolism. The last petition of the Our Father is continued into a quietly spoken[97] embolism ("insertion") that asks once more before Communion for deliverance from evil of any kind (*Libera nos ab omnibus malis*) — those consequences of sin having a lasting effect (*praeteritis*), present afflictions (*praesentibus*), or impending temptations (*et futuris*) — and, as a prayer for peace (*da propitius pacem in diebus nostris*),[98] leads over to the subsequent ceremonies of peace (greeting of peace: *Pax Domini sit semper vobiscum*; *Agnus Dei . . . dona nobis pacem*; the priest's preparation for Communion: *Domine Jesu Christe*). As heavenly intercessors, Mary as well as both of the founders of the Church in Rome, Peter and Paul, are invoked, but also St Andrew, who, as the brother of St Peter, was especially venerated in Rome already from the time of the fifth century. Since the Byzantine Church traces her founding back to this Apostle, his being named together with the Princes of the Apostles is also a sign of communion with the Eastern Church. During this prayer the priest holds the paten,[99] placed vertically over the purificator outside of the corporal, in order to cross himself with the paten at the words *da propitius pacem* as a sign that Christ established this peace on the Cross (cf. Col 1:20). After he has reverently kissed the paten, as a holy vessel upon which the

96 Cf. Augustine, *Sermo Denis* 6,3 [= *sermo* 229,3] (*Miscellanea Agostiniana* I, 32 / Augustine, *Sermons*, trans. by E. Hill, *The Works of St Augustine* III/6 [Hyde Park, NY: New City Press, 1993], 267).

97 The placement of this prayer in the section of the Mass that represents the Passion of Christ before His Resurrection (symbolized in the subsequent commingling of the Body and Blood of Christ) made the quiet praying of the embolism seem more appropriate, as during the Canon, around the turn of the millennium.

98 Simultaneously a continuation of the *diesque nostros in tua pace disponas* from the *Hanc igitur* of the Canon.

99 In a Solemn High Mass it is accepted by the deacon from the subdeacon, who has been holding it in a veil since the Offertory, and presented to the priest.

Body of Christ will rest, he slides the Host, which has been lying on the corporal up to this point, onto the paten, which now takes its place in front of the chalice.

The breaking and mingling. During the closing formula of the embolism *Per eundem Dominum nostrum Jesum Christum*, etc., the priest breaks the host above the chalice in order to indicate that this contains the Blood that poured out of Christ's sacrificed Body on the Cross, especially from His opened side (cf. Jn 19:34). Then three crosses are made over the chalice with the small particle (*consignatio*) while the priest says: *Pax* ✠ *Domini sit* ✠ *semper vobis*✠*cum*. After the people's reply (*Et cum spiritu tuo*) the particle is lowered into the chalice (*commixtio*). The unification of the Body and Blood[100] of Christ is regarded—just as at the *Per ipsum* of the final doxology of the Canon—as a symbol of the Resurrection, insofar as in Holy Communion is received the Body of the risen Christ, whose word is also recalled in the preceding greeting of peace. The following silent prayer of the priest (*Haec commixtio, et consecratio Corporis et Sanguinis Domini nostri Jesu Christi*)[101] asks for the life-giving power of Holy Communion (*fiat accipientibus nobis in vitam aeternam*), which was already preached as the "medicine of immortality" at the beginning of the second century.[102]

The *Agnus Dei*. After the completion of the commingling, the choir sings the Agnus Dei while the priest recites the words with a small bow, his gaze directed toward the broken host, striking his breast three times with his right hand. The Agnus Dei was introduced as an element of the Eastern liturgy at the end of the seventh century, originally as a longer chant accompanying the rite of breaking the bread in the celebration of the

---

100   According to biblical and ancient notions, the blood is the seat of the soul.

101   The term *consecratio* does not here mean a sacramental consecration of the already changed species, but is rather to be understood in a larger sense; cf. Jungmann, *Missarum sollemnia* II, 394n39: "The two species are 'consecrated' by their commingling to represent the Risen One, and thus shall give eternal life"; idem, *The Mass of the Roman Rite* II, 316n27: "As a matter of fact, we can follow Brinktrine in speaking of a consecration rite, in which the word 'consecration' is understood in a wider sense"; M.J. Scheeben, *Über die Eucharistie und den Messkanon*, ed. and comm. by M. Stickelbroeck (Regensburg: Verlag Friedrich Pustet, 2011), 102–11.

102   Cf. Ignatius of Antioch, *Epistula ad Ephesios* 20,2 (Fischer 160f. / *Epistles of St Clement and St Ignatius*, 68): φάρμακον ἀθανασίας, *pharmakon athanasias*.

Mass.[103] The invocation has commonly been repeated three times beginning in the twelfth century. Instead of *miserere nobis, dona eis requiem* is said in Masses for the Dead (for the third repetition: *requiem sempiternam*). The sacrificed lamb, typologically prefigured in the Old Testament paschal lamb (cf. Ex 12:1–14), prophetically foreshadowed as an image of the suffering servant of God (cf. Isa 53:7), witnessed by John the Baptist as being fulfilled in Christ (cf. Jn 1:29), explained by Peter as the redemptive power of the Blood of Christ (cf. 1 Pet 1:19), and finally standing victorious in the center of the vision of the heavenly throne (cf. Rev 5:6), is a symbol saturated with rich biblical reminiscences of the redemptive sacrificial death of Christ.[104] With the threefold invocation as well as the request for mercy and peace, the Mass simultaneously proves itself to be the realization of that sacrifice on the Cross and an application of the salvation there obtained.

Prayer for peace and kiss of peace. Following the last words of the *Agnus Dei*, the priest prays the prayer of peace (*Domine Jesu Christe, qui dixisti apostolis tuis*) with a small bow and his folded hands resting on the altar. This prayer serves as a preparation for the administering of the Pax or, alternately, replaces this ceremony when it is omitted. Observed since the beginning of the eleventh century, this prayer follows Christ's promise of peace given in the cenacle during the Last Supper (cf. Jn 14:27), contrasts personal sins with the abundant faith of the Church that exceeds individual failure (*ne respicias peccata mea, sed fidem Ecclesiae tuae*),[105] and conceptually follows on the *Te igitur* of the Canon, from which it has taken certain words (*pacificare, coadunare*). In a Solemn High Mass, the

---

103 Cf. Grégoire, "Le 'Sanctus' et l'Agnus Dei,'" 163–75.

104 Cf. Schnitzler, *Messe* II, 266: "The Agnus Dei of the Mass resembles a golden ring on which the gems of divine revelation shine through the Old and New Testament, through Moses, Isaiah, the Baptist, and the evangelist John. The Agnus Dei of the Mass is the arch of a mighty bridge that stretches from the distant shores of the Paschal Vigil of the Chosen People in Egypt over the river of mercy in the history of salvation, to descend again on the distant otherworldly shore of Eternity. The Agnus Dei resembles a crystal in which the colorful lights of the Church's mystery of salvation, the Easter Mystery, sparkle, the purple lights of the blood and the golden glow of victory."

105 In the NOM changed to *peccata nostra*. For the consequences of this modification, cf. J. Ratzinger, *The Ratzinger Report: An Exclusive Interview on the State of the Church*, trans. by S. Attanasio / G. Harrison (San Francisco: Ignatius Press, 1985), 51–53. For general differences cf. R. Kahl, "Alte und neue Pax," UVK 42 (2012): 145–48.

priest, together with the deacon, kisses the altar, as this peace is not an expression of human goodwill ("not as the world giveth": Jn 14:27), but comes from Christ. The priest then gives the deacon the kiss of peace, a stylized embrace preserving decorum, with the words *Pax tecum*; the deacon (or assisting presbyter) responds *Et cum spiritu tuo*, and performs the same ceremony with the subdeacon, who in turn passes it on to all of the clergy present in the chancel in hierarchical order. In Masses for the Dead, the prayer and the kiss of peace are omitted, since "these [Masses] are offered for their repose, not our present peace."[106] In the Roman rite, the Pax functions not only as a preparation for Holy Communion (cf. Mt 5:23f.), but also as a completion of the act of sacrifice, insofar as the unity of the mystical Body of Christ is identified and produced through the Eucharistic sacrifice (*signum unitatis et vinculum caritatis*).[107]

Holy Communion. i) *Preparatory prayers.* Since the end of the eleventh century, these prayers, which the priest speaks in a bowed attitude with his folded hands lying on the altar, have been located in their current arrangement in the missals, yet they are each separately observed already in the ninth century (*Domine Jesu Christe*) and the tenth century (*Perceptio Corporis tui*). Originating in the Gallico-Frankish Church, these private prayers of preparation that the priest spoke in the first person singular were selected from a multitude of similar set phrases and included in the Roman liturgy.[108] The fact that Holy Communion, which itself is followed by much shorter prayers, is prepared for with longer prayers such as these, which are also excellently suited for use by the faithful,[109] manifests the Church's belief that it is especially a prayerful preparation for the reception of the Sacrament of the Altar that determines the amount of grace bestowed on the communicant. The first prayer (*Domine Jesu Christe*) contains in its

---

106 Thomas Aquinas, *STh* III, 83,4, in *Summa Theologiae*, vol. 59, trans. by Th. Gilby, 159. In remembrance of Judas' kiss, the kiss of peace is omitted on Holy Thursday.

107 Thus, for example, in the Secret of Corpus Christi: "Graciously bestow on Thy Church, we beseech Thee, O Lord, the gifts of unity and peace which are mystically shown forth in the offerings now made." Cf. Brinktrine, *Messe*, 268–72.

108 Cf. M. Daras, "Les Prières préparatoires à la Sainte Communion," in *Le Canon de la Messe*, 251–63 (covers all prayers from *Domine Jesu Christi qui dixisti* to *Domine, non sum dignus*).

109 Cf. P. Lebrun, *Explication de la Messe* [LO 9] (Paris: Éditions du Cerf, 1949), 551f.; Batiffol, *Leçons sur la messe*, 323f.

few words a succinct summary of the divine work of salvation (*Fili Dei vivi, qui ex voluntate Patris, cooperante Spiritu Sancto, per mortem tuam mundum vivificasti*) and requests as fruits of Holy Communion forgiveness of sins, true fulfillment of the commandments, and perseverance until the end (*libera me per hoc sacrosanctum Corpus et Sanguinem tuum ab omnibus iniquitatibus meis, et universis malis: et fac me tuis semper inhaerere mandatis, et a te numquam separari permittas*). The second prayer (*Perceptio Corporis tui*) begins in the style of the Pauline admonition (cf. 1 Cor 11:29), humbly asks (*quod ego indignus sumere praesumo*) to be preserved from an unworthy Communion, and then asks for its protective and salutary effects for the soul and body (*prosit mihi ad tutamentum mentis et corporis, et ad medelam percipiendam*).[110]

ii) *The celebrant's Communion.* After genuflecting, the priest takes both halves of the sacred Host, together with the paten, and speaks (since the eleventh century) a slightly adjusted psalm verse (*Panem caelestem accipiam, et nomen Domini invocabo*: cf. Ps 115:4), which, similar to the remaining accompanying words, gives emphasis to the dignity and significance of the holy action and preserves the taking of the mysteries from thoughtless performance. Subsequently, he speaks three times in a low voice, while striking his breast with his right hand, *Domine non sum dignus*, and follows quietly with the next words (*ut intres sub tectum meum, sed tantum dic verbo, et sanabitur anima mea*). The triple repetition intensifies the urgent profession and request. The formula entered the liturgy in the eleventh century and became generally used in the thirteenth century. The altering of the quotation from Mt 8:8 (*et sanabitur puer meus*) was presumably done in view of Ps 40:5 (*sana animam meam, quia peccavi tibi*). The priest crosses himself with the sacred Host (from the thirteenth century), says *Corpus Domini nostri Jesu Christi custodiat animam meam in vitam aeternam. Amen*, and receives the Body of the Lord while bowing deeply, and remains for a short time in silent thanksgiving. Then he uncovers the chalice, genuflects, and removes with the paten any particles of Host that may be lying on the corporal, brushing

110 Critical of the merely facultative use of the prayers of preparation in the NOM, G. May, *Die alte und die neue Messe. Die Rechtslage hinsichtlich des Ordo Missae* [Sonderdruck UVK 1975/1976] (Sankt Augustin: Richarz Verlag, ⁴1991), 67.

these "pearls," as they are referred to in the Eastern liturgy,[111] into the chalice. As an expression of thanks, the priest prays the psalm verse *Quid retribuam Domino pro omnibus, quae retribuit mihi?* (Ps 115:12) and takes the chalice again with a prayer taken from the psalms (*Calicem salutaris accipiam, et nomen Domini invocabo*: Ps 115:4). Thereupon he blesses himself with the chalice in the form of a cross and, holding the paten under the chalice, receives the Precious Blood with the words *Sanguis Domini nostri Jesu Christi custodiat animam meam in vitam aeternam. Amen.*

iii) *Communion of the faithful.* After a Confiteor before Holy Communion had first become common in the liturgies of certain orders (twelfth/thirteenth centuries), Pope Pius V established the custom for the rite of the Mass of 1570. The Confiteor at the beginning of the Mass is primarily a preparation for the celebrant and assistant, that is, the acolyte, so that an admission of guilt on the part of the faithful immediately before Communion is reasonable. The Confiteor is spoken by the acolyte (sometimes together with the people), or at a High Mass chanted by the deacon while bowing, followed by the priestly prayer of forgiveness (*Misereatur vestri...*) and the minor absolution (*Indulgentiam, absolutionem, et remissionem peccatorum vestrorum...*).[112] The priest then shows the people the sacred Host with the ciborium or paten and speaks the *Ecce Agnus Dei, ecce qui tollit peccata mundi*, and then says three times, with the faithful, *Domine non sum dignus ... sed tantum dic verbo et sanabitur anima mea.* The *Ecce Agnus Dei* is first witnessed at the Council of Aix in 1585, where it was prescribed along with the accompanying rite. Communion under both species was common in the Western Church until the twelfth/thirteenth centuries, but then fell out of practice for mainly practical reasons, combined with a deepened dogmatic understanding of the Real Presence, according to which the entirety of Christ is present under the form of bread *per concomitantiam*. The Council of Constance in 1415 officially suppressed

---

111 Cf. John Chrysostom, *Eclogae ex diversis homiliis* 47 (PG 69, 898); *Collectiones Canonum Coptiae* (H. Denzinger, *Ritus orientalium* I [Würzburg: Stahel, 1863], 95): "May God forfend that any of the pearls or consecrated particles adhere (*sc.*, to the fingers) or fall to the ground."

112 The Communion Confiteor is no longer required in the MRom 1962, after it was removed with the reform of the rubrics (*Rubricarum instructum*, Nr. 503) of July 25, 1960. It has nevertheless remained in common use.

Communion of the chalice for the laity.[113] For the classical rite, Communion in the mouth while kneeling is prescribed.[114] Accompanied by an acolyte holding a Communion paten so that no particle may fall to the ground, the priest distributes the hosts to the faithful kneeling at the Communion rail, first blessing each communicant with a host and quietly speaking: *Corpus Domini nostri Jesu Christi custodiat animam tuam in vitam aeternam. Amen.* This formula of administration (ninth century) recalls Christ's Eucharistic promise: "He that eateth my flesh and drinketh my blood hath everlasting life: and I will raise him up on the last day" (Jn 6:54).

Even though Communion on the tongue came into common use in the Western Church only during the ninth century, and reception of Communion while kneeling became usual only during the eleventh century, this form still represents the result of an organic development from early Christian practice,[115] which was characterized by veneration of the Blessed

---

113 DH 1198–1200.

114 For the NOM as well, Communion on the tongue is the ordinary form for receiving Communion. The practice of Communion in the hand was permitted after its improper introduction in certain countries (Netherlands, Belgium, France, Germany), but this option is not founded upon a law, but rather upon an indult (act of grace), that is, an exception from the effective law. Cf. the Instruction *Memoriale Domini* (AAS 61 [1969]: 541–45, 543 / trans.: *Documents on the Liturgy, 1963–1979. Conciliar, Papal, and Curial Texts* [Collegeville, MN: Liturgical Press, 1982], 645): "Further, this way of distributing communion [*sc.*, on the tongue], which must now be regarded as the normal practice, more effectively ensures that communion is distributed with the required reverence, decorum, and dignity; that there is less danger of disrespect for the Eucharistic elements, in which 'in a unique way Christ is present, whole and entire, God and man, substantially and continuously' (Instruction *Eucharisticum Mysterium*, no. 9); finally that the caution is exercised which the Church has always counseled regarding the particles of the consecrated bread." Cf. J.R. Laise, "Communion in the Hand—An Erroneous Reading of *Memoriale Domini*," in *Theological and Historical Aspects of the Roman Missal* (CIEL UK, 2000), 233–48; idem, *Communion in the Hand: Documents and History* (Boonville / NY: Preserving Christian Publications, ²2018).

115 Cf. M. Lugmayr, "Die Praxis der Handkommunion auf dem Prüfstand," FKTh 25 (2009): 139–54, 143, 152f.; idem, *Handkommunion. Eine historisch-dogmatische Untersuchung* (Buttenwiesen: Stella Maris, 2001), 18–44; idem, "Die heutige Form der Handkommunion," *Theologisches* 37 (2007): 129–34; idem, "Die Geschichte des Ritus der Kommunionausteilung": *Verehrung und Spendung der Heiligen Eucharistie*. Vorträge des zweiten internationalen Kolloquiums: Geschichtliche, kanonische und theologische Arbeiten über die römisch-katholische Liturgie [CIEL: Notre-Dame-du-Laus, Oktober 1996] (Ditzingen: Laienvereinigung für den Klassischen Römischen Ritus in der Katholischen Kirche e.V., 1997), 59–81; A. Schneider, *Dominus Est—It Is the Lord: Reflections of a Bishop of Central Asia on Holy Communion*, trans. by N.L. Gregoris (Pine Beach, NJ: Newman House Press, 2008).

Sacrament and took place in an attitude of worship that bore witness to faith in Christ's true presence. St Augustine said: "No one eats of that flesh without first worshipping it."[116] From Cyril of Jerusalem is found the instruction, "draw near... bending, and saying with an air of worship and reverence, *Amen*."[117] To justify the practice of Communion in the hand, some refer readily to the example of the early Church, where some texts clearly speak of Communion being laid in the hands of the faithful.[118] The most important evidence is found in the *Mystagogical Catecheses* of Bishop Cyril of Jerusalem at the end of the fourth century. The bishop instructed those newly baptized during Eastertide on how one should receive the Blessed Sacrament:

> Coming up to receive, therefore, do not approach with your wrists extended or your fingers splayed, but making your left hand a throne for the right (for it is about to receive a King) and cupping your palm, so receive the Body of Christ; and answer: "Amen." Carefully hallow your eyes by the touch of the sacred Body, and then partake, taking care to lose no part of It. Such a loss would be like a mutilation of your own body. Why, if you had been given gold-dust, would you not take the utmost care to hold it fast, not letting a grain slip through your fingers, lest you be by so much the poorer? How much more carefully, then, will you guard against losing so much as a crumb of that which is more precious than gold and precious stones![119]

It is significant that the Eucharist, laid on the right hand, is not then received by means of the less-valued left hand, but rather directly by the mouth. What

---

116   Augustine, *Enarrationes in Psalmos* 98, 9 (CCL 39, 1385 / Augustine, *Expositions on the Psalms*, trans. by M. Boulding, *The Works of St Augustine* III/8 [Hyde Park, NY: New City Press, 2002], 474): "*nemo autem illam carnem manducat, nisi prius adoraverit.*"

117   Cyril of Jerusalem, *Mystagogicae catecheses* 5,22 (FC 7, 164 / *The Works of Cyril of Jerusalem*, vol. 2: Lenten lectures. Mystagogical lectures. Sermon on the paralytic. Letters to Constantius. Fragments. Indices, trans. by L. P. McCauley / A. A. Stephenson, *The Fathers of the Church* 64 [Washington, DC: Catholic University of America Press, 1970], 203).

118   Cf. Lugmayr, *Handkommunion*, 20–23.

119   Cyril of Jerusalem, *Mystagogicae catecheses* 5,21 (FC 7, 162 / *The Works of Cyril*, 2:203).

appears at first glance to be Communion in the hand reveals itself on closer examination to be Communion in the mouth, with the right hand serving as a sort of paten.[120] Bishop Cyril's description shows that "the attitude of the communicant is, then, not one of taking and capturing, but rather of reverent and humble reception, accompanied by a sign of adoration."[121]

Kneeling, genuflection, or three deep bows have been witnessed since the sixth century as expressions of adoration before receiving Communion.[122] Furthermore, pictorial representations of the practice show the hands veiled or laid one upon the other in the form of a cross for the reception of Communion, as also indicated in various instructions. Sources from the sixth/seventh centuries find that the priest directly placed the Lord's Body in the mouths of the faithful.[123] This custom spread ever wider and came into common use in the West during the ninth century.[124] This

---

120   Cf. Lugmayr, *Handkommunion*, 35f.; idem, "Praxis," 141; R. Spaemann, "Liturgie — Ausdruck des Glaubens," F. Breid (ed.), *Die heilige Liturgie: Referate der "Internationalen Theologischen Sommerakademie 1997" des Linzer Priesterkreises in Aigen/M.* (Steyr: Verlag Wilhelm Ennsthaler, 1997), 36–71, 42f.: "If, at very least, the communicants would (as was the case in the ancient Church) bring the palm into which they had received the host to their mouth, instead of using the fingers of the other hand to pick it up, then there would still be visible something of the peculiarity of this food, and it would be clear that the reception of the fruit from the tree of the Cross is the opposite of the grasp with which the people in paradise seized the forbidden fruit"; idem, "Bemerkungen eines Laien, der die alte Messe liebt," A. Gerhards (ed.), *Ein Ritus, zwei Formen. Die Richtlinie Papst Benedikts XVI. zur Liturgie* (Freiburg i. Br.: Verlag Herder, 2008), 75–102, 93: "Today's Communion on the tongue bears more resemblance to the ancient Church's communion in the hand, as far as the awesome care in dealing with the sacred species is concerned."

121   Lugmayr, *Handkommunion*, 27–33; idem, "Praxis," 142f.

122   Cf. Lugmayr, "Praxis," 142.

123   Cf. Gregory I, *Dialogi* 3,3,2 (SCh 260, 268 / St Gregory the Great, *Dialogues*, trans. by O.J. Zimmerman, *The Fathers of the Church* 39 [New York, NY: Fathers of the Church, Inc., 1959], 117). According to K. Gamber, *The Modern Rite: Collected Essays on the Reform of the Liturgy*, trans. by H. Taylor (Farnborough: Saint Michael's Abbey Press, 2002), 59, the abolition of communion in the hand had already begun in the fifth/sixth centuries. Cf. M. Righetti, *Manuale di storia liturgica* III, 736.

124   Cf. the instruction from the Synod of Rouen (ca. 878), can. 2 (Mansi 10, 1199f.): "*Nulli autem laico aut feminae eucharistiam in manibus ponat, sed tantum in os eius*" [For no layman or woman may the Eucharist be placed in his/her hands, but only in his/her mouth]. On questions of the dating and historicity of the Synod, cf. Lugmayr, *Handkommunion*, 23f. Already around the year 400 the direct consumption of the received Host was required; cf. Provincial Synod of Toledo, can. 14 (Mansi 3, 1000): "*Si quis autem acceptam a sacerdote eucharistiam non sumpserit, velut sacrilegus propellatur*" [If however anyone shall not consume

form was the most appropriate for hindering the misuse of the consecrated Host, its profanation through superstitious or magical practices. Another expression of care and veneration is the Communion paten, which, however, was only commonly prescribed in 1929,[125] though it was already in use in particular places much earlier (fourteenth century). Of older origin is the Communion cloth that was either spread before the kneeling communicants by two acolytes (since the thirteenth century) or laid over the Communion rail (since the sixteenth century) in order to catch falling particles. Although the universal use of the paten may seem to render this cloth no longer necessary, its continuing use in traditional communities serves as an additional reminder of the holiness of the divine banquet spread before the faithful, and symbolically connects the altar rail to the clothed altar.

If the Church still clings to this superior practice as a general principle, but in actuality the exception—that is, Communion in the hand—has become the rule, then the classical rite of the Mass can claim to correspond faithfully to the very requirements intended by liturgical law. Ultimately, the point is that the method of receiving Communion and the careful treatment of the Eucharistic species should make evident the Church's faith in the Real Presence.[126] It is precisely the practice of Communion on the tongue while kneeling that contradicts the atmosphere of the everyday and profoundly conforms to the mystery: one is not taking common bread with his own hand, but receiving the Body of Christ that the Church gives to the faithful.

For a meeting with the Redeemer's divine Person, the outward sign of kneeling—witnessed many times in the biblical portrayals of encounters with the Risen Christ (cf. Mt 28:9; Lk 24:52)—is singularly appropriate. If the Church prescribes that the faithful must kneel for the moment of

---

the Eucharist received from a priest, let him be driven forth as sacrilegious].

125   Instruction of March 26, 1929 (AAS 21 [1929]: 635). Note that this instruction states that the communion cloth is still prescribed to be used in conjunction with the communion plate. The spreading of a linen cloth for Communion was still mentioned in the *Rituale Romanum* of 1954 (the last universal edition published before 1964). J. B. O'Connell reiterates this prescription as late as his 1964 edition of *The Celebration of Mass*. It therefore should be used universally.

126   Cf. Lugmayr, "Praxis," 139.

the consecration, then it is indeed liturgically appropriate also to kneel for the moment of Holy Communion, at which time Christ comes as close as possible to the faithful.[127] Receiving Communion while kneeling is a sign of deep reverence; it is a manifest expression of a living faith in the sacramental presence of Christ and of humble reception of the divine gift.[128] Furthermore, kneeling together at the Communion rail emphasizes the Communion of the faithful with each other in an impressive manner.[129]

Ablutions. The thorough purification of the paten, Communion paten, chalice, and the fingers of the priest forms an expression of reverent faith in the Real Presence, even in the smallest particles of the Host and the drops of Precious Blood left in the chalice. The current form is almost identical to the order prescribed at the beginning of the fourteenth century, even to the finest detail. After any possible particles left behind on the corporal have been collected with the paten and brushed into the chalice — the Communion paten is also purified in the same way — some wine is poured into the chalice and consumed by the celebrant,[130] while he holds the paten under the rim of the chalice and prays: *Quod ore sumpsimus, Domine, pura mente capiamus: et de munere temporali fiat nobis remedium sempiternum.* "May that which we have received with the mouth, O Lord, be taken hold of with a pure mind, and let this temporal gift become for us an everlasting remedy." The very old prayer, already seen in the sixth century as a Postcommunion, beautifully shows that Holy Communion is not ordinary food, but rather while it is received with the

127 Cf. Lugmayr, "Praxis," 154.

128 On the meaning of kneeling, cf. J. Ratzinger, *The Spirit of the Liturgy*, trans. by J. Saward (San Francisco: Ignatius Press, 2000), 115–22 (= idem, *Theology of the Liturgy*, 184–94).

129 Cf. H.-L. Barth, *"Nichts soll dem Gottesdienst vorgezogen werden" (Benediktregel Kap. 43). Aufsätze zur Liturgiereform* [Respondeo 15] (Siegburg: Franz Schmitt Verlag, 2002), 102: "The *communio*-character of the Eucharistic reception was excellently expressed through the common, calm, and collected kneeling at the same communion rail."

130 Cf. P. Guéranger, *Explanation of the Prayers and Ceremonies of Holy Mass*, trans. by L. Shepherd, published as *The Traditional Latin Mass Explained* (Brooklyn: Angelico Press, 2017), 107: "The Priest must always drink from the same side of the chalice; and for this reason, a small cross is always engraven on its foot. Without this precaution, the Priest would be liable, if he were not very attentive, to wipe off, with the purificator, the Precious Blood still wet on the lip of the chalice."

mouth, it nourishes the soul. Then the priest goes to the Epistle side and purifies the fingers that have touched the Body of the Lord, and while the wine and water flow over his fingertips he speaks another ablution prayer—already observed in the seventh century as a Postcommunion in the plural form—*Corpus tuum, Domine, quod sumpsi, et Sanguis, quem potavi, adhaereat visceribus meis: et praesta, ut in me non remaneat scelerum macula, quem pura et sancta refecerunt sacramenta: Qui vivis et regnas in saecula saeculorum. Amen.* "May Thy Body, O Lord, which I have taken up, and [Thy] Blood, which I have drunk, cleave to my inmost being; and grant that no stain of wickedness may remain in me, whom these pure and holy sacraments have refreshed: Thou who livest and reignest for ever and ever. Amen." After the purification, the tips of the thumb and index finger are no longer held together.

Communion chant. After the chalice is veiled, the priest proceeds to the Epistle side and prays the Communion antiphon, a verse that was originally the antiphon (*antiphona ad communionem* [*populi*]) for a psalm that accompanied the Communion of the faithful and was originally (fourth century) sung by them, but later by a schola, and usually in a shortened form, similar to the Introit and Offertory chants (twelfth/thirteenth centuries). At a High Mass, the choir sings the Communion chant during the Communion of the faithful. In the Early Christian period Psalm 33 was primarily sung, especially due to verse 9 (*Gustate et videte, quoniam suavis est Dominus*), but later other psalms were included. Therefore the text of the antiphon is found to be taken not only from the psalms, but also from the Gospel of the day[131] as well as other biblical[132] or non-biblical[133] texts. Regarding content, the verse concerns either Holy Communion[134] or more often the feast itself with

---

131 Thus, for example, on the feast of the Sacred Heart of Jesus: Jn 19:34. Cf. A. Fortescue, "Communion-Antiphon," *The Catholic Encyclopedia* IV (New York: Robert Appleton Company, 1908): 169f.

132 Thus, for example, on the feast of Pentecost: Acts 2:2,4.

133 Thus, for example, on the feast of St Ignatius of Antioch, Bishop and Martyr (Feb. 1): *Epistle to the Romans* 4:1 (Kleist, *Epistles of St Clement and St Ignatius*, 82).

134 Thus, for example, Thursday of the First Week in Lent: "*Panis, quem ego dedero, caro mea est pro saeculi vita*" [The bread that I will give is My flesh for the life of the world]; Passion Sunday: "*Hoc corpus, quod pro vobis tradetur: hic calix novi Testamenti est in meo sanguine,*

its Epistle[135] or Gospel,[136] the liturgical season,[137] or the occasion of the celebration of the Mass.[138]

The Conclusion

Postcommunion. St Augustine stated as a rule for the liturgy of his time: "After they have done this and have partaken of the sacrament, the giving of thanks brings all to an end."[139] The Postcommunion originally concluded the celebration of the Mass ([*oratio*] *ad concludendum*) before the appearance of the *Ite missa est* and the closing blessing. Similarly to the Collect, the prayer is introduced by kissing the altar and the exchanged greeting *Dominus vobiscum–Et cum spiritu tuo*, and is spoken or sung at the Epistle side and expanded by a commemoration when called for. The Postcommunion prayers have the same structure as the Collect and are stylistically similar in clarity, conciseness, and elegance. Regarding content, various accents may be distinguished. In part, these prayers unite gratitude for the reception of Holy Communion with the request for the beneficial effect of the sacramental grace.[140] Other closing prayers refer

---

dicit Dominus: hoc facite, quotiescumque sumitis, in meam commemorationem" [This is My Body which shall be delivered for you: this chalice is the new testament in My Blood, saith the Lord: do this, as often as you receive it, in commemoration of Me].

135 Thus, for example, on Easter Sunday: *"Pascha nostrum immolatus est Christus, alleluia: itaque epulemur in azymis sinceritatis et veritatis, alleluia, alleluia, alleluia"* [Christ our Pasch is immolated, alleluia: therefore let us feast with the unleavened bread of sincerity and truth].

136 Thus, for example, on Epiphany: *"Videmus stellam eius in Oriente, et venimus cum muneribus adorare Dominum"* [We have seen His star in the East, and are come with gifts to adore the Lord].

137 Thus, for example, on the Sundays in Advent.

138 Thus, for example, in the Masses for the Dead: *"Lux aeterna luceat eis, Domine: Cum Sanctis tuis in aeternum: quia pius es. Requiem aeternam dona eis, Domine..."* [May light eternal shine upon them, O Lord: With Thy saints for ever, for Thou art merciful. Eternal rest grant unto them, O Lord...]

139 Augustine, *Epistula* 149,16 (CSEL 44, 363 / Augustine, *Letters*, trans. by R. Teske, *The Works of St Augustine* II/2 [Hyde Park, NY: New City Press, 2003], 368): *"Quibus peractis et participato tanto sacramento, gratiarum actio cuncta concludit."* Cf. A. Fortescue, "Postcommunion," *The Catholic Encyclopedia* XII (New York: Robert Appleton Company, 1911): 318f.

140 Thus, for example, the Sixth Sunday after Epiphany: *"Caelestibus, Domine, pasti deliciis: quaesumus, ut semper eadem, per quae veraciter vivimus, appetamus"* [Being nourished, O Lord, with heavenly delights, we beseech Thee that we may ever hunger after those things

to the mystery of the feast for that day.[141] Further prayers harmoniously combine the mystery of the Eucharist with the feast[142] or liturgical season.[143] In synopsis, the texts of these prayers offer a magnificent proclamation of the Sacrament of the Altar with theological depth and poetic beauty.[144]

Prayer over the people. On the weekdays of Lent, an old prayer of blessing has survived that was used, before the introduction of the closing blessing in its current form, to bless the people at each Mass in a special manner before they left the church to return to their everyday duties. This *Oratio super populum* became gradually less frequent during the year, however, and under Pope Gregory the Great it was limited to the weekdays in Lent. In this use, which continues even today, it serves as a supplementary prayer for strengthening the faithful with additional blessings during the time of increased spiritual warfare.[145] After an *Oremus*, the priest (or deacon)

---

by which we truly live]; Eleventh Sunday after Pentecost: "*Sentiamus, quaesumus, Domine, tui perceptione sacramenti, subsidium mentis et corporis: ut, in utroque salvati, caelestis remedii plenitudine gloriemur*" [Having received Thy holy sacrament, we beseech Thee, O Lord, that we may feel supported in soul and body; that being saved in both, we may glory in the fullness of the heavenly remedy].

141 Thus, for example, on the feast of Pentecost: "*Sancti Spiritus, Domine, corda nostra mundet infusio: et sui roris intima aspersione fecundet*" [May the outpouring of the Holy Spirit purify our hearts, O Lord, and by the inward sprinkling of His heavenly dew may they be made fruitful].

142 Thus, for example, the Second Mass of Christmas: "*Huius nos, Domine, sacramenti semper novitas natalis instauret: cuius Nativitas singularis humanam repulit vetustatem*" [May the newness of this mystery of Thy birth ever restore us, O Lord, for Thy singular birth has driven out human obsolescence].

143 Thus, for example, Wednesday of the Third Week in Lent: "*Sanctificet nos, Domine, qua pasti sumus, mensa caelestis: et a cunctis erroribus expiatos, supernis promissionibus reddat acceptos*" [May the heavenly table of which we have partaken sanctify us, O Lord, and purifying us from all errors, render us worthy of lofty promises].

144 Cf. Batiffol, *Leçons sur la messe*, 325: "One must say about the *Postcommunion* prayers of the Roman liturgy what we said about the other prayers: for piety, they are a safe and strong discipline, moderate and peace-giving, that we must learn to love. They are rather short, certainly, but they can be points of meditation. With them we do not stray into a false lyricism: they lead to action without loosening the union with God. They invite the believer to make his life a thanksgiving: *Da, quaesumus, ut in gratiarum semper actione maneamus.*" Cf. (Docteur) Havet, "La Postcommunion, Conclusion du Drame Sacré," *Le Canon de la Messe*, 265–85; Schnitzler, *Messe* II, 299–305 ("Die Sakramentslitanei der Postcommunio").

145 Cf. L. Eizenhofer, "Untersuchungen zum Stil und Inhalt der römischen *Oratio super populum*," EL 52 (1938): 258–311.

speaks *Humiliate capita vestra*, so that the people kneel while the prayer is said. It is characteristic of these prayers that in many old texts the priest does not include himself but rather prays as a mediator between God and the people on behalf of the faithful (*populus tuus, ecclesia tua, familia tua*).

The dismissal (*Ite, missa est*). The solemn dismissal of the faithful with the *Ite missa est* is observed since the seventh/eighth centuries, though it may be as old as the Latin Mass itself. In the style of ancient formulas for dismissal from a secular or ecclesiastical gathering, the word *missa* in this context means "dismissal."[146] After the preceding *Dominus vobiscum–Et cum spiritu tuo*, the priest, or deacon, turns to the people with the call, *Ite missa est*, and they give thanks for the graces received in the celebration of the Mass with *Deo gratias*. This was the original closing formula with which the old Roman Mass ended until the eleventh century. It was later replaced on certain days — in the Masses without a Gloria[147] — with *Benedicamus Domino* ("Let us bless the Lord"), which the priest says while turned toward the altar, and which, at least according to the *Missale Romanum* 1962, is still used as a conclusion in those Masses that are followed by a procession or the like (i.e., Holy Thursday, Corpus Christi). In the Masses for the Dead since the twelfth century the closing formula is *Requiescant in pace* ("May they rest in peace"). Here the priest or deacon remains turned toward the altar, as the request is on behalf not of the people, but of the dead. The faithful answer *Amen*, thereby demonstrating that the Church's prayer for the dead functions in the form of an intercession. During the octave of Easter, the *Ite missa est* is followed by a double *Alleluia*.

The prayer *Placeat tibi*. The next prayers originate from private meditations and only became elements of the official *Ordo* of the Mass over the years.

The prayer *Placeat tibi, sancta Trinitas, obsequium servitutis meae* is of Gallican origin (ninth century), possibly having been used as a prayer to

---

146   Cf. Avitus of Vienne (ca. 500), *Epistula 1* (PL 59, 199): "*In ecclesiis palatiisque sive praetoriis missa fieri pronuntiatur, cum populus ab observatione dimittitur*" [In churches and in palaces as well as in military headquarters, 'missa' is announced whenever a gathering is dismissed from its duty]. Cf. A. Fortescue, "Ite missa est," *The Catholic Encyclopedia* VIII (New York: Robert Appleton Company, 1910): 253f.

147   The rule from the eleventh century until the rubrical reform of 1960. Nevertheless, like many other pre-1960 customs, this practice is returning in our times.

accompany the kissing of the altar, and is directed to the Trinity. It became common in Rome in the eleventh century, being included in the first printing of the Roman Missal (1474) where it came after the final blessing, but under Pope Pius V it was moved prior to the blessing as a prayer of preparation that the priest speaks while bowing deeply, his folded hands lying on the altar. The *Placeat tibi* summarizes once more all of the prayers of the celebration of the Mass, as it begs for the merciful acceptance of the homage (*obsequium servitutis meae*) and of the sacrifice that was offered up (*praesta, ut sacrificium, quod oculis tuae maiestatis indignus obtuli, tibi sit acceptabile*) as well as its beneficial effect for the priest and people (*mihique et omnibus, pro quibus illud obtuli, sit, te miserante, propitiabile*). Especially the last word clearly emphasizes the expiatory character of the sacrifice of the Mass.[148]

Final blessing. A final blessing is first witnessed in its current form during the eleventh century. Over the course of the twelfth century, it found acceptance in Rome as well. Previously, the *Oratio super populum* or the Postcommunion served as the final prayer of blessing. The current position of the final blessing after the *Ite missa est* is due to the fact that it probably developed from the blessing given by a bishop as he returned to the sacristy from the altar. A standardization of the various forms and formulas was enacted under Pope Pius V. After kissing the altar, the priest lifts his eyes and hands to the Cross, from which all blessings originate, joins his spread hands and deeply bows his head while praying aloud *Benedicat vos omnipotens Deus*. Then he turns to the people and gives the blessing with the sign of the Cross, as he continues *Pater et Filius* ✠ *et Spiritus Sanctus*. The people answer *Amen*. In the Masses for the Dead the blessing is dispensed with, as these Masses are primarily celebrated for the departed and all blessings of the living are omitted.

The Last Gospel. The Last Gospel constitutes a final distinctive feature of the classical rite. After the *Ite missa est* and the blessing that follows comes the reading of the prologue to the Gospel of John. This proclamation

---

148 Cf. May, *Die alte und die neue Messe*, 67n244: "The related word 'propitiatorium' is in particular theologically important by its frequent use at the Council of Trent (e.g.: CT VI, 745, 750, 768 etc.)."

became a fixed element of the Roman rite of the Mass only much later. Pope Pius V first introduced the Last Gospel into the Missal, but in so doing he only regulated and codified a much older custom. The Last Gospel is first found in 1256 in the missals of the Dominican Order, where the priest spoke it after a private Mass either while unvesting or afterward. The use of this reading spread during the thirteenth and fourteenth centuries, as many faithful requested hearing this Gospel after Mass, because a special blessing was ascribed to it, but which furthermore from its substance was the most appropriate close of the celebration of the Mass, as it once more gratefully professed faith in the Word of God, His Incarnation, and His works, so full of grace and truth.

St Augustine refers to a philosopher of his time who remarked that the opening words of this Gospel should be written in golden letters and located in the most prominent place in every church.[149] Even though the mystery of the Incarnation of the *Logos* remained as yet inaccessible to the late-ancient Platonist, the connection between St John's Gospel and the sacrifice of the Mass was profoundly grasped by the religious sense of later epochs. Is not the mystery of the Incarnation repeated, in a way, in every church, in every Mass? As the divine *Logos* descended into the Virgin Mary's womb, Christ descends to the altar through the priest's words of consecration. St Thomas Aquinas profoundly recognized this analogy between the Incarnation and the Eucharist when he did not create a new Preface for the Office of Corpus Christi, but instead selected the Preface of Christmas.[150] What is true of the mystery of the Incarnation may be said as well of the Sacrament of the Altar: "so that knowing God visibly, we may be drawn by Him to the love of things invisible" (*ut, dum visibi-liter Deum cognoscimus, per hunc in invisibilium amorem rapiamur*). The Incarnation substantiates the sacramental principle: the invisible in the visible, the spiritual in the material, the divine in the human, the eternal in the temporal. As the Incarnation is the prerequisite for the Eucharist, so the Eucharist is the continuation of the Incarnation. Pope Leo the Great

---

149 Cf. Augustine, *De civitate Dei* 10,29 (CCL 47, 306 / Augustine, *The City of God*, trans. by W. Babcock, *The Works of St Augustine* I/6 [Hyde Park, NY: New City Press, 2012], 341).
150 Cf. M. Mosebach, "The Last Gospel," in *Heresy of Formlessness*, 117–20.

expressed this in the words: "What was to be seen of our Redeemer has passed over into the sacraments."[151]

With the Gospel of John constituting the epilogue of the sacrifice of the Mass, the Church makes her own the words of the Evangelist: "We have seen His glory" (Jn 1:14). The Last Gospel thus becomes a grateful acknowledgement by those who looked upon the Host, lifted up by the priest after the consecration. "The aim of the prologue is contemplation, the retrospective beholding of a lived reality."[152] The Prologue continues: "We saw His glory... full of grace and truth," which recalls the request of the prayers at the foot of the altar: "Send forth Thy light and Thy truth" (Ps 42:3). What is requested from God at the beginning of the celebration of the Mass with the words of longing from the Old Testament, and what has been accomplished in the proclamation of God's Word and in the action of the sacrifice, is once more gratefully acknowledged at the close with the word of the Evangelist. Thus Holy Mass is encompassed by a petition and its fulfillment. The Last Gospel, the beginning of the Gospel of John, constitutes a magnificent summary of the entire Mass, a *summa eucharistica*: "And the Word was made flesh, and dwelt among us" (Jn 1:14).

The Leonine prayers. According to the *Ritus servandus in celebratione Missae* of the 1962 *Missale Romanum*, Holy Mass ends with the Last Gospel. At a Low Mass the priest kneels at the foot of the altar before exiting and prays with the acolyte a series of petitionary prayers (three *Ave Marias*, *Salve Regina*, versicle, oration, invocation of St Michael the Archangel, and invocation of the Sacred Heart of Jesus), which were prescribed at various times of ecclesiastical affliction and changed many times, that is, extended and provided with new intentions.[153] Beyond

---

151   Leo I, *Sermones* 74,2 (CCL 138 A, 457 / St Leo the Great, *Sermons*, trans. by J. P. Freeland / A. J. Conway, *The Fathers of the Church* 93 [Washington, DC: Catholic University of America Press, 1996], 326): "*Quod itaque Redemptoris nostri conspicuum fuit, in sacramenta transivit.*"

152   Mosebach, "Last Gospel," 120.

153   Pope Pius IX had decreed a first version of such prayers in 1859 for the embattled Papal States. Pope Leo XIII extended this prayer for the entire Church during the struggle for ecclesiastical freedom in 1884 and in 1886 added the common intention of the conversion of sinners. Under Pope Pius X in 1904, an invocation of the Sacred Heart, repeated three

the immediate reasons for their origin, these prayers have an enduring meaning for the great concerns of the church[154] in the battle that surrounds us in the world at this time and in every age.[155]

---

times, was included. Pius XI ordered in 1930 that this prayer be said for the free exercise of religion in Russia. Under Pope Paul VI these prayers were disestablished in 1964. Cf. J. Pizzoni, "De precibus post missam imperatis," EL 69 (1955): 54–60; Shaw, *Liturgical Restoration*, 195–203.

154   Thus, for example in the prayer *Deus refugium nostrum* (O God, our refuge and our strength): "*pro conversione peccatorum, pro libertate et exaltatione sanctae Matris Ecclesiae*" [for the conversion of sinners and for the freedom and exaltation of Holy Mother Church].

155   Thus the prayer "*Sancte Michael Archangele, defende nos in proelio.*"

6

The Liturgical Year

THE BEAUTY OF THE CYCLE OF
THE LITURGICAL YEAR

"What an immense fund of poetry, what an incomparable estate of art the Church possesses!" Thus wrote the French author Charles-George Huysmans (1848–1907) in his autobiographical novel *En Route* (1895).[1] Not least because of his encounter with the beauty of the liturgy as it was celebrated by the Benedictine nuns in their cloister chapel on the Rue Monsieur in Paris,[2] he found his way back to the Catholic Faith. He describes what the liturgical year meant for him personally in a scene of the novel where the main character observes with his mind's eye a year in that church, with all its hymns, Sequences, psalms, and various other songs, and compares it with the precious crown of King Recceswinth that rests in Paris's Musée de Cluny:

> The liturgical year was, like it, studded with crystals and jewels by its admirable canticles and its fervent hymns set in the very gold of Benedictions and Vespers. It seemed that the Church had substituted for that crown of thorns with which the Jews had surrounded the temples of the Savior, the truly royal crown of the Proper Seasons, the only one which was chiselled in a metal precious enough, with art pure enough to dare to place itself on the brow of a God.[3]

---

1 J.-K. Huysmans, *En Route*, trans. W. Fleming, with an introduction by David Blow (Sawtry, UK: Dedalus, 2002), 281.

2 Due to its sublime liturgy, this convent was a center of attraction and a meeting place of many Catholic intellectuals at the beginning of the twentieth century (among others, P. Claudel, F. Mauriac, J. Rivière, G. Marcel, J. Maritain). Cf. *Témoignages anciens et nouveaux réunis par les Moniales de Jouques*, nouvelle édition (Jouques: Éditions du Cloître, 1988).

3 Huysmans, *En Route*, 277–78.

It is not only the magnificent poetry and hymns that constitute the beauty of the liturgical year, but also the way and manner in which the Church sees fit to celebrate certain feasts. Careful gradations, preceding attunements (vigils), longer preparations with dramatic climaxes (Septuagesima, Quadragesima, Passiontide, Holy Week, the Easter Triduum), deliberate lingering (octaves), and occasional pauses (quarterly Ember days) are the means that serve the liturgy in structuring the liturgical year and differentiating the celebrations according to their meaning. Add to this that the liturgical seasons harmoniously merge with the rhythm of the natural year determined by the course of the sun, while the succession of light and darkness becomes a symbol for the battle between the Light of the World and the powers of darkness, and the character of each particular season lends a cosmic dimension to the liturgical mysteries of the feasts.[4]

GRADATIONS

The liturgical days of the year (Sundays, ferias, vigils, feasts, and octaves) are arranged into four classes according to the reform of the rubrics in 1960.[5]

---

4 Cf. J. Tyciak, *Jahreskranz der Güte Gottes. Das Jahr der Kirche* (Mainz: Matthias-Grünewald-Verlag, 1953), 19f.: "Again and again we therefore feel the path of the sun in the ecclesiastical year. The Church celebrates Easter on Sundays after the first spring full moon. Christ himself is the living God, whose resurrection establishes the spring of a new world. In the summer, she celebrates the feast of the Pentecostal ardor; at the time of the wheat blossoms and the ripening vines, the feast of the vine and the wheat [Corpus Christi]; the ecclesiastical autumn joins clearly the autumnal natural rhythm, and in the winter time, with its desire for the light, light plays a special role in the liturgy. The vigil days are full of this, and Christmas in its trilogy follows the rhythm of the course of the sun. In the early spring with its storms, the Church speaks of the storm on the sea and reads the Gospel of sowing at the time of sowing. After the summer solstice, it celebrates the feast of the Baptist, who decreased so that Jesus might increase, and at the winter solstice the feast of the rising of the new light, the *Oriens ex alto* (dawn from on high). The feast of Epiphany not only commemorates the theophany in the Church, but sees in the star of the wise a picture of luminous radiance throughout the whole of creation"; cf. S. Stricker, *Das Kirchenjahr: Mysterium. Gesammelte Arbeiten Laacher Mönche* (Münster: Aschendorff Verlag, 1926), 63–78, 75–77.

5 Pope Pius V had introduced five categories (*festum duplex* I Class/II Class; *festum duplex/semiduplex/simplex*), which were increased by one category (*duplex maius*) under Pope Clement VIII, so that it, together with the various classes of octaves, made up a highly sophisticated arrangement: *festum duplex* I Class with a first order privileged octave (Easter, Pentecost); *festum duplex* I Class with a second order privileged octave (Epiphany, Corpus Christi); *festum duplex* I Class with a third order privileged octave (Christmas, Ascension

These classes indicate their rank (*praestantia*) and determine precedence (*praecedentia*) in case of the coincidence of two offices on the same day, designating when an office of lower rank must yield to one of higher degree, and either be entirely omitted, only commemorated, or transferred to a different day.[6] Thus, for example, there are first class Sundays (Advent, Lent, Passiontide, Easter Sunday, Low Sunday, and Pentecost Sunday) that have precedence over all other feasts, even those of first class (e.g., the Annunciation). All remaining Sundays of the year are second class, and in the case of falling on the same day, they have precedence over all second class feasts (e.g., the Visitation on July 2). The weekdays (ferial days) are divided into four classes that guarantee the precedence of the *temporale* (the cycle of time) over the *sanctorale* (the cycle of the saints) and prevent ordinary feasts of the saints (III Class) from overshadowing the liturgical seasons (e.g., Advent, Lent, and Passiontide). The gradation of the feasts of the saints also demonstrates a careful determination of their significance (I Class: e.g., the Apostles Peter and Paul, June 29; II Class: e.g., St Laurence, August 10; III Class: e.g., St Pius X, September 3).

A feast's rank not only emphasizes its significance and regulates cases of coincidence, but also, in fact, influences the manner of its celebration. The number and type of assistants or acolytes, the selection and splendor

---

and Sacred Heart); *festum duplex* I Class with common octave (e.g., Assumption, All Saints); *festum duplex* II Class (e.g., Apostles); *duplex maius* (e.g., Mary Magdalen, founders of prominent orders); *festum duplex* (prominent Saints, e.g., Athanasius, Pius V); *festum semiduplex* (secondary saints, as for example, Pope Anacletus); *festum simplex* (lesser-known Saints, as for example the martyr Pantaleon). The term *duplex* dates back to the Middle Ages when canons of the cathedrals celebrated a doubled evening prayer, that is, one of the day (*de feria*) and one of a high feast that fell on the same day. Later, this term continued to designate the order of rank, even for feasts without doubled offices.

6 Cf. D. v. Hildebrand, *Liturgy and Personality* (s.l.: The Hildebrand Project, 2016), 62: "The hierarchy of values is also expressed in the fact that a secondary feast yields to the greater feast and makes way for it. It is the achievement of what we have defined above as the sign of true personality: the lesser value inwardly makes way for the greater value. People who are not familiar with the spirit of the Liturgy think that this precise gradation of feasts, and the exact regulations governing which feast takes precedence over another, are but a form of juridical pedantry which should have no place in the religious sphere. But those who penetrate deeper will recognize that a great and central principle is here exemplified, a principle which should also influence the attitude toward the cosmos in the life of the individual, so that his life may really be in tune with the objective *logos* of being."

of the vestments, the number of lit candles on the altar, the melodies for the texts (*tonus simplex, solemnis, solemnior*), and others aspects are determined or suggested by the classification.[7]

PREPARATION AND PROGRESSION
Vigil

The vigil is the day preceding a certain high feast, serving as a preparation for it. Evolving from the Easter Vigil—the *Mater omnium sanctarum vigiliarum*[8]—nocturnal services on Pentecost and the Ember days, and commemorative services at the graves of the Martyrs, were added.[9] Soon the vigils, including the celebration of the Eucharist, were moved up to the preceding evening (fourth/fifth century). The actual feast day received its own Mass. Later the vigil Masses were shifted to the afternoon (twelfth century), and finally to the morning (fourteenth century).

The 1962 *Missale Romanum* contains various vigil days divided into three classes, regulating their precedence over other days and feasts or commemorations: I Class: the Eves of Christmas and Pentecost; II Class: Vigil of the Ascension, Assumption (August 14), Birth of St John the Baptist (June 23), as well as Peter and Paul (June 28); III Class: Vigil of St Laurence (August 9).

---

7 Cf. ibid.: "The rank of each feast corresponds to the objective scale of its mystery. This implies the inner melody which fills the entire Liturgy of the day, the degree of splendor, of joy, of glorification, the weight of commemoration, the entire display of festivity and jubilation. All this is expressed vividly in the fact that certain parts of the Liturgy appear only in connection with a certain degree of festivity, such as the *Credo* in the Mass, the *Te Deum* in Matins, the Alleluia and its variations, a Sequence in the greatest feasts, and the proper Prefaces. Further, this spirit is reflected in the thought content of the individual texts of various feasts as in the *Haec dies quam fecit Dominus* ('This is the day the Lord has made') of Easter and in the often repeated *Hodie* of Christmas. Again, we find this spirit in the atmosphere of the entire linguistic expression, the width and breadth of a feast's celebration, in its being preceded by a vigil in which its dawn is anticipated, and in its prolongation by an octave. And we also find it in the fact that all other feasts are displaced because of the greatness and splendor of the feast in question as expressed in the degree of 'exclusiveness' of an octave; all this, moreover, is reflected in the modes of the plain chant, the celebration of high Mass with deacon and subdeacon and incense, and even in the outward decorations required by the feast, the display of candles, and so on."

8 Augustine, *Sermo* 219 (PL 38, 1088 / Augustine, *Sermons*, trans. by E. Hill, *The Works of St Augustine* III/6 [Hyde Park, NY: New City Press, 1993], 198): "the mother of all holy vigils."

9 Cf. A. Baumstark, *Nocturna laus. Typen frühchristlicher Vigilienfeier und ihr Fortleben* [LQF 32] (Münster: Aschendorff Verlag, 1957), 17–104.

Septuagesima, Quadragesima, Passiontide

The classical liturgy of the Roman Church, like that of the Eastern Church, recognized from its earliest days (sixth century) a pre-Lenten period that preceded Quadragesima, made up of three Sundays (Septuagesima, Sexagesima, Quinquagesima).[10] With pastoral wisdom and empathy, the Church prepares her faithful for the beginning of the season of Lent, which in turn leads into an even more intensified preparation for the feast of Easter with Passion Sunday (fifth Sunday of Lent) before the beginning of Holy Week, which culminates in the *Triduum Sacrum*. The following description clearly shows with what delicate pedagogy the Church gradually leads her faithful toward the high point of the liturgical year:

> The first, as it were, rather cautious introduction occurs in the two and a half weeks of the time before Lent; it is—on all Sundays and the weekdays without feasts—characterized by the liturgical color violet and the omission of the Gloria and Alleluia verse; the Sundays, however, still contain the common Preface for Sunday, namely that of the Most Holy Trinity. But even on feasts of the saints (as well as any Friday dedicated to the Sacred Heart of Jesus falling during this time) a difference is present: even here the Alleluia verse is replaced by the Tract.... Lent forms the second stage—more precisely, until the Saturday before Passion Sunday. During Lent we are introduced to the solemnity of this time: the Preface for Lent makes its entrance and is used even on feasts of the saints (if they do not have their own Preface), and the weekdays, each possessing its own formulary of the Mass, have such an importance that they take precedence over the normal feasts of the saints; only the feasts of St Joseph and the Annunciation have precedence over the Lenten weekdays, and if they fall on a Sunday in Lent, they are transferred to the following day. The subsequent Passiontide is even more urgently arranged—already sensibly noticeable through the

10 *Quinquagesima* is the fiftieth day before Easter; both of the other Sundays are named after an older notation because they divide the days before Easter into a seventh or sixth "tithe," *in septuagesima* or *in sexagesima*. Cf. L. Pristas, "Parachuted into Lent: The Suppression of Septuagesima," *Usus Antiquior* 1 (2010): 95–109.

veiled crucifix. Now the Preface of the Holy Cross is a feature, even on feasts of the saints.... And we are led one step higher in Holy Week; here on Sunday, Tuesday, and Wednesday the Passion is read as the Gospel. There is no longer room for the commemoration of any other feast; the feasts of St Joseph and the Annunciation are transferred to the week after Easter if they fall during this week; the same would apply in the case of a patron saint falling in this week. All other feasts in the respective year entirely fall away. Holy Week finds its point of culmination in the *Triduum Sacrum*, in which all is directed toward Good Friday, and there again, in turn, all is directed toward the Lord's words, "It is accomplished." The gentle hand of Mother Church leads us up a mountain and brings us to the summit.[11]

Octaves

The octave is the extended celebration of a feast with its conclusion on the eighth day. It allows for a deliberate lingering-over of the feast, so that the celebrated mystery can be more deeply contemplated for the entire week. If Easter in the first place had an octave week (4th century), Christmas was given at first an octave day (6th century) and later an octave week, which, however, did not displace the older feasts. Later the octave of Pentecost entered (end of the sixth century). An octave of the feast of Epiphany was observed in Jerusalem already in the fourth century, while the calendar for the Western Church first features one in the eighth century. After the Middle Ages saw a considerable increase in octaves, especially for the feasts of saints, Pope Pius V arranged for a significant decrease with the reform of the Breviary (1568). After the reform of the rubrics in 1960, only the three great feasts of Christmas, Easter, and Pentecost have designated octaves.[12] Today the octave of Pentecost exists only

11 Cf. Kaschewsky, "Die Rubriken," 363f.

12 Critical of the elimination of the octave of Epiphany as well as the "Sundays after Epiphany," no longer contained in the MRom 1970, which allowed for a lingering over the "oldest feast of Christ the King in the Church," cf. H.-L. Barth, "Der Stern aus Jakob und der Stern von Betlehem in Bibel und christlicher Tradition," idem (ed.), *Wahrheit und Schönheit*, 197–271, 270f. For the interpretation of the Kingship of Christ on these Sundays, cf. P. Parsch,

in the 1962 *Missale Romanum*. Without a doubt, Pentecost belongs to the mystery of Easter as its conclusion after fifty days, but the mystery of the feast possesses its own wealth of meaning that deserves to be considered and celebrated through an octave week. As the Sundays in the following season are not simply called "Sundays in the Christian Year," whose reckoning begins after the conclusion of the cycle of Christmas, but rather are designated as "Sundays after Pentecost," the naming already demonstrates the importance that the traditional liturgy ascribes to the Holy Ghost for the life of the Church, as, since earliest times, He has been considered the "soul" of the mystical Body of Christ.[13]

Ember days

The special celebration of the Ember days—Wednesday, Friday, and Saturday at the start of each of the four seasons (*quattuor tempora*)—is of genuine Roman origin.[14] The old Christian tradition of repeated fasts during the year likely merged with heathen celebrations of the seasons[15] on the occasion of the three-fold harvest of grain, wine, and olives. From here developed the custom since the third/fourth centuries of setting aside one week each quarter of the year for spiritual assembly and renewal with fasting, prayer, and an exceptional divine service on Wednesday and Friday—the traditional days of stations and fasting—along with a vigil culminating in a celebration of the Mass during the night between Saturday and Sunday in St Peter's. The nocturnal divine worship was later moved up to Saturday morning. Even today, the use of six readings recalls the original vigil. There were originally only three such times, in the months of June, September, and December, and so a fourth Ember week was added in spring, which at first

---

The Church's Year of Grace, trans. by William G. Heidt OSB (Collegeville, MN: The Liturgical Press, ²1962), 288f., 305f.

13   Cf. Augustine, *Sermo* 267,4 (PL 28, 1231 / Augustine, *Sermons*, trans. by E. Hill, *The Works of St Augustine* III/7 [Hyde Park, NY: New City Press, 1993], 276).

14   Cf. L. Fischer, *Die kirchlichen Quatember. Ihre Entstehung, Entwicklung und Bedeutung in liturgischer, rechtlicher und kulturhistorischer Hinsicht* [Veröffentlichungen aus dem Kirchenhistorischen Seminar, Munich IV/3] (Munich: Lentner, 1914); A. de Waal, "Geist und Geschichte der Quatember," *Der Katholik* 91.7 (1911): 401–11; 91.8 (1911): 37–55.

15   Jewish influences are also possible; cf. Zech 8:19, where a fast during the fourth, fifth, seventh, and tenth months is clearly indicated.

fell during the week immediately preceding the then three-week season of Lent, but which, after that season was extended, found its current place in the first week of Quadragesima. The remaining Ember days, which existed before the introduction of the Advent season and of the octave of Pentecost, now fall during the third week of Advent (after St Lucy, December 13), during the octave of Pentecost, and traditionally during the week after the Exaltation of the Holy Cross (September 14), although the *Codex Rubricarum* of 1960 shifts its celebration slightly later. The sermons of Pope Leo I (440–461), who already spoke of a traditional, even apostolic heritage, demonstrate how conscientiously the Roman Church observed these customs in the fifth century. At the end of the fifth century under Pope Gelasius I (492–496), the Ember days became fixed days for conferring the major orders—at first, only in December—which in this manner are prepared for by a week of prayer and fasting by the entire community (cf. Acts 13:3).[16]

Apart from Lent, the Ember days are the only week days that have their own Mass formularies in the *Proprium de tempore*. The texts are determined by the character of the particular season of the liturgical year. The readings for the Ember days in autumn contain references to the Jewish day of atonement and feast of tabernacles, which in the typological meaning on the one hand recognize the necessity of penance and on the other hand instill trust in God's Providence—the Providence that allowed the people of Israel to dwell in tents for forty years, each day providing them with manna. As a time of intensified prayer and fasting, the quarterly return of the three Ember days, with their additional liturgical formularies, offers a regular opportunity for mental and spiritual renewal and deepening,[17] which at the same time serves as an even more pointed preparation for the high feasts (in the case of Advent or Lent) or as a follow-up of a high

16 Cf. B. Kleinheyer, *Die Priesterweihe im römischen Ritus. Eine liturgiehistorische Studie* [Trierer Theologische Studien 12] (Trier: Paulinus-Verlag, 1962), 35–47; I. Schuster, *The Sacramentary*, vol. I, 329–31, 337–45; Fischer, *Quatember*, 102–25. In Lent the investure of the virgins consecrated to God was also combined with the Ember days.

17 Cf. De Waal, "Geist und Geschichte der Quatember," 55: "Let us again teach the faithful to regard the Ember days as days of penance and atonement for the missteps of the past quarter, as days of giving thanks as well as making pleas for corporal benefits; for that is the original purpose of this arrangement. Let us teach them again to pray for our seminaries and novitiates; for that was the second and even higher purpose."

feast (in the case of Pentecost), and also facilitates a pause and short retreat from the regular course of the months (fall Ember days).[18] If nothing else, a review of the early Christian origins of the Ember days and the practices associated with them — prayer, fasting, almsgiving, and vigils — impressively demonstrates to what degree the golden age of the Church during the first centuries was owed to the elevated spiritual level of the faithful.

Stational liturgy

Since the mid-fifth century, under Pope Hilary (461–468), on certain distinguished days of the liturgical year, the so-called stational liturgy took place in one of the old Roman churches. The stational liturgy later received its classical form under Pope Gregory the Great (509–604), and the names of the stational churches were included in the missal up to and including the 1962 issuance of the *Missale Romanum*.[19] The *statio* was the location where people gathered for divine worship, but also described the gathering itself, expressing the vigilance of God's soldiers in spiritual combat (cf. Eph 6:11–18) with a term derived from the vocabulary of the Roman military ("sentinel").[20] According to a determined schedule, the bishop of Rome celebrated the liturgy together with the clergy of the titular churches as well as the faithful from the entire city, or delegations of their regions, sometimes in this church, sometimes in that, in order to emphasize the unity of the Roman congregation.[21] The pope would proceed with a

18   Cf. L. Dobszay, *Restoration*, 130: "The four times three days are, as it were, the *decima* [tithe] of the 12 months of the year. Adrift among various occupations, cares, the frailties of life — and with God's grace — the Church halts the flow of time and reflects in a religious way upon all that happens with and to us."

19   Cf. J.P. Kirsch, *Die Stationskirchen des Missale Romanum* [EcOra 19] (Freiburg i. Br.: Verlag Herder, 1926); H. Grisar, *Das Missale im Lichte römischer Stadtgeschichte* (Freiburg i. Br.: Verlag Herder, 1925); R. Zerfass, "Die Idee der römischen Stationsfeier und ihr Fortleben," LJ 8 (1958): 218–29; U. Nersinger, *Liturgien und Zeremonien*, 346–57.

20   Cf. Tertullian, *De oratione* 19,5 (CCL 1, 268 / Tertullian, *Disciplinary, Moral, and Ascetical Works*, trans. by E.J. Daly, *The Fathers of the Church* 40 [New York, NY: Fathers of the Church, Inc., 1959], 175): "*Si statio de militari exemplo nomen accepit, nam et militia Dei sumus...*" Cf. C. Mohrmann, "Statio": eadem, *Études sur le latin des Chrétiens* III (Rome: Edizioni di Storia e Letteratura, 1965), 307–30.

21   Cf. Zerfass, "Stationsfeier," 220: "Out of the Christian community of Rome, which originally was but one, a series of parishes emerged with the growth of the faithful — in the 5th century there are 25 such *tituli*.... Thus, the celebration of the Eucharistic station

great entourage from his residence in the Lateran Palace to the stational church, while the people repaired to that place from various regions. Occasionally another church was a place of assembly (*Collecta*), where a first prayer would be recited, and from there the solemn procession would move to the stational church while singing psalms and praying litanies.[22] The custom of the stational liturgy remained until the beginning of the popes' residence in Avignon (1305).[23]

Despite altered liturgical circumstances, the 1570 *Missale Romanum* still contained stational memoranda on 87 days,[24] which, along with the calendar of the saints, preserved local Roman color. Among these days are all the days of Lent, the most important Sundays as well as the great feasts of Our Lord and of the saints. In many cases, connections may be found between the current formulary of the Mass and the corresponding stational church. That is, the church frequently was chosen because it corresponded to the liturgical topic of the day or the feast. On the other hand, the place influenced the choice of hymns or readings. Often, therefore, just a glance at the corresponding stational church provides an adequate understanding of the formulary of the Mass.[25]

---

liturgy becomes a unifying bond for the city's Christian community, whose solidity was threatened by its own growth. The original form of the Mass, during which the bishop in the midst of his congregation, surrounded by his clergy, offers the sacrifice, is thus maintained for centuries beyond the ideal epoch of a 'founding generation' (in this case: the primitive church) by the principle of the wandering location [i.e., a stational church visited by its bishop]. At the same time, in accordance with the nature of the celebration of the Mass as the highest form of realization of the Christian community, the inner, hierarchical structure of this church in the bishop, the clergy, and the people is vividly demonstrated to the individual believer—without the need of legal formulas—simply by celebrating together the Eucharist, the *sacramentum unitatis*."

22 Cf. R. Hierzegger, "Collecta und Statio," ZKTh 60 (1936): 511–54.

23 At the beginning of the twentieth century there were efforts in Rome to revive the old celebration of the stations once again. Cf. Nersinger, *Liturgien und Zeremonien* I, 358–68.

24 Due to the three Masses on Christmas there are a total of 89 formularies with stational indications.

25 Cf. Grisar, *Missale*, 2: "So the question of how the Gospel of the resurrection of Lazarus was chosen for Friday after the fourth Sunday of Lent at the Mass is answered by the words 'Statio ad S. Eusebium.' The ancient titular church of St Eusebius lies at the esquiline necropolis of ancient Rome; the surrounding great territory of the dead invited the procession of the faithful of Rome to the memory of the departed and of the eternal resurrection. And why, in the Gospel on Monday after the first Sunday of Lent, is the scene of

Accordingly, Pope Gregory placed the time of preparation leading up to Lent under the protection of the three great patrons of the city of Rome, as he chose the three great patriarchal basilicas of St Laurence, St Paul, and St Peter for the Sundays of Septuagesima, Sexagesima, and Quinquagesima. The texts of these Mass formularies make multiple references to those saints.[26] To take another example, the Wednesday of the second week of Lent is celebrated in the stational church of St Cecilia.[27] The Introit (*Ne derelinquas me*) can be understood equally as a song of penance and as the cry of this early Christian martyr in the face of her enemies. The Epistle depicts the queenly figure of Esther, who, together with Mardochai, appears as a powerful advocate of her people to implore God's assistance against the enemy (cf. Est 13:8–11, 15–17 Vulg.) and as a type of this early Christian saint. The final words of that prayer, "Shut not the mouths of them that sing to thee," recall the tradition according to which St Cecilia, when the pagan music began to play at her wedding feast, sang to the Lord in her heart: *Fiat cor meum immaculatum, ut non confundar* (May my heart be immaculate so that I be not destroyed).[28] As the legendary *passio* relates, Cecilia converted her husband Valerian and his brother Tiburtius and suffered martyrdom with them. Thus the Gospel, in which

---

the Last Judgment presented to us with punishment for the wicked and rewarding the works of mercy? Because the station church, S. Petrus ad vincula, directly adjoins the buildings of the Roman court, i.e., the town's prefecture. The powerful memories of this place, where also St Peter, as it is widely accepted, temporarily lay in chains and was convicted, suggested the choice of the Gospel of the judgment. And further the Gospel of the Samaritan woman at Jacob's well on Friday after the third Sunday of Lent at the station of S. Laurentius in Lucina is explained by the simple fact that in this church there was a highly revered well, which was of the utmost importance for the city, which at that time was extremely poor in water, and that relics of the Palestinian Jacob's well were kept in Rome."

26 Thus the *Introitus, Lectio, Graduale,* and *Tractus* of Septuagesima Sunday refer to the martyrdom of St Laurence; on Sexagesima Sunday the Collect, Epistle, and Gospel refer to St Paul. Cf. Grisar, *Missale,* 54–57.

27 Cf. I. Herwegen, *Das Kunstprinzip der Liturgie* (Paderborn: Junfermann, ²/³1920), 15: "The memory of the virgin martyr pervades the liturgical texts in a barely noticeable yet delicious way, like the scent of incense"; Grisar, *Missale,* 29f.: "In an image from Pope Paschal I, an angel crowned St Cecilia in this church, with Tiburtius and Valerianus around her. Might a similar painting or a similar mosaic in the apse have influenced the choice of the Gospel?"

28 Cf. I. Schuster, *The Sacramentary (Liber Sacramentorum),* trans. by A. Levelis-Marke (London: Burns & Oates, 1925), vol. II, 85–86; cf. also the quotation from idem, *The Sacramentary,* vol. II, 59, quoted below, p. 219, n73.

Salome brings her sons James and John to Christ to beg a place for them in the kingdom of heaven (cf. Mt 20:17–28), becomes a reflection of the stational saint who, together with her two brothers in the faith, drank the cup of sorrow of which Christ speaks in the day's Gospel.

The indications of the old Roman stational churches contained in the Missal are not merely helpful from a historical viewpoint for the deeper understanding of many Mass formularies. They are, in fact, still meaningful today, insofar as they remind the celebrating local congregation that they are part of a greater whole, just as the stational liturgy celebrated with Christ's vicar expressed this to the Roman Christians.[29] As the solemn entrance into the stational church was ever a symbol of the entrance into the heavenly Jerusalem,[30] whose likeness is in the House of God and which becomes mystically present in the liturgy, the stational indications in the Missal place the heavenly Church of the saints before our eyes as the focal point of all earthly celebrations.[31] The stational celebration is furthermore a special manner of honoring the saints, insofar as the faithful are able to enter into an intimate relation with them. Significantly, the indications in the Missal do not state, e.g., *Statio ad Ecclesiam S. Laurentii* (stational liturgy at the Church of St Laurence), but rather *Statio ad S. Laurentium* (stational liturgy at St Laurence, in the sense of "with" or "toward" him).

29   Cf. J. Tyciak, *Jahreskranz*, 23: "If the liturgy still indicates the station church to us even today, it wants to remind us of this pneumatic unity.... Each community assembled before the altar expands to the community of the great universal Church. The life of all affects our own weak praying and thanking. Thus the station liturgy gives us a true broadening of the heart."

30   Cf. Durandus, *Rationale divinorum officiorum* IV,6,15f. (CCM 140, 277f.): "*Cum autem ad aliquam ecclesiam processionaliter tendimus, tunc quasi ad terram promissionis accedimus. Cum vero ecclesiam cantantes intramus, quasi gaudentes ad patriam pervenimus ... optantes ut de mundo revertamur ad patriam et de una Ecclesia ad aliam, scilicet de militante ad triumphantem*" [When we walk to a church in procession, it is as if we draw near to the Promised Land. When we enter the church singing, it is as if we arrive rejoicing to our native country... wishing that we return to our native country from the world, and from the one Church to the other, that is, from the militant to the triumphant Church].

31   Cf. Tyciak, *Jahreskranz*, 24: "The *Caelestis urbs Jerusalem* ('heavenly city of Jerusalem,' an expression from the hymn of the Dedication of a Church) descends in the liturgical worship and presents itself in the house of the Lord. The solemn entering of the earthly church into the temple of the Lord signifies a mysterious participation of the faithful in the liturgical worship and the community of the transfigured."

In a consecrated House of God the saint is present, so that the faithful may personally resort to him, and through the sacrifice of Christ, enter into such a close relationship with him that the words and graces referring to the saint are simultaneously also promised to them. By way of example, the Communion antiphon of Easter Monday states: "The Lord is risen, and hath appeared to Peter"; thus, the congregation actually or spiritually gathered at St Peter's — *Statio ad S. Petrum* — may apply these words to themselves, as they encounter the Risen Christ in the celebration of the sacrifice.

In such ways, the stational indications primarily show the Roman roots from which the liturgy of the Latin Church has grown, but more than historical reminiscences, they are spiritual signposts that direct the individual celebrations of the Mass to the *one* sacrifice of the Catholic Church. They make its heavenly dimension transparent, and at the same time, in the remembrance of the stational saint, put a special mystagogue in place for the celebration of the sacrifice.[32]

---

32 Cf. Tyciak, *Jahreskranz*, 24f.: "Therefore we do not see in the indication of the station a mere historical memory, a bygone antiquity no longer meaningful today, but a living reality that embraces the congregation, the universal Church, the shrine, and the saints. Over time and space, every cultic community surrounding the altar enters into the great unity of the Church of nations in the holy sacrificial celebration and stands in a lively community through Christ with all the saints, especially the blessed of the particular station church. So today we can celebrate the station liturgy in the spirit of the old Church as a true walk in holy procession to the heavenly Church, to the celebration of the second coming of Christ . . ."

7

Direction of Prayer

HISTORICAL DEVELOPMENT

Directing the celebration *versus altare* (turned toward an East-facing altar) is among the great constants in the history of the classical rite of the Mass. For almost 1,900 years the celebrant looked eastward at the altar — not turned *away* from the assembled people, but rather turned *toward* the Lord, in collaboration with them. This positioning of the officiant is in no way specific to the Christian cult, but is rather a constant in the history of religion as well.

Already in pagan antiquity the sacrificing priest stood before (not behind) the altar. His gaze was directed toward the sanctuary and the image of the deity who received the sacrifice. It was similar in the Temple of Jerusalem. Here, too, the priest stood before the great altar of burnt offerings in the temple court at the presentation of the victim, whereby his gaze was directed toward the Holy of Holies in the inner temple, the place that was considered to be the dwelling of the Most High. When offering a sacrifice, the person always turned himself toward the one to whom he offered the sacrifice, not those for whom or with whom he offered it.[1]

That the priest at the altar should turn himself toward the people was first postulated by Luther, but it is not known that he ever practiced it himself.[2] As opposed to those of the Reformed Church, however,

---

1   Cf. K. Gamber, *Zum Herrn hin! Fragen um Kirchenbau und Gebet nach Osten* (Regensburg: Verlag Friedrich Pustet, 1987), 57.

2   Cf. M. Luther, *Deutsche Messe und Ordnung des Gottesdienstes*, 1526 (WA 19, 80): "But in the true Mass among genuine Christians, the altar would not have to remain so, and the priest would always turn to the people, as without doubt Christ did at the Lord's Supper. Well, that will be so in good time." Cf. K. Gamber, "Celebrating the Mass *Versus Populum*: Liturgical and Sociological Aspects," idem, *The Reform of the Roman Liturgy: Its Problems and Background*, trans. by K.D. Grimm (San Juan Capistrano, CA / Harrison, NY: Una Voce Press [i.a.], 1993), 77–89, 77f.; idem, "Celebration 'Turned Towards the People,'" *The Modern Rite*, 25–34, 25.

Lutheran congregations generally maintained a common orientation of prayer toward the altar for their services. Except for isolated attempts, a celebration *versus populum* remained always foreign in the Eastern Orthodox Church. At least at the anaphora, the Eucharistic prayer, there was and is only one common direction of prayer for both the priest and people.[3] Even members of the Anglican High Church consider the direction of prayer toward the apse (*versus apsidem*), that is, toward the altar, as an important support of their efforts to reclaim the sacrificial character of the Eucharist.[4] In the Catholic Church, celebration toward the people (*versus populum*) was favored as early as the eighteenth century by proponents of the Enlightenment, but it was little practiced.[5] Only in the 1920s did the Youth Movement and the Liturgical Movement begin to propagate this practice,[6] yet Pope Pius XII opposed these efforts, stating that "one would be straying from the straight path were he to wish the altar restored to its primitive table form,"[7] inasmuch as this change would allow for a celebration toward the people. Vatican II's Constitution on the Liturgy did not address the question of the direction of celebration,

3 Cf. Gamber, "Celebrating the Mass *Versus Populum*," 79; U.M. Lang, *Turning Towards the Lord. Orientation in Liturgical Prayer* (San Francisco: Ignatius Press, 2005), 97f.

4 Cf. A. Nichols, *Looking at the Liturgy: A Critical View of Its Contemporary Form* (San Francisco: Ignatius Press, 1996), 96f. For similar tendencies within the Oxford movement in the nineteenth century, cf. Lang, *Turning Towards the Lord*, 112f.

5 Cf. Lang, *Turning Towards the Lord*, 119f.

6 Cf. Gamber, "Celebrating the Mass *Versus Populum*," 79; Lang, *Turning Towards the Lord*, 120f.

7 Pius XII, *Mediator Dei* (AAS 39:454 / Seasoltz, *Documentation*, 125). Further experiments, especially in France during the 1950s, led to Paul Claudel's "historical protest"; see Paul Claudel, "La messe à l'envers": *Supplément aux œuvres complètes* I (Lausanne: L'Age d'Homme, 1990), 294f. (originally: *Le Figaro*, Jan. 29, 1955). Cf. P. Claudel, *Journal* II (Paris: Gallimard, 1969), 842 (Aug. 15, 1953): "From the viewpoint of the liturgy, it is a complete misinterpretation. The priest at Mass is only the people's representative. We are the ones who say Mass with him. From time to time he invites us to cooperation by turning to us: *Dom[inus] vobiscum, Orate fratres*. Now Mass is no longer our work, it is a spectacle that is offered to separated people, as in earlier days. We have suffered a degradation. Instead of being priests, we are no more than assistants, spectators. The Latin Mass is not made for that and as a work of art it suffers terrible damage. Not to mention this odious mixture with French. It looks a lot like a Protestant cult. Trouble and sadness." Cf. M. Levatois, *La messe à l'envers. L'espace liturgique en débat* (Paris: Éditions Jacqueline Chambon, 2009), 155–57.

and thus neither desired nor demanded changes.[8] The burden of proof, therefore, lies with those who demand a change to the centuries-old direction of divine worship.

Luther had already invoked the Last Supper practice of Jesus for his corresponding demand. A new type of pictorial representation that began to assert itself from the thirteenth century and is familiar from Leonardo Da Vinci's *Last Supper* may have been formative for his conception of the events of the time: Jesus sitting at the rear side of a table in the midst of the Apostles, facing the observer of the scene.[9] If Mass were made to correspond to this artistic presentation, the priest should stand at the altar across from the people and turn his gaze on them. This argument, however, is based on a misapprehension of ancient table manners as they would have been practiced at the Last Supper. There was at that time either a round or a semicircular table at whose open front side the food would be brought, while those partaking of the meal sat or reclined at the rear semicircle of the table. The place of honor was not in the middle, but rather on the right side. The one presiding over a meal never had another partaker across from his place. These original arrangements are shown in the oldest representations of the Last Supper until the Middle Ages.[10] If this finding alone prevents the derivation of celebrating *versus populum* from Jesus' practice at the Last Supper,[11] a look

8 On further development and justification of the changes, cf. H.-L. Barth, "*Nichts soll dem Gottesdienst vorgezogen werden*," 153f.; M. Davies, *The Catholic Sanctuary and the Second Vatican Council* (Rockford, IL: TAN Books and Publishers, 1997); idem, *Pope Paul's New Mass* [Liturgical Revolution III] (Dickinson, TX: Angelus Press, 1980), 397–417; J. Fournée, "Missa versus Deum," UVK 9 (1979): 17–27, 85–96, 86; Levatois, *La messe à l'envers*, 59–81; P.B. Wodrazka, "Die Zelebration 'versus orientem' bzw. 'versus absidem.' Ein chronologischer Durchgang durch die postkonziliaren kirchlichen Dokumente (in Auszügen)," *Theologisches* 37 (2007): 99–114; A. Lorenzer, *Das Konzil der Buchhalter. Die Zerstörung der Sinnlichkeit. Eine Religionskritik* (Frankfurt a. M.: Fischer-Taschenbuch-Verlag, 1984), 198–207.

9 Cf. Gamber, "Celebration 'Turned Towards the People,'" 26; Lang, *Turning Towards the Lord*, 93f.

10 One of the most famous representations is the mosaic in Sant' Apollinare Nuovo in Ravenna (around 500); reproduction by Gamber, *Zum Herrn hin*, 26; Lang, *Turning Towards the Lord*, 62.

11 Cf. Davies, *The Catholic Sanctuary*; Lang, *Turning Towards the Lord*, 61f.; L. Bouyer, *Liturgy and Architecture* (Notre Dame, IN: University of Notre Dame Press, 1967), 53f.

at the historical beginnings of the Eucharistic celebration demonstrates yet more that the primitive Church's congregation in no way repeated the Last Supper as such and did not consider the meal as the original ritual form of the Eucharist.

EASTWARD PRAYER ORIENTATION

Crucial for the question of the direction of celebration in the early Church was the fundamental eastern orientation of prayer. This orientation is already found in pagan antiquity and in Judaism, though in the latter an alignment toward Jerusalem later prevailed. For Christians, on the other hand, prayer toward the east became definitive for private as well as liturgical practice.[12] In this orientation, the gaze was ever focused eastward, in the direction of the rising sun.[13] The eastern direction was associated with a rich symbolism that reaches from the beginnings of the history of mankind until the second coming of Christ, equally encompasses the Old and New Testaments, and shows quite plainly the work of salvation in its many facets to those who pray. At the end of the time of the Church Fathers, St John Damascene (first half of the eighth century) summarized the rich symbolism of the Christians' eastern orientation of prayer:

> It is not without reason or by chance that we worship toward the east.... Since God is spiritual light and Christ in sacred Scripture is called "Sun of Justice" (Mal 4:2) and "Orient" (Lk 1:78), the east should be dedicated to His worship.... Also, the divine David says: "Sing to God, ye kingdoms of the earth: sing ye to

---

12   Cf. Lang, *Turning Towards the Lord*, 35–56; Jungmann, *The Early Liturgy*, 134–38; M. Wallraff, *Christus verus Sol. Sonnenverehrung und Christentum in der Spätantike* [JAC.E 32] (Münster: Aschendorff Verlag, 2001), 60–88; E. Keller, *Eucharistie und Parusie. Liturgie- und theologiegeschichtliche Untersuchungen zur eschatologischen Dimension der Eucharistie anhand ausgewählter Zeugnisse aus frühchristlicher und patristischer Zeit* (Fribourg/Switzerland: Academic Press, 1989), 119–47; Dölger, *Sol Salutis*, 136–242; M.J. Moreton, "Εἰς ἀνατολὰς βλέψατε: Orientation as a Liturgical Principle," StPatr 17/2 (1982): 575–90.

13   Cf. S. Heid, "Gebetshaltung und Ostung in frühchristlicher Zeit," RivAC 82 (2006): 347–404, 378; idem, "Haltung und Richtung. Grundformen christlichen Betens," IKaZ 38 (2009): 611–19, 612f.

the Lord; who mounteth above the heaven of heavens, to the east" (Ps 67:33f.). And still again, Scripture says: "And the Lord has planted a paradise in Eden to the east; wherein He placed man whom He had formed," and whom He cast out, when he had transgressed, "and made him to live over against the paradise of pleasure" (Gen 2:8; 3,24 LXX), or in the west. Thus it is that, when we worship God, we long for our ancient fatherland and gaze toward it.... As a matter of fact, when the Lord was crucified, He looked toward the west, and so we worship gazing toward Him. And when He was taken up, He ascended to the east and thus the Apostles worshiped Him and thus He shall come in the same way as they had seen Him going into heaven (cf. Acts 1:11), as the Lord Himself said: "As lightning cometh out of the east and appeareth even into the west: so shall also the coming of the Son of man be" (Mt 24:27). And so, while we are awaiting Him, we worship toward the east. This is, moreover, the unwritten tradition of the Apostles, for they have handed many things down to us unwritten.[14]

From among these diverse motifs, the second coming of Christ at the end of time stands out. Turning toward the east was a bodily expression of the living expectation of the *parousia* of the Lord, which possesses its cosmic symbol in the blaze of light of the rising sun.

The Early Christian construction of churches sought, as far as possible, to conform to this principle of praying toward the east and orienting the apse in that direction. Where this proved topographically or structurally impossible and the entrance to a basilica faced the east, the celebrant stood behind the altar in order that the performance of the sacrifice of the Mass might be directed toward the east nevertheless. This verifiable practice, above all in the Roman basilicas (St Peter's, among others), led to the erroneous conclusion that in the early Church there

---

14 John of Damascus, *De fide orthodoxa* 85 (IV 12) (PTS 12, 190f. / St John of Damascus, *Writings*, trans. by F. H. Chase, *The Fathers of the Church* 37 [Washington, DC: Catholic University of America Press, 1958], 352–54).

was certainly a celebration *"versus populum."*[15] This assumption, which attempted to provide archeological corroboration for the corresponding liturgical endeavors of the time, has in the meantime been clearly and scientifically disproved.[16] Countless studies have proved that while the arrangement of the liturgical space in Christian antiquity was versatile, a celebration toward the people was never intentionally pursued.[17] In early Christian times, the praying congregation's line of vision was considered to be not so much toward the altar, where there were neither crucifix nor candlesticks, nor developed and ritualized gestures of the celebrant (genuflections, kisses of the altar, signs of the Cross, elevation), as rather toward the image of the exalted Christ, or the heavenly Cross, as the mosaics in the apse impressively presented it.[18] Here it was not merely a matter of a decorative presentation of Christ, but rather "of His epiphanic presence as the counterpart to the praying congregation."[19] Even in basilicas with the entrance facing east, the priest and people were not face-to-face in the sense of reciprocally looking at each other. The image of Christ enthroned in Heaven or of His glorious Cross in the apse dome enabled an "imaginary eastern orientation" of prayer in

---

15 Thus, especially, O. Nussbaum, *Der Standort des Liturgen am christlichen Altar vor dem Jahre 1000. Eine archäologische und liturgiegeschichtliche Untersuchung* [Theoph. 18] (Bonn: Peter Hanstein Verlag, 1965).

16 Cf. J.A. Jungmann, "Review of O. Nussbaum, *Der Standort des Liturgen*," ZKTh 88 (1966): 445–50; M. Metzger, "La place des liturges à l'autel," RevSR 45 (1971): 113–45; Lang, *Turning Towards the Lord*, 56–66; Gamber, *Zum Herrn hin*, 40f.; idem, "Die Hinwendung nach Osten bei der Messfeier im 4. und 5. Jahrhundert," idem, *Liturgie und Kirchenbau. Studien zur Geschichte der Messfeier und des Gotteshauses in der Frühzeit* [SPLi 6] (Regensburg: Verlag Friedrich Pustet, 1976), 7–27.

17 Cf. Lang, *Turning Towards the Lord*, 85f.; J. Ratzinger, *Theology of the Liturgy* (*Collected Works* 11), xvif.; Bouyer, *Liturgy and Architecture*; J. Lara, "*Versus Populum* Revisited," *Worship* 68 (1994): 210–21; J. Braun, *Der christliche Altar*, 2 vol. (Munich: Alte Meister Guenther Koch & Co., 1924).

18 Cf. Heid, "Gebetshaltung," 368f., 385; idem: "Haltung und Richtung," 615f.; Gamber, *Zum Herrn hin*, 16; E. Peterson, "Das Kreuz und das Gebet nach Osten," idem, *Frühkirche, Judentum und Gnosis. Studien und Untersuchungen* (Freiburg i. Br.: Verlag Herder, 1959), 15–35; as to the Cross as eschatological sign of Christ's return (Mt 24:30), cf. M. Reinecke, "L'orientation de l'autel: histoire et théologie": *La liturgie, trésor de l'église. Actes du premier colloque d'études historiques, théologiques et canoniques sur le rite catholique romain* [Notre-Dame-du-Laus, Octobre 1995] (Paris: CIEL, 1996), 187–217, 205–8.

19 Heid, "Gebetshaltung," 370.

these cases.[20] Many prayers of the Roman Canon as well (*elevatis oculis in caelum*; *supra quae propitio ac sereno vultu respicere digneris*; *jube haec perferri per manus sancti Angeli tui in sublime altare tuum*) reflect the early Christian awareness that the liturgy is celebrated before the opened heavens in the view of God.[21]

In the early Middle Ages, in Carolingian times, the strict eastern orientation of the houses of God prevailed. The Western, Latin churches did not adopt the plan of Roman basilicas with an east-facing entrance, but rather Rome came into accord with the Frankish practice of the apse strictly facing east, which had become common in Western Europe and found its high point in Romanesque and Gothic architecture.[22] The Council of Trent introduced a new phase in the arrangement of the liturgical space: the eastern orientation was retained as a matter of principle, but with episcopal approval other church orientations — except toward the North — were permitted.[23] In visual correspondence to the Tridentine dogmatic apologia for the Eucharistic Real Presence, the tabernacle now found its central location on the altar (*in media altaris parte*), while the chancel or sanctuary, though enclosed by a small balustrade or grille, was still wide open to the view of the faithful, allowing an unobstructed view of the performance of the sacrifice of the Mass at the high altar.[24] The inner "orientation" of the sacred space, uniting priest and people in a common alignment with the main altar, crucifix, and tabernacle, substituted for an

20   Cf. Lang, *Turning Towards the Lord*, 85f.; Heid, "Gebetshaltung," 379–82, 389f.

21   Cf. Gregory I, *Dialogi* 4,60,3 (SCh 265, 202 / St Gregory the Great, *Dialogues*, 273): "For, who of the faithful can have any doubt that at the moment of the immolation, at the sound of the priest's voice, the heavens stand open and choirs of angels are present at the mystery of Jesus Christ? There at the altar the lowliest is united with the most sublime, earth is joined to heaven, the visible and invisible somehow merge into one."

22   Cf. Levatois, *La messe à l'envers*, 25–27; C. Vogel, "Versus orientem. L'orientation dans les *Ordines Romani* du haut moyen-âge," *Studi medievali* III/1 (1960): 447–69; Lang, *Turning Towards the Lord*, 87.

23   Cf. Charles Borromeo, *Instructionum fabricae et suppellectilis ecclesiasticae libri* I,10 (ed. by S. della Torre / M. Marinelli / F. Adorni [Monumenta studia instrumenta liturgica 8] (Vatican City: Libreria Editrice Vaticana, 2000), 28); Lang, *Turning Towards the Lord*, 95–97; Levatois, *La messe à l'envers*, 29.

24   Cf. Levatois, *La messe à l'envers*, 28–51; the Roman Jesuit church "Il Gesù" is considered an architectonical archetype of Catholic reform, ibid., 30f.

outward eastern orientation. If, furthermore, the eastern orientation of a church, by reason of the symbolism of light associated with it, represents the ideal situation, in which the cosmic dimension of the Eucharist is revealed also through the architecture, then certainly a common direction of prayer for the priest and the people, independent of that, still remains greatly meaningful for the proper basic understanding of the celebration of the Mass.[25]

THEOCENTRISM AND SACRIFICIAL CHARACTER

The celebration *versus altare* is a Eucharistic theology made visible. The inner direction of Eucharistic prayer manifests itself in the outward orientation. Even someone who is unfamiliar with the Mass could recognize by the direction of the celebration *versus altare* that the priest precedes the people and prays to God together with them. The instruction of the early Church that prayer at the altar always be addressed to the Father (*Cum altari assistitur, semper ad Patrem dirigatur oratio*),[26] although originally directed against the tendency of including a direct salutation of Christ within the Mass, also demonstrates that visual contact between the priest and the faithful at that moment does not fundamentally conform to the intended purpose of liturgical prayer. The celebration *versus altare* emphasizes in a visual manner that the prayers are directed not toward the faithful, but rather toward God. The principal purpose of the liturgy is not dialogue, but collective worship. This orientation of prayer expresses the theocentric character of the liturgy.[27] The classical orientation of celebration opposes all tendencies to reduce holy worship to pedagogy and to replace doxology with catechesis. It similarly

---

25 Cf. Jungmann, *Missarum sollemnia* I, 333n15; idem, *The Mass of the Roman Rite* I, 255n15; Gamber, *Liturgie und Kirchenbau*, 26f.

26 Council of Hippo (393), can. 21 (*Breviarium Hipponense*: CCL 259, 39). Cf. J. A. Jungmann, *The Place of Christ in Liturgical Prayer*, trans. by A. Peeler (Collegeville, MN: Liturgical Press, 1989), 144f.

27 Cf. J. Ratzinger, "Préface," K. Gamber, *Tournés vers le Seigneur* (Le Barroux: Éditions Sainte-Madeleine, 1993), s.p.: "This orientation of prayer expresses the theocentric character of the liturgy, it obeys the call: Let us turn to the Lord." R. L. Burke, "The Theo-Centric Character of Catholic Liturgy," *The Thomist* 75 (2011): 347–64.

prevents the liturgical immanentism[28] that results when the position of the priest and people across from each other creates a circle enclosed on itself, in which the celebrant becomes the actual point of reference for the assembled faithful, and they for him, thus suggesting the "idea of an autonomous, complacent community."[29] The common orientation of prayer prevents a static self-referentiality within the liturgical congregation. It is rather a visual expression that each Mass is celebrated in expectation and anticipation of Christ's Second Coming. Led by the priest, the people of God proceeds as in a procession toward the coming Lord.[30] The inner dynamic of the liturgical action urges an outward alignment by the priest and people in prayer.

This applies equally to the eschatological dimension of the celebration of the Mass and to its sacrificial character. As the priest leads the pilgrims, the people of God, on the common journey toward Christ's Second Coming, he also stands at the forefront of the faithful before God, to bring Him the Church's prayers and sacrifices. A witness to one of Padre Pio's Masses wrote afterward: "In this crowd one could only just hear the murmur of his praying. He truly became the mediator for mankind before the face of God, the most sublime peak of finite creation before the infinite!"[31] This quotation demonstrates what the question of the orientation of prayer is ultimately about: Is the Mass primarily understood as a sacrifice or as a meal? Is the priest the congregation's representative before God or the congregation's partner in dialogue? Is the celebrant directed to God as the sacrificing priest, or to the assembled congregation as the "president"?

---

28   Cf. Nichols, *Looking at the Liturgy*, 97: "the danger, namely, of a congregation's covert self-reference in a horizontal humanistic world. In contemporary 'Catholic communalism,' it has been said: 'Liturgical *Gemütlichkeit*, communal warmth, friendliness, welcoming hospitality, can easily be mistaken for the source and summit of the faith.'" (Quotation: T. Day, *Where Have You Gone, Michelangelo? The Loss of Soul in Catholic Culture* [New York, NY: Crossroad, 1993], 107). Cf. Lang, *Turning Towards the Lord*, 102–4.

29   Ratzinger, *Feast of Faith*, 142 (*Theology of the Liturgy*, 390).

30   Cf. Ratzinger, *Spirit of the Liturgy*, 79–81 (*Theology of the Liturgy*, 48–50); Lang, *Turning Towards the Lord*, 100–2, 108f.

31   Fournée, "Missa versus Deum," 95. Cf. Second Vatican Council, SC 33: "Moreover, the prayers addressed to God by the priest, who presides over the assembly in the person of Christ, are said in the name of the entire holy people and all those present." Trans.: *Documents on the Liturgy, 1963–1979*, 11.

The orientation of celebration, therefore, has fundamental consequences for the content and understanding of the Mass. It has been rightly emphasized: "The essential issue regarding the position of the priest at the altar is . . . the sacrificial character of the Mass. The one performing the sacrifice turns toward Him to whom he offers the sacrifice; thus he stands at the altar 'ad Dominum', toward the Lord."[32] Since the third century, the terms *prosphora, anaphora*, and *oblatio* have commonly been used to describe the Eucharist, demonstrating the characteristic sacrificial dynamic of offering and bringing sacrifices to God, which finds its visible expression in the common direction of prayer.[33] The classical direction of celebration emphasizes the sacrificial character of the Eucharist, creates a harmony between theology and ceremony, and prevents the disintegration of preaching and of liturgical symbolism.[34]

CONCENTRATION AND DISCRETION

Finally, the celebration *versus altare* leads both the priest and the assembled faithful to a deeper personal union with the Eucharistic mystery.

32   Gamber, *Zum Herrn hin*, 61; cf. ibid., 57: "A meal is celebrated in the (family) circle under the chairmanship of the householder, while a sacrifice is made in all religions by a specially commissioned celebrant. . . . The celebrant is lifted out of the crowd and has his place in front of it, in front of the altar, in the presence of the deity. People have always turned toward the one who received the sacrifice, and not toward those present." Cf. idem, "Celebrating the Mass *Versus Populum*," 85–89; idem, "Celebration 'Turned Towards the People,'" 32f. Cf. Jungmann, *Missarum sollemnia* I, 333n15; idem, *The Mass of the Roman Rite* I, 255n15: "But the basic principle that at prayer all—including even the celebrant—should take a God-ward stance, could easily be at work here too, in establishing the celebrant's position at the altar. If Mass were only a service of instruction or a Communion celebration, the other position, facing the people, would be more natural. But it is different if the Mass is an immolation and homage to God"; idem, "Review of O. Nussbaum," 448: "The more apparent the concept of sacrifice becomes in the Mass, the more regularly the eastern orientation is demanded for the celebrant, wherever the altar may stand"; Lang, *Turning Towards the Lord*, 109–15.

33   Cf. J. A. Jungmann, "Der neue Altar," *Der Seelsorger* 37 (1967): 374–81, 377; J. Betz, "Die Prosphora in der patristischen Theologie": B. Neunheuser (ed.), *Opfer Christi und Opfer der Kirche. Die Lehre vom Messopfer als Mysteriengedächtnis in der Theologie der Gegenwart* (Düsseldorf: Patmos-Verlag, 1960), 99–116.

34   Cf. Lang, *Turning Towards the Lord*, 115: "The sacrificial character of the Eucharist must find an adequate expression in the actual rite. Not even the best mystagogical catechesis can make up for the decline in the understanding of the Mass among Catholics, if the liturgical celebration sends out signs to the contrary." Cf. Gamber, *Zum Herrn hin*, 58, 61.

Though the traditional form of the Mass is often reproached for being a "clerical liturgy," insofar as the actions of the priest, which the people can only more or less follow, stand in the foreground, it may be countered that, paradoxically, the orientation of celebration *versus altare* more perfectly allows the priest to retreat behind his liturgical function, while the position of the priest opposite the congregation ushers in every possible sort of neo-clericalism.[35] "A priest at the altar has no face," wrote Gertrude von Le Fort in her *Hymns to the Church*,[36] indicating in these few words with what discretion the classical rite of the Mass ensheaths the celebrating priest in favor of the *repraesentatio Christi*.[37] When turned toward the altar, the priest is never tempted to perform like an actor before an audience,[38] and

35 Cf. Fournée, "Missa versus Deum," 26, 93, 95; Gamber, *Zum Herrn hin*, 53f.; Spaemann, "Liturgie—Ausdruck des Glaubens," 36–71, 58; Bouyer, *Liturgy and Architecture*, 110f.

36 Gertrud v. Le Fort, *Hymnen an die Kirche* (Munich: Ehrenwirth Verlag, ⁵1948), 22.

37 R. Spaemann, "Gedanken eines Laien zur Reform der Reform," IKaZ 38 (2008): 82–89, 83: "The old liturgy is less focused on the priest's person than the new one." Cf. E. Recktenwald, "Die alte Liturgie bewahren?": N. Esser (ed.), *Dem Schönen und Heiligen dienen, dem Bösen wehren* (Sinzig: Sankt-Meinrad-Verlag, 1997), 90–105, 99: "This retreat [into the ritual] serves to visualize the divine reality that comes from God—the earthly liturgy is the image of the heavenly liturgy—and to make way for the action of the main celebrant, namely, Christ himself—the priest acts *in persona Christi*. The celebrating priest becomes the more unimportant in his individual personality the more priestly his action is. In the heart of the Holy Mass, during the Canon, in which the transubstantiation and thus the descent of the one eternal High Priest occurs, the priest no longer has a face: he stands—yes!—with his back to the people, he speaks what every other priest speaks at this point, he becomes in his person completely unimportant and replaceable, because he makes room for the One for whose sake alone the believer takes part in the sacred liturgy. To emphasize eye contact with the priest at this point therefore means the utmost misunderstanding of the priestly function in its proper sense. In the highest priestly act, the priest is pure instrument and perviousness for the One."

38 Cf. Dobszay, *Restoration*, 92f.: "The change of physical direction became a change in psychological orientation. He began to say the Mass not *for* (*pro*) but *to* or *at* the people. He began trying to influence what had become for him an audience, through gestures: head or eye movements during the holiest parts of the Mass; the priest became a president, or rather an actor or media-man for the assembly. This 'direct contact' was often accompanied with fraternizing manners.... The rearrangement of the sanctuary... transformed the liturgical ethos in general and the liturgical mentality of the priests in particular. The priest surely mentally *imagined* but did not *experience* in his innermost being what it actually means to step up to the throne of the Most High God, to bring there the prayer and the sacrifice of God's people in the name of Christ. The typical manners and concerns of a community leader or even a schoolteacher were now uppermost in his mind."

thus he remains free of a false dependence, in order to concentrate entirely on the holy actions without distraction and to unite himself interiorly with the celebrated mystery.

Furthermore, this orientation of celebration also allows the faithful to unite themselves more intensively with the actions on the altar. In his plea for the preservation of the traditional manner of celebration, Paul Claudel wrote: "It is certainly true that in the traditional liturgy, a great, poignant, and moving part of the Holy Sacrifice is denied to the view of the faithful, but not to their hearts and to their faith."[39] The argument that better visibility will facilitate access to the Mystery of Faith does not bear weight. On the one hand, the central *mysterium fidei* is the consecration, which as such remains withdrawn from our bodily eyes: "The only view by which it is possible to observe the mystery is the interior vision of Faith."[40] On the other hand it remains questionable to what extent other elements, such as the priest's Communion or the purification of the chalice, should be absolutely visible to the people. Here the classical orientation of celebration possesses superior discretion and aesthetics.[41] By concealing and cloaking much of what happens at the altar, the traditional liturgy prevents the faithful from fixing their gaze on the exteriorly visible, attending to the gestures of the celebrant as such, and mistaking visibility of rite for transparency of mystery.

The question of whether the liturgy is ultimately directed toward God or toward man, whether it is theocentric or anthropocentric, concerns not only the direction of celebration, but also the use of a sacred language.

---

39   P. Claudel, "La messe à l'envers," *Figaro Littéraire*, Jan. 29, 1955.

40   Fournée, "Missa versus Deum," 88.

41   Cf. Fournée, "Missa versus Deum," 88; Lorenzer, *Konzil der Buchhalter*, 192; Gamber, *Zum Herrn hin*, 55.

8

Sacred Language

LATIN

Origin and character of sacred language

The phenomenon of a sacred language is found in all religions. Such a language was used by the Greek oracles of ancient times and can be found in ancient Roman pagan prayers, whose formulas date back to distant antiquity, occasionally having become unintelligible even to the priest himself,[1] though still used in order to remain true to ancestral tradition. At the time of Christ, the Jews used the language of Old Hebraic for their services, though it was incomprehensible to the people.[2] In the synagogues, only the readings and a few prayers relating to them were written in the mother tongue of Aramaic; the great, established prayer texts were recited in Hebrew. Although Christ adamantly attacked the formalism of the Pharisees in other respects, He never questioned this practice.[3] Insofar as the Passover Meal was primarily celebrated with Hebrew prayers, the Last Supper was also characterized by elements of a sacred language.[4] It is therefore possible that Christ spoke the words of Eucharistic consecration in the Hebrew *lingua sacra*.[5] Other world religions also recognize sacred

---

1 Cf. Quintilian, *Institutio oratoria* 1,6,40 (Bibliotheca Teubneriana 46): "*Saliorum carmina vix sacerdotibus suis satis intellecta. Sed illa mutari vetat religio*" [The hymns of the Salii are barely understood by their own priests; and yet their religion prohibits them {the hymns} from being changed].

2 F. van der Meer, "Der Boykott des Latein," UVK 4 (1974): 19–22, 21: "Christ did not hear Aramaic in the house of His Father, but the language of David."

3 Cf. L. Bouyer, *The Liturgy Revived: A Doctrinal Commentary of the Conciliar Constitution on the Liturgy* (Notre Dame, IN: University of Notre Dame Press, 1964), 96f.

4 Discussions on the Constitution on the Sacred Liturgy in favor of the vernacular wrongly referred to the supposed celebration of Christ's Last Supper exclusively in Aramaic. Cf. *Acta Synodalia Sacrosancti Concilii Oecumenici Vaticani II*, vol. 1, periodus prima, Pars I (Vatican City: Typis Polyglottis Vaticanis, 1970), 378; M. Davies, *Pope John's Council*, 332.

5 Cf. J. Jeremias, *The Eucharistic Words of Jesus*, trans. by N. Perrin (London: SCM Press, 1966), 196–97.

languages that differ from everyday idioms. The Muslims use classical Arabic for their prayers. The Buddhists employ Pali, and the Hindus Sanskrit. Even within Christianity various dedicated languages of worship have developed.[6] Thus the Orthodox Greeks celebrate their liturgy in ancient Greek and the Russians in Church Slavonic. In addition, there is the use of Armenian, Coptic, and Syrian. Though originally these were certainly the living, vernacular language, over the course of time they grew ever more distant from everyday speech and finally assumed the character of a proper language of worship. Even Anglican services use the melodious Elizabethan English found in the *Book of Common Prayer*.

Thus, if sacred languages existed in numerous cultures and almost all epochs of history, and still continue to exist, this fact is an expression of a fundamental human need. In the background stands a particular religious experience that shapes and changes speech and language. It is the experience of something supernatural, divine, transcendent, and wholly other, to which man seeks to respond by using a language that differentiates itself from the form of everyday speech by means of a sacred stylization.[7] Here lies the origin of the so-called hieratic or "priestly" languages.[8] Far from creating a language barrier, the sacred language calls to mind that religion has "something else" to say to man.[9] The sacred language prevents man from dragging the divine down to his own level, and instead lifts man up to the divine, which it does not, however, reveal and expose completely to the human understanding, but instead indicates as a mystery.

The characteristics of a sacred language include (1) a conscious distancing from the words of colloquial language, which makes the "complete otherness" of the divine felt; (2) an archaizing or at least conservative tendency to favor antiquated expressions and adhere to certain speech forms from centuries ago, as is well-suited for the worship of an eternal

6   Cf. D. Viain, "Les langues liturgiques": *La Messe en question*. Actes du Ve Congrès Théologique de Sì Sì No No, Paris, April 2002 (Villegenon: Courrier de Rome, 2002), 339–80, 341–49; L. Godefroy, "Langues liturgiques," DThC 8/2 (1925): 2580–91; P. Guéranger, *Institutions liturgiques* III, 51–160.

7   Cf. C. Mohrmann, "Sakralsprache und Umgangssprache," eadem, *Études sur le latin des chrétiens* IV (Rome: Edizioni di Storia e Letteratura, 1977), 161–74, 171f.

8   Cf. Mohrmann, "Sakralsprache," 171; eadem, *Liturgical Latin*, 1–26, 52.

9   Cf. Nichols, *Looking at the Liturgy*, 102f.

and unchanging God; (3) the use of foreign words that evoke religious associations, as, for example, the Hebrew and Aramaic forms of the words *alleluia, Sabaoth, hosanna, amen, maranatha* in the Greek books of the New Testament; and finally, (4) syntactic and phonetic stylizations (e.g., parallelisms, alliterations, rhymes, and rhythmic sentence endings) that clearly structure the train of thought, are memorable and allow for easy recollection, and strive for tonal beauty.

In order to understand the essence and meaning of a sacred language, it is important to be aware that language has multiple functions.[10] First, it is a medium of communication that allows for the transmission of thoughts or information. Here intelligibility is vital. Beyond this, however, language is a form of expression. By means of language, man can give expression to his feelings and experiences, even his entire being. Thus, for example, singing a song does not convey information, but rather expresses sentiments, creates an atmosphere, and brings about fellowship. Considered from the standpoint of linguistics, prayer belongs more to the realm of expression than to that of communication.[11] This applies not only to personal prayer, but also to collective prayer. Insofar as the sacred language in the liturgy is primarily directed toward God, it does not especially aim at imparting information in the sense of human communication. Here the language serves rather as a bridge between the profane world and the transcendent God. The sacred language, as a simultaneously human and stylized speech, seeks to create an atmosphere that both reflects and evokes a certain religious attitude in those who pray.[12]

Tendencies toward a conscious separation from everyday language are already demonstrated in the early liturgical texts of the Greek language, where biblical elements of style from the Septuagint along with Hebrew and Aramaic expressions were combined with literary forms of the Hellenistic tradition.[13]

---

10   Cf. Mohrmann, "Sakralsprache," 163f.
11   Cf. Mohrmann, "Sakralsprache," 164.
12   Cf. Mohrmann, "Sakralsprache," 172.
13   Cf. Mohrmann, *Liturgical Latin*, 15, 21–26, 23: "The whole of the earliest Eucharistic terminology is deliberately isolated from the language of everyday life . . . and the modern liturgists who would like to view the earliest Eucharistic celebration as a 'gathering round

The beginnings of the Latin liturgical language

In Rome the Eucharist was originally celebrated in Greek. As already demonstrated in St Paul's Epistle to the Romans, composed in Greek, Christendom had found its first faithful within the Greek-speaking community of this cosmopolitan city, whose inhabitants, for the most part, came from eastern Mediterranean regions. Alongside these were the upper class of Romans who were always anxious to adopt Greek culture. Although the number of Latin-speaking Christians continually grew and Latin gradually became the common language of the Church in Rome by the middle of the second century,[14] apostolic Greek still remained the language of the liturgy, at least the Canon of the Mass, for two centuries.[15]

Latin initially found entrance into the Roman liturgy's readings in the form of translations of the Bible.[16] The Latinization of the liturgy prior to this had already begun in North Africa, where Latin translations of the Bible originated in the middle of the second century. But even these developments were not simply a colloquial element within the divine worship. These texts also possessed a sacred stylizing, insofar as the Latin translations bore a strong biblical complexion through a certain literalism, that is, a close following of the scriptural forms of speech, and in this way they acquired a peculiarly foreign style, soon felt to be holy.[17] The final transition to the Latin liturgical language, having already been initiated in a longer process, was completed in Rome in the middle of the fourth century and was broadly finalized under Pope Damasus I (366–384).[18]

---

the kitchen table' certainly do not find support in the testimony of the earliest terminology."

14 Cf. C. Mohrmann, "Les origines de la latinité chrétienne à Rome," *Études sur le latin* III, 67–126; eadem, *Liturgical Latin*, 27–29; eadem, "Die Rolle des Lateins in der Kirche des Westens," *Theologische Revue* 52 (1956): 1–18, 1f.

15 Cf. C. Mohrmann, "Linguistic Problems in the Early Church": eadem, *Études sur le latin des chrétiens* I (Rome: Edizioni di Storia e Letteratura, 1961), 103–11, 111.

16 Cf. Mohrmann, *Liturgical Latin*, 75.

17 Cf. Mohrmann, "Sakralsprache," 166; eadem, "Rolle des Lateins," 2f.

18 Cf. Mohrmann, *Liturgical Latin*, 44f.; Jungmann, *Missarum sollemnia* I, 65; idem, *The Mass of the Roman Rite* I, 50f.; Th. Klauser, "Der Übergang der römischen Kirche von der griechischen zur lateinischen Liturgiesprache": idem, *Gesammelte Arbeiten zur Liturgiegeschichte, Kirchengeschichte und Christlichen Archäologie*, ed. by E. Dassmann [JAC.E 3] (Münster: Aschendorff Verlag, 1974), 184–94, 185.

What reasons were there for the lateness of this Latinization of the Roman liturgy?[19] Initially, it was the conservative tendency inherent in each liturgy to resist any change in the language of worship and to seek to preserve what was established. The Roman mentality, moreover, always distinguished itself by a strong consciousness of tradition (*tenax antiquitatis*), which cautiously opposed all innovations. Furthermore, an appreciation for the sacred formation of the holy texts was the inheritance of old Roman religiosity. In order to conform to the requirements of a hieratic style, Christian Latinity first had to be perfected to a certain degree and be capable of rising above everyday speech. After the first and second centuries, when the substance of the Christian message stood in the foreground and the instrument of language was still considered or used with a certain indifference, a distinct consciousness awoke at the beginning of the fourth century of the value and meaning of the linguistic form of expression. If the development of a Christian sacred language thoroughly drew on particular elements of style of old Roman traditions,[20] then such an impartial use of Rome's cultural inheritance was conceivable only in the later peacetime of the Church (from 313 on) when the pagan religion no longer presented a serious threat to Christianity; and just as confidently as the Church introduced the spoils of heathen temples into her own basilicas, she made the stylistic forms of ancient prayer texts her own. Finally, the Latinization of the liturgy was part of an extensive project to evangelize the late ancient culture, pursued by the Roman popes of the fourth century, Damasus in particular, by means of substantial construction projects and the creation of a Christian calendar (354).[21] The use of Latin as a sacred language that stylistically tied in with old Roman traditions would especially have won over to the Christian Faith the influential elite of the empire, who at this time had just begun

19   Cf. Mohrmann, *Liturgical Latin*, 45f., 74, 76; eadem, "Notes sur le latin liturgique": eadem, *Études sur le latin des chrétiens* II (Rome: Edizioni di Storia e Letteratura, 1961), 93–108, 97–100; eadem, "Rolle des Lateins," 5–8.

20   Cf. Mohrmann, *Liturgical Latin*, 58–62; eadem, "Notes sur le latin liturgique," 102f.; eadem, "Rolle des Lateins," 7f.; Jungmann, *The Early Liturgy*, 126f.

21   Cf. U. M. Lang, "Rhetoric of Salvation: The Origins of Latin as the Language of the Roman Liturgy," idem (ed.), *The Genius of the Roman Rite. Historical, Theological, and Pastoral Perspectives on Catholic Liturgy* (Chicago / Mundelein, IL: Hillenbrand Books, 2010), 22–44, 32f.

to discover anew their texts of classical literature. The Church had at its disposal a language of prayer whose content was renewed by revelation and at the same time formally bound to the Roman tradition.

The introduction of Latin into the Roman liturgy, then, certainly did not indicate the abandonment of the principle of a sacred language. In that sense, Latinization cannot be understood as an argument for the vernacular, as though with the change of the liturgical language, the Church in Rome were simply accounting for the fact that the majority of the faithful by then were no longer Greek-speaking, but Latin-speaking Christians.[22] The Latin of the liturgy was identical with neither the classical Latin of Cicero nor the colloquial language, Vulgar Latin. It was, at least in the texts of prayers, a highly stylized form of language, which was not readily understandable to the average Roman of the fourth and fifth centuries: "No Roman had ever spoken in the language or style of the Canon or the prayers of the Roman Mass."[23] It was rather a language that sought to awaken the experience of the sacred and to raise man above the things of this world to God. This rising up to God was accomplished neither by a complete renunciation of language (holy silence, *silentium mysticum*) nor in the form of glossolalia, the gift of tongues (cf. 1 Cor 14:2), which no longer possessed its communicative character; rather, it was accomplished by means of a sacred language that drew from biblical sources as well as from the hieratic idiom of pagan Rome and, not least of all, also made use of ancient rhetoric.[24] As a glance at the historical development demonstrates, the Church did not slip Latin on as a garment that could be replaced with another at any time. Rather, the Roman Church artistically forged for herself her own Latin for her liturgy, and in it she uniquely expressed her identity.[25]

---

22   As according to the thesis of Th. Klauser, *A Short History of the Western Liturgy* (London: Oxford University Press, 1969), 21–24.

23   Mohrmann, "Sakralsprache," 166; eadem, *Liturgical Latin*, 53f., 74.

24   Cf. C. Mohrmann, "Relations entre langue et religion," *Études sur le latin* I, 123–37, 137.

25   Cf. A. Schönberger, "Eine *apologia pro latinitate* aus Meisterhand," UVK 33 (2003): 294–318, 302; B. Lécureux, "Latein—die Sakralsprache der römischen Kirche," UVK 31 (2001): 259–84, 276–80; eadem, *Le Latin—langue de l'Église* (Paris: Éditions Pierre Téqui, 1998), 68–72; Viain, *Langues liturgiques*, 369.

Advantages of liturgical Latin

What are the characteristic traits that make Latin, more than any other language, suitable for serving the Roman Church as the official language in liturgy and teaching? Pope Pius XI defined these qualities accurately and succinctly: "The Church ... of its very nature requires a language that is universal, immutable, and non-vernacular."[26]

Universality. The unity of the Latin liturgical language is, first of all, "a manifest and beautiful sign of unity" in the Church.[27] The universality of the Catholic Church, which transcends all national bounds, is expressed in the universality of the Latin language of worship. A uniform liturgical language is capable not only of representing the unity of the Church across peoples, races, and languages, but also of preserving and promoting it. This unity is not only symbolized by Latin, but in a certain way is also effected by it.

The connection of individual churches with Rome, the center of the Universal Church, is manifested and strengthened by the use of this city's native tongue. It can be historically proved that the connection with Rome lessened proportionally as the bond of the common Latin language loosened.[28] The Latin liturgical language opposes such centrifugal tendencies and reinforces the *Romanitas* of the Catholic Church.

If the Constitution on the Liturgy (SC 48) desired "that Christ's faithful, when present at this mystery of faith, should not be there as strangers or silent spectators," it is paradoxically exactly the Latin language of worship

---

26   Pius XI, Apostolic Letter *Officiorum Omnium* (AAS 14 [1922]: 449–58, 452): "*Ecclesia ... sermonem suapte natura requirit universalem, immutabilem, non vulgarem.*" Cf. John XXIII, Apostolic Constitution *Veterum Sapientia* (AAS 54 [1962]: 129–35, 131: "Finally, the Catholic Church has a dignity far surpassing that of every merely human society, for it was founded by Christ the Lord. It is altogether fitting, therefore, that the language it uses should be noble, majestic, and non-vernacular." Trans.: http://www.papalencyclicals.net/John23/j23veterum. htm). For individual characteristics, cf. Viain, *Langues liturgiques*, 368–378; Schönberger, "Eine *apologia pro latinitate*," 309–16; Lécureux, *Latin*, 21–95.

27   Pius XII, *Mediator Dei* (AAS 39:545 / Seasoltz, *Documentation*, 124).

28   Cf. F. Hettinger, *Aus Kirche und Welt* I: Rom und Italien (Freiburg i. Br.: Verlag Herder, [6]1911), 345; H.-L. Barth, "Latein—Universale Kultsprache der Katholischen Kirche": N. Esser (ed.), *Dem Schönen und Heiligen dienen, dem Bösen wehren* (Sinzig: Sankt-Meinrad-Verlag, 1997), 152–64, 157–59. On the correlation between heresy, schism, and the vernacular in the Eastern Church, cf. Schönberger, "Eine *apologia pro latinitate*," 299f.; Viain, *Langues liturgiques*, 345f.

that frequently removes this danger, while the use of the vernacular in many ways reinforces it, when, for example, Catholics in a foreign country assist at a Mass but do not understand the native language. They are then virtually obliged to be present at this mystery of faith as strangers and silent spectators. In an age of mobility, mass-tourism, and globalization, the unity of the language of worship could convey the experience to the faithful that each Catholic is at home in every Catholic church in the world. Everywhere he hears the familiar prayers and chants. Any priest, wheresoever he travels, can celebrate the holy Mass with the faithful at any altar. The common liturgical language lends itself to uniting Catholics of various nations and cultures and to overcoming language barriers.[29] Precisely at such a worship service, at which faithful from all over the world participate, the use of Latin prevents discrimination against any living language or the favoring of one particular nation over another. Rather, it enables all of the participants without exception to praise God in unison.

The Latin language of worship does not simply manifest and produce the unity of the Church that crosses over regions in the present age. Linguistic unity possesses not only a synchronic dimension, but also a diachronic one, since the community of believers spans not only physical space, but also time. Even the previous generations of earlier centuries belonged to this community of faith. Latin is therefore a bond of unity on the horizontal as well as the vertical plane.[30] Latin, as the language of worship, creates a time-transcending unity, as it binds together countless generations of supplicants from a multitude of ages, from over one and a half thousand years, into one common language. The faithful of the twenty-first century pray to God with the same words with which Christians of late antiquity and of the Middle Ages have prayed to God: *Gloria in excelsis Deo, Credo in unum Deum, Agnus Dei*. The words of the Latin liturgical language are, so to speak, imbued with the spiritual experiences of countless saints and mystics.[31] Its centuries-long usage makes the continuity of the Faith tangible.

---

29 Cf. Lécureux, *Latin*, 86: "This is, again, a fact, if not a principle: Latinity and catholicity are practically always synonymous."

30 Cf. Lécureux, *Latin*, 8, 124f.

31 Cf. A. Rosmini, *Die fünf Wunden der Kirche* (Paderborn: Verlag Ferdinand Schöningh, 1971), 29: "the growing trust of someone who knows how to pray to God with the same

Immutability. The immutability of the Latin language of worship also lends itself in a special manner to making the liturgy into an authentic testimony of faith. "The use of the Latin language ... is ... an effective antidote for any corruption of doctrinal truth," wrote Pope Pius XII in his liturgical encyclical *Mediator Dei*.[32] In contrast to modern languages, which are constantly evolving, liturgical Latin is no longer subject to change.[33] While the meaning of words continually changes in a living language, as they receive new nuances or lose their original significance, Latin words everywhere and at all times retain the same meaning. The words that express the most important truths of the Faith must not be allowed to be subjected to different interpretations. In the Apostolic Constitution *Veterum Sapientia*, Pope John XXIII emphasized the dangers to the truths of the Faith that could spring from the changeability of living language, contrasting it with the protective role played by an unchangeable liturgical language:

> Modern languages are liable to change, and no single one of them is superior to the others in authority. If the truths of the Catholic Church were entrusted to an unspecified number of them, the

words, with which through many centuries countless saints and our fathers in Christ have worshiped Him..."

32   Pius XII, *Mediator Dei* (AAS 39:545 / Seasoltz, *Documentation*, 124): "*Latinae linguae usus ... est ... remedium efficax adversus quaslibet germanae doctrinae corruptelas.*" Cf. P. Guéranger, *Institutions liturgiques* III, 73; J.C. Hedley, *The Holy Eucharist* (London / New York: Longmans, Green, 1911), 200: "Had the Church from the beginning adopted the principle of a vernacular Liturgy for each nation or people ... it would have been morally impossible thus to keep the liturgical prayers on a level with the changing and developing language of the peoples of Europe. The task would have been too vast, and too hard to organize. Misunderstanding, heterodoxy, heresy, arising from the incompetence or the willfulness of translators and adaptors, would have taxed the vigilance of the Church's pastors to such an extent that disaster would only have been averted by a standing miracle."

33   Cf. Cf. Lécureux, *Latin*, 22–25. Cf. Horace, *De arte poetica* 60–63 (Bibliotheca Teubneriana, 296f.): "*Ut silvae foliis pronos mutantur in annos, / prima cadunt: ita verborum vetus interit aetas, / et iuvenum ritu florent modo nata vigentque. / debemur morti nos nostraque...*" ("As the forests shed their leaves, as the year declines, and the oldest fall, so perish those former generations of words, while the latest, like infants, are born and thrive. We're destined for death, we and ours..." Trans.: http://www.poetryintranslation.com/PITBR/Latin/HoraceArsPoetica.htm#anchor_Toc98156241).

meaning of these truths, varied as they are, would not be manifest to everyone with sufficient clarity and precision. There would, moreover, be no language that could serve as a common and constant norm by which to gauge the exact meaning of other renderings. But Latin is indeed such a language. It is set and unchanging. It has long since ceased to be affected by those alterations in the meaning of words that are the normal result of daily, popular use.[34]

Thus, in contrast to living languages, liturgical Latin is capable of manifesting and guaranteeing the fundamental immutability of the deposit of Faith (*depositum fidei*). The unvarying form of the language corresponds to the unvarying substance of the Faith. The unchanging Latin language possesses something of the firmness and irreversibility of Catholic dogma. The unchanging liturgical language thus mirrors something of God's eternity. In a certain sense, liturgy is timeless; it transcends the constant growth and decay of the moment. In the liturgy, eternity enters time. A sacred language that is not subject to change suggests an idea of this mystery.

Liturgical Latin is immune to the problems inevitably associated with modern language. Apart from the problem of inadequate, biased, or false translations,[35] the continual changing and development of the vernacular

---

34   John XXIII, *Veterum Sapientia*: "*Si enim catholicae Ecclesiae veritates traderentur vel nonnullis vel multis ex mutabilibus linguis recentioribus, quarum nulla ceteris auctoritate praestaret, sane ex eo consequeretur ut hinc earum vis neque satis significanter neque satis dilucide, qua varietate eae sunt, omnibus pateret; ut illinc nulla communis stabilisque norma haberetur, ad quam ceterarum sensus esset expendendus. Re quidem ipsa, lingua Latina, iamdiu adversus varietates tuta, quas cotidiana populi consuetudo in vocabulorum notionem inducere solet, fixa quidem censenda est et immutabilis*" (AAS 54:131 / trans.: http://www.papalencyclicals.net/ John23/j23veterum.htm).

35   Cf. Viain, *Langues liturgiques* 374: "If heresy does not originate from a translation, it nevertheless profits from it, as a wicked parasite thrives on a diminished and withered organism." Cf. L. Bianchi, *Liturgia. Memoria o istruzioni per l'uso? Studi sulla trasformazione della lingua dei testi liturgici nell'attuazione della riforma* (Casale Monferrato: Edizioni Piemme, 2002); H.-L. Barth, "Tendenziöse Übersetzungen lateinischer Texte aus Liturgie und Lehramt," idem, "*Nichts soll dem Gottesdienst vorgezogen werden*," 50–57; R. Kaschewsky, "Tendenzen in den Orationen des Neuen Missale II. Die deutschen Übersetzungen der Sonn- und Feiertagsorationen," UVK 12 (1982): 89–110; H. Hitchcock, "Authentic Liturgy versus the Tower of Babel: The Dawn of a 'New Era,'" *Faith and Liturgy* (CIEL, 2002); A. Rose, "Réflexions sur le problème des traductions liturgiques," ibid., 321–28.

obliges ever new adaptations and revisions of the liturgical texts.[36] A continual change in the sacred realm, however, contradicts its essence, insofar as the liturgy, at its core, thrives on enduring constancy. The surrender to changing modes of speech is fatal for any liturgy. Perpetual variability has a destabilizing effect on piety, which is, as is well-known, a habit, and therefore requires permanence and consistency.[37] Moreover, changes in the language facilitate the impression that the Faith itself has changed or could change. The enduring constancy of the language of worship and independence from ever-changing "linguistic games" are, however, an impressive testimony of the "faith once delivered to the saints" (*semel traditae sanctis fidei*: Jude 3).

Beauty and transcendence. Finally, as *sermo non vulgaris*, non-vernacular diction, the Latin liturgical language possesses a special dignity, beauty, and transcendence. "Your speech is like the metal of your bells," wrote the poet Gertrude von Le Fort in her *Hymns to the Church*.[38] Here the Church also proves to possess a thorough understanding of human nature, as in this way she helps her faithful to detach themselves from their everyday language, where each word recalls profane realities, and to feel, even sensibly, that "wholly Other" sought by all piety. In colloquial speech, each word typically possesses one exact meaning, which is determined by its everyday use and which inevitably allows the here and now to enter the imagination of one who uses these words.[39] A sacred language, on

---

36   While the Collect for the feast of Corpus Christi experienced no changes for more than five hundred years, in the last thirty years there have been six different versions in the new Italian Missals (1970, 1973, 1983, 1991, 1995, 2002). Cf. P. Siffi, *La Messa di san Pio V. Osservazioni sul Rito Tridentino in risposta ai critici del Motu Proprio* (Genoa / Milan: Marietti, 2007), 59–61. Translations provided in daily missals can afford to be adaptable and revisable because the "weight" of the liturgical worship does not rest on them; they are merely aids to entering into rites of worship that enjoy a permanent linguistic identity.

37   Cf. Viain, *Langues liturgiques*, 374f.

38   G. v. Le Fort, *Hymnen an die Kirche*, 28.

39   Cf. D. Crouan, *Réflexions sur la liturgie. La question de la langue culturelle* (Paris: Éditions Pierre Téqui, 1987), 100–2; idem, *La Messe en latin et en grégorien* (Paris: Éditions Pierre Téqui, 2006), 69: "Everyday language seems far too immersed in the banal to be able to transmit concepts that can be linked to the divine, and to foster a free, deep, and personal dialogue between the soul and the One who transcends it, in the context of an act that is not, strictly speaking, a personal one, since it involves an approach made in Church."

the other hand, alienated from the everyday, can loose these intellectual chains of common ideas and translate man to another world, whether the words transcend intellectual comprehension and permit the experiencing of the otherworldly, or the deep meaning of the words awakens a wealth of associations and resonances. The realization of the sacrifice of the Cross and union with the celestial liturgy demand a language that stands above the banalizing idioms of everyday speech and makes perceptible the mysteries completed on the altar. *Cottidiana vilescunt* runs an ancient proverb: familiarity breeds contempt. The language of worship prevents the desacralization of the liturgical action. It does not sink into trivial ordinariness, but its supernatural meaning is rather illuminated through its rich eloquence. It is not a glaring light, however, in which the sacred language makes the holy action shine; rather, it resembles the mysterious semi-darkness of a Gothic cathedral, which neither fully reveals the mystery to the eyes, nor fully withdraws it. The sacred language spreads a delicate veil over the truths of the Faith, which protects the holy mystery and eludes hasty comprehensibility. "The language, the gestures, the vestments, the rite, everything that surrounds the religious act and that differentiates it from the common and profane, does not lead away from God: on the contrary, it allows Him to be more strongly felt!"[40]

The nobility, majesty, and sacrality of the liturgical language result, not least of all, from the wealth of meaning that the individual terms of the Latin language possess, as well as from the clarity of style that character-izes the prayers, which, in measured and ordered strict trains of thought, gracefully declare before God the concerns of man without verbosity, exuberance of emotion, or ambiguous sentimentality.[41]

Only on the foundation of the Latin language could such literary works of art as the Roman prayers, with their combination of elegance and con-ciseness, have been created.[42] Trained in the system of rules of ancient

---

40 B. Capelle, "Plaidoyer pour le latin," QLP 31 (1950): 65–71, 71.

41 Cf. Lécureux, "Latein," 274–76; eadem, *Latin*, 64–67.

42 Cf. A Benedictine Monk [i.e., G. Calvet], *The Sacred Liturgy* (London: Saint Austin Press, 1999), 82: "perhaps one day we will see academic theses on the rhetorical beauty of the prayers of the Church." M. Mosebach, *Heresy of Formlessness*, 76, refers to *Kindlers Literaturlexikon* IV (1968), col. 2721: "They [the orations] are artifacts of high theological

rhetoric, Roman popes such as Leo the Great, as well as unknown authors, created prayer formulas with sonorous phrases, finely balanced sentences, and solemn rhythms of sequence (*cursus*).[43] The wealth of meaning, the precision, and the harmony of the original Latin cannot be conveyed in any modern language without sacrificing quality.

Comprehensibility and participation. A frequent objection against the use of a sacred language is that it impedes comprehension of the liturgical texts and interferes with the faithful's *participatio actuosa*.[44] The liturgy, however, is not the expression of private piety but the Church's public worship. The liturgy primarily aims at the glorification of God and the sanctification of man. The essence of Catholic worship is latreutic and sacramental. Although the Mass contains "great education" (*magnam eruditionem*) within itself,[45] the faithful's religious education and subjective edification are in no way its primary ends. These, rather, comprise a secondary element that is only the consequence of the objective action. The demand for a comprehensible vernacular language more importantly underestimates that in the Mass, inexpressible mysteries are accomplished that no man can perfectly comprehend. This mysterious character of the Mass should find expression in a sacred language. A language that is not commonly understood suggests to the faithful that they stand before a mystery that eludes total transparency. In contrast, vernacular language counterfeits an understanding that is absolutely not real. Instead, the oft-requested catechesis and sermons to the faithful, explaining the sense

---

expressiveness, fashioned according to the canons of Late Latin art prose, of monumental simplicity and acute precision. They are so perfect that they remained essentially unchanged, and today they still constitute the form of prayer of the Catholic Church."

43 Cf. Klauser, *A Short History of the Western Liturgy*, 37–44; Mohrmann, *Liturgical Latin*, 66–68; H. Reinfelder, "Zum Stil der lateinischen Orationen," JLW 11 (1931): 20–34; M. G. Haessly, *Rhetoric in the Sunday Collects of the Roman Missal: With Introduction, Text, Commentary and Translation*, Diss. Ursuline College for Women, Cleveland, OH (St Louis, MO: The Manufacturers Printery, 1938); J. Pascher, *Eucharistia*, 365 (example of the *cursus*); J. Cochez, "La structure rythmique des Oraisons," in *La Préparation de l'Eucharistie*, 140–50.

44 Cf. Schönberger, "Eine *apologia pro latinitate*," 316f.; Viain, *Langues liturgiques*, 378f.; Godefroy, "Langues liturgiques," 2589f.; Hedley, *Holy Eucharist*, 201f.

45 Council of Trent, sess. XXII, cap. 8 (DH 1749): "Although the Mass contains much instruction for the faithful, the Fathers did not think that it should be celebrated in the vernacular indiscriminately (can. 9)."

and meaning of the rites and prayers, are more efficacious than seeking such an alleged understanding of liturgical texts by the use of the native tongue.[46] Since the Church has held fast to the Latin liturgical language, she has ever thought very highly of the mental capabilities even of the common people, who, with suitable instruction, are certainly capable of attentively following a Latin Mass. Whoever disputes this possibility thinks too little of the faithful's readiness to learn.[47] There is a wealth of impressive examples of how strongly the parishioner's mentality was formed by the Latin liturgy over the centuries[48] and how little the Latin was a serious obstacle to actively celebrating this liturgy.[49]

This profound influence results not least of all from the fact that in addition to a literal understanding of the liturgical texts, there is also an intuitive, holistic conception of the holy action. The participation here is not fixated on the word or limited to the intellect, but is rather the interaction of words and gestures, of colors and sounds, whereby intellect, sense, and disposition are simultaneously addressed. In this way, even

46   Council of Trent, sess. XXII, cap. 8 (DH 1749): "The holy Council ... orders that pastors and all who have the care of souls must frequently, either by themselves or through others, explain during the celebration of the Masses some of the readings of the Mass and, among other things, give some instruction about the mystery of this most holy sacrifice, especially on Sundays and feast days." *Pontificale Romanum*. Editio princeps (1595–1596), ed. by M. Sodi and A. M. Triacca [Monumenta Liturgica Concilii Tridentini 1] (Vatican City: Libreria Editrice Vaticana, 1997), 622 (617 in the original): Ordo ad synodum. Cf. P. Guéranger, *Institutions liturgiques* III, 81–83.

47   Cf. T. Casini, *The Torn Tunic: Letter of a Catholic on the "Liturgical Reform"* (Hawthorne, CA: Christian Book Club of America, s.a.), 28f.; R. Amerio, *Iota unum. A Study of the Changes in the Catholic Church in the XXth Century*, trans. J. Parsons (Kansas City, MO: Sarto House, 1996), 612: "The stamping out of Latin is, furthermore, at odds with the egalitarian spirit which pervades the modern world and the modern Church. Egalitarians want to raise the cultural level of the masses, but the abandonment of Latin displays a kind of despising of the people of God, as if they were unworthy in their coarseness to be elevated to a level at which they could appreciate the sublime and poetical, and it damns them instead to drag everything down to the lowest common denominator."

48   Cf. Amerio, *Iota unum*, 613; Guéranger, *Institutions liturgiques* III, 77f.

49   G. Morin, "Vom Geiste und der Zukunft der katholischen Liturgie," *Hochland* 25 (1928): 252–68, 259, explains how, thanks to the active liturgical life of his Norman homeland, "at seventeen I had learned by heart, complete and by myself, the most complicated pieces of the *Antiphonarium* and the *Graduale*, without ever having owned either of the thick volumes containing the words and music." Cf. Spaemann, "Bemerkungen eines Laien," 75–102, 82f.; J. H. Newman, *Loss and Gain* (London: Burns & Oates, 1962), 243.

the believer who has never learned Latin, but has frequently heard it, can translate the liturgical language into the "dialect of his heart" and arrive at a deeper understanding.[50] Thus Pope Pius XII specifically approved of forms of liturgical participation that do not directly follow the texts of the celebration of the Mass, but are related to the meaning of the rites.[51] Already in 1526, the theological College of the Sorbonne in Paris, which at that time possessed great authority in assessing theological questions, censured the critical statements made by the humanist Erasmus of Rotterdam on the prayer of the common people in a language unintelligible to them. It defended the practice of the Church and defined the meaning of the liturgical prayers not exclusively as intellectual instruction, but especially as the affective orientation toward God.[52]

---

50   Cf. Crouan, *La Messe en latin*, 59f.: "Therefore, when they are assisted, emphasized, amplified, expressed by the corresponding gestures of the liturgical rite . . . the Latin words, arriving at the ear of the faithful, become capable of triggering a mechanism of spontaneous translation of a language never learned. The faithful then translates into his 'cordial dialect'—the dialect of his heart—this Latin never learned but so often heard."

51   Cf. Pius XII, *Mediator Dei* (AAS 39:561 / Seasoltz, *Documentation*, 136): "Who, then, would say . . . that all these Christians cannot participate in the Mass nor share its fruits? On the contrary, they can adopt some other method which proves easier for certain people; for instance, they can lovingly meditate on the mysteries of Jesus Christ or perform other exercises of piety or recite prayers which, though they differ from the sacred rites, are still essentially in harmony with them."

52   Cf. C. du Plessis d'Argentré, *Collectio iudiciorum de novis erroribus* II (Paris: Cailleau, 1728), 62: "*Per quae sane constat non in sola verborum intelligentia fructum orationis consistere; perniciosum quoque esse errorem existimantium solum ad erudiendum intellectum fidei* [recte: *fieri*, according to M. Fiedrowicz], *orationem vocalem, cum praecipue fiat talis oratio ad inflammandum affectum, ut pio et devoto animo in Deum modis praedictis se erigendo mens reficiatur, et obtinendo quae petit sua intentione non frustretur, mereatur itidem intellectus illuminationem quemadmodum et caetera alia utilia aut necessaria, qui nimirum fructus longe uberiores sunt, quam sola verborum intelligentia, quae absque excitatione affectus in Deum, parum affert utilitatis*" (quoted in Guéranger, *Institutions liturgiques* III, 164; cf. 122–24) [Therefore it is perfectly clear that the benefit of the liturgical prayer consists not only in the understanding of the words; it is a dangerous error to think that vocal prayer serves only to educate the intellect. On the contrary, such prayer mainly contributes to inflame the affections, so that the worshipper, rising up with a pious and devout heart to God in the aforementioned ways, will be edified, and obtaining his wishes, he will not be frustrated in his intentions; and in addition, the intellect acquires illumination together with other useful or necessary things, all of which benefits are far more abundant than the understanding of the words alone, which does not achieve much advantage without the arousal of the affection for God].

Questioning and defending the liturgical language. Since the time of the Reformation, the words of the Apostle Paul have been used to support a general comprehensibility of the texts used in divine worship: "In the church I had rather speak five words with my understanding, that I may instruct others also, than ten thousand words in a tongue" (1 Cor 14:18).[53] This statement was originally directed against the glossolalia of the charismatics in Corinth. Ambrosiaster, an unnamed commentator on St Paul at the time of Pope Damasus (366–384),[54] applied the Apostle's words to any incomprehensible foreign language when he pleaded for the liturgical use of the vernacular in Rome, that is, the transition from Greek to Latin.[55]

St Paul's words, however, were directed only against inherently unintelligible discourse, such as glossolalia, which cannot edify the congregation; he in no way eliminated the possibility of a sacred language that is comprehensible in principle.[56] Ambrosiaster, writing in Rome, was certainly referring to Latin-speakers who sang in Greek without understanding the words, though he added that this was ultimately legitimate: "The Spirit given in baptism knows what the soul is praying when it speaks or prays in an unknown tongue."[57] This early Christian witness begins by proving

---

53 Cf. Paul VI, "Allocution in the General Audience of Nov. 26, 1969," *L'Osservatore Romano*, Nov. 27, 1969.

54 Ambrosiaster, *In epistulam primam ad Corinthios* 14,13–19 (CSEL 81/2, 152–55). Cf. L. Lentner, "Das geschichtliche Phänomen der Kultsprache": Th. Bogler (ed.), *Sakrale Sprache und kultischer Gesang* [LuM 37] (Maria Laach: Ars Liturgica Buch- und Kunstverlag, 1965), 37–61, 45f.

55 Thus Klauser, "Übergang zur lateinischen Liturgiesprache," 188–90; idem, *A Short History of the Western Liturgy*, 22f.; A. Fürst, *Die Liturgie der Alten Kirche. Geschichte und Theologie* (Münster: Aschendorff Verlag, 2008), 52.

56 Cf. Barth, "Latein," 160; Lécureux, *Latin* 102; Z.-C. Jourdain, *La Sainte Eucharistie* II (Paris: Hippolyte Walzer, Libraire-Éditeur, 1897), 548–50; L.A. Bocquillot, *Traité historique de la liturgie sacrée ou de la Messe* (Paris: Chez Anisson, Directeur de l'Imprimerie Royale, 1701), book I, chap. 14: "This is so clear that I cannot be surprised enough that the Protestant ministers found among them rather simple and credulous minds, to make them believe that St Paul had in advance condemned the present use of all the churches in the world" (quoted in Jourdain, *La Sainte Eucharistie* II, 550).

57 Ambrosiaster, *In epistulam primam ad Corinthios* 14,14f. (CSEL 81/2, 153): "*Spiritus ergo, qui datur in baptismo, scit quid oret animus, dum loquitur aut perorat lingua sibi ignota; mens autem, qui est animus, sine fructu est. Quem enim potest habere profectum, qui ignorat quae loquatur? . . . Cum quis hac lingua loquitur quam novit, tam spiritu quam mente orat, quia non solum spiritus eius, quem dixi datum in baptismate, scit quod oratur, sed et animus*

the coexistence of an everyday language and one of worship. Then he clearly distinguishes between a spiritual and an intellectual dimension of prayer. He who prays in a familiar language prays with spirit (*spiritus*) and intellect (*mens*). He who prays in a foreign language is also able to pray. Owing to the grace of baptism there is the possibility of a spiritual prayer, even if the intellect is not directly included in the process. The spiritual merit of Christian prayer is independent of its intellectual merit. While the so-called Ambrosiaster desired the use of a Latin liturgical language in Rome for the sake of comprehension, he simultaneously emphasized the legitimacy of a sacred language that is — at first — foreign to the believer.[58]

Until the Reformation, the liturgical language question did not arise either practically or theoretically in the Western Church.[59] Liturgical Latin was supported by the common use of this language in higher education, ecclesiastical and governmental administration, and cultural life in general. Only when the living medieval Latin vanished from educated circles and yielded to Humanist Latin, oriented toward classical antiquity, did academics like Erasmus of Rotterdam in the sixteenth century question the exclusive use of liturgical Latin in favor of the principle of common comprehensibility.[60] Such efforts, however, had no great consequences, as in the meantime Protestant reformers from this region had carried out many dramatic changes to the practice of divine worship. The protest against a language no longer understood by the faithful and the demand for a celebration of divine worship in the vernacular were the same aspirations of all of the heresies of the Middle Ages (Albigensian, Waldensian, Wycliffite, and Hussite) that preceded the reformers of the sixteenth century (Luther,

---

simili modo, et de psalmo non ignoratur" [The Spirit, which is given in baptism, does know that for which the mind prays, when the tongue speaks or prays in an unknown language; but the intellect, which is of the mind, remains without benefit. For what profit can someone have who does not know what he is saying? . . . When someone is speaking in the language he knows, he prays in the Spirit as well as in his intellect, because not only does his Spirit, which (as I said) was given in baptism, know that for which he prays, but the mind likewise, and he is not ignorant about the psalm].

58 Cf. Mohrmann, *Liturgical Latin*, 49f.; eadem, "Notes sur le latin liturgique," 98f.

59 Cf. Viain, *Langues liturgiques*, 352.

60 Cf. Godefroy, "Langues liturgiques," 2584f.; Lentner, "Phänomen der Kultsprache," 54f.; Mohrmann, "Sakralsprache," 170.

Zwingli, and Calvin) and prepared the way for Protestantism.[61] For its pro-ponents, the introduction of the native language was indispensable, insofar as it accustomed the people to the fact that profound changes to the liturgy were indeed possible.[62] Where the Eucharist was no longer considered to be a sacrifice and no longer possessed its primary character of homage, but rather had only a didactic and edifying function; where there was no longer an intermediary priesthood, but rather only the guidance of divine worship by a delegate or representative of the congregation; and where the sacraments no longer operated through their mere execution (*ex opere operato*), but rather only through the faith of the recipient, inspired by the Word—in such a situation the sacred language must yield to the vernacular, which sought to instruct, and which enabled a sort of "concelebration" by the entire congregation.

In order to confront mistaken ideas and defend the Catholic understand-ing of worship and sacrament, the Church felt compelled at the Council of Trent to condemn the requirement that "Mass should be celebrated only in the vernacular" (can. 9)[63] and to advocate Latin as the liturgical language,[64] whose perpetuation was a visible expression of the Holy Mass's primary character of worship and of the fact that sacramental grace was

61 Cf. L. Eisenhofer, *Handbuch der katholischen Liturgik* I (Freiburg i. Br.: Verlag Herder, 1932), 155–59; V. Thalhofer, *Handbuch der katholischen Liturgik* I (Freiburg i. Br.: Verlag Herder, 1883), 408–10; A. Doerner, *Sentire cum Ecclesia* (Mönchengladbach: Kühlen, 1941), 336f.; idem, "Die lateinische Kultsprache—und die Gegner der Kirche," UVK 18 (1988): 216–37; Godefroy, "Langues liturgiques," 2585f.; Guéranger, *Institutions liturgiques* III, 155–59.

62 Cf. M. Davies, *Cranmer's Godly Order*, 163: "The introduction of the vernacular even before the imposition of the new services was, in itself, 'indeed a revolution.' It changed the entire ethos of the Mass, and proved to be an effective instrument for revolutionary change as it accustomed the people to the idea that radical changes could be made in the way that they worshipped. The principal feature of the Catholic liturgy had been stability."

63 Sess. XXII, can. 9 (DH 1759): A direct reply to the teachings of Calvin, who stated, "the Mass ought to be celebrated in no other language than the vernacular—one which all understand (*missam non nisi in lingua vulgari, quam omnes intelligant, celebrare debere*)." Cf. Lentner, "Phänomen der Kultsprache," 57.

64 Sess. XXII, cap. 8 (DH 1749). Cf. H. A. P. Schmidt, *Liturgie et langue vulgaire. Le problème de la langue liturgique chez les premiers réformateurs et au Concile de Trente* [Analecta Grego-riana 53] (Rome: Aedes Universitatis Gregorianae, 1950); Th. Freudenberger, "Die Messliturgie in der Volkssprache im Urteil des Trienter Konzils": R. Bäumer (ed.), *Reformatio Ecclesiae*. Festschrift E. Iserloh (Paderborn: Verlag Ferdinand Schöningh, 1980), 679–98; Godefroy, "Langues liturgiques," 2585f.; Lentner, "Phänomen der Kultsprache," 55–60.

not principally due to subjective faith, but rather to God's operation, mediated by the priest. Further deliberations by the Council Fathers in support of the Latin liturgical language, though they did not find their way into the official decrees, nevertheless show other arguments behind the Council's decision:

> The Latin language, in which Masses are celebrated in the West, is by far the most suitable, especially since it is common to many nations. There appears to be no doubt that if Masses were performed in the common language of each individual people, the divine mysteries would be treated with less reverence. There is also a danger that various errors could then develop in many translations and could allow it to appear that the various mysteries of our Faith, which are wholly simple, are diverse.[65]

Rationalistic tendencies in the eighteenth and nineteenth century once again prompted Catholic Enlightenment philosophers in Germany and Josephinist Austria to demand the introduction of the vernacular into divine worship.[66] According to the ideals of the Enlightenment, Christianity was reduced to an institution for the promotion of morality and humanitarianism; since divine worship was understood as primarily a place of moralizing instruction, a sacred language proper to worship had no right to exist. The decrees of the Synod of Pistoia (1768), which sought to introduce profound liturgical reforms — including the strict introduction of the vernacular, as demanded by the French Jansenists, among others — were

---

65   Sess. XXII (Aug. 6, 1562), cap. 4 (CT VIII [Freiburg i. Br.: Verlag Herder, 1919], 753).

66   Cf. Thalhofer, *Handbuch der katholischen Liturgik* I, 108–16; see for example A. Vierbach, *Die liturgischen Anschauungen des Vitus Anton Winter. Ein Beitrag zur Geschichte der Aufklärung* [Münchener Studien zur historischen Theologie 9] (Munich: Verlag J. Kösel & Verlag Friedrich Pustet, 1929), 90–92. Despite a certain affinity to the ideas of the Enlightenment, Bishop J.M. Sailer realized the problem of too high expectations concerning the vernacular language: "Whoever wants to reform divine worship should start by educating enlightened, godly priests.... Do not expect too much from the German language.... With all the new hymn-books and liturgical experiments, the Protestant churches are getting more and more empty. The same may happen to ours, too. I fear that we will drive out our old churchgoers without gaining much by the newly attracted." J.M. Sailer, *Neue Beiträge zur Bildung des Geistlichen*, Sämtliche Werke 19 (Sulzbach: Seidel, 1839), 353, 355, 366.

completely controlled by this rationalistic spirit. Pope Pius VI rejected the propositions of that Tuscan national synod with the bull *Auctorem Fidei* of August 28, 1794, and condemned the claims of the Jansenist Quesnel, which were incorporated into the documents, that the use of a sacred language deprived the common people of the possibility of uniting themselves with the voice of the entire Church and contradicted the apostolic practice and God's own intention.[67]

During the twentieth century, it was primarily Pope Pius XII who emphasized the irreplaceable value of the Latin liturgical language as "a manifest and beautiful sign of unity, as well as an effective antidote for any corruption of doctrinal truth."[68] While the pope did concede the use of the vernacular for the other liturgical rites,[69] he sharply criticized the expansion of this practice to the celebration of Mass.[70] Pope John XXIII also decreed in his Apostolic Constitution *Veterum Sapientia* that Latin was the compulsory language of worship, as well as the Catholic Church's language of administration and scholarship.[71] Along the same lines, the provisions of Vatican II's Constitution on the Liturgy indicate: "Particular law remaining in force, the use of the Latin language is to be preserved in the Latin rites."[72] In the subsequent statement that "the use of the mother tongue ... may be of great advantage to the people" (SC 36:2; cf. 54), the Council Fathers referred to the doctrinal portion of divine worship

---

67   DH 2666: "No. 66. The proposition that asserts that 'it is contrary to the apostolic practice and the counsels of God not to prepare easier ways of uniting the voice of the people with that of the whole Church'; if understood <to mean> that the use of the common language should be introduced into the liturgical prayers, <is> false, rash, destructive to the order prescribed for the celebration of the mysteries, easily productive of numerous evils." Cf. Eisenhofer, *Handbuch der katholischen Liturgik* I, 158; A. Gerhards, "Die Synode von Pistoia 1786 und ihre Reform des Gottesdienstes": M. Klöckener / B. Kranemann (eds.), *Liturgiereformen — Historische Studien zu einem bleibenden Grundzug des christlichen Gottesdienstes* I (Münster: Aschendorff Verlag, 2002), 496–510, 501, 508.

68   *Mediator Dei* (AAS 39:545 / Seasoltz, *Documentation*, 124).

69   Ibid.: "*In non paucis tamen ritibus vulgati sermonis usurpatio valde utilis apud populum exsistere potest.*"

70   *Mediator Dei* (AAS 39:544 / Seasoltz, *Documentation*, 124).

71   *Veterum Sapientia*, in AAS 54 [1962]: 129–35 / trans.: *On Latin as the Official Language of the Church* (Washington, DC: National Catholic Welfare Conference, 1962).

72   SC 36,1: "*Linguae latinae usus, salvo particulari iure, in Ritibus latinis servetur.*" Trans.: *Documents on the Liturgy, 1963–1979*, 11.

(Epistle and Gospel) and by no means to the celebration of the Mass in general, as demonstrated by the remarks that follow in the document. By farther-reaching concessions to the local language,[73] the majority of the Council Fathers had in mind particular situations in individual mission countries,[74] and not, there can be no doubt, a virtual abandonment of the language of worship throughout the Universal Church.[75]

Biblical translations in the *Missale Romanum*. The majority of biblical texts in the Roman liturgy of the Mass are taken from the Vulgate created by St Jerome.[76] One exception is the Book of Psalms, with which the learned Church Father dealt in various attempts as translator, having been charged by Pope Damasus with a revision of the insufficient older Latin translations (*Vetus Latina*). Jerome based his first text revision (383) on the "common edition" (κοινὴ ἔκδοσις, *koinē ekdosis*) of the Septuagint, the Greek translation of the Old Testament. For this first cursory revision, which changed the texts already naturalized in the liturgy as little as possible and which was limited to the correction of obvious errors, the name *Psalterium Romanum* first became common in the mid-eighteenth century.[77] This *Psalterium* was used in the liturgy of the city of Rome until the time of Pope Pius V and afterwards was still used for the Divine Office

---

73 SC 54: "Wherever a more extended use of the mother tongue within the Mass appears desirable, the regulation laid down in art. 40 of this Constitution is to be observed." Trans.: *Documents on the Liturgy, 1963–1979*, 15.

74 Cf. Casini, *The Torn Tunic*, 84: "But also here you yourself made a condition, that places should be taken into account [*pro conditione locorum*]. I am sure I do not know whom you had in mind — Hottentots, Zulus, the Mau-Mau, Red Indians? — any but the inhabitants of the land of Cicero and Virgil, where 'to speak Latin' still means, in popular parlance, 'to speak plainly.'"

75 For further development cf. Barth, *Die Mär vom antiken Kanon*, 76–85; L. Salleron, *La nouvelle Messe* (Paris: Nouvelles éditions latines, ²1981), 19–22, 73–94; M. Davies, *Pope Paul's New Mass*, 368–76; idem, *Pope John's Council*, 331–38, 368–70.

76 Cf. Eisenhofer, *Handbuch der katholischen Liturgik* I, 161; Thalhofer, *Handbuch der katholischen Liturgik* I, 404; idem, *Erklärung der Psalmen und der im römischen Brevier vorkommenden biblischen Cantica, mit besonderer Rücksicht auf deren liturgischen Gebrauch* (Regensburg: Verlag Manz, 1914), 15–17; F. Stummer, *Einführung in die lateinische Bibel* (Paderborn: Verlag Ferdinand Schöningh, 1928), 80–88.

77 On the controversial discussion of whether the Roman Psalter is in fact identical with St Jerome's first recension of the Psalms, cf. A. Robert / A. Feuillet, *Einleitung in die Heilige Schrift* I. Allgemeine Einleitungsfragen und Altes Testament (Wien / Freiburg / Basel: Verlag Herder, ²1966), 595n306.

of St Peter's. However, texts from the Roman *Psalterium* can still be found in the chants (Introit, Gradual, Tract, Offertory, and Communion) of Sundays and feasts of older origin,[78] as well as in antiphons and responsories from older offices in the Breviary, where the texts from St Jerome's second recension of the Psalms (386) could not match the older, familiar melodies, or where these were regarded as unchangeable.[79] For this second revision of the *Vetus Latina* Psalter (386), St Jerome, residing in Bethlehem at the time, used the so-called Hexaplaric recension of the Septuagint — an adaptation of the Greek text of the Bible produced by Origen between 228 and 245, which guaranteed a greater authenticity of the Greek version of the Old Testament books by means of further translations.[80] Because Jerome's second revision of the Psalms, which remained equally true to the original Greek and to the "*lingua rustica*" of the previous Latin translation "in order not to discourage the reader's interest by excessive novelty,"[81] was first used in Gaul, it received the name of *Psalterium Gallicanum* during the ninth century. From Gaul, this *Psalterium* gained circulation throughout the entire Church. Owing to its inclusion in the Vulgate and in the Roman Breviary, it gained a special importance.[82] Despite occasional shortcomings

78   See also, for example, the Introit antiphon (*Vetus Latina*) for the Third Mass of Christmas: "*Puer natus est nobis, et filius datus est nobis, cuius imperium super humerum eius; et vocabitur nomen eius magni consilii Angelus.*" Cf. Is 9:6 Vulg.: "*Parvulus enim natus est nobis, et filius datus est nobis; et factus est principatus super humerum eius; et vocabitur nomen eius Admirabilis, Consiliarius, Deus fortis.*"

79   The Missals which appeared in Venice since 1596, which consistently featured the later Vulgate texts, were placed on the Index.

80   Cf. B. Botte, "Les anciennes versions de la Bible," MD 53 (1958): 88–109, 95; L. Mortari (ed.), *Il Salterio della Tradizione. Versione del Salterio Greco dei LXX* (Turin: Piero Gribaudi editore, 1983), 26n71.

81   Jerome, *Epistula* 106,12 (CSEL 55, 255): "*Ubicumque sensus idem est, veterum interpretum consuetudinem mutare noluimus, ne nimia novitate lectoris studium terreremus.*" Cf. A. Thibaut, *La révision hexaplaire de saint Jérôme: Richesses et déficiences des anciens psautiers latins* [Collectanea Biblica Latina 13] (Rome / Vatican City: Abbaye St Jerome, 1959), 107–49, 146; C. Mohrmann, "The New Latin Psalter: Its Diction and Style," *Études sur le latin* II, 109–32, 111: "The greatest stress was laid upon liturgical conservativism"; E. Pannier, "Psaumes (Livre des)," *Dictionnaire de la Bible* 5 (1912): 807–38, 828.

82   A later translation of the Psalms, the so-called *Psalterium Pianum* or the "Bea Psalter," based on the original Hebrew texts, was issued by order of Pope Pius XII through the Pontifical Biblical Institute, and was authorized (*si libuerit*) for the liturgical office by the Motu Proprio *In Cotidianis Precibus* (AAS 37 [1945]: 65–67 / Seasoltz, *Documentation*, 104–7)

and some passages that are difficult to understand, this translation possesses an incomparable significance by reason of its centuries-long usage, whereby it has shaped the prayer of countless generations as well as the language and literature of the entire Western Church.[83] Moreover, this *Psalterium* unites the Western Church with the Eastern Church, insofar as Psalms is the one book of the Old Testament not translated from Hebrew, but rather from Greek.[84] Finally, this *Psalterium* is based on that version of the Psalms quoted by the Evangelists in the New Testament, especially in the accounts of the Passion and Resurrection, so that ultimately the Vulgate Psalms express the unity of the Old and New Testament.[85] The third and last Psalm translation by St Jerome (392), which was the first based on the Hebrew texts (*Psalterium secundum Hebraeos*), could not be received into the liturgy in place of the *Psalterium Gallicanum*, as the latter was already deeply rooted in the Latin Church's divine worship, and even minor variations of familiar wording in the text provoked fierce resistance by the faithful, according to St Augustine.[86] St Jerome himself was thoroughly aware of the various requirements that dictated the liturgical use

---

on May 24, 1945, though it was never prescribed. Cf. A. Bea, *La nuova traduzione latina del salterio: origine e spirito* (Roma: Pilotta, 1945). Critical of the break with Christian Latinity, which was abandoned in favor of the classical style for the purpose of a supposedly easier comprehensibility, was C. Mohrmann, "The New Latin Psalter," 109–32; eadem, "Quelques observations linguistiques à propos de la nouvelle version latine du psautier," *Études sur le latin* III, 196–225; "Le Nouveau Psautier," MD 5 (1946): 60–106; Reid, *Organic Development*, 131–33.

83 Cf. Mohrmann, "The New Latin Psalter," 111f.: "The *Gallicanum* has great beauty, a beauty consecrated by its agelong use in the Church's liturgy and one which is embedded as an inalienable possession in the religious thought and sentiment of the West. From the fourth century down to our own day this version of the psalms has left its imprint on the language and literature of our Western world. These are traditional values that should not be despised, and when people speak scornfully of the positive 'nonsense sentences' of the *Psalterium Gallicanum*—there are really very few of these—they should reflect that generations and generations have been so impressed by the sheer beauty of this version emanating from the infancy of Western Christianity that they have little difficulty in putting up with its occasional unintelligibility."

84 Cf. Mortari (ed.), *Salterio della Tradizione*, 31; S. Heitz, "Vorwort": *Mysterium der Anbetung. Göttliche Liturgie und Stundengebet der Orthodoxen Kirche* I (Cologne: Luthe-Verlag, 1996), xxf.

85 Cf. Mortari (ed.), *Salterio della Tradizione*, 35f.

86 Augustine, *Epistula* 71,5 (CSEL 23, 253 / Augustine, *Letters*, trans. by R. J. Teske, *The Works of St Augustine* II/1 [Hyde Park, NY: New City Press, 2001], 284).

of biblical texts on the one hand and biblical argumentation against the Jews on the other hand.[87]

Besides respect for the traditional texts, there were theological reasons for preserving the translation of the Psalms that followed the Septuagint. The translation into Greek that originated in the mid-third century before Christ during the Hellenic Diaspora of the Jews substantially differed in several places from the original Hebrew text.[88] It reflected an advanced stage of revelation that possessed a distinct expectation of the Messiah, a universal perspective of salvation, as well as a deepened eschatology, or hope of resurrection, and thus presented a kind of "preparation for the Gospel" (*praeparatio evangelica*).[89] The Septuagint "forms a new text of the Old Testament," and is an interpretation of the sacred text, a sacred text itself, and a source of new theological notions.[90] In many cases, the Septuagint's wording alone can indicate why and in what sense the Church adopted and interpreted a specific text. Not infrequently it is the variation from the Hebrew text that constitutes the reason for the use of a psalm in a particular place in the liturgy.[91]

---

87 Jerome, *Praefatio in Librum Psalmorum iuxta Hebraeos*: Biblia Sacra iuxta Vulgatam Versionem [ed. by R. Weber and B. Fischer] (Stuttgart: Deutsche Bibelgesellschaft, ³1983), 769: "*aliud sit in ecclesiis Christo credentium Psalmos legere, aliud Iudaeis singula verba calumniantibus respondere.*"

88 Not infrequently does the Septuagint actually present a better tradition than the later Masoretes, who, only beginning in the sixth century after Christ, codified definitively, by means of vocalization for instance, the Hebrew text that consisted only of consonants (radicals), and thus often had multiple meanings.

89 Cf. Mortari (ed.), *Salterio della Tradizione*, 37–52; G. Bertram, "Praeparatio evangelica in der Septuaginta," *Vetus Testamentum* 7 (1957): 225–49; H.-L. Barth, *Ist die traditionelle lateinische Messe antisemitisch?* [Brennpunkt Theologie 7] (Altötting: Sarto-Verlag, 2007), 143–51; idem, *Ipsa conteret. Maria die Schlangenzertreterin: Philologische und theologische Überlegungen zum Protoevangelium (Gn 3,15)* (Ruppichteroth: Canisius-Werk, 2000), 203–7, 233–40.

90 G. Bertram, "Der Sprachschatz der Septuaginta und des hebräischen Alten Testamentes," *Zeitschrift für die Alttestamentliche Wissenschaft*, NF 16 (1939): 85–101, 101; Mortari (ed.), *Salterio della Tradizione*, 35, 44.

91 Thus, for example, the Introit verse from Ps 138:17 (Vulg.) for the feast of an Apostle: "*Mihi autem nimis honorati sunt amici tui, Domine: nimis confortatus est principatus eorum*" ("Thy friends, O God, are made exceedingly honorable; their principality is exceedingly strengthened"); cf. by contrast Ps 139:17 according to the Jerusalem Bible: "How hard for me to grasp your thoughts, how many, God, there are!" The same is true for the Introit antiphon from Ps 138:18 (Vulg.) for Easter Sunday: "*Resurrexi et adhuc tecum sum*" ("I arose, and am

The remaining Old Testament texts of the Roman Missal, especially from the Prophets, follow the Vulgate text that St Jerome translated directly from the Hebrew in 392 (not Baruch, Wisdom, Sirach, and I–II Maccabees). In spite of all of his scholarly efforts to achieve a faithful rendering of the Hebrew text (*hebraica veritas*), St Jerome respected the devotion of wider circles to the traditional biblical text, especially for liturgically and dogmatically relevant texts and phrases, as they were familiar from the Septuagint.[92]

The Vulgate forms an inalienable component of the Latin Church's tradition. Since the first centuries it was used not only in the liturgy, but also by the Church Fathers, councils, theologians, and canon lawyers of the Middle Ages.[93] The Council of Trent decreed the authority and authenticity of the Vulgate in public readings, disputations, sermons, and exegeses, and gave reason for the theological, not philological, inerrancy of this translation, with its centuries-long use in the Church.[94] The Vulgate text thus embeds the classical Roman liturgy harmoniously and indissolubly in the overall structure of this tradition, in linguistic terms as well.

Furthermore, the Vulgate also possesses a specific character that gives an adequate form of expression to the mysteries of the liturgy. Not infrequently it was poets who sensitively noticed the inimitable peculiarity of this translation of the Bible:

> Aside from Messianic texts as such, which contemporary critics and translators are making every effort to diminish in number and importance, the Scriptures contain many allusions and faint echoes to delight hearts and ears made sensitive by love. For God was willing to confide many things to us only through whispers.

still with Thee"); cf. by contrast Ps 139:18 according to the Jerusalem Bible: "If I come to an end, I am still with you." See Shaw, *Liturgical Restoration*, 151–59.

92 Cf. Thibaut, *Revision hexaplaire*, 146.

93 Cf. P. Salmon, "Introduction," *Richesses et déficiences des anciens psautiers latins*, 5–21, 20: "The official Bible offered to all has always remained the Vulgate, not by the fact of a narrow conservatism, but because this text was part of the Tradition. Used since the first centuries in the liturgy, in the councils, in the official acts of the Magisterium, by the Holy Fathers, the theologians, the canonists, the Vulgate entered the treasury of the Church: it is now part of these acquired values whose entirety and variety constitute her richness."

94 DH 1506.

From this point of view, nothing can ever replace our matchless Vulgate. All else is flat, cold, and coarse by contrast—like Virgil translated by a fourth-year student.... We are indeed fortunate to have such a translation of the Bible as the Vulgate. I personally am almost willing to consider this poetic monument the masterpiece of that Latin language.... The test of bread is nourishment, the test of a remedy is healing, and the test of life is animation. The Vulgate has always proved itself to be, for saints and sinners alike, an inexhaustible source of instruction, enthusiasm, consolation, and enlightenment. It is something like the Eucharist, which is the root of paradise and the very language of our intercourse with God.[95]

GREGORIAN CHANT

Formation

Gregorian chant is the unison liturgical song of the Church in the Latin language, generally unaccompanied by musical instruments. Its treasury contains thousands of songs that developed over the centuries. For the majority of these pieces, the names of the composers are as little known as the exact time and the exact place of their origin. Precisely because the concrete origin of these hymns remain concealed under the veil of anonymity, Gregorian chant was able to become the song entirely belonging to the Roman Church.[96]

Although the Gregorian repertoire only emerged in the mid-eighth century, its roots reach much further back into the past. The psalm singing of the synagogue as well as the example of Christ and the Apostles, who also recited the designated number of psalms in the Upper Room, form the oldest foundations of Christian cultic singing. It soon borrowed certain elements from the secular musical art of the Greeks in order to gain form, shape, and beauty.

95 P. Claudel, *Ich liebe das Wort* (Recklinghausen: Paulus Verlag, 1955), 27, 64; cf. 50 (French original: idem, *J'aime la Bible* [Paris: Les éditions Fayard, 1955]). Cf. V. Larbaud, *Sankt Hieronymus, Schutzpatron der Übersetzer* (Munich: Kösel-Verlag, 1955), 58f.: "That the Vulgate is truly the work of a genius is evident from the very qualities we see in it: that firmness, that greatness, that majestic simplicity of style and expression. And from the crumbs of this feast, in which the Orient was served to the Occident, generations of readers, writers, poets have nourished themselves and will continue to nourish themselves."

96 Cf. Second Vatican Council, SC 116.

Gregorian chant, in the strict sense, was the result of a merging of Roman and Gallico-Frankish traditions, which at the same time also took place on the ritual level in the form of the so-called Roman-Frankish mixed liturgy. The center of that fusion during the eighth century lay between the Rhine and Moselle Rivers, in the region of Metz, the heart of Carolingian Europe. While the Roman liturgy here principally contributed the texts—mostly taken from the Bible—the core of the Gregorian melodies originates from the Gallican tradition. Though the old Roman liturgical music was certainly rich in its texts, expressing in a fitting way the mysteries of particular feasts through carefully chosen words of Scripture, it remained from a musical standpoint rather poor, extremely sober, and monotonous. The old Gallican liturgical music, on the other hand, with regard to content, was partly characterized by oriental influence, with its poetic exuberance occasionally less exact and diffuse on the doctrinal level, but musically rich, magnificent, and splendid. Thus Gregorian chant in its original inventory was the fruit of a union in which two currents of tradition combined their respective best attributes: from the Roman tradition the quality of text, and from the Gallican tradition the beauty of the music.[97] Although the basic principles of Roman chant were preserved, the Gallican musicians provided it with the decorations with which they were familiar. Rome, in turn, recognized this further-developed chant as its own property and adopted it into its liturgy.

As a consequence of this fusion, the basic components of the chant of today emerged during the second half of the eighth century in the northwest of Frankish Gaul. Afterward, the Gregorian style of singing spread throughout all of Europe in the ninth century, quickly replacing all remaining chants by reason of its exceptional quality. The Emperor Charlemagne promoted this development, as he considered the Roman chant to be a unifying factor that gave his empire and the people belonging to it a cohesiveness that was oriented toward Rome, the center of this unity. The majority of melodies were developed between the ninth and eleventh centuries, the classical epoch of Gregorian chant. Enriching

---

97   Cf. Crouan, *La Messe en latin*, 17f.; H. Courau, "Der Gregorianische Gesang und Europa," UVK 27 (1997): 30–43, 34–37.

hymns, Sequences, and tropes joined the original forms of recitative, psalmodic, and responsorial styles.

Pope Gregory the Great (590–604), whose name graced the plainchant (*cantus gregorianus*) since at least the ninth century, was considered a fore-runner of this process of growth and proliferation.[98] The prologue to the Gregorian Antiphonary, which is attributed to one of Gregory's successors, Pope Hadrian (d. 795), states: "Following the repertoire of the Fathers, he renewed and increased the chants that serve the liturgical year."[99] In the mid-ninth century, a biographer attributed the compiling of the Roman antiphonary to Pope Gregory. According to this testimony, it was a matter of compiling already existing compositions from various times and authors, which were collected, adapted, and standardized.[100] The body of source material certainly does not allow for a more exact specifying of Gregory's role in the development of Roman liturgical music and for ascribing the

98 For the so-called "Gregorian Question," i.e., whether the pope himself (re-)organized the Roman chant or later times wished to declare a specific form of chant as genuinely Roman with the authority of his name, cf. K. Hodes, *Der Gregorianische Choral. Eine Einführung* (Langwaden: Bernardus-Verlag, ³1990), 9–13; idem, "Der der römischen Liturgie eigene Gesang—Entstehung und Geschichte des Gregorianischen Chorals," *Sinfonia sacra* 4 (1996): 7–28, 14–17; J. Dyer, "Gregor I.": L. Finscher (ed.), *Die Musik in Geschichte und Gegenwart. Allgemeine Enzyklopädie der Musik* 7 (Kassel [i.a.]: Bärenreiter-Verlag, 2002), 1562–64 (with bibliography); D. Johner / M. Pfaff, *Choralschule* (Regensburg: Verlag Friedrich Pustet, ⁸1956), 238–42; J.P. Schmit, *Geschichte des Gregorianischen Chorals* (Trier: Paulinus-Verlag, 1952), 61–86; A. Heinz, "Papst Gregor der Große und die Liturgie," LJ 54 (2004): 69–84, 78–80 (= idem, *Lebendiges Erbe. Beiträge zur abendländischen Liturgie- und Frömmigkeitsgeschichte* [Tübingen: A. Francke Verlag, 2010], 57–71).

99 *Patrum monumenta sequens, renovavit et auxit carmina* (Antiphonarius ordinatus a S. Gregorio per circulum anni, ed. J.M. Tommasius, *Opera omnia* V (Rome: Ex typographia Palladis, 1750), 1). For the interpretation of this quotation, cf. H. Leclercq, "Antiphonaire," DACL 1/2 (1924): 2440–61, 2451f.; G. Morin, "En quoi consista précisément la réforme grégorienne du chant liturgique," RBen 5 (1890): 193–204; H. Courau, "Grégoire-le-Grand, le Saint, le Pape du chant liturgique": Schola Saint Grégoire (ed.), *Saint Grégoire-le-Grand. Chant grégorien. Art et prière de l'Église. Historique de la Schola* (Paris: Éditions Pierre Téqui, 2004), 11–45, 40. For further statements of the magisterium on Gregory's patronage, see Courau, "Der Gregorianische Gesang und Europa," 37n8.

100 Johannes Diaconus, *Vita sancti Gregorii* 2,6 (PL 75, 90): "*Antiphonarium centonem cantorum studiosissimus nimis utiliter compilavit.*" Cf. M. Huglo, "L'antiphonaire: Archétype ou répertoire original?": *Grégoire le Grand*: Chantilly, centre culturel Les Fontaines, 15–19 Sept. 1982 [Colloques internationaux du Centre National de la recherche scientifique] (Paris: Éditions du Centre National de la recherche scientifique, 1986), 661–66.

composition of individual pieces to him.[101] Nevertheless, with his reverence for past tradition, the careful organization of a school of liturgical music (*schola cantorum*) at the Lateran Basilica and at St Peter, as well as his fundamental concern for the order and beauty of the liturgy, Pope Gregory created the same forward-looking principles that enabled the development and later perfection of the Latin chant.

The medieval iconography in illustrations of the Gregorian antiphonary (tenth/twelfth centuries), which depicts the pope composing the melodies attributed to him under the inspiration of the Holy Ghost, conveys that those living during that time period were convinced of the divine origin of this liturgical music and Pope Gregory's decisive role in its arrangement.[102] Dom Baron OSB insightfully describes how this spiritual origin of Gregorian chant can be more precisely understood:

> The Holy Ghost has granted special assistance to those who were instructed to watch over the development of Gregorian chant. If the Holy Ghost must aid in the accomplishment of the smallest good work, how much more must He have helped those who were to give this music its definitive expression in the liturgy! For this was precisely the objective of their efforts: from these texts, of which most were inspired in the highest sense, they must uncover the expression buried within, placed there by the Holy Ghost, and must specify it with a melodic formula that united the faithful in sentiment even as the words united them in thought. And this, not only for one part, for one Mass, or for one Office, but rather for the entire liturgy of the entire year. In a word, it

---

101   In the prologue to Monza's Gradual (eighth century) it states (R.-J. Hesbert, *Antiphonale Missarum sextuplex* [Brussels: Vromant & Cie., 1935], 2): "*Gregorius praesul . . . renovans monumenta patrumque priorum tum composuit hunc libellum musicae artis scolae cantorum*" ("Bishop Gregory renewed the inheritance of the Fathers and composed this book of musical art for the schola of singers.") *Componere* at this time only meant "to compile." Not until the seventeenth century did it signify "to compose" in the current sense.

102   Cf. Courau, "Grégoire-le-Grand," 44: "Through this dove, an entire epoch affirms the divine origin of sacred chant through the emblematic personality of the holy pope who, in fact, played such a great role in its organization"; idem, "Die keusche Trunkenheit des Geistes als Kriterium des liturgischen Gesangs," UVK 31 (2001): 3–13, 10–13.

was a matter of determining what the religious sentiment of the mystical life of Christ should be, day after day, and expressing it in a song that was capable of allowing anyone who sang it or heard it to enter into Christ's interior disposition. One will easily admit that such a task exceeds the powers of the human mind and could only be accomplished with the assistance of the Spirit of Christ. What kind of assistance was this? It cannot be easily said. It is certain that the Holy Ghost did not deliver the chant to the Church all at once, in a finished manner. After the time of the charismatic gifts was past, this was no longer the method of His actions. He allowed the chant to develop according to circumstances and requirements; He imparted to those who were instructed the qualities that were required for judging and acting in the suitable moment.[103]

Liturgical advantages

Over the course of centuries, Gregorian chant became *the* music of the Roman liturgy. It was referred to as "the supreme model for sacred music"[104] and even to this day it is considered to be "the Roman Church's very own sacred song, and pre-eminently so,"[105] as recognized by the Second Vatican Council: "The Church acknowledges Gregorian chant as specially suited to the Roman liturgy: therefore, other things being equal, it should be given chief place in liturgical services."[106] This primacy is a result of the particular way Gregorian chant conforms to the requirements that Pope Pius X discerned for liturgical music in general when he emphasized that it "should possess, in the highest degree, the qualities proper to the liturgy, namely, sanctity and goodness of form,

103   L. Baron, *L'expression du chant grégorien. Commentaire liturgique et musical des messes des dimanches et des principales fêtes de l'année* I (Plouharnel / Morbihan: Abbaye Sainte-Anne de Kergonan, 1947), xxvif. (English trans. is based on the German trans. of the author).

104   Pius X, Motu proprio *Tra le Sollecitudini* (ASS 36 [1903/04]: 333 / Seasoltz, *Documentation*, 5).

105   SCR, *De Musica Sacra et Sacra Liturgia*, n. 16 (AAS 50:636 / Seasoltz, *Documentation*, 260): "*Cantus gregorianus est cantus sacer Ecclesiae romanae proprius et principalis.*"

106   SC 116: "*Ecclesia cantum gregorianum agnoscit ut liturgiae romanae proprium: qui ideo in actionibus liturgicis, ceteris paribus, principem locum obtineat.*"

from which spontaneously springs its other character, universality."[107] In what, then, do the sanctity, perfection of form, and universality of Gregorian chant consist?

Sanctity. Because this music was created solely for the liturgy and is accomplished in it as a pure prayer and praise of God, Gregorian plainchant possesses a sacred character in its essence. The edification of the faithful is only its secondary aim and is ever bound up with the first. Gregorian chant is not an optional, exchangeable accompaniment to the action of divine worship, but rather is a component of the liturgy itself, "the servant, as it were, of the sacred liturgy."[108] In contrast to the other kinds of liturgical songs inserted into liturgical ceremonies or even superimposed where silence would be called for, Gregorian chant developed from the very ceremonies and is their intended musical counterpart. Action and singing are intertwined by an indissoluble and harmonious bond:

> The processional chants that accompany liturgical processions (the Introit, Gradual, Offertory, and Communion), the responsories of the Ordinary of the Mass that interweave the prayers of the priest and the laity, and the reciting tone of the readings and orations—all these create a ladder of liturgical expression on which the movements, the actions, and the content of the prayers are brought into a perfect harmony.[109]

Arising from the understanding of the Mass as a sacrifice offered up to God, this music seeks to serve the sacrifice and to become itself the Church's prayer of sacrifice. Through its exclusively prayerful character,

---

107   Pius X, *Tra le Sollecitudini* (ASS 36:332, 389 [Latin] / Seasoltz, *Documentation*, 5). Quoted in Pius XII, Encyclical Letter *Musicae Sacrae Disciplinae* (AAS 48 [1956]:15 / Seasoltz, *Documentation*, 225).

108   Pius XII, *Musicae Sacrae Disciplinae* (AAS 48:12 / Seasoltz, *Documentation*, 223): "*sacrae liturgiae quasi administra.*" Cf. G. Mercier, *La Liturgie, culte de l'Église. Sa nature, son excellence, ses principes fondamentaux, ses éléments constitutifs. Le rôle des autres formes de dévotion* (Mulhouse: Éditions Salvator, 1961), 119.

109   M. Mosebach, *Heresy of Formlessness*, 22f.; cf. J. Laas, "Vom Verstehen sakraler Musik—Der Gregorianische Choral als universelle Sprache," UVK 33 (2003): 339–66, 352–56.

Gregorian chant ensures a theocentric understanding of the liturgy.[110] Contrary to all anthropocentric tendencies, this form of sacred music preserves the cultic dimension of the liturgy, whose primary aim is to glorify God: "Gregorian chant is something sacred. It exists only for God without ever seeking to direct attention toward itself or to please. It knows only one aim: to serve, to be forgotten itself in order to lead souls to God."[111] As Gregorian chant neither seeks to impress nor puts itself on display, but only wishes to be the servant of the Word of God, it resembles St John the Baptist who prepared the way for the *Logos*.[112]

Gregorian chant has become the liturgical music of the Church *par excellence* not least of all by reason of its being strictly related to the words of Holy Scripture. Pope Pius XII wrote: "This chant, because of the close adaptation of the melody to the sacred text, is not only most intimately conformed to the words, but also in a way interprets their force and efficacy and brings delight to the minds of the hearers."[113] The texts of Gregorian chant are formed almost exclusively from Sacred Scripture.[114] Plainchant is almost "a Bible in music,"[115] "Holy Writ put into music, as it were," "sonorous revelation."[116] The words selected from Scripture were only slightly changed, mostly through shortening, extension, restructuring, or joining with other passages. Thus Gregorian chant constitutes a unique reading of Scripture and becomes its own *locus theologicus*, insofar as it reveals a

110   Cf. J. Overath, "Die theologische und pastorale Bedeutung des Cantus Gregorianus," *Musicae Sacrae Ministerium* 18 (1981): 14–29, 18.

111   Dom J. Gajard OSB, Lecture given on October 23, 1938, quoted in H. Courau, "Der gregorianische Choral—integrierender Bestandteil der römischen Liturgie," UVK 24 (1994): 282–93, 289.

112   Cf. N.N., "Der Gregorianische Choral," UVK 20 (1990): 250–55, 252. Cf. Dom J. Claire OSB, quoted in Crouan, *La Messe en latin*, 197: "And it is precisely this exclusive service that definitely tears the melody away from itself, which consecrates it, makes it sacred, fulfilling literally the word of the Gospel ... : 'If any man will come after me, let him deny himself, and follow me.'"

113   Pius XII, *Musicae Sacrae Disciplina* (AAS 48:15 / Seasoltz, *Documentation*, 225).

114   Cf. M. Berry, "La musique liturgique: sacrée ou profane?," *Liturgie et sacré* (CIEL, 2003), 237–48.

115   S. Tamburini, *Il fascino della Liturgia Tradizionale* (Verona: Fede & Cultura, 2009), 37: "The Gregorian chant, a true Bible in music."

116   Laas, "Vom Verstehen sakraler Musik," 339, 359.

special meaning of the sung text.[117] In Gregorian music there exists such a symbiosis of words and music that they cannot be separated from each other. The melody first receives its own meaning from the text; the text's depth of meaning is unlocked by the melody.[118]

The Gregorian melodies were composed with great care and wisdom in order to illuminate the meaning of the sacred words. It is not without cause that Gregorian chant is referred to as an *"exégèse musicale"* of the biblical words[119] and an "inspired commentary on Sacred Scripture."[120] Even where the melodies are richly embellished and the melismatic sections appear to have been developed only for their own sakes, they nevertheless serve the text, though on a higher plane. They draw the attention to the central words of a sentence, express its inner wealth of significance, and illuminate its meaning and emotiveness.[121] Gregorian chant succeeds in doing this in its own unique way: the word creates its own melody, while all musical elements of the chant emerge in homogeneous and direct ways from the Latin word. Gregorian chant is the music already latently contained in the words that emerges outward and becomes perceptible.[122] The melody lends "wings to the word,"[123] in a sense, and gives the Word of God the power to penetrate the soul,

---

117 Cf. J. Hourlier, *Reflections on the Spirituality of Gregorian Chant*, trans. G. Casprini and R. Edmonson (Solesmes: Abbaye Saint-Pierre de Solesmes, 1995), 7–8.

118 Cf. A. Le Guennant, "Lettre-Préface": Baron, *L'expression du chant grégorien* I, s.p.: "The word and the sound are linked closely, indissolubly. Now, in such a case, the text gives the melody its impulse, direction, and character; it determines its rises and falls; on the other hand, the melody has the function of amplifying the literal or mystical meaning of the text, of discovering the emotion that is certainly present there but would not be communicated directly to us unless melody sets it free. Thanks to it, what the text states or implies is projected outside, in full clarity: to say it all with one word, the melody is here *expression*, in the etymological sense of the term." Examples in Laas, "Vom Verstehen sakraler Musik," 356–59; A. Forest, "Grégorien et prière," Schola Saint Grégoire (ed.), *Saint Grégoire-le-Grand. Chant grégorien. Art et prière de l'Église. Historique de la Schola* (Paris: Éditions Pierre Téqui, 2004), 47–66.

119 Crouan, *La Messe en latin*, 93: "Gregorian chant is a musical exegesis of the sacred text whose words, sentences, and profound meaning it manifests."

120 Dom J. Gajard OSB, quoted in Forest, "Grégorien et prière," 58.

121 Cf. Crouan, *La Messe en latin*, 91f.

122 Cf. Baron, *L'expression du chant grégorien* I, xxif.

123 Cf. N.N., "Der Gregorianische Choral," 251.

and to speak alike to the heart and to the mind.[124] What Pope Pius X wrote about liturgical music in general applies in the greatest measure to Gregorian plainchant:

> It tends to increase the decorum and the splendor of the ecclesiastical ceremonies, and since its principal office is to clothe with befitting melody the liturgical text proposed for the understanding of the faithful, its proper end is to add greater efficacy to the text, in order that by means of it the faithful may be the more easily moved to devotion and better disposed to receive the fruits of grace associated with the celebration of the most holy mysteries.[125]

It is exactly in this way that Gregorian chant is able to serve the faithful as a properly understood *participatio actuosa*.[126] Thus, as with the other liturgical prayers, a literal understanding of the texts is in no way an essential requirement; rather, there is an intuitive perception of liturgical music that can awaken the listener's piety. As St Thomas Aquinas writes: "For even if they (*sc.*, the hearers) do not understand what is sung, yet they understand why it is sung, namely, for God's honour; and this is enough to arouse their devotion."[127]

Perfection of form. In addition to the sanctity of Gregorian plainchant,

---

124 Cf. A. Le Guennant, "Lettre-Préface": Baron, *L'expression du chant grégorien* I, s.p.: "In sung prayer, the text provides man with the nourishment necessary for his mind: *intellectum illumina*; music gives him what his heart needs: *affectum inflamma*. So they both contribute, in concert, to the full development of the human being in his relationship with God."

125 Pius X, *Tra le Sollecitudini* (ASS 36:332 / Seasoltz, *Documentation*, 4f.). Cf. Crouan, *La Messe en latin*, 81; K. Gamber, *Fragen in die Zeit. Kirche und Liturgie nach dem Vatikanum II* [SPLi Beiheft 24] (Regensburg: Verlag Friedrich Pustet, 1989), 70: "without Gregorian chant and its mystical beauty, the Roman liturgy, simple in its rites and prayers, lacks the splendor necessary to allow the faithful to experience the numinous."

126 Cf. Pius X, *Tra le Sollecitudini* (ASS 36:333 / Seasoltz, *Documentation*, 5f.): "Efforts must especially be made to restore the use of the Gregorian chant by the people, so that the faithful may again take a more active part in the ecclesiastical offices, as they were wont to do in ancient times"; Pius XI, Apostolic Constitution *Divini Cultus* (AAS 21 [1929]: 39f. / Seasoltz, *Documentation*, 62); Pius XII, *Mediator Dei* (AAS 39:588–90 / Seasoltz, *Documentation*, 135f.). Cf. Mercier, *Liturgie*, 112–17.

127 Thomas Aquinas, *STh* II–II, 91, 2 ad 5, in *Summa Theologiae*, vol. 39 (2a2ae. 80–91): Religion and Worship, trans. by K. D. O'Rourke (Oxford: Blackfriars Publications [i.a.], 1964), 251.

Pope Pius X noted the "goodness of the form" (*bontà delle forme*) as a further characteristic. For the author André Frossard, member of the *Académie française*, Gregorian chant was that "free singing of the soul, which came to us from that time when the Church was still in league with beauty."[128] At the end of his life, Mozart said that he would gladly renounce his entire body of compositions if only he could be capable of composing the Introit of the Requiem Mass.[129] Gregorian chant's beauty relies on, not least of all, its simplicity, clarity, and transparency for the liturgical mystery. The unison singing dispenses with any kind of instrumental accompaniment and is satisfied with the simplest melodic means. It does not seek to call attention to itself by any kind of effects. It demands that each singer have no wish to stand out from the other members of the choir, but instead forget himself for the good of the whole and blend with the voices of the others. Although full of life, the melodies are ever balanced and restrained, simultaneously delicate and haunting, as smooth as they are assertive, and filled with a marvelous diversity of nuances.

Because of these characteristics, Gregorian chant promotes interior contemplation. Where this music expresses human emotions, they lose their fervid, unrestrained character in order to present themselves clearly and calmly in these melodies, imbued with God's peace.[130] Far from ecstatic emotional exuberance, rousing rhythms, or deafening loudness, Gregorian melodies facilitate a form of contemplative prayer that transcends simple intellectual understanding of the sung words, while it silently fathoms their depth and leads contemplation to adoration.[131] For this reason, Gregorian chant is referred to as "singing silence" and "musical contemplation."[132]

---

128   A. Frossard, *Le Parti de Dieu — Lettre aux évêques* (Paris: Les éditions Fayard, ²1993); quoted in A. Schönberger, "Was André Frossard an der neuen Liturgie missfällt," UVK 24 (1994): 94–96, 96.

129   Cf. M. Legrais, "Esthétique du chant grégorien," *Sedes sapientiae* 55 (1996): 15–32, 16. Some claim that Mozart said "he would gladly exchange all his music for the fame of having composed the Gregorian Preface": see *Catholic Encyclopedia* (1911), s.v. 'ecclesiastical music'.

130   Cf. N.N., "Der Gregorianische Choral," 253; A.-M. Henry / G. Nawroth / D. Delalande, *Der Gregorianische Choral: Die Katholische Glaubenswelt* I (Freiburg i. Br.: Verlag Herder, 1960), 212–37, 221f.

131   Cf. Forest, "Grégorien et prière," 47–66.

132   W.-M. de Saint-Jean, *Silence sacré et intériorité dans la liturgie* (Versailles: CIEL, 2004), 88; idem, "Silence et intériorité dans la liturgie," *Liturgie et sacré* (CIEL, 2003), 273–350, 348.

Universality. From the characteristics of Gregorian chant described thus far emerges the universal character of this music, which not only unifies the present Church of the Roman rite worldwide *"una voce"* (in one voice), but also makes tangible the continuity of the faith throughout history by its almost 1,500-year-old tradition. In contrast to later forms of liturgical music, which in many cases were esteemed and practiced only in their places of origin in Europe, Gregorian chant has enjoyed great popularity among the faithful everywhere, even in regions outside of Europe, especially in Africa.[133] The universal reception and spread of Gregorian chant was made possible by the fact that it owes its origin to the confluence of diverse musical traditions of Jewish, Greek, Roman, and Gallican origin, but at the same time, despite these diverse elements, it found an inner unity by gradually abandoning everything individual, personal, differentiating, everything that was only the expression of one particular people, one particular fashion, and one particular taste, and by retaining only that which sought to unify, which moved the root of the soul and spoke to its innermost life, which, ultimately, is the same in all people. Thus emerged a song with a universal character that corresponds to all peoples and all times. It was no longer the voice of one or another, but the voice and the work of the universal Church.[134]

The authoritativeness of Gregorian chant is not ultimately based on rubrics or legislative decrees from the popes. Rather, this music owed its universal standing to the *consensus populi*, the *sensus Ecclesiae*, as manifested by the centuries-long tradition of the Western Church,[135] which beheld therein the highest exemplar of any kind of sacred music.[136] The normativity of Gregorian plainchant is based on the essence of sacred music itself. At

---

133 Cf. P. Lopy, "Gregorianischer Choral in Afrika—eine Befragung in Senegal," UVK 24 (1994): 293–99.

134 Cf. Baron, *L'expression du chant grégorien* I, xxvii.

135 Cf. Hourlier, *Spirituality of Gregorian Chant*, 34f.

136 Cf. Pius X, *Tra le Sollecitudini* (ASS 36:333 / Seasoltz, *Documentation*, 5): "Upon these grounds the Gregorian chant has always been regarded as the supreme model for sacred music, so that the following rule may be safely laid down: The more closely a composition for church approaches in its movement, inspiration and savour the Gregorian form, the more sacred and liturgical it is; and the more out of harmony it is with that supreme model, the less worthy it is of the temple."

the celebration of the Mass or the Divine Office, the music is not an arbitrary embellishment that merely serves exteriorly to enhance the beauty of divine worship; it is rather a fundamental component of the Catholic liturgy, because earthly homage represents heavenly homage. More than any other music, Gregorian chant expresses this representational aspect because it enters into a sphere from which every naturalistic means of expression is expelled. "The chant of the Church we call Gregorian is an echo of the chant arising in the heavenly Jerusalem."[137]

---

137 A Benedictine Monk [G. Calvet], *The Sacred Liturgy*, 34. Cf. de Saint-Jean, *Silence sacré et intériorité*, 88; idem, "Silence et intériorité," 349: "The Gregorian melody, this wing that raises us up to God, resonates, in inspired praise, His own Word revealed to us. And its path, from our earthly temples to the eternal Sanctuary, crosses our souls with secret and deep harmonies which nourish the life-giving desire for Heaven."

9

Rituality and Sacrality

RITE

Guarantee of synchronic and diachronic unity

In the context of the liturgy, "rite" refers to the regulation of the official prayer of the Church, whereby the exterior forms of divine worship, i.e., the corresponding texts and actions, are firmly declared.[1] The rite thus encompasses the binding forms of a particular cult as it is celebrated in one part of the Church, a ritual family. The rite is not the sacred action itself, but rather the sum of the practical norms and formulas that regulate the particular liturgical functions and are observed in carrying them out. The rite is the interaction of words and prayers, gestures and signs (ceremonies), as well as rubrics (regulatory statutes for speaking the prayers and completing the actions).[2] The Church has always overseen and given final approval of the rites. After the Council of Trent, Pope Sixtus V created the Sacred Congregation of Rites (1588).[3]

The traditional *Ordo Missae* is based on a meticulously regulated rite, which leaves no room for arbitrary innovating, but rather seeks to guarantee the untouchableness of the liturgical action. In a serious misjudgment of the deep significance of rituality in general, the traditional liturgy was accused, especially during the 1960s and '70s, of fossilization or ossification,

---

1   On the origin of the term from early Christian usage, cf. Thalhofer, *Handbuch der katholischen Liturgik* I, 370f.

2   Cf. L. Dobszay, *Restoration*, 3: "When we speak of the 'Tridentine Rite' or 'Dominican Rite,' we refer to the system of a *full* liturgical order. In this sense a 'rite' is the content, the entire fixed material, of the liturgy. It is more than the sum of single elements; rather, it is their complexity in an organic structure. The single parts mutually suppose and indicate each other; they are in line with a common conception, a unitary style. This cohesion is the result not of some kind of engineering process, but of a continually cultivated, controlled tradition, always improved according to necessity."

3   Cf. McManus, *Congregation of Sacred Rites*; R. Naz, "Rites, S. Congrégation des," DDC 7 (1958/65): 691–94; Jungmann, *Missarum sollemnia* I, 183f.; idem, *The Mass of the Roman Rite* I, 139.

of stiffening into ritualism, of a legalistic mentality, and of rubrical fixation. Requests for changes were made by those seeking to introduce creativity and spontaneity in place of this rituality, and these requests quickly proved to be excessive demands. The consequences are known everywhere and sufficiently described elsewhere.[4] In the meantime, however, a change of thinking has begun.

Social and cultural sciences have newly discovered the meaning of ritual and have once more emphasized its significance for mankind. The traditional liturgy has always been convinced of this truth, though in the past theology and catechesis obviously did not always develop these insights for the appreciation of the faithful in such a way that they would recognize liturgical rituality as a good worth protecting and unhesitatingly defending.

Rituals, as the social sciences teach, belong to the life of man. They are pre-shaped and repeatable forms of execution for specific situations that relieve individuals of the necessity of always newly inventing the appropriate form. These forms of execution communicate security and stability, and going beyond mere actions that serve only to accomplish a purpose, they give beauty and meaning to what is being done. Rituals, as religious science teaches, especially belong to the realm of religious performance. Wherever man confronts the divine in order to pay homage, there are prescribed forms, established as "custom," well-tried and socially accepted, that govern and order the relations of man to the divine power.[5]

Since rituals make up a universal religio-historical phenomenon, the Christian liturgy is not excluded from it. Here, as well, there are

---

4 Cf. Ratzinger, *Feast of Faith*, 324 (*Theology of the Liturgy*, 67f.): "It is also worth observing here that the 'creativity' involved in manufactured liturgies has a very restricted scope. It is poor indeed compared with the wealth of the received liturgy in its hundreds and thousands of years of history. Unfortunately, the originators of homemade liturgies are slower to become aware of this than the participants."

5 Cf. Ratzinger, *Spirit of the Liturgy*, 159 (*Theology of the Liturgy*, 98): "In the second century, the Roman jurist Pomponius Festus, who was not a Christian, defined *ritus* as an 'approved practice in the administration of sacrifice' (*mos comprobatus in administrandis sacrificiis*). He thereby summed up in a precise formula one of the great realities in the history of religion. Man is always looking for the right way of honoring God, for a form of prayer and common worship that pleases God and is appropriate to his nature." The classical definition comes from the commentator on Virgil Servius (ca. AD 400), *Aen.* 12,836a: "*mos institutus religionis caerimoniis consecratus.*"

rituals — pre-shaped, sanctified, symbolic forms. On the one hand, these reach back to the past, handed down as "custom," providing consistency, making that which is approved repeatable, and linking us, as well as the Faith itself, with the community of faithful of centuries past.[6] On the other hand, these rituals remain identical in the present and thus make recognizable that which is celebrated elsewhere in the same manner. Liturgical rites thus possess a diachronic element, as they transcend and consolidate time, and a synchronic element, as they unite region and place, people and languages in the present.[7]

This unifying power of rites is clearly expressed in the thoughts of Paul Claudel, the great French Catholic poet (1868–1955), who had a profound conversion experience during Christmas Vespers in the Cathedral of Notre-Dame in Paris (1886). In a small work about the Mass (1917) he looks back on the many stations of his diplomatic life:

> Was it in Notre-Dame one day at the dark Mass
>   at seven in the morning,
> That Genevieve blessed her city in the fog,
>   driven from sleep by the foreign cry of the tugboats?
> Was it in Boston's greasy alleys? Was it in China,
> Where the priest still wears on his head
>   the bushel invented by the last of the Mings?
> Or in Prague, in one of the beautiful Baroque churches,
>   in the shine of laughing gold,
> Filled with angels who are settled everywhere
>   like a flock of birds?
> In snow-filled Frankfurt, or in Hamburg,
>   where the rain slams against the windows?

---

6   Cf. K. Gamber, "Liturgy, Our Home: The Need for an Unchanging Liturgy," idem, *Reform of the Roman Liturgy*, 105–11. Cf. A Benedictine Monk [G. Calvet], *The Sacred Liturgy*, 67f.

7   Cf. Y. M.-J. Congar, *Tradition & Traditions: The Biblical, Historical, and Theological Evidence for Catholic Teaching on Tradition*, part I, trans. by M. Naseby / part II by Th. Rainborough (San Diego, CA / Needham Heights, MA: Simon & Schuster, 1966), 429: "Ritual, as a means of communication and of victory over devouring time, is also seen to be a powerful means for communion in the same reality between men separated by centuries of change and affected by very different influences."

Or in I know not what chapel, between two trains,
    swallowed up among sinister little shops?
In the plumes of smoke as from burning tar,
    or on a limpid morning like gold,
There always lies upon the altar a book containing
    all knowledge of life and death.[8]

There always lies a book upon the altar—this is the exhilarating experience of a Catholic who relies on tradition: regardless of where I am, regardless of which country I am in, regardless of which church or chapel I visit, everywhere the same language is spoken, everywhere on this day the same saints are commemorated, everywhere the same Mass is prayed. "You Are at Home Everywhere" [*Überall bist du zuhaus*] is the title of a lovely illustrated German book from the 1950s about the life of the Catholic Church throughout the whole world. The classical liturgical rite, with its strict uniformity and prevention of any arbitrary act, enables precisely this: Catholics are at home everywhere, for there is the same Missal on every altar. Everywhere the priest follows the same rubrics, everywhere the same prayers are recited, and everywhere the same Faith is celebrated. The rite thus enables the synchronic unity of the Church, the unity of all faithful in the present, wherever they may be.

Claudel's words, "There always lies a book upon the altar," can also be understood with an emphasis on "always." Not only everywhere, but at all times a book, the same Missal, lies and has lain on the altar. The traditional rite is not only identical on the synchronic level, world-wide, but also on the diachronic level, across time. Despite many developments and modifications, the classical rite remained largely constant in its substance over the course of centuries. In the first chapter, John Henry Newman was cited as saying: were Athanasius and Ambrose to come into our time and into our city, they would turn from many imposing churches and would "ask the way to some small chapel where Mass was said."[9] Why?

---

8 P. Claudel, *Die Messe des Verbannten* [Christliche Meister 13] (Einsiedeln: Johannes-Verlag, 1981), 25f.

9 Cf. p. 51 above.

There always lies a book upon the altar, it has always been in its substance the same Missal, the same prayer, the same faith. Thus the rite creates a synchronic as well as a diachronic unity of the Church. It creates the space-transcending unity of the present and the time-transcending unity that binds the past and present together. The rite guarantees that we celebrate "what has been believed everywhere, always, and by all. This is truly and properly 'Catholic.'"[10]

On the meaning of the intangible

As a predetermined form, the rite is a reminder that the liturgy must always be the entering into something prescribed and that the Mass is nothing other than the realization of Christ's sacrifice on Calvary. Since the rite's primary aim is to be the reenactment of Christ's already-completed sacrifice on the Cross, there can be no room for free design and constant changes. A rite that has been formed over centuries has extinguished the traces of subjective, self-invented, and self-made elements. Whoever enters into such an order will learn that he enters that place where he is able to encounter God's mystery. The rite creates an objective space, removed from human interference, which consequently makes the intangible — God's presence — perceptible. Every violent interference with the rite destroys this space, a space that the worshiper must sense to be inviolable in order to be able to encounter that which ultimately does not come from man, but from God.[11]

It also belongs to the ritual unspontaneity and untouchableness of the liturgy that it should not be subject to constantly changing human mentalities, as this would require that its forms of expression be continually

---

10 Vincent of Lérins, *Commonitorium* 2,5 (CCL 64, 149 / Vincent of Lérins, *Commonitories*, 270).

11 Cf. M. Mosebach, *Häresie der Formlosigkeit* (cf. p. 53, n6 above), 219f.; J. H. Newman, "Ceremonies of the Church," Sermon 7 in *Parochial and Plain Sermons*, II, 77f.: "Rites which the Church has appointed, and with reason — for the Church's authority is from Christ — being long used, cannot be disused without harm to our souls." Similar to the negative consequences of the change to time-honored laws: Thomas Aquinas, *STh* I–II, 97,2, in *Summa Theologiae*, vol. 28 (1a2ae. 90–97): Law and Political Theory, trans. by Th. Gilby (Oxford: Blackfriars Publications [i.a.], 1966), 144–49.

adapted to them.[12] The traditional rite of the Mass has always resisted the temptation of regarding the fundamentally legitimate concern for intelligibility or "reasonable worship" (λογικὴ λατρεία, *logikē latreia*: Rom 12:1) as a demand for modern man, with his alleged capacity for understanding, to become the measure of the liturgy and to adapt it accordingly.[13] Ongoing changes would be the inevitable consequence if there did not exist a reliable criterion for the manner, degree, and frequency thereof.[14]

12   Cf. Pius X, Encyclical Letter *Pascendi Dominici Gregis* (DH 3493), on modernist demands that the liturgy must follow the laws of evolution in order to survive.

13   Cf. L. Bouyer, *Das Handwerk des Theologen* (Einsiedeln: Johannes-Verlag, 1980), 49: "Things have been made easy, on the pretext of complying with the wishes of the faithful. No effort has been made to open up their minds to the authentic word of God in the authentic tradition. More and more, therefore, the liturgy has become an expression of the participants as they are and not as God would have wanted them to be: transformed into the Son through the liturgical process. Forgetting this, worship becomes a simple consecration of humanity as it is, uncritical and above all, unaltered." J. Hitchcock, *The Recovery of the Sacred* (San Francisco: Ignatius Press, 1995), 58: "When disaffected worshippers said, 'The Mass doesn't do anything for me,' liturgists no longer responded, as they once had, by insisting that the Mass is a deep mystery into whose spirit the individual must seek to penetrate by prayer, study, patience, and humility. They, rather, acknowledged that the Mass would indeed have to be changed to make it capable of speaking to a wide audience. A crucial shift of the profoundest importance was thus negotiated, but its seriousness was little noted at the time."

14   For corresponding concerns on the eve of liturgical reform, cf. Bishop D. Staffa, "Allocution concerning the conciliar schema 'On the Holy Liturgy in General' in the Congregatio generalis VI on Oct. 24, 1962" (*Acta Synodalia*, vol. I. Periodus prima, pars I, 428f.): *Additur sacram Liturgiam esse aptandam mutatis temporibus et circumstantiis. Hic quoque ad consectaria debemus attendere: mores enim, immo vultus ipsius societatis, hodie praesertim, celeriter mutat et celerius mutabitur; quod placitis multitudinis hodie videtur consentaneum, post triginta vel ad summum quinquaginta annos iam apparebit incongruum; concludendum ergo esset post triginta vel quinquaginta annos integre aut fere integre Liturgiam iterum esse reformandum. Hoc mihi videtur logicum iuxta praemissa, sed minime decorum pro sacra Liturgia, minime utile pro dignitate Ecclesiae, minime tutum pro integritate et unitate fidei, minime favens unitati disciplinae* [They add that sacred liturgy has to be accommodated to the change of times and circumstances; but here, too, we must take into account the consequences. For the customs and even the character of society itself, especially nowadays, change swiftly and will change even more swiftly in the future. What today seems suitable to the sentiments of the crowd will, after thirty or at most fifty years go by, already seem unsuitable. It will, therefore, be concluded in thirty or fifty years' time that the liturgy should once again be reformed entirely or almost entirely. This, to me, seems logical [as a conclusion] from the premises (i.e., the prooemium and first chapter of *Sacrosanctum Concilium*), but this diminishes the glory of the sacred liturgy, is not at all useful for the dignity of the Church, in no way upholds the integrity and unity of the faith, and by no

The traditional liturgy follows a different principle. It does not seek to adapt itself to mankind, but aims rather that man should insert himself into it and be assimilated to it. It does not use his everyday speech, but invites him to learn its timeless language. It does not bring mankind's world of today into the divine worship, but wishes to draw man into its own world.[15] How easily this is possible and how fascinating this can be has been vividly and impressively described by many who have discovered the traditional liturgy today.[16]

RUBRICS

Guarantors of non-arbitrariness

Up to and including its 1962 edition, the Roman Missal provided virtually no possibility of freedom of choice. It fully followed the principle: "The greatness of the liturgy depends . . . on its unspontaneity."[17] The guar-

---

means supports unity of discipline]. Cf. Davies, *Pope John's Council*, 347: "Papal teaching on the need to adapt the liturgy to keep pace with modern times is conspicuous only by its absence [prior to Vatican II]—and this is hardly surprising when this alleged 'need' is examined in a dispassionate and rational manner. When do times become modern? What are the criteria by which modernity is assessed? When does one modernity cease and another modernity come into being?"

15　Cf. Th. M. Kocik, *The Reform of the Reform? A Liturgical Debate: Reform or Return* (San Francisco: Ignatius Press, 2003), Appendix IV: A. Nichols, "Salutary Dissatisfaction," 195–219, 199: "Even were it the case, however, that the Church public is by and large adequately satisfied with the form of worship customarily offered to them in the modern Roman rite, it is still possible to assert that they should *not* be. The Church is not a business, whose management can rest content if its customers express satisfaction. To 'feel comfortable with a worship situation' is an infallible sign that we have missed the real meaning of the liturgy in its sacrality, its difference, its supernatural power. If we are to use commercial analogies here, then we must say of the Church that she is in the business of making people realize they have needs they have barely dreamed of. Because we are made in the image of God, made to tend to our divine archetype when he appears to us in the suffering and glorified God-man Jesus Christ, we have a need precisely *not* to be confirmed in our ordinary everyday personas by the easy uplift of a worship that consists in quickly appropriated words and sounds. By an apparent paradox, we need the liturgy *not* to be intrusively relevant to the secular roles that the society of a fallen world constructs for us. We need the liturgy to *estrange* us from our ordinary workaday selves by enabling us to find a new identity in those voices that speak there of adoration, purification, and the endless transcendence of the peace beyond all understanding of the City of God."

16　Cf. the description by Ratzinger, *Milestones*, 18–20.

17　Ratzinger, *Spirit of the Liturgy*, 166 (*Theology of the Liturgy*, 103).

antors of this unspontaneity are the rubrics, the instructions[18] printed in red in the Missal, specifying how the prayers are to be said and how the sacred actions are to be carried out. By reason of their precise regulation of interaction with the sacred, the rubrics, along with Scripture, amount to a *locus theologicus*, a source of theological knowledge concerning the mystery of the Eucharist.

The Missal codified by Pope Pius V following the Council of Trent governed even the smallest details of the liturgical rite, not leaving anything to chance or the celebrant's discretion, by use of precise instructions in the rubrics. This reveals a better knowledge of human nature than that of those who, as they triumphantly bade farewell to alleged rubricism, transformed "the serious rules of the sacred game"[19] into a playground of creative capriciousness. As was once appropriately said, the rubrics are "Rahab's scarlet cord, an escape route from the catastrophe of *ad libitum* contingencies." Like the red cord that Rahab hung from her window at the behest of Joshua's spies in order to protect her house from destruction during the capture of Jericho (cf. Josh 2:18–21), the red instructions of the Missal protect the celebrant from succumbing to the overwhelming diversity of possibilities and sinking into the chaos of that which is ever newly-discovered or spontaneously created. Paradoxically, it is precisely the meticulous regulation of all liturgical actions that, given a certain familiarity, ultimately allows a nearly effortless exercise of the same.[20]

18   On the origin of the term from the Roman legal terminology and its later application also to the *Rubricae Generales* written in black in the MRom 1570 cf. Thalhofer, *Handbuch der katholischen Liturgik* I, 378; furthermore cf. Mosebach, *Heresy of Formlessness*, 131–33; Kaschewsky, "Die Rubriken."

19   Cf. R. Guardini, *The Spirit of the Liturgy* [with an introduction by J.M. Pierce / trans. by A. Lane] (New York, NY: Crossroad, 1998), 71.

20   Cf. A. Fortescue, *The Ceremonies of the Roman Rite Described* (London: Burns, Oates and Washbourne, ²1937), xxiii: "Probably the first impression which these descriptions of ceremonies would produce on a stranger is that of enormous complication. Really this is much less than it seems. In general, actions are far less conspicuous when done than when described in words. Most Catholics hardly notice these things when they go to church. The ministers and servers who do them constantly become so used to them by long habit that they too do them almost without thought.... It is worth noticing that, the more exact details of direction are, the less complicated their performance becomes. When each person knows exactly what to do, when they all agree and do their parts confidently and silently, the effect of the ceremony is immeasurably more tranquil than when there is doubt, confusion or discussion."

The objectivity inherent in the classical rite is due not least to the fact that the celebrating priest is bound to the liturgical texts and there is no possibility of improvisation. This binding is especially brought out by the practice of having the assisting presbyter at a solemn Pontifical Mass or the master of ceremonies at a High Mass point the celebrant precisely to the texts or prayers to be said at certain times. As it is not only newly ordained priests but also experienced priests who are led through the Missal in this manner, it is clear that "this ritual of pointing actually manifests the celebrant's submission to the traditional order of prayer: it is not something created by him. Here again the cult wishes to be understood and experienced as something given, not made by the man of the moment."[21]

It is not only the prayer texts that are strictly predetermined by the rite. The rubrics determine each gesture of the priest at the altar (the position of the body, head, arms, or fingers) in the finest detail. Even the putting on of the liturgical vestments is exactly directed in numerous instructions. Which pieces of the vestments are put on, with or without having been kissed, is as determined as the order of sleeves in putting on the alb or the proper crossing of the stole, whose right end the priest always places over the left. The manner in which the priest approaches the altar is exactly prescribed: with lowered eyes, dignified tread, and upright posture (*oculis demissis, incessu gravi, corpore erecto*). The spreading of arms and hands is regulated according to width and height: they should neither reach beyond the width nor over the height of the shoulders, and the palms should turn toward each other. The rite dictates the position of the fingers, the differentiated forms of bows, as well as the number and different kinds of genuflections (*in plano, in gradu*).[22] With regard to the position of the eyes, it specifies when they should be lowered (*Dominus vobiscum*, Final Blessing), when they should be raised and directed toward the altar crucifix (*Te igitur*, among others), and when they should be consistently directed toward the Most Blessed Sacrament (*Pater Noster*). The volume of speaking while the priest prays the Canon is such that he can hear his own voice, but without being heard by those nearby.[23]

---

21   Mosebach, *Heresy of Formlessness*, 128.
22   That is, on the ground; on the altar step.
23   Cf. *Rubricae generales Missalis Romani* (1962), no. 500.

Objectification and de-individualization

All of these meticulously detailed regulations, none of which tolerates any deviation or arbitrariness, have only one aim: when the priest acts on the altar *in persona Christi*, and speaks the words of consecration in the name of Christ, lending Him his voice, it is entirely suitable that everything personal, individual, and subjective retreat and be reduced to a minimum, so that he may place himself fully in the role of Christ the High Priest.[24] The removal of the individual makes clear that it is another who is acting:

> A priest at the altar has no face, and the arms that
> raise the Lord are without dust or ornament,
> For whom God calls to speak, him He calls to be silent,
> and whomever His Spirit ignites, disappears.[25]

This is precisely the aim of the strict rite and the rubrics, which at first glance seem legalistic: the silencing of one's own words, so that God may have His say; the extinguishing of individual vagaries to make room for God's incursion[26] and enable His stepping into the present moment. The strict regulation of the rubrics also guarantees the dignity of the liturgical action, as it entirely separates it from the personal mannerisms of the

---

24 N.N., *Christian Order*, April 1974, 240f.; quoted in Davies, *Pope Paul's New Mass*, 2f.: "I remember how, when, as a young priest, I was preparing to say my first Mass, I was drilled most strictly and told to drill myself in such a way that every word and gesture of mine at the altar of sacrifice would be exactly correct. Everything—tone of voice, blessings, bows, genuflections, turn-rounds to the people, height and breadth at which one held extended arms—had to be as laid down in the rubrics, exactly correct. Why? Because, at the altar, one was performing the noblest action open to a human being: the sacrifice of God's Son to God. It followed, both logically and theologically, that one had to bring to it every ounce of reverence of which a human being was capable. ... Human nature being what it is, individual idiosyncrasies would come out to take from reverence, if priests were left to themselves in the matter of words and gestures at Mass. It followed that idiosyncrasies had to be cut to a minimum. Hence, the rubrics, which bound all priests at Mass, depersonalizing them, so to say, in the interests of the reverence which men had to put forth when they offered sacrifice to God. How else could they acknowledge adequately in their hearts their total dependence on Him Who had made them from nothing, except that they manifested it in every bodily gesture that was theirs at Mass?"

25 G. v. Le Fort, *Hymnen an die Kirche*, 22.

26 Cf. Ratzinger, *Spirit of the Liturgy*, 168f. (*Theology of the Liturgy*, 104f.).

celebrant,[27] who, completely subjected to the ritual's specifications, possesses only minimal leeway for directing the attention of the faithful to himself through his personal strengths or weaknesses. Finally, the rubrics protect the Church's most prized possession from deformations, trivializations, and subjectivizations.

The controversy over the prescriptive or descriptive character of the rubrics, argued by theologians since the end of the sixteenth century, reveals just how great an importance has ever been ascribed to these functions of the rubrics.[28] If the rubrics are ultimately regarded not as mere advice for a dignified and appropriate completion of the liturgical action, but rather as instructions that oblige the officiant in conscience, that is — depending on the matter — under a grave (*sub gravi*) or venial (*sub levi*) sin, then this demonstrates once more the conviction that the liturgy deserves protection and that the most reliable guarantee of this is in the Church's standards, which are not subject to negotiation.

CEREMONIES
Through the visible to the invisible

> Let us recall: before the Council, the historically evolved chore-
> ography of a sacred dance unfolded at the altar with meaning-
> ful (but not rationalistically clear) gestures, with the recitative
> speech of the Latin texts, and with the intonation of hymns and
> songs which the choir answered. This performance also included
> multi-level candlesticks in front of the altarpieces, surrounded by
> flowers, occasionally interspersed with ornamental pieces from

27 Cf. Davies, *Pope Paul's New Mass*, 154: "In the traditional Mass the rubrics insured the celebrant subordinated his personality to the celebration. His every word, every gesture, was meticulously regulated. This is why, providing the rubrics were observed, a badly celebrated Mass was almost impossible. Hurried, unedifying celebrations may have occurred — but they were certainly the exception. The rubrics insured that normally every celebration was recollected, prayerful, and dignified. The fact that much of the Mass was said in a very low voice made no small contribution to this edifying situation. Before the Council it would have been most unusual to hear a member of the congregation remark that a Mass had been either dull or lively. The Mass was the Mass, and that was that."

28 Cf. Thalhofer, *Handbuch der katholischen Liturgik* I, 379–81.

the treasury of the Church. The action at the altar was a unity of sacred, veiled texts, songs, ritualized gestures, music, smoke of incense, and solemn space used as a "theater" in that exquisite sense that dates back to antiquity. The liturgical reform has pierced this unity to the heart. What the Council issued was no modification, but a qualitative reversal. A seminar invented *ad hoc* took the place of a presentative symbolic structure.[29]

This description arises from an accurate observation of the classical liturgy and vividly demonstrates the impressive impact that the interactions of words and gestures, hymns and symbols are capable of developing in the sacred space. Of special importance here are those performances that receive the name of "ceremonies." Although the term *caerimonia* was originally synonymous with *ritus*, its linguistic usage narrowed after the Council of Trent, such that "ceremonies" primarily referred to those exterior forms of worship that did not originate from divine institution but rather were introduced by the Church; it thereafter only indicated those actions and determined forms of symbolic or mimetic nature.[30] Prayers and readings thus do not belong to the ceremonies, but can instead be accompanied by them (e.g., spreading and folding of hands, bowing the head, incensing, and so on).

The Council of Trent (Session XXII in 1562) explained the purpose of the ceremonies by describing the way in which they objectively make the sacrifice instituted by Christ appear more solemn and splendid, and subjectively make it more vivid and impressive for the faithful:

> And as human nature is such that it cannot easily raise itself up to the meditation of divine realities without external aids, Holy Mother Church has for that reason duly established certain rites, such as that some parts of the Mass should be said in quieter tones (can. 9) and others in louder; and she has provided ceremonial

---

29 A. Lorenzer, *Das Konzil der Buchhalter. Die Zerstörung der Sinnlichkeit. Eine Religionskritik* (Frankfurt a. M.: Fischer-Taschenbuch-Verlag, 1984), 191.

30 Cf. Thalhofer, *Handbuch der katholischen Liturgik* I, 371–73.

(can. 7), such as mystical blessings, lights, incense, vestments, and many other rituals of that kind from apostolic discipline and tradition, by which both the majesty of so great a sacrifice is emphasized and the minds of the faithful are aroused by those visible signs of religion and piety to the contemplation of the sublime mysteries hidden in this sacrifice.[31]

A few years later, Cardinal Robert Bellarmine SJ explained the meaning of the ceremonies in exactly this sense by stating that body-bound man can only grasp the greatness of intellectual religion when it is not "naked mysteries" that are introduced to him, but instead mysteries adorned and clothed with exterior brilliance so that he may intellectually grasp them with greater reverence.[32] In the same way, the learned liturgist and later Cardinal G. Bona OCist described the function of these actions in 1663:

For although the ceremonies themselves can claim no perfection or sanctity in their own right, they are, nevertheless, the outward acts of religion, designed to rouse the heart, like signals of a sort, to veneration of the sacred realities, and to raise the mind to meditation on the supernatural. They serve to foster piety, to kindle the

---

31   Council of Trent, sess. XXII, cap. 5 (DH 1746).

32   R. Bellarmine, *Disputationes de controversiis christianae fidei*, controversia 8, lib. 2, c. 31 [*Opera omnia* III] (Paris: Vivès, 1870 [repr. Frankfurt a. M.: Minerva-Verlag, 1965]), 500f.: "*Quinta* (sc., ratio) *est conservatio religionis. Id enim caerimoniae praestant, ne religio vilescat, et contemnatur, et sic paulatim pereat. Nam excellentia religionis nostrae praecipua, quia spiritualis est, non facile perspicitur a nobis, qui corporei sumus. Ideo non proponuntur nuda mysteria, sed vestiuntur, et ornantur, ut externam quamdam maiestatem sensibus obiciant, et per eam maiori cum reverentia ab ipsa mente percipiantur*" [The fifth (reason) is the conservation of religion. The ceremonies fulfil the task of not allowing religion to become vile and contemptible, so that it would eventually perish. For the superior excellence of our religion, owing to its spiritual nature, is not easily apprehended by us who are of a bodily nature. And for this reason, no bare mysteries are put before us, but they are clothed and adorned, in order to present some majesty to the senses, and thus be perceived by the mind with greater reverence]. Similarly, Newman, "Ceremonies of the Church," *Parochial and Plain Sermons* II, 74f.: "Scripture gives the *spirit*, and the Church the *body*, to our worship; and we may as well expect that the spirits of men might be seen by us without the intervention of their bodies, as suppose that the Object of faith can be realized in a world of sense and excitement, without the instrumentality of an outward form to arrest and fix attention, to stimulate the careless, and to encourage the desponding."

flame of charity, to increase our faith and deepen our devotion. They provide instruction for simple folk, decoration for divine worship, continuity of religious practice. They make it possible to tell genuine Christians from their false or heretical counterparts.[33]

The principle of *per visibilia ad invisibilia* ("through the visible to the invisible") serves as a basis for all of these considerations,[34] as it is found in the Preface for Christmas: *Dum visibiliter Deum cognoscimus, per hunc in invisibilium amorem rapiamur.*[35]

Perfection of form and intensification of liturgical gestures

The ceremonial regulations have various functions. A few serve to confer beauty and perfection of form on the execution of the ritual, such as the detailed instructions for the position of the hands when the celebrant crosses either himself or the Eucharistic offerings or when he blesses the faithful, or the exact regulation of the sequence, required arm movements, and steps with which the priest should incense the high altar. Other ceremonial gestures lend greater poignancy to the prayers they accompany, as for example striking the breast at the *mea culpa* of the Confiteor or lifting the hands at the *Sursum corda*. Further gestures serve as expressions of veneration, be it bowing when the Holy Name of Jesus or other holy names are spoken, genuflecting before the consecrated offerings, or kissing holy objects such as the altar and paten. The ceremonies of the traditional liturgy of the Mass thus comprise a rich repertoire of ritualized gestures[36] that distinguish it from the

---

33   J. Bona, *De divina psalmodia*, cap. 19 § III,1: *Opera omnia*, 563. Quoted in Pius XII, *Mediator Dei* (AAS 39:531 / Seasoltz, *Documentation*, 144). Similarly J.J. Olier, *L'esprit des cérémonies de la messe. Explication des cérémonies de la grand'messe de paroisse selon l'usage romain*, Préface (Perpignan: Édition Tempora, 2009), 39f.

34   Cf. Thomas Aquinas, *STh* II–II, 81,7, in *Summa Theologiae*, vol. 39 (2a2ae. 80–91): Religion and Worship, trans. by K.D. O'Rourke (Oxford: Blackfriars Publications [i.a.], 1964), 26–29; *STh* III, 60,4, in *Summa Theologiae*, vol. 56 (3a, 60–65): The Sacraments, trans. by D. Bourke (Oxford: Blackfriars Publications [i.a.], 1975), 12–17; *ScG* 3,119.

35   "So that knowing God visibly, we may be drawn by Him to the love of things invisible." Cf. B. Capelle, "La Préface de Noël," QLP 18 (1933): 273–83.

36   Cf. R. Suntrup, *Die Bedeutung der liturgischen Gebärden und Bewegungen in lateinischen und deutschen Auslegungen des 9. bis 13. Jahrhunderts* (Munich: Wilhelm Fink Verlag, 1978);

Novus Ordo Missae through a stark differentiation and intensification. For example, there are different forms of bowing. The classical liturgy differentiates between the bowing of the head and of the body. The latter can be a deep bow (*inclinatio profunda*) as during the Confiteor, or a medium bow (*inclinatio media*) as after the Confiteor at the prayer *Deus, tu conversus*. The head can be bowed deeply, half, or lightly, corresponding respectively to when the name of Jesus, Mary, or another saint or reigning pope is spoken. The hierarchically arranged forms of inclination here correspond perfectly to the liturgical teaching on the differing levels of honor accorded to God Himself (*cultus latriae*: adoration), the Mother of God (*cultus hyperduliae*: special veneration), and particular individuals (*cultus duliae*: simple honor).[37]

On the ceremonial level, this subtle differentiation is expressed, for example, when the celebrant, before the mixing of the water and wine, blesses the water with the sign of the Cross, as it symbolizes the faithful, but he does not bless the wine, as that is a symbol of Christ. In reverse, the acolyte, when passing the two cruets, kisses them out of respect for the mystery their contents signify.[38] Moreover, at Masses for the dead, the blessing of water is omitted, as the Church no longer possesses the power of the keys over the souls in Purgatory, and instead can speak for them only as an intercessor.[39]

H. Lubienska de Lenval, *La Liturgie du Geste* (Tournai / Paris: Éditions Casterman, ²1957); P. Christophe, *Beauté des gestes du Chrétien* (Paris: Éditions du Cerf, 2009); F. Cassingena-Trévedy, *Te igitur. Le missel de Pie V. Herméneutique et déontologie d'un attachement* (Geneva: Ad Solem Éditions, 2007), 69: "Provided that it is really lived with love, and no longer performed in a cranky and mechanical way, the richness of gestures in the Tridentine celebration, with its signs of the cross, its kisses, its genuflections, eminently favors, in the deepest sense of the term, the *commitment* of the celebrant in the act he carries out: in a movement at once gymnastic and spiritual, it draws the gift of his own body, the real presence of his body (that is to say, of his whole being) to the Body he presents; gesture after gesture, sign after sign, it sews and binds the celebrant to the altar of the Lord and recalls his body to the Body."

37   Cf. Thalhofer, *Handbuch der katholischen Liturgik* I, 295f., 394.

38   Cf. *Ritus servandus in celebratione Missae* VII,4. The missal rubrics do not give every detail, something commented upon by rubricians. So while the missal rubric does not mention the kissing of the water cruet, every rubrician mentions it in connection with serving Low Mass (see, inter alia, J.B. O'Connell, L. O'Connell, LeVavasseur-Haegy-Stercky, Callewaert, Van der Stappen, and Martinucci).

39   Cf. Guéranger, *The Traditional Latin Mass Explained*, 39f.

In addition, certain prayers are ceremonially intensified by accompanying gestures or repetitions. The Confiteor impressively demonstrates how spiritual acts translate into bodily gestures, but at the same time are also strengthened and deepened by the exterior form of expression. At the Confiteor, the priest bows deeply, an expression of humble admission of guilt and, simultaneously, a symbol of "*homo incurvatus in seipsum*" (man turned in on himself), of the sinner bent in on himself, no longer looking up toward Heaven, but rather looking only to what is earthly. Only after the subsequent intercession by the acolyte (*Misereatur tui omnipotens Deus...*) does the priest straighten himself from this posture. At the Confiteor, he folds his hands as a symbol of composure, of surrender to God, and of begging for grace and forgiveness. The triple striking of the breast at the *mea culpa*, already recognized as a gesture of sorrow in Greek antiquity and witnessed as a sign of contrition in the Gospel (cf. Lk 18:13), seeks to strike at the sins rooted in the heart and shatter the source of all sins, the pride of the sinful heart, so that God may create a new and pure heart within (cf. Ezek 36:26; Ps 50:12).[40] The genuflection at *Et incarnatus est* during the Credo and at *Et verbum caro factum est* in the Last Gospel strikingly call to mind that the mystery of God's Incarnation constitutes the pivotal point of the entire history of the world and requires an appropriate response: a physical gesture acknowledging Christ.[41] The triple *Domine, non sum*

---

40   Cf. N. Gihr, *The Holy Sacrifice of the Mass: Dogmatically, Liturgically and Ascetically Explained* (Saint Louis, MO / London: Herder, 1949), 362n1: "This threefold gesture is beautifully expressed in the *Dies irae*: Oro supplex (= joining of the hands) et acclinis (= profund inclination of the body), cor contritum quasi cinis (= striking of the breast)."

41   Cf. Ratzinger, *Feast of Faith*, 74f. (*Theology of the Liturgy*, 328f.): "The hymn to Christ in Philippians 2:6–11 speaks of the cosmic liturgy as a bending of the knee at the name of Jesus, seeing in it a fulfillment of the Isaian prophecy (Is 45:23) of the sovereignty of the God of Israel. In bending the knee at the name of Jesus, the Church is acting in all truth; she is entering into the cosmic gesture, paying homage to the Victor and thereby going over to the Victor's side. For in bending the knee we signify that we are imitating and adopting the attitude of him who, though he was 'in the form of God,' yet 'humbled himself unto death.' In this way, by combining the prophetic word of the Old Covenant and the manner of life of Jesus Christ, the Letter to the Philippians has taken up the sign of kneeling, which it regards as the appropriate posture for Christians to adopt at the name of Jesus, and has given it a cosmic significance in salvation history. Here, the bodily gesture attains the status of a confession of faith in Christ: words could not replace such a confession." On kneeling as an answer to the moments of divine epiphany throughout the entire liturgy, cf. Mosebach, *Heresy of Formlessness*, 90–94.

dignus, accompanied by a striking of the breast, is not an unnecessary repetition, but a form that facilitates the attaining of the proper disposition required for the reception of the Most Blessed Sacrament. Other gestures that accompany the intonation and recitation of the Gloria and Credo make the interior lifting up of the prayer visible in the spreading and raising of the hands or the directing of the eyes upward, and allow the expression of interior acts of adoration (*adoramus te / simul adoratur*), thanksgiving (*gratias agimus tibi*), and petition (*suscipe deprecationem nostram*) to be expressed not only verbally, but also by the physical movements of the bowing of the head in veneration of the divine Persons (*Deo / Deum*) and names (*Jesum Christum*). In the same way, the Offertory prayers are intensified in their expressive power through gestures corresponding to their content—lifting of the eyes (*Suscipe, sancte Pater / Offerimus tibi*) and bowing (*In spiritu humilitatis / Suscipe, sancta Trinitas*). The symbolic wealth of expression found in the prayer gestures at the beginning of the Canon (*Te igitur*) is explained in the following description:

> At the beginning of the Canon, immediately before the start (and not only with the start) of the prayer, the celebrant extends (*extendit*) his hands, lifts them, and then immediately folds them again. The spreading of the hands (previously in the form of a cross) right at the start of the Canon is intended to characterize it as the *repraesentatio passionis Domini* and should recall the Savior, praying with outstretched arms on the Cross; the lifting of the hands is a manifest expression of the elevation of the mind, which should continue through the entire Canon, which formerly bore the name "Prayer" *kat' exochen* [par excellence]; the immediate folding of the hands allows the Canon, this prayer *in sensu eminenti* [in the most significant sense], to appear urgent, the lifting of the eyes (toward Heaven or the altar crucifix) then indicates the directing of the prayer toward God. The immediate lowering of the gaze in connection with the deep bow before the altar expresses that the prayer of the Canon is pervaded by an awareness of sin and guilt and thus it is carried out with a humble attitude, similar to that of the publican in the Temple.

Among the other gestures, the laying of the priest's folded hands upon the altar indicates that it is nevertheless a prayer of the Mediator and is performed in closest association with the one sacrifice of the altar.[42]

The signs of the Cross, which in various forms accompany many prayers or are accompanied by them, emphatically connect the sacrifice on the Cross, which obtained forgiveness of sin and eternal life, to particular parts of the celebration of the Mass, e.g., the request for forgiveness after the Confiteor (*Indulgentiam, absolutionem, et remissionem peccatorum*), the close of the Credo (*et vitam venturi saeculi*), and the reception of Communion (*Corpus Domini nostri Jesu Christi custodiat animam tuam in vitam aeternam*). The sign of the Cross made at the close of the Sanctus during the words *Benedictus qui venit in nomine Domini* recalls that the entrance into Jerusalem began Our Lord's Passion, to which, as a mystery to be realized, vivid witness is given again and again on the altar with profound numerical symbolism, above all by the numerous signs of the Cross made over the bread and wine, or the Body and Blood, respectively, during the prayers of the Canon.[43] Even in the slightest gestures, for instance the thumbs crossed over each other in a cross at the spreading of the hands over the Eucharistic offerings (*Hanc igitur oblationem*), the sign of salvation is present in order to indicate Christ as the sacrificial lamb.

In the priest's gestures that accompany the words of consecration, his actions *in persona Christi* acquire, on the ceremonial level, the most manifest significance, as here these actions become a perfect matching of Christ's actions during the institution of the Sacrament of the Altar at the Last Supper.[44]

---

42 Thalhofer, *Handbuch der katholischen Liturgik* II (Freiburg i. Br.: Verlag Herder, 1890), 199.

43 Cf. Mosebach, *Heresy of Formlessness*, 75f.

44 Cf. C. Folsom, "Gestures Accompanying the Words of Consecration in the History of the *Ordo Missae*": *The Veneration and Administration of the Eucharist*: Proceedings of the Second Colloquium of the International Centre of Liturgical Studies, 9–11 October 1996 (Southampton: The Saint Austin Press, 1997), 75–94.

Richness of symbolism

Not all ceremonies, however, are as direct and clear in meaning as those described thus far. Why, for example, is the Epistle read from one side of the altar and the Gospel from the other side? Why does the priest turn with a half circle from the altar to the people at each *Dominus vobiscum*, turning back around to the altar with a half circle movement, while at the *Orate fratres* he completes a full circle turn, turning back toward the altar in the other direction? Why is it that during the incensing of the bread and wine on the altar the censor is passed over the offerings in the form of a cross twice in a clockwise rotation, and a third time counter-clockwise? Why is the paten concealed under the corporal after the offering and only pulled out again after the *Pater noster*?

These are just a few examples of how much in the traditional rite of the Mass is not readily understandable, but is made accessible only by knowledge of its historical development. Such knowledge of the genesis of particular ceremonies, however, is not unproblematic. The further and more precisely one investigates the centuries-old history of the rite of the Mass, the clearer one thing becomes: what appears to have come to us from time immemorial and was regarded by earlier epochs as untouchable (as they often lacked information that was recovered later) proves to be historically circumscribed, the result of contingent factors, and a relic of practical requirements that once existed but have not existed for a long time now. The further historical liturgical research progressed, the greater became the temptation of using knowledge of the genesis of particular rites and ceremonies in order to question their value.[45] Such relativism or skepticism toward historical developments does not, however, agree with the constant conviction of the Church that in the course of history an organic

---

45 Thus, for example, B. Durst, *Das Wesen der Eucharistiefeier und des christlichen Priestertums* [Studia Anselmiana 32] (Neresheim: Ulrichsbuchhandlung, 1953), 155: "*Per quem haec omnia.* This prayer seems to be a blessing prayer . . . blessing of natural produce from the earliest days of the Roman Canon to the late Middle Ages. But since, in our time, such a blessing of natural produce no longer takes place, it would not seem unfounded for this prayer to be entirely omitted at this point." It was with similar arguments that the elimination of the Last Gospel, for example, was demanded, whose incorporation into the rite of the Mass is owed to the function of blessing attributed to the Prologue to the Gospel of John, so greatly treasured in the Middle Ages.

development of liturgy occurs under the assistance of the Holy Ghost.[46] Pope Pius XII, in his liturgical encyclical *Mediator Dei*, already warned against an excessive archaeologism or antiquarianism, which enthusiastically idealized all that is old and would have liked to dismiss later forms of development as superimpositions and incrustations, and which sought to reduce worship at all costs to its earliest forms, thus depriving it of all the beauties it accumulated over the centuries.[47]

46 Cf. Recktenwald, "Die alte Liturgie bewahren?," in Esser, *Dem Schönen und Heiligen dienen*, 100f.: "The knowledge of the historical conditions of ritual details seduces us into assuming that their importance, justification, and inner meaningfulness are of the same contingency as the constellation of those conditions. In fact, it is precisely the essence of the rite that makes its value emancipated from the contingency of its genesis. . . . Basically, we have always known that all of these details and all the texts were created somewhere for some reason. But the ignorance about *what* time in *which* place and on *which* occasion they originated, allowed us no judgment and thus no judging about the rite. And so we were closer to the truth than those who were subject to seductive conclusions. For example, because of their knowledge of the later, namely the medieval origins of the Offertory prayers, they were inclined to conclude that these prayers were less original and therefore deserved to be abolished. For the assumption of decreasing dignity over the years implies the denial of the continual action of the Holy Spirit in the Church, and thus of a Spirit-driven progress in general. . . . The knowledge of the historical origins pretends to be a knowledge of disposition, thus suggesting a power of disposition and destroying the consciousness of the sacrality and inviolability. . . . This means that the more the liturgical historian delves into his discipline, the more he needs a deeper faith in the action of the Holy Spirit and in the supernaturalism of the Church. Only this faith saves him from the temptation to replace his faith in the holiness of the rites by his historical knowledge of their genesis, and thus to present it as an enlightenment concerning a naive faith to be overcome. Exactly with this pretense, however, were the results of research concerning the history of liturgy often brought to the attention of the people of God, who were declared, ironically, to have 'come of age.'"

47 Cf. Pius XII, *Mediator Dei* (AAS 39:545f. / Seasoltz, *Documentation*, 124f.); Paul VI, Encyclical Letter *Ecclesiam Suam*: "No one should deceive himself into thinking that the Church, which has now become a vast, magnificent, and majestic temple built to the glory of God, should be reduced to the modest proportions which it had in its earliest days, as though this minimal form were the only one that is genuine and lawful" (AAS 56 [1964]: 630 / trans.: http://w2.vatican.va/content/paul-vi/en/encyclicals/documents/hf_p-vi_enc_06081964_ecclesiam.html). Cf. A.-G. Martimort, *L'histoire et le problème liturgique contemporain: Études de Pastorale Liturgique* [LO 1] (Paris: Éditions du Cerf, 1944), 97–126, 119f.: "It is important to avoid the attitude of an 'archaeologist.' The history of the Church is not stopped at a given time; it is no more a question of settling in the thirteenth century than it is of returning to the fifth; we must be aware of the needs of our time, and give them satisfaction by drawing on the lessons of the past, but without rejecting the definitive enrichments of this past—of all of this past, although sometimes it is necessary to make an effort of discernment in order not to mix the final contributions and the transitional elements in this past." Cf. Un moine de

Already in the nineteenth century, Dom Prosper Guéranger OSB had sharply criticized similar tendencies as a characteristic of the so-called anti-liturgical heresy:

> All sectarians without exception begin by claiming the rights of antiquity. They wish to free Christianity of all that has sunk into falsehood and has become unworthy of God because of man's error and passions. They only wish for the primordial and they assert the claim that they are returning back to the cradle of Christian institutions. To this end they shorten, obliterate, and cut away. Everything falls under their blows; whoever expectantly wishes to see before his eyes divine worship in its original purity finds himself besieged with new formulas which are but a day old and indisputably penned by men, as their authors are still living.[48]

Apart from the fact that some "results" of research into liturgical history often proved to be unsupported and quickly outdated, they are hardly suitable for determining the Church's *lex orandi*. In contrast to the tendencies of a certain liturgical archaism, which sought to purify a supposedly classical form of the Roman liturgy of so-called medieval overgrowths,[49] the ceremonial elaboration in the Middle Ages has in the meanwhile been experienced as a valuable enrichment of the Roman rite of Mass.[50]

Fontgombault, *Une histoire de la messe* (Feucherolles: La Nef, 2009), 79–87; Kocik, *The Reform of the Reform?*, 214–25; Archbishop W. Godefray, "Allocution in the Congregatio generalis V (fifth general congregation) on Oct. 23, 1962": *Acta Synodalia Sacrosancti Concilii Oecumenici Vaticani II*, vol. 1. Periodus prima, pars 1 (Vatican City: Typis Polyglottis Vaticanis, 1970), 374.

48 Guéranger, *Institutions liturgiques* I, 399f.

49 Cf. J. Ratzinger: "This archaism has often made us close our eyes to the good things which have been evolved in later developments and has caused us to set the taste of one period up on a pedestal; admittedly, it was a splendid period which rightly commands the greatest respect and affection, but its taste can no more be made a matter of absolute dogma than the taste of any other period" ("Catholicism after the Council," trans. by P. Russell, *The Furrow* 18 [1967]: 10); idem, *The Ratzinger Report*, 131f.

50 Cf. Ratzinger, *Spirit of the Liturgy*, 90 (*Theology of the Liturgy*, 55f.): "The changes in the Middle Ages brought losses, but they also provided a wonderful spiritual deepening. They unfolded the magnitude of the mystery instituted at the Last Supper and enabled it to be experienced with a new fullness."

Moreover, particular liturgical elements that were originally introduced because of practical requirements or other reasons determined by history could take on new, symbolic meanings in later epochs, which allow them to transcend time and make them worth protecting.[51]

For example, at the elevation of the Host and chalice, according to the instructions of the rubrics, the servers are to lift the priest's chasuble, which was necessary originally because of the design of the medieval bell chasuble and its heavy, richly-ornamented material.[52] Today this custom is retained, despite modified forms of vestments, not least of all because of its beautiful and symbolic meaning when one recalls the woman with an issue of blood who was healed by touching the hem of Christ's garment (cf. Mt 9:20f.) and then sees in this gesture a symbol of the sanctifying power that emanates from the Sacrament of the Altar.

Other customs have not only received a symbolic meaning retrospectively, but also owe their development to the symbolism itself. For example, the custom of placing the closed missal on the altar in such a way that the clasp faces toward the altar crucifix, apart from reasons of convention so that the missal does not turn its back toward the crucifix, results from the biblical symbolism of opening the book, which is reserved for the lion of the tribe of Judah who conquered on the Cross (cf. Rev 5:5).[53]

The Middle Ages saw the development of countless allegorical and symbolic explanations of the Mass, which interpreted the individual rites and ceremonies emblematically in order to find in the course of the celebration a symbolic summary of the history of salvation, that is, the life

---

51   Cf. May, *Die alte und die neue Messe*, 14: "The knowledge of the historical origin of a prayer or custom does not say anything about its liturgical significance and pastoral fruitfulness in the present. What was originally introduced for a specific reason may turn out to stand above time. Liturgical elements that have a specific meaning from a historical viewpoint can give them up and gain another meaning. By no means is the older stage always more genuine and more evident than the more recent." Cf. Z.-C. Jourdain, *La Sainte Eucharistie* III (Paris: Hippolyte Walzer, Libraire-Éditeur, 1900), 407–14.

52   Cf. *Ritus servandus in celebratione Missae* VIII,6. Cf. Jungmann, *Missarum sollemnia* II, 266; idem, *The Mass of the Roman Rite* II, 213f.

53   Cf. Thalhofer, *Handbuch der katholischen Liturgik* II, 57n3: "In the Missal and by special decree of the Congregation of Rites (Sep. 7, 1816), it is prescribed for the private Mass that the priest himself opens the Missal, and he too shall close it again, as a representative of the One, of whom is said: *ipse aperit, et nemo claudit, claudit, et nemo aperit* (Rev 3,7)."

of Christ.[54] This certainly expresses the conviction—regardless of what appears to be a mostly arbitrary interpretation of detail today—that the rite of the Mass is capable of making the work of salvation transparent in all of its wealth[55] and that not even a single custom or ceremony lacks a deeper symbolic meaning.[56] The spiritual interpretation of the Bible, unlike historical-critical exegesis, is not satisfied with inquiry into the historical conditions of formation, but further asks what message Scripture contains

54 Cf. P. Rorem, *The Medieval Development of Liturgical Symbolism* (Bramcote [i.a.]: Grove Books, 1986); A. Härdelin, "Liturgie als Abbreviatur der Heilsökonomie": *Atti del Congresso Internazionale: Tommaso d'Aquino nel suo settimo centenario* [4. Problemi di teologia] (Naples: Edizioni domenicane italiane, 1976), 433–43; R. Messner, "Zur Hermeneutik allegorischer Liturgieerklärung," ZKTh 115 (1993): 284–319; A. Häussling, "Messerklärung (expositiones missae)": idem, *Christliche Identität aus der Liturgie. Theologische und historische Studien zum Gottesdienst der Kirche.* Ed. by M. Klöckener, i.a. [Liturgiewissenschaftliche Quellen und Forschungen 79] (Münster: Aschendorff Verlag, 1997), 142–50; A. Franz, *Die Messe im Deutschen Mittelalter* (Bonn: Nova & Vetera, 2003 [repr. of Freiburg i. Br.: Verlag Herder, 1902]), 333–514; C. Barthe, "The 'Mystical' Meaning of the Ceremonies of the Mass: Liturgical Exegesis in the Middle Ages," U.M. Lang (ed.), *Genius of the Roman Rite*, 179–97; C. Barthe, *La messe. Une forêt de symboles* (Versailles: Via romana, 2011); idem / D. Millet-Gérard, "Introduction": Guillaume Durand, *Le sens spirituel de la liturgie. Rational des Divins Offices.* Livre IV de la Messe (Geneva: Ad Solem Éditions, 2003), 7–65; J.F. White, "Durandus and the Interpretation of Christian Worship": G.H. Shriver (ed.), *Contemporary Reflections on Medieval Christian Tradition: Essays in Honor of Ray C. Petry* (Durham, NC: Duke University Press, 1974), 41–52; C. Barthold, "Introduction," Durandus, *Rationale* (Mülheim/Mosel: Carthusianus Verlag, 2012), xx–xlviii.

55 Cf. the Secret of the Ninth Sunday after Pentecost: "*Quoties huius hostiae commemoratio celebretur, opus nostrae redemptionis exercetur*" [For as often as this memorial sacrifice is offered, the work of our redemption is wrought]. Quoted in Second Vatican Council, SC 2.

56 Cf. Durandus, *Rationale divinorum officiorum*, prooemium 1 (CCM 140, 3): "*Quecumque in ecclesiasticis officiis, rebus ac ornamentis consistunt, divinis plena sunt signis atque mysteriis, ac singularia celesti sunt dulcedine redundantia, si diligentem tamen habeant inspectorem, qui norit mel de petra sugere oleumque de durissimo saxo*" [Whatever is established in ecclesiastical services, vessels, and ornaments is full of divine signs and mysteries, and each of them is overflowing with heavenly sweetness, provided there is a diligent observer who knows to suck honey out of the rock and oil out of the most solid stone]. This is already almost verbatim from Innocent III, *De sacro Altaris Mysterio*, prologus (PL 217, 774B / MSIL 15, 55). Cf. Mosebach, *Heresy of Formlessness*, 20: "We often smile at the way medieval people were fond of explaining mundane things in a spiritual way. For instance, if the nave of a church was not quite square with the chancel, people said that the whole church represented the crucified Lord, and the slightly crooked chancel was his head, fallen to one side. I think this is how we *should* look at things. It is the most effective way of filling a rite with prayer and thus uniting form and content."

for the believing reader of today.[57] By analogy, the traditional rite of the Mass also makes its riches accessible to him who begins to understand its timeless language of symbolism and who allows himself to be led through the holy ceremonies from the visible to the invisible.

If the classical liturgy uses the senses as a means to speak to man, all of these means have certainly been taken from the world — light, color, sounds, incense, the language of signs. These means, however, do not seek to bind human senses to the world, but rather to lift them up and allow them to discern the invisible in the visible, the heavenly in the earthly, and the eternal in the temporal. The preface of the Liturgical Constitution (SC 2) beautifully describes a "dynamism of transcendence"[58] into which the liturgy should lead man. It is concerned with crossing over from the human to the divine, from the visible to the invisible, from action to contemplation, from the present to the future and eternal. The classical form of the liturgy perfectly conforms to this dynamic of crossing over, as in its rite it is always concerned with the movement from man to God, from the exterior to the interior, from below to above, from the now to that which is to come.[59]

COHERENCE OF FORM AND CONTENT

The dynamic of crossing over from the visible to the invisible is especially guaranteed in the traditional liturgy through the correspondence between form and content. The postulate of the coherence of cultic forms is much more than a question of mere liturgical aesthetics.[60] Rather, it is entirely a matter of the fundamental requirements of the act of worship. The exterior forms of veneration and adoration that belong to the classical rite of the Mass are the best way of guaranteeing the corresponding

---

57   Cf. M. Fiedrowicz, *Theologie der Kirchenväter. Grundlagen frühchristlicher Glaubens-reflexion* (Freiburg i. Br.: Verlag Herder, ²2010), 97–187.

58   J. Ratzinger, "Fortieth Anniversary of the Constitution on the Sacred Liturgy: A Look Back and a Look Forward," idem, *Theology of the Liturgy* (*Collected Works* 11), 574–88, 577, 586.

59   Critical questions on the NOM concerning these aspects are formulated by A. M. Card. Stickler, "Erinnerungen und Erfahrungen eines Konzilsperitus der Liturgiekommission," in Breid (ed.), *Die heilige Liturgie*, 160–95, 193f.

60   Cf. Mosebach, *Heresy of Formlessness*, 14: "People of aesthetic sensibility, much scorned and suspect, are the recipients of a terrible gift: they can infallibly discern the inner truth of what they see, of some process, of an idea, on the basis of its external form."

interior attitudes.[61] Prayers of preparation, genuflections, and bows are not trifles that could be omitted without diminishing the faithful completion of the holy action. The interior encounter with the sacred must manifest itself outwardly, involving and being supported by an exterior form. The traditional liturgy insists that interior sentiments are plausible only if at the same time they appear in an outwardly appropriate manner. In the same way, the liturgy is aware of the formative power that the sensible can exercise on the spiritual condition.[62]

With the number of its sacred signs, the beauty of its altars, the preciousness of its chalices and vestments, and its ceaseless expressions of reverence, the classical rite guarantees this correspondence of interior belief and exterior form. This rite is, so to speak, safeguarded against a possible discord between that which one believes and that which one sees. Here is found the perfected unity and harmony between that which is to be performed and the way in which it is performed. The classical rite does not require anything to be believed that one does not — symbolically — see.

This correspondence of content and form is created above all by the multiple signs of reverence, which demonstrate the presence of God,[63]

---

61   Cf. Dobszay, *Restoration*, 215: "The traditional gestures transmitted to us through the classical Roman rite have a special role, even in our days: they are able to give shape to the priest's mind in liturgy. The majority of these motions are not addressed to the congregation. They make sense only if the priest believes that he is performing a service before God.... The priest who follows the rubrics and goes through these motions, gestures and hand positions attentively is compelled in his mind 'to stay within the sanctuary.'"

62   Cf. Augustine, *De cura pro mortuis gerenda* 5,7 (CSEL 41, 632 / St Augustine, *Treatises on Marriage and Other Subjects*, trans. by Ch. T. Wilcox, *The Fathers of the Church* 27 [New York, NY: Fathers of the Church, Inc., 1955], 360): "Those who pray by using the members of the body, as when they bend the knees, when they extend the hands, or even prostrate themselves upon the ground, or whatever else they do in a visible manner, they do that which indicates that they are suppliants although their invisible will and the intention of their heart is known to God, for He has no need of such outward signs to indicate that the human mind is in a state of supplication to Him. By doing this a man excites himself more to a proper state for praying and lamenting more humbly and fervently, and, somehow or other, since these movements of the body cannot be made except by a previous movement of the mind, by these same actions of the visible man, the invisible soul which prompted them is strengthened. Then, by reason of this the devotion of one's heart is strengthened, because he has resolved that these prayers be made and has made them."

63   Cf. T. Guillard, "Le missel romain, porteur du sacré," *Liturgie et sacré* (CIEL, 2003), 351–60; D. Marc, "Du respect de l'Église pour les vases sacrés, les saintes espèces et les

involving either the Real Presence of the consecrated Eucharistic species, the sacramental representation of the priest acting *in persona Christi*, or symbolic visualization by means of sacred things such as the altar.[64] Prayers, genuflections, bows, and incensing create a choreography of reverence in the liturgical interplay, which is further developed by actions involving the vestments, missal, chalice, and paten: kisses,[65] purifications before use,[66] subsequent purifications,[67] and veiling and unveiling.[68]

In every imaginable way, the traditional rite of the Mass expresses veneration and worship of the presence of God in the Sacrament of the Altar. The quietness of the Canon envelops the mystery of the consecration with a veil of reverential silence. Everything that comes into contact with the Body of Christ is marked with the greatest reverence. Before taking hold of the host, the celebrant lightly brushes the tips of the index fingers of both hands on the front corners of the corporal. In the same way after the consecration, he brushes any possible clinging particles

---

parcelles d'hostie consacrée," *Présence du Christ dans la liturgie*. Actes du sixième colloque d'études historiques, théologiques et canoniques sur le rite romain [Versailles, Novembre 2000] (Versailles: CIEL, 2001), 345–57; J.-Y. Hameline, "Célébrer dévotement après le concile de Trente," MD 218 (1999): 7–37. John Paul II, "Salutatory address to the plenary assembly of the Congregation for Divine Worship (Sep. 21, 2001)," *Notitiae* 37 (2001): 401–4, 402: "In the Roman Missal, called the Missal of St Pius V, as in several Eastern liturgies, there are very beautiful prayers with which the priest expresses the most profound sense of humility and reverence before the sacred mysteries: they reveal the very substance of the liturgy."

64 Cf. J. Nebel, "Die 'ordentliche' und die 'ausserordentliche' Form," 191: "The traditional *usus* knows a consistent and peculiar reverence to the altar, which has at least since the High Middle Ages also found a detailed expression [in gestures]. Access to the altar must first be requested by the celebrant in the prayers at the foot of the altar, after which point his relation to the altar is so 'strong' that he never omits to kiss it before turning away from the altar. The relation to the altar also determines the exact position of the hands or forearms that touch the altar at certain moments, but not at other moments. The altar is also the place of the consecration; the paten, on the other hand, is associated exclusively with the meal-aspect of the Eucharist..." Cf. Davies, *Pope Paul's New Mass*, 389–95.

65 At the putting on of particular vestments; the beginning of the Gospel in the missal after its proclamation; the paten at the *Libera nos*.

66 The inside of the chalice before pouring in the wine; the paten before it is kissed at the *Libera nos*.

67 Chalice, paten, and ciborium after Holy Communion.

68 Use of the chalice veil; the subdeacon holding the paten with a veil during the Canon, or covering it with the corporal. For "revelation through veiling," cf. Mosebach, *Heresy of Formlessness*, 149–58.

from his thumbs and index fingers into the chalice, and subsequently holds these fingers together until the Purification so that not even the smallest particle may go astray. For this reason his hands must remain on the corporal when he genuflects or kisses the altar, and the purification of the fingers takes place over the chalice, on top of the corporal. The corporal itself, upon which the Body of Christ rested, is folded in a special way for the protection of any possibly remaining particles, and kept safe in the burse. The chalice is always covered with the pall to protect the Blood of Christ from any possible impurities. The altar is covered with three linens to absorb the Precious Blood, should any spill from the chalice. Immediately after the consecration, each of the transubstantiated species is worshiped by the priest with a genuflection, and a second genuflection follows after the elevation of the host and that of the chalice. Each further change to the consecrated species — the removal of the pall at the elevation of the chalice, the breaking of the host, turning away from the altar and turning toward the faithful — is always accompanied by further genuflections. All of these instructions manifest the Church's faith in the Real Presence of Christ, which all particles of the consecrated species contain, small and inconspicuous though they may be. St Thomas Aquinas gave poetic expression to this belief of the Church in the Sequence for Corpus Christi, *Lauda Sion*: *Fracto demum sacramento / Ne vacilles, sed memento / Tantum esse sub fragmento / Quantum toto tegitur.*[69]

In the Missal's introduction, following the ritual instructions on the course of the Holy Mass (*Ritus servandus*), comes a separate section, *De Defectibus*, which addresses in detail all kinds of interruptions, emergencies, and accidents. In this way, these regulations, which are covered more comprehensively and exactly in appropriate rubrical handbooks,[70] seek to ensure

---

69   "If at length the sacrament is broken, / do not falter, but remember, / how much is under one fragment, / as much as hidden in the whole." Cf. in general, J.-H. Tück, *A Gift of Presence. The Theology and Poetry of the Eucharist in Thomas Aquinas*, trans. by S. Hefelfinger (Washington, DC: The Catholic University of America Press, 2018); the translation of *Lauda Sion* is on pp. 217–18.

70   Cf. P. J. B de Herdt, *Sacrae Liturgiae Praxis iuxta Ritum Romanum* II (Louvain: Vanlinthout, ⁴1863), 153–226. The statements of *De Defectibus* of the MRom are substantially found in Thomas Aquinas, *STh* III, 83,6 ad 1–6, in *Summa Theologiae*, vol. 59, trans. by Th. Gilby, 178–83.

that the sacred action can always be continued with the greatest possible reverence and dignity even under the most adverse circumstances, as defects or disturbances need not be met with imprudent improvisation, but with procedures that have been approved or thought through with practical sense.[71]

The traditional rite is rightly designated as a "school of reverence":

> It translates this feeling into language, music, movement, and silence, in the manner in which the liturgical vessels are manufactured, such as the linen which comes into contact with the offerings, and in the instructions for the spiritual and physical preparation for the celebration of the holy mysteries.... The inner resplendence of this rite does not demand cathedrals — rather it has made possible the building of cathedrals and even in the catacombs created the invisible cathedral of veneration.[72]

SACRALITY AND BEAUTY
Entrance into the sphere of holiness

With its interior radiance, which led to the raising of the cathedrals, the classical rite of the Mass resembles the king's daughter described in the psalm (44:14f.), whose glory is internal (*omnis gloria eius filiae regis ab intus*), but who, at the same time, wears gilded and colorful garments (*in fimbris aureis, circumamicta varietate*). The psalmist goes on to state: "After her shall virgins be brought to the king" (*adducentur regi virgines post eam*), an entourage that resembles the varied arts that place their best and most beautiful creations in the service of God, thus becoming a part of divine

---

71 Cf. Mosebach, *Heresy of Formlessness*, 131f.: "It is in the nature of the rubrics to envisage all imaginable mishaps that could impede the course of the Mass: the death of the priest before, during, or after transubstantiation; poisoning of the altar wine; fire; the arrival of enemy troops; flood; severe frost that causes the wine to freeze in the chalice; and the priest's vomiting after receiving Communion. There is positively nothing that could shake the spirit of the rubrics! They take into account every kind of disturbance of mind or body and have detailed, carefully weighed answers for all eventualities."

72 M. Mosebach, "Ein Apostolat der Ehrfurcht": Priesterseminar St Petrus (ed.), *Von der Liturgie und dem Geheimnis der heiligen Messe* (Wigratzbad: Priesterseminar St Petrus, 1996), 10–15, 13, 15. Cf. B. Deneke, "Die Bezeugung der eucharistischen Realpräsenz — Ein Vergleich," UVK 45 (2014): 7–23.

worship themselves. The traditional rite of the Mass is one of the great inspiring forces in the history of art, which sought to manifest the interior splendor of the liturgy in an exterior way by means of architecture and music, sculpture and painting, embroidery of vestments and goldsmithery. Over the course of centuries, the classical rite of the Mass not only prompted the development of countless works of art; in its historically perfected form, the Mass constitutes a work of art in and of itself.[73] The traditional liturgy's own beauty is the result of the harmonious interplay of sacred space, language, and music, of magnificent and sublime texts, stylized gestures, dignified strides, precious sacred vessels, costly vestments, and richly ornamented missals and evangelistaries. All these different elements come to inner unity through their common ordering to the glorification of God,[74] whose beauty is reflected in the liturgy. The material beauty of these elements that support divine worship serves the formal beauty of the liturgy, which consists in facilitating the prayerful lifting up of the Church to God.[75]

73   Cf. I. Schuster, *The Sacramentary*, vol. II, 59: "If, therefore, we wish to appreciate the full artistic beauty of the Roman Liturgy, it is not enough to read, nor even to meditate upon the words of the Missal, for these are like the text of some great drama, the full significance of which cannot be fully grasped until one sees it interpreted on the stage. In the same manner, the Roman Liturgy must be seen and heard in the basilicas, with the music, the sacred vestments, the ritual, and the processions which render it so rich and varied, so sublime and impressive. When carried out as the *Caeremoniale Episcoporum* and the *Missale Romanum* prescribe, the liturgy is seen to be so great a masterpiece of heavenly grace and beauty that no art can ever produce its equal." Cf. P. Gardeil, "On disait autrefois 'Beau comme la messe,'" C. Barthe (ed.), *Reconstruire la liturgie* (Paris: François-Xavier de Guibert, 1997), 65–78, esp. 69. Cf. the petition of 56 English intellectuals and artists: "Appeal to preserve the Roman Catholic Mass in its traditional form" (*Times* July 6, 1971), reprinted with biographical notes in Shaw, *The Case for Liturgical Restoration*, 213–16.

74   Cf. M. Festugière, *La Liturgie catholique. Essai de synthèse, suivi de quelques développements* (Maredsous: Abbaye de Maredsous, 1913), 150: "On this ensemble of admirable variety, the thought of the service of God confers an incomparable unity. The beauty of the liturgy is therefore the result, one and complex, of a large number of perfectly coordinated factors."

75   Cf. Festugière, *Liturgie*, 174f.: "The true beauty of the liturgy is its *formal beauty*. Therefore the liturgy is beautiful when it has the necessary qualities to create an *ascending current* of souls or rather loves, a current of social prayer. Moreover, for the creation of such a current to be favored or even made possible, the *material beauty* of the liturgy—realized to a certain degree—is a necessary condition. All lavishness and skills of art must be sought and placed at the service of worship that are capable of increasing its formal beauty—while anything else must be pushed aside. Furthermore, centuries have created in liturgy certain traditions which are equivalent to inviolable rules." Cf. I. Herwegen, *Das Kunstprinzip*

When and insofar as architecture, language, song, vestments, and movement leave behind the everyday and renounce all that is banal, they facilitate the existence of the sacred sphere, in which the presence of God is mystically felt.[76] It is an indication of the sacred that it belongs to the realm of the world on the one side and to the realm of God on the other. God sets apart created realities — particular places, times, people, actions, and things — in order to direct these toward Himself in a special manner, or to make Himself present there in a special way.[77] Thus the created reality in this place receives a sacred character and becomes a place of encounter with the divine.

In view of the history of this world, which since its beginning has borne the signature of closing itself off from God, and is thus the history of progressive de-sacralization, sacrality signifies the return of God into the world and its history.[78] If the phenomenon of sacrality can be found in all world religions,[79] the Catholic Church, in contrast to Protestantism, was always convinced that she did not live from the death of all sacred phenomena, but rather that she could find in God's revelation all that man sought after in the other religions. Thus, in the universally observed

---

der Liturgie, 18f.; D. v. Hildebrand, *Trojan Horse in the City of God: The Catholic Crisis Explained* (Manchester, NH: Sophia Institute Press, 1993), 229–39; D. Crouan, *L'art et la liturgie. Essai sur les rapports constants unissant l'art et la liturgie au cours des siècles* (Paris: Éditions Pierre Téqui, 1988).

76 Cf. G. Calvet, "Grandeur de notre univers liturgique," *Itinéraires* 350 (1990): 209–53, 220: "Beauty has the essential purpose of raising us to the level of the sacred."

77 Cf. Thomas Aquinas, *STh* II–II, 99,1: "*Sacrum dicitur aliquid ex eo quod ad divinum cultum ordinatur. . . . ex hoc quod aliquid deputatur ad cultum Dei, efficitur quoddam divinum, et sic ei quaedam reverentia debetur quae refertur in Deum*," in *Summa Theologiae*, vol. 40 (2a2ae. 92–100): Superstition and Irreverence, trans. by F. O'Meara and M.J. Duffy (Oxford: Blackfriars Publications [i.a.], 1968), 115 ["Something is called sacred because it is appointed for divine worship. . . . it is invested with a quality of divinity from being appointed for the service of God, and thus a certain reverence is due to it, which reverence is referred to God"]. Cf. J. Pieper, *In Search of the Sacred*, trans. L. Krauth (San Francisco: Ignatius Press, 1991), 22–23, 25; B. Neiss, "Le sacré . . . réflexions préliminaires sur une notion oubliée": *Liturgie et sacré* (CIEL, 2003), 11–19.

78 Cf. M. Levatois, *La messe à l'envers. L'espace liturgique en débat* (Paris: Éditions Jacqueline Chambon, 2009), 100f. with reference to L. Bouyer, "Faut-il en finir avec le sacré?": Card. Renard / L. Bouyer / Y. Congar / J. Daniélou (eds.), *Notre foi* (Paris: Éditions Beauchesne, 1967), 33.

79 Cf. D. Barsotti, *Liturgie als Mitte* (Einsiedeln: Johannes-Verlag, 1961), 8: "The deepest concern and purpose of every cult in the historical religions of mankind is the restoration of lost sacredness."

religious expressions of the sacred — places, times, and languages[80] — there is a specifically Christian manifestation of sacrality; the liturgy would be destroyed if this sacrality were abandoned.[81] "The language, the gestures, the vestments, the rite, everything that surrounds the religious act and differentiates it from the common and profane, does not lead away from God: on the contrary, it allows Him to be more strongly felt!"[82]

The conscious egress from the realm of the profane and entrance into the sphere of the sacred is expressed in the prayers at the foot of the altar when the priest prays the verses of the psalm: *Discerne causam meam de gente non sancta* (Distinguish my cause from the nation that is not holy).[83] This separation from the profane is an unalterable requirement for the *Introibo ad altare Dei*, for the entrance into the sanctuary, into the sacred space, the symbolic and veiled presence of God:

> As long as it has reached a certain loftiness, all sacred liturgy tends, by means of ritual, to raise us above the banal and the everyday, not for the sake of an aesthetic goal, but to show the faithful that the action taking place comes from God. It signifies that something heavenly comes down to touch the earth.[84]

Pope Gregory wrote at the end of the sixth century concerning this:

> At the moment of the immolation, at the sound of the priest's voice, the heavens stand open and choirs of angels are present at

---

80   Cf. Neiss, "Le sacré," 15f.

81   Cf. Hitchcock, *Recovery of the Sacred*; D. Torevell, *Losing the Sacred: Ritual, Modernity and Liturgical Reform* (Edinburgh: T. & T. Clark, 2000).

82   Capelle, "Plaidoyer pour le latin," 71.

83   Cf. R. de Mattei, *La Liturgia della Chiesa nell' epoca della secolarizzazione* (Chieti: Edizioni Solfanelli, 2009), 66f.: "If there is a moment and a place where the secularized world has not penetrated, this place, this moment is the traditional Mass. After the words '*introibo ad Altare Dei*,' the frothy tide of secularization that spoils and pollutes everything stops at the door of the sanctuary, does not penetrate the immaculate enclosure, where a pure and stainless victim is offered and immolated to God. All the expressions that follow confine a space, dividing the *gens sancta* from the *gens non sancta*."

84   A Benedictine Monk [G. Calvet], *Four Benefits of the Liturgy* (London: Saint Austin Press, 1999), 21.

the mystery of Jesus Christ. There at the altar the lowliest is united with the most sublime, earth is joined to heaven, the visible and invisible somehow merge into one.[85]

Reflection of heaven

No way is better suited to making this heavenly dimension of the liturgy perceptible to the faithful than the *via pulchritudinis* (way of beauty). Tradition vividly describes this in the baptism of Clovis, King of the Franks, on Christmas Day (498/499) in Rheims. The processional route was decorated with expensive curtains and colorful cloths and was filled with fragrances of every kind. The sound of hymns, spiritual songs, and litanies filled the air. The crowd cheered the King and the holy bishop Remigius. The enchanting brilliance of the ceremony prompted Clovis to ask the bishop if this were the kingdom he had promised to him. The holy Remigius replied that this was not yet that kingdom, but was only the beginning of the path that led to it.[86] In this sense, the beauty of the liturgy is always the start of a path upon which, from the very beginning, lies a reflection of that which the eyes will see in its entirety at the destination. Therefore the liturgy of the Church on earth, still on its pilgrimage (*Ecclesia peregrinans*), should and must always reflect something of the splendor of the Church triumphant (*Ecclesia triumphans*) and make visible in the beauty of earthly divine worship the glory of the heavenly Jerusalem.

The power of conversion that emanates from such a beautiful liturgy is demonstrated by a depiction in the so-called Nestor's Chronicle, according

---

85   Gregory I, *Dialogi* 4,60,3 (SCh 265, 202 / St Gregory the Great, *Dialogues*, 273. Cf. Cassingena-Trévedy, *Te igitur*, 75f.: "We enter the Tridentine liturgy ... a 'meta-world,' as a sort of region beyond, here below. Basically, the experience to which the great and true Tridentine celebration invites is homogeneous with that which is constantly suggested by the catechesis and homiletics of the 4th and 5th centuries, that of John Chrysostom and Theodore of Mopsuestia, not to mention the two *Hierarchies* of Pseudo-Dionysius that belong to the same milieu: it is a properly *mysterious* experience, based on a radical crossing, an irreversible passage from one world to another world. This is the essential and constitutive *orientation* of the Tridentine celebration and its most beautifully traditional character. 'The priest is here. Life is far away. This is Mass,' says Paul Claudel: John Chrysostom does not say anything other than that when, beginning the little pre-anaphoric dialogue, he invites the faithful to 'now set aside all cares of life,' the *biōtika*."

86   Cf. Hinkmar, *Vita Sancti Remigii* 15 (Monumenta Germaniae Historica. Scriptores rerum Merovingicarum 3, 296).

to which the Grand Prince Vladimir of Kiev, in search of the one true God, sent delegates to question Muslims, Jews, and Greeks and bring back reports of their manners of divine worship. At the Hagia Sophia in Constantinople (987), these delegates attended a liturgy that surpassed all the others they had seen in splendor and beauty:

> From this moment on we no longer knew whether we were in Heaven or on earth, for certainly there is no such splendor and no such beauty anywhere on earth. We cannot describe it, we only know that God dwells there among those people, and their worship surpasses that of every other place. For we cannot forget that beauty.

This they reported upon their return to their ruler, who, as a result, agreed to be baptized, and raised Christianity to the religion of the state.[87] Thus the liturgy not only describes the glory of heaven in its texts, but also allows a reflection of that glory to shine forth in its own beauty. Upon seeing the traditional rite of the Mass, even an outside observer can immediately sense that here the presence of God is believed and celebrated.[88] In the classical rite the impression of the sacred is simply *given*, and certainly as far as possible made independent of the person of the celebrant. In so doing, this rite proves itself superior to all other forms in which this impression is to a great extent dependent upon the personal style of celebration (*ars celebrandi*).[89] A liturgy whose sacred character was dependent on the priest's piety would have disavowed itself.

Even before the liturgy addresses itself to man's intellectual powers, it captures his soul with its beauty. It is not without reason that the beauty of divine worship is described as being the great portal of the Church:

---

87 Cf. P. Hauptmann / G. Stricker (ed.), *Die Orthodoxe Kirche in Russland. Dokumente ihrer Geschichte (860–1980)* (Göttingen: Vandenhoeck & Ruprecht, 1988), 62f.; T. Ware, *The Orthodox Church* (Harmondsworth: Penguin Books, 1967), 269; R. Trautmann (ed.), *Die altrussische Nestorchronik* (Leipzig: Markert & Peters, 1931), 58–86.

88 Cf. W. Hoeres, "Verratene Schönheit. Die traditionelle Liturgie und der Vorwurf des Ästhetizismus," UVK 39 (2009), 164–76, 174f.

89 Cf. J. Nebel, "Die 'ordentliche' und die 'ausserordentliche' Form," 193.

One enters into the Church of God, the great temple of Truth, through two doors: the one of Wisdom, the other of Beauty. It seems to me that the narrow door is that of Wisdom, the wide one, in contrast, through which millions enter, is the door of Beauty. The Church always keeps both open. From time to time she receives the rare philosopher and thinker, who crucify her with their thoughts; in contrast there is a countless flock which unceasingly swarms to her because of her colors, her music, her smile, as man seeks the warmth and light of the sun in spring.[90]

For centuries past, the beauty of the liturgy was the wealth of the poor as well,[91] who in their churches possessed for their own what in later times is presented only in museums.[92] In her greatest times, the Church has always resisted the illusion that she could convincingly proclaim the truth if at the same time her intrinsic splendor, beauty as *splendor veritatis*, was not there for all to see.[93]

90   F. Lelotte, *Heimkehr zur Kirche. Konvertiten des 20. Jahrhunderts*, 4 (Lucerne: Rex-Verlag, 1959), 146: quotation from the religious historian P. Vincent McNabb.

91   Cf. Ratzinger, *The Ratzinger Report*, 130: "In the solemnity of the worship, the Church expressed the glory of God, the joy of faith, the victory of truth and light over error and darkness. The richness of the liturgy is not the richness of some priestly caste: it is the wealth of all, including the poor, who in fact long for it and do not at all find it a stumbling block"; W. Hoeres, *Der Aufstand gegen die Ewigkeit. Kirche zwischen Tradition und Selbstzerstörung* (Stein am Rhein: Christiana-Verlag, 1984), 77f.

92   Cf. A.M. Weiss, *Natur und Übernatur. Geist und Leben des Christentums* 3/2 (Freiburg i. Br.: Verlag Herder, ³1897), 998f.: "Let us think of the collections that are now crammed into the overcrowded museums of our big cities from the looted churches. Now, of course, they are lost to the people. There was no better way to rob the people of taste and education. . . . In former times, these treasures and thousands of them, now destroyed by fierce anger, stood in the churches year in, year out, in the view of the people. The church gave the order. The people paid with joy. Every day they saw them with devotion. They could study them at leisure. They formed their taste thereon. They learned to imitate them."

93   A Benedictine Monk [G. Calvet], *The Sacred Liturgy*, 62: "We may use a photographic image to say that it is beauty that fixes truth. The truth of doctrine is often more betrayed by gradual insipidity than by spiritual error pure and simple." Cf. M. Mosebach, "Das Paradies auf Erden — Liturgie als Fenster zum Jenseits," UVK 43 (2013): 201–14; in English, "The Liturgy as a Window to Another World," trans. Faith Ann Gibson, published on the Rorate Caeli weblog on May 19, 2015.

PARTICIPATIO ACTUOSA
Concept and Meaning

Since the beginning of the twentieth century, the popes have repeatedly called for a conscious and lively participation of the faithful in the liturgy, yet without any far-reaching reforms for this purpose appearing necessary. The traditional rite of the Mass clearly possessed the spiritual resources for facilitating such participation, provided that the faithful fulfill their corresponding requirements. The Liturgical Constitution of the Second Vatican Council, under the motto of *participatio actuosa* (SC 14, 19, 30, 50), repeatedly demanded a lively participation by the faithful in divine worship, though their descriptions of this—"conscious, active, with spiritual gain, full of devotion" (SC 11, 48)—are as vague as Paul VI's corresponding statements as to whether or not the traditional rite of the *Missale Romanum* (1962) conformed to these demands.[94]

The term *participatio actuosa* dates back to a phrasing (*partecipazione attiva*) used by Pope Pius X, who urged the re-introduction of the singing of Gregorian chant by the people, "so that the faithful may again take a more active part in the ecclesiastical offices."[95] Pope Pius XI adopted these ideas and spoke of "taking an active part (*actuose participando*) in the venerated mysteries and the public solemn prayers of the Church."[96] Thus he stipulated: "It is most important that when faithful assist at the sacred ceremonies . . . they should not be merely detached and silent spectators, but, filled with a deep sense of the beauty of the liturgy, should sing alternately with the clergy or the choir, as it is prescribed."[97] In his encyclical *Mediator Dei*, Pope Pius XII paid extensive attention to the faithful's participation, expressly identified as *participatio actuosa*,[98] when he declared that its

---

94 Cf. P. Kwasniewski, *Noble Beauty, Transcendent Holiness. Why the Modern Age Needs the Mass of Ages* (Kettering, OH: Angelico Press, 2017), 191–213; G. Celier, "Une réforme injustifiée?": *La Messe en question*. Actes du Ve Congrès Théologique de Sì Sì No No, 239–60, 253–60.

95 Pius X, *Tra le Sollecitudini* (ASS 36:333 / Seasoltz, *Documentation*, 5f.); the expression "partecipazione attiva" can be found in the Italian text (ASS 36:331 / Seasoltz, *Documentation*, 4); the Latin translation says only *participatio* (ASS 36:388).

96 Pius XI, *Divini Cultus* (AAS 21:35 / Seasoltz, *Documentation*, 59).

97 Pius XI, *Divini Cultus* (AAS 21:40f. / Seasoltz, *Documentation*, 62).

98 Pius XII, *Mediator Dei* (AAS 39:523, 552, 560 / Seasoltz, *Documentation*, 108f., 129–37);

primary expression was the conscious union with the sacrifice of Christ, the High Priest.[99] The quoted texts demonstrate the presence of the topic in the pronouncements of the Magisterium as well as the sufficiency that was recognized in the traditional rite of the Mass in that regard.

It was misleading translations and erroneous interpretations of *participatio actuosa* that first cast doubt on that quality of the traditional rite. This inevitably occurred where the Latin adjective *actuosus* was identified as *activus*. "Active" is, however, the classical antonym of "contemplative."[100] Active participation is thus taken to mean participation that incorporates as many agents as possible in exterior activities (among others: singing, reading aloud, presenting the gifts, and shaking hands).[101] The adjective

---

particularly, cf. 589: "*quo actuosius fideles divinum cultum participent*"; 592: "*Christiana plebs Liturgiam tam actuose participet.*" Cf. B.-M. Laisney, "Active Participation in the Liturgy, in Accordance with the Prescriptions of *Mediator Dei*," *Liturgy, Participation and Sacred Music.* The Proceedings of the Ninth International Colloquium of Historical, Canonical and Theological Studies of the Roman Catholic Liturgy [Paris, November 2003] (Rochester: CIEL UK, 2006), 57–80.

99 Pius XII, *Mediator Dei* (AAS 39:551f. / Seasoltz, *Documentation*, 129): "Through this active and individual participation (*actuosa singulorum participatione*), the members of the mystical Body not only become daily more like their divine Head, but the life flowing from the Head is imparted to the members.... All the faithful should be aware that to participate in the Eucharistic sacrifice is their chief duty and supreme dignity, and that not in an inert and negligent fashion, giving way to distractions and daydreaming, but with such earnestness and concentration (*tam impense tamque actuose*) that they may be united as closely as possible with the High Priest, according to the apostle: 'Let this mind be in you which was also in Christ Jesus' (Ph 2:5). And together with him and through him let them make their oblation, and in union with him let them offer up themselves." Likewise SCR, *De Musica Sacra et Sacra Liturgia* (AAS 50:637f. / Seasoltz, *Documentation*, 261): "This participation should, above all, be interior, exercised in devout attention of the mind and in the affection of the heart. Through this, the faithful 'closely join the supreme Priest... and together with him and through him offer [the sacrifice], and consecrate themselves together with him' (*Mediator Dei*)."

100 Cf. Augustine, *De civitate Dei* 8,4 (CCL 47, 219f.): "*una pars* (sc., sapientiae) *activa, altera contemplativa dici potest.*" Augustine, *The City of God*, I/6, 246: "its (sc., Wisdom's) one part may be called active and its other contemplative."

101 Critical of this, Ratzinger, *Spirit of the Liturgy*, 174f. (*Theology of the Liturgy*, 108f.). On the consequences of the English translation "active participation" and respective misunderstandings, cf. P. Crane, *Gnosis auf dem Vormarsch. Hintergründe der Liturgie-Reform* (Kisslegg: Fe-medienverlag, ²1995), 38–40 (= *Christian Order* [ed. by P. Crane, London], February 1990, 95–102); N. Bux, *Benedict XVI's Reform: The Liturgy between Innovation and Tradition*, trans. by J. Trabbic (San Francisco: Ignatius Press, 2012), 118: "When certain liturgists want to

actuosus rather possesses the connotation of an eager, intense involvement on an interior level.[102]

Participatio actuosa is thus fulfilled where the faithful interiorly and spiritually connect with the liturgical action. It is about a cooperation that allows what is externally heard (*Oremus*; *Sursum corda*) or observed (*Ecce Agnus Dei*) to become inner processes. *Participatio actuosa* therefore implies the faithful's interior, prayerful concentration on the sacrifice of the Mass. The Latin term for participation once more recalls that the realized sacrifice of Christ is the real *actio* in which the faithful should take part, by spiritually and prayerfully uniting themselves to the offering of the sacrificed Logos.[103]

Precisely because the traditional rite of the Mass tightly restricts the possibilities for the faithful to participate externally, insofar as the central liturgical actions are reserved for the celebrant and the ministers, it opens the way for an even more intense internal participation in the sacred action that would only be obstructed by merely external performances. It belongs to the wisdom of the traditional liturgy that it never sought to define this interior participation of the faithful in a single form, but rather considered various methods to be legitimate. Against tendencies in the Liturgical Movement to elevate conscious participation in the official prayer texts as the sole criterion of devout participation, Pope Pius XII also advocated for forms of participation that regarded less the liturgical texts

---

defend their idea or taste, they say: 'The people must participate.' It is a neo-clericalism that has infected even the laity."

102 Cf. B. McElligott, "Active Participation": C. Francis / M. Lynch (eds.), *A Voice for All Time: Essays on the Liturgy of the Catholic Church since the Second Vatican Council* (Bristol: Association for Latin Liturgy, 1994), 18–28, 19: "By using the word 'active' for *actuosa* the Church's intention has been misunderstood, and generally, if perhaps unconsciously, taken to mean bodily activity, whereas what the Church really asks is full, sincere mental activity, expressed externally by the body"; ibid., with reference to C. Lewis / C. Short, *A Latin Dictionary* (Oxford: Clarendon Press, 1962), s.v. actuosus: "full of activity, very active (with the acc. idea of zeal, subjective impulse)."

103 Cf. Ratzinger, *Spirit of the Liturgy*, 171–75 (*Theology of the Liturgy*, 106–9). For "laymen's participation in the liturgical sacrificial oblation at Mass," cf. Barth, *Die Mär vom antiken Kanon*, 112–20. In general, cf. B.-M. Laisney, "Die echte 'aktive Teilnahme' an der Liturgie," UVK 26 (1996): 147–59; idem, "'Aktiv' an der Messe teilnehmen," UVK 26 (1996): 231–40; idem, "Sich mit der Messe vereinen," UVK 27 (1997): 203–15; *Liturgy, Participation and Sacred Music* (CIEL UK, 2006).

than the meaning of the rite as a whole.[104] In typical Catholic vastness, a great variety of individual possibilities for participation accompany the rubrical strictness of the rite[105] that do not need to be regulated in any way,[106] but should be respected. Even being silently present and merely watching do not necessarily indicate a lack of interior involvement. The very act of listening, be it with the ears or with the heart, is assuredly a form of active participation.[107] Finally, the silence, be it during the Canon or at a Low Mass, allows an intense participation[108] and certainly enables a special manner of sharing in the mystery celebrated, a combination of interior and exterior worship, and a hushed union with Christ's sacrifice. In the same way, the silent execution of many rites calls for a personal appropriation on the part of the believer, for whom an exterior audibility of texts would not, at any rate, imply an interior apprehension of meaning.[109]

104   Cf. Pius XII, *Mediator Dei* (AAS 39:561 / Seasoltz, *Documentation*, 136); quoted on p. 167, n51 above. Similarly, SCR, *De Musica Sacra et Sacra Liturgia* (AAS 50:641 / Seasoltz, *Documentation*, 265). Cf. H.-L. Barth, "Bereitete Papst Pius XII. die nachkonziliare Liturgiereform vor?," idem, "*Nichts soll dem Gottesdienst vorgezogen werden*," 84–163, 143–46.

105   Cf. Mosebach, *Heresy of Formlessness*, 93f.: "The believer can 'participate actively' in a variety of ways. He can follow the priest step by step along the high road of the mysteries, subordinating his prayers, as the priest does, to the traditional gestures — standing, bowing, moving to one side or the other, and so on. But he can also simply contemplate the work of Christ that is carried out in Holy Mass; in doing this he does not necessarily have to join in every one of the liturgy's prayers, but may silently and in solitude adore the miracle that is taking place before his eyes. It is one of the greatest paradoxes of [the traditional] Holy Mass that, with all its liturgical strictness, it particularly facilitates prayer that is radically personal and contemplative."

106   Descriptions of failed regulations are provided by Lorenzer, *Konzil der Buchhalter*, 198f.

107   Cf. J. and R. Maritain, *Liturgy and Contemplation*, trans. J. Evans (New York: P. J. Kenedy, 1960), 86: "As regards participation in the liturgical life of the Church, and although the expression 'active participation' has in actual fact taken the sense of participation externally manifested, it is important to observe here that to *listen*, whether with the ear or with the heart, is from the philosophical point of view as 'active' as to *speak*."

108   Cf. SCR, *De Musica Sacra et Sacra Liturgia* (AAS 50:641 / Seasoltz, *Documentation*, 264f.); Second Vatican Council, SC 30. Cf. W.-M. de Saint Jean, "Silence et intériorité dans la liturgie," *Liturgie et sacré* (CIEL, 2003), 273–350, 320–22.

109   Cf. J. Nebel, "Die 'ordentliche' und die 'ausserordentliche' Form," 187f.: "Especially by the silent performance of many rites and prayers, one avoids a situation in which the faithful in their participation are, so to speak, 'served' and run the risk of no longer sufficiently feeling the need to engage themselves in a personal prayer. With the silent performance of the rites, the participation of the faithful in the liturgical acts depends much more strongly on their personal spiritual engagement, their uniting themselves spiritually with the sacred action. It

Earthly contemplation

Participatio actuosa, as required and encouraged by the traditional liturgy, is opposed to all pragmatism that primarily understands man as an active being who must use the world as a resource, and as a result must also "create and design" the liturgy.[110] In contrast, the traditional understanding of *participatio actuosa* involves a different concept of man. To all activism that arises from a modern mentality, the classical liturgy opposes a contemplative encounter with reality, which the great thinkers of pre-Christian antiquity described as the proper purpose of man, who finds his fulfillment in beholding (θεωρία, *theōria*) the highest good, the beautiful.[111] Similarly in the Christian tradition, knowing is always the most intense form of grasping reality and the most noble form of possession.[112] This is as true for the *visio beatifica* as for "earthly contemplation," which sees a reflection of the Creator in the creature and is the highest possible form of happiness on earth.[113] A vital requirement for this is love, insofar as he is happy who sees that which he loves.[114] Thus contemplation is described as "loving awareness" and "beholding the beloved."[115]

---

is precisely in this way that the faithful, in their dignity and maturity, are taken seriously as baptized Christians."

110 Cf. Hoeres, "Verratene Schönheit," 168f.

111 Cf. Plato, *Symposium* 211d–212a. Cf. J. Pieper, "Was heisst Glück? Erfüllung im Schauen": idem, *Buchstabier-Übungen: Aufsätze, Reden, Notizen* (Munich: Kösel-Verlag, 1980), 131–49, 139f.

112 Cf. Augustine, *De diversis quaestionibus LXXXIII*, 35,1f. (CCL 44A, 51f. / Augustine, *Responses to Miscellaneous Questions*, trans. by B. Ramsey, *The Works of St Augustine* I/12 [Hyde Park, NY: New City Press, 2008], 49f.): "*nihil est aliud habere quam nosse. . . . Quid est aliud beate vivere nisi aeternum aliquid cognoscendo habere?*" ("But to possess that is nothing but to know it. . . . What does it mean to live blessedly if not to possess something eternal through knowledge of it?"); Thomas Aquinas, *Super librum de causis* 18, ed. by J.G. Heller (Freiburg i. Br.: Verlag Herder, 2017): "*habere aliquid in se formaliter et non materialiter, in quo consistit ratio cognitionis, est nobilissimus modus habendi aliquid*" ("the most noble way of possessing something is to possess something in oneself as a form and not as a material, and therein the definition of cognition consists"). Cf. J. Pieper, "Was heisst Glück?," 142f.; idem, *Happiness and Contemplation*, trans. R. and C. Winston (South Bend, IN: St. Augustine's Press, 1998), 58–67.

113 Cf. Thomas Aquinas, *STh* I–II, 3,5, in *Summa Theologiae*, vol. 16 (1a2ae. 1–5): Purpose and Happiness, trans. by Th. Gilby (Oxford: Blackfriars Publications [i.a.], 1969), 74 ["The imperfect beatitude we can have at present is primarily and chiefly centered on contemplation"]. Cf. Pieper, *Happiness and Contemplation*, 76–88.

114 Cf. Pieper, *Happiness and Contemplation*, 70.

115 Cf. ibid., 72.

With its transparency for the mystery of God, the classical rite of the Mass stipulates that "earthly contemplation" is an appropriate form of participation.[116] To what extent such a "simple gazing look,"[117] a hushed quiet for the purpose of knowledge, is in keeping with the liturgy is demonstrated by a further insight from the same Western and Christian tradition. Knowing can be defined as "the most noble form of possessing" also because it hereby performs an assimilation: the objective world, insofar as it is known, comes to be one with the knower, who, by his understanding, gains a share of a foreign being, that is, possesses the form of the foreign being, whose likeness is formed within him.[118] The forming of such a likeness is also the goal of the liturgy:

> All the elements of the liturgy, then, would have us reproduce in our hearts the likeness of the divine Redeemer through the mystery of the Cross, according to the words of the Apostle of the Gentiles, "With Christ I am nailed to the Cross. I live, now not I, but Christ liveth in me" (Gal 2:19f.). Thus we become a victim, as it were, along with Christ, to increase the glory of the eternal Father.[119]

116 Cf. Hoeres, "Verratene Schönheit," 175f.: "The application of these ideas to the traditional, so-called Tridentine Mass is easy. If anywhere, we have here the perfect unity of content and form, a manifestly sacred form and a statement that consists in the presence of the numinous par excellence, the Son of God, who as the eternal High Priest and Lamb of God offers himself to the Father. All the actions and gestures, the incense, the numerous genuflections and bows, the care and awe that prevents even the smallest of particles from being lost, the solemn Gregorian chant, here serve the purpose of approaching the incomprehensible mystery and illustrating its presence. The perception is so immediate and at the same time so transparent that even an outsider feels immediately that God's presence is being celebrated here. This unique spectacle before the face of God, who becomes present here, of its own accord implies that the proper participation in it is an adoring and silent contemplation. This silence full of amazement is not disturbed by diverse forms of participation . . . unless one misunderstands that term in a purely acoustic sense!"; idem, *Der Aufstand gegen die Ewigkeit*, 61–65.

117 Pieper, *Happiness and Contemplation*, 74.

118 Cf. Thomas Aquinas, *STh* I, 14,1, in *Summa Theologiae*, vol. 4 (1a. 14–18): Knowledge in God, trans. by Th. Gonall (Oxford: Blackfriars Publications [i.a.], 1964), 7: "This will become evident if we note that the difference between knowing and non-knowing subjects is that the latter have nothing but their own form, whereas a knowing subject is one whose nature it is to have in addition the form of something else; for the likeness of the thing known is in the knower." Cf. Pieper, *Happiness and Contemplation*, 65–66.

119 Pius XII., *Mediator Dei* (AAS 39:559 / Seasoltz, *Documentation*, 134).

Lessening the possibilities of exterior assistance allows for an interior concentration on the real *actio*, the sacramental realization of Christ's sacrificial action, which deserves the faithful's intense participation.

From communal participation arises that deep communion of the faithful with one another that grows from the participation of many in Christ's one sacrifice, a communion that may not be pursued as a sensation for its own sake, nor one that can be generated by group dynamics.[120] It is the distinct theocentrism of the traditional rite that creates a common perspective for all and thus brings about their inner unity.

---

120   Cf. W. Hoeres, *Gottesdienst als Gemeinschaftskult — Ideologie und Liturgie* [Distinguo 1] (Bad Honnef: Johannes Bökmann, 1992), 12–16.

PART III

Theology

10

The Traditional Rite of the Mass as Celebrated Dogma

PAUL CLAUDEL WROTE TO HIS FRIEND JACQUES RIV-ière, a young philosopher seeking God: "The liturgy and the zealous attendance of the Church's divine worship will teach you more than all of your books. Immerse yourself in this limitless pool of magnificence, certitude, and poetry."[1] Claudel knew whereof he spoke. As an unbeliever he visited the cathedral of Notre Dame in Paris on Christmas Day in 1886, and within a matter of seconds he felt an unshakable certainty of God's existence and left the church a convert.[2] He did not know a single priest and had no Catholic friends to whom he could have turned in order to be introduced to the Catholic Faith. He eagerly read religious texts. He later wrote:

> But the greatest book that was placed before me and instructed me was the Church. Praised be the great and glorious Mother at whose knee I have learned everything! I spent all of my Sundays in Notre Dame, and as often as possible I went there during the week. In those days, when I was as ignorant in questions of the Faith as one can be of Buddhism, the sacred drama unfolded here before my eyes with a majesty that surpassed all of my imaginings. Ah, this was not the miserable language of devotional books! It was the deepest, most magnificent poetry, these the most noble gestures that have ever been entrusted to human beings. I could never tire of watching the drama of the Mass, every movement of the priest wrote itself deeply into my mind

---

1 P. Claudel, *Briefwechsel mit Rivière, 1907–1914* [ed. by R. Grosche / trans. by H. Szász] (Munich: Kösel-Verlag, ²1955), 67f. [May 25, 1907].

2 Cf. P. Claudel, *Der Strom. Ausgewählte Prosa* (Frankfurt a. M.: Ullstein Verlag, 1955), 172 (from: *Contacts et circonstances* [Paris: Éditions Gallimard, 1940]).

and heart. The celebration of the Requiem Mass, the Christmas Mass, the drama of each particular day of Holy Week, the sublime hymn of the Exultet, next to which the most inebriated sounds of a Sophocles and a Pindar appeared insipid to me, everything forced me down in reverence and joy, in gratitude, repentance, and deepest adoration . . . [3]

Whoever reads this description understands why Claudel could say: "The epitome of Catholicism, the delicate and substantial point that summarizes it all, is the Eucharist."[4] In a similar way, he wrote in his work on the Mass: "There always lies upon the altar a book containing all knowledge of life and death."[5] In fact, from the morning of creation, as described in the first pages of Genesis and presented to us in the first reading of the Easter Vigil, until the heavenly Jerusalem, as depicted in the Apocalypse of John and proclaimed in the Epistle for the dedication of a church, from the lamenting *De profundis* of the absolution for the dead ("Out of the depths I have cried to Thee, O Lord") to the rejoicing Alleluia of Easter morning, "all knowledge of life and death" is "included" and kept in the traditional Roman Missal.

As the biblical readings present to us the great events of the story of salvation, the feasts of the saints bring to mind the Church's history over the centuries. In the orations, the central dogmatic truths are expressed as well as the principles of Christian morality and asceticism. The *Missale Romanum* presents a unique summary of the entire Catholic Faith. M. Mosebach aptly observes: "A priest, shipwrecked on a remote island with nothing but the Missal of Trent, could produce, with it, the whole patrimony of Catholicism."[6] This special quality belongs to it not only because it is a so-called "complete missal," containing the Epistles and Gospels, which, in contrast, the new *Ordo* takes instead from a separate book, the

---

3 P. Claudel, *Der Strom*, 175 (from: *Contacts et circonstances* [Paris: Éditions Gallimard, 1940]); cf. Claudel, *Der Strom*, 179 (from: *L'épée et le miroir* [Paris: Éditions Gallimard, 1939]).

4 P. Claudel, Letter to André Gide of Dec. 8, 1921, quoted in A. Läpple, *Lesebuch zum katholischen Erwachsenenkatechismus* (Aschaffenburg: Paul Pattloch Verlag, 1986), 430.

5 P. Claudel, *Die Messe des Verbannten*, 26.

6 Mosebach, *Heresy of Formlessness*, 124.

lectionary. The special quality of the classical missal — according to which it contains all the mysteries of life and death — is based on the fact that there, and only there, no longer in the new version, can one find prayer texts that bring the specifically Catholic into sharp relief. In this way, the classical rite of the Mass is shown to be "dogma celebrated." The prayers of this liturgy "are entirely governed by and interwoven with dogma."[7]

7   R. Guardini, *The Spirit of the Liturgy*, with an introduction by J.M. Pierce / trans. by A. Lane (New York, NY: Crossroad Publishing Co., 1998), 21.

11

Orations

THIS IS BEAUTIFULLY DEMONSTRATED IN THE ORA-
tions (*Collecta*, *Secreta*, and *Postcommunio*), which are, stylistically speaking,
sublime works of art.[1] These "greatest jewels of [the Church's] liturgical
treasure"[2] are among the oldest components of her spiritual inheritance
and are steeped in dogma. They almost create a *Summa theologiae in nuce*
that succinctly expresses the Catholic Faith without omission.[3] Only in
the orations of the classical rite are contained and preserved numerous
ideas that, although they belong irrevocably to the Catholic Faith, are
understated or entirely lost in later modified versions: detachment from
the temporal and desire for the eternal; the Kingship of Christ over the
world and society; the battle against heresy and schism, the conversion
of non-believers, the necessity of the return to the Catholic Church and
genuine truth; merits, miracles, and apparitions of the saints; God's wrath
for sin and the possibility of eternal damnation.[4] All of these aspects are

---

1 Cf. Mosebach, *Heresy of Formlessness*, 76f.

2 A Benedictine Monk [G. Calvet], *The Sacred Liturgy*, 79.

3 Cf. D.J. Olewinski, "Défense et propagation de la foi dans le missel tridentin": *Foi et
liturgie* (CIEL, 2002), 369–450.

4 Critical comparisons with the texts of the NOM are provided by R. Kaschewsky, "Tendenzen in den Orationen des Neuen Missale," UVK 10 (1980): 304–37; L. Pristas, "The Collects
at Sunday Mass: An Examination of the Revisions of Vatican II," *Nova et Vetera* [Eng. ed.] 3.1
(2005): 5–38; eadem, *Collects of the Roman Missals. A Comparative Study of the Sundays in
Proper Seasons Before and After the Second Vatican Council* [T&T Clark Studies in Fundamental
Liturgy] (London: Bloomsbury, 2013); eadem, "The Post-Vatican II Revision of the Lenten
Collects," U.M. Lang (ed.), *Ever Directed Towards the Lord: The Love of God in the Liturgy of
the Eucharist Past, Present, and Hoped For* (London / New York: T & T Clark, 2007), 62–89;
L. Bianchi, "A Survey of the Theology, History, Terminology, and Syntax in the Prayers of
the Roman Missal," *Theological and Historical Aspects of the Roman Missal* (CIEL UK, 2000),
127–64; E. Guillou, "Les oraisons de la nouvelle messe et l'esprit de la réforme liturgique,"
Fideliter 86 (1992): 58–75; F. Knittel, "La lèpre du modernisme—L'encyclique *Pascendi* et la
nouvelle liturgie": *Actualité de l'encyclique Pascendi de Saint Pie X. Actes du Symposium pour
le centenaire de l'encyclique Pascendi, Paris 9–11 November 2007* (Suresnes: Éditions Clovis,

deeply rooted in the biblical message and have distinctively shaped Catholic piety for almost two thousand years.

REALISM OF THE WORLDVIEW AND IDEA OF MAN

The criticism of so-called negative themes and polemic features of the classical orations reflects more the modern *Zeitgeist* than any theological imbalances that require correction.[5] In fact, each prayer formula manifests an extremely realistic perception of the condition of the world and its people.[6] St Augustine wrote in his work *The City of God* (18:51) that from the time of Abel "even to the end of this world, the Church has gone forward on pilgrimage amid the persecutions of the world and the consolations of God." The orations are the insistent echo of this history-spanning experience. Thus the Church tirelessly asks God to protect the faithful from all adversities (*ab omnibus semper tueantur adversis*),[7] to defend them from all dangers (*a cunctis nos defende periculis*),[8] and to free them from all threatening evils (*a cunctis malis imminentibus ... liberemur*).[9]

2008), 133–99; Bianchi, *Liturgia*, 57–70, 119–60; A. Cekada, *The Problems with the Prayers of the Modern Mass* (Rockford, IL: TAN Books and Publishers, 1991); J. van der Ploeg, "'Neue' oder 'alte' Messe?," *Theologisches* 23 (1993): 471–80, 474–80.

5 Thus M. Augé, "Le collette del proprio del tempo nel nuovo messale," EL 84 (1970): 275–98, 297: "Then we have to underline the corrections made to the Collects of Lent to render the content more consistent ... with the mentality of the man of today"; cf. 278, 287; similarly, C. Braga, "Il nuovo Messale Romano," EL 84 (1970): 249–74, 272. Critical of this, Bianchi, "A Survey," 127–29.

6 Cf. H. Richens, "The Close of the Gregorian Era," C. Francis / M. Lynch (eds.), *A Voice for All Time. Essays on the Liturgy of the Catholic Church since the Second Vatican Council* (Bristol: Association for Latin Liturgy, 1994), 109–27, 125: "It seems that much of the distaste for negative themes derives from the immediate post-Conciliar euphoria, now rapidly dispersing. While all Christians are animated by the hope of the good news brought by the Gospels, they were conscious enough, in the formative stages of the Roman rite, of the world in turmoil and of human weakness and sin. Today the turmoil is with us still."

7 Postcommunion on the feast of St Mark, April 25.

8 Secret of the feast of St Chrysogonus, November 24.

9 Collect of the feast of Sts Cosmas and Damian, September 27. For further examples, see Knittel, "Lèpre du modernisme," 158–62. Similarly, the Collect of the feast of the Most Precious Blood, which Pope Pius IX introduced as a response to the growing aggression toward the Church. Cf. P. Milcarek, "Memory, Presence and Contemplation — The Feasts of Our Lord in the Traditional Roman Missal," *The Presence of Christ in the Eucharist*. The Proceedings of the Sixth International Colloquium of Historical, Canonical and Theological Studies on the Roman Catholic Liturgy [Versailles, November 2000] (Kingston & Surbiton: CIEL UK,

It is not only by exterior adversity that the Church is widely besieged. In the classical orations the battle against sin occupies a good deal of space, for it offends God's majesty (*qui maiestatem tuam graviter delinquendo offendimus*),[10] wounds the soul (*culpae vulnera*),[11] drags it down with its weight (*qui peccatorum nostrorum pondere premimur*),[12] and holds it captive (*sub peccati iugo vetusta servitus tenet*).[13] The sinner's will to convert manifests itself in worthy fruits of repentance (*dignos paenitentiae fructus facere*),[14] deep remorsefulness (*nos eorum consociari fletibus*),[15] and reparation (*dignae quoque satisfactionis exhibeamus officium*).[16] Thus the holy Curé of Ars is wonderful not only because of "his pastoral zeal" (NOM), but also "his constant prayer and penance."[17] By underlining the significance of bodily fasting (*inchoata ieiunia . . . observantiam quam corporaliter exhibemus*),[18] the orations of Lent recall that the interactions between body and soul constitute an anthropological constant to be held up to the faithful in the Church's prayer at all times, if this prayer is to be more than merely a reflection of what is practiced (or not practiced) at a given moment.[19]

2001), 55–70. For a statistical comparison of terms between MRom 1962 and MRom 1970, see Bianchi, "A Survey," 158–60.

10   Collect of the feast of St Bruno, October 6.

11   Postcommunion of the feast of the Immaculate Conception, December 8.

12   Collect of the feast of Pope St Gregory I, March 12.

13   Collect of the third Mass of Christmas Day. See Bianchi, "A Survey," 158–60.

14   Collect of the feast of St Raymond of Peñafort, January 23.

15   Collect of the feast of the Seven Founders of the Servite Order, February 12.

16   Collect of the feast of the Sacred Heart of Jesus. Further examples in Knittel, "Lèpre du modernisme," 166–68.

17   Collect of the feast of the Curé of Ars, August 8 (formerly August 9).

18   Collect of the Friday after Ash Wednesday.

19   Cf. Pristas, "Lenten Collects," 88f.: "Our liturgical prayer does not, at least tradition-ally, present a mirror image of the faithful. Rather, liturgical prayer shows us what we are to be and to do. . . . Hidden in the revisers' supposition that modern persons do not fast and their disinclination to urge fasting in the collects of Lent is a conviction that modern persons are somehow different from those of earlier generations—that is, their human nature itself is somehow different—so that the means which God gave earlier generations for obtaining great spiritual graces are not available to the modern person. This is patently absurd. The nature possessed by modern persons is the same nature that the Son of God assumed and that all whom he redeemed share. And therefore the same intimate relationship between body and soul that is recognized by our ascetical traditions to be a fact of human nature

Because the traditional orations see man's situation as deeply affected by original sin and emphasize the resulting weaknesses of creatures (*infirmitas, fragilitas, humilitas, error, servitus, tenebrae*), God's grace does not become a mere ingredient in a Pelagian sense, and thus become obsolete so that man would be able to live and function without this grace. In the Missal of Pius V, any discourse on grace is always related to a description of the fundamental human condition of sinfulness, and thus recognizes grace as necessary for salvation.[20] The intensity of the plea for God's help is also expressed in these prayers in emphatic imperatives (*excita; veni; aurem tuam precibus nostris accommoda; illustra mentis nostrae tenebras; da; concede; succurre; ad defensionem nostram dexteram tuae maiestatis extende*), which once again connect human need and divine assistance.[21] The Catholic teaching on grace is clearly witnessed in these prayers. They are frequently an echo of that dogmatic clarification with which the Church described the nuances of the interaction between divine grace and human action during the Semipelagian controversy of the fifth century.[22]

The traditional orations do not recognize an uncritical openness toward the world,[23] but rather tirelessly call to mind the distance demanded in the Gospel. Characteristic of this is the Postcommunion of the Second Sunday of Advent: "Filled with the food of spiritual nourishment, we humbly entreat Thee, O Lord, that by our partaking of this Mystery, Thou wouldst

---

exists in modern persons also. And the fact that the very Son of God fasted in the flesh presents a compelling reason why we should also. The revised Lenten collects that neither expect, nor insistently invite, us to fast have done us a distinct disservice."

20 Cf. Collect of the Third Sunday of Advent: "*mentis nostrae tenebras gratia tuae visitationis illustra*"; Collect of the Fourth Sunday of Advent: "*per auxilium gratiae tuae . . . nostra peccata.*" Cf. Bianchi, "A Survey," 131–34; idem, *Liturgia*, 119–38; Pristas, "Collects at Sunday Mass," 26–36.

21 Cf. Bianchi, "A Survey," 134: "In the place of these imperatives, in Paul VI's Missal the final or consecutive subjunctive prevails. Thus, even on the level of syntax, we pass from the cry of petition, from a dynamic of pure petition, to a basically descriptive phraseology"; idem, *Liturgia*, 132f.

22 Cf. fifth Collect of Ember Saturday in Lent: "*Actiones nostras, quaesumus, Domine, aspirando praeveni, et adiuvando prosequere, ut cuncta nostra oratio et operatio a te semper incipiat et per te coepta finiatur*"; Collect of Easter Sunday: "*vota nostra, quae praeveniendo aspiras, etiam adiuvando prosequere*"; Collect of the Sixteenth Sunday after Pentecost: "*Tua nos, quaesumus, Domine, gratia semper et praeveniat et sequatur.*"

23 Cf. Kaschewsky, "Tendenzen," 323f.

teach us to despise the things of earth, and to love those of Heaven (*terrena despicere et amare caelestia*)."[24] How little such a request concerns a falsely-understood contempt for the world is demonstrated by the Church's great cultural achievements in all epochs of her history. To what extent the classical orations entirely correspond to the spirit of the New Testament can be demonstrated by a few exemplary quotations: "Whosoever therefore will be a friend of this world becometh an enemy of God" (Jas 4:4). St Paul warns: "Be not conformed to this world" (Rom 12:2). Many similar texts could be cited[25] in order to show that the classical orations in no way originate from a specifically medieval mentality ("escapism," "vale of tears") but rather genuinely breathe the spirit of the Gospel.

The doctrine of the Kingship of Christ is equally deeply rooted in the Old and New Testament.[26] Rather than being limited to merely a spiritual level and understood only eschatologically (NOM),[27] the feast of Christ's kingship in the *Missale Romanum* 1962 recalls His inalienable right of sovereignty over nations and society, so that "all the families of the nations, rent asunder by the wound of sin, may be subjected to the sweet yoke of His rule" (Collect), as only the Christian faith can forever guarantee the good of the state and of the people.[28] Similarly, worldly titles of the saints

24 Similarly: Collect of the feast of St Peter Damian, February 23; Collect of the feast of St Casimir, March 4; Postcommunion of the feast of the Sacred Heart of Jesus; Postcommunion of the feast of St Paulinus of Nola, June 22; Collect of the feast of St Henry, July 15; Collect of the feast of St Francis, October 4; Collect of the feast of St Hedwig, October 16; Collect of the feast of St Elizabeth of Hungary, November 19. Cf. Knittel, "Lèpre du modernisme," 139, 178–81.

25 Cf. Barth, "*Nichts soll dem Gottesdienst vorgezogen werden*," 133f.; Ploeg, "'Neue' oder 'alte' Messe?," 476.

26 On the introduction of the feast of the Kingship of Our Lord Jesus Christ, cf. Pius XI, Encyclical Letter *Quas Primas* (AAS 17 [1925]: 593–610 / trans.: Seasoltz, *Documentation*, 36–46). For the theological and political dimensions of Christ's kingship, cf. Dom Gérard OSB, *Demain la Chrétienté* (Le Barroux: Éditions Sainte-Madeleine, ²2005), 109–25.

27 In contrast to the NOM version, which is reserved for the last Sunday of the liturgical year, the traditional version is observed on the last Sunday in October, immediately before the feast of all the saints who labored and suffered to bring about Christ's rulership in this world.

28 Collect of the feast of Christ the King: "*Omnipotens Deus, qui in dilecto Filio tuo, universorum Rege, omnia instaurare voluisti: concede propitius, ut cunctae familiae gentium, peccati vulnere disgregatae, eius suavissimo subdantur imperio.*" Cf. H.-L. Barth, "Religionsfreiheit oder Toleranz? Gedanken zum Verhältnis von Staat und Kirche," *Civitas* 3 (2008): 13–39, 31–37; Ploeg, "'Neue' oder 'alte' Messe?," 478f.; Guillou, "Les oraisons," 71–73. On the relation of the feast of Christ the King to the feast of Epiphany, cf. Barth, "Der Stern aus Jakob," idem

are not suppressed or concealed in the classical orations, as it was certainly the faithful exercise of their earthly offices by which kings (Collect of the feast of St Louis, August 25), queens (Collects of the feasts of St Elizabeth of Portugal, July 8, and St Margaret of Scotland, June 10), and emperors (Collect of the feast of St Henry, July 15) became saints.[29]

THE CHURCH MILITANT

The Church here on earth is not simply "on the pilgrim's way," but it is rather a militant Church (*ecclesia militans*).[30] Her ranks are called to battle. The prayers identify those enemies and adversaries that the Church militant must continually encounter in the temporal as well as the spiritual life. On the feast of the Confessor St John of Capistrano (March 28), whose endeavors enabled the Christians to achieve victory over the Turkish army in 1456 at Belgrade, the Collect speaks of God working through him to "enable [His] faithful people to triumph over the enemies of the Cross by the most holy Name of Jesus" and therefore requests "that by his intercession we may overcome the snares of our spiritual enemies."[31] The confessor-bishop St Patrick proclaimed God's glory not only to the "Irish people" (NOM), but to the "*gentibus*" (nations or heathens),[32] who fiercely resisted in order to retain their ancestral cult under the leadership of the Druids. In the same way the confessor-bishop St Augustine of Canterbury not only "[led] the English peoples to the Gospel" (NOM), but also "shed upon the English people the light of the true faith,"[33] as he cast out the darkness of earlier error. The holy bishop St Irenaeus of Lyons, who effectively confronted the threat of the heresy of Gnosticism in the second century with his writing *Adversus Haereses*, not only "[confirmed] true doctrine and the peace of the Church" (NOM), but also "[overcame] heresies by the truth of doctrine

---

(ed.), *Wahrheit und Schönheit*, 197–271, 270f.

29 For further examples see Knittel, "Lèpre du modernisme," 142, 193–95.

30 Collect of the feast of St Ignatius of Loyola, July 31, cf. the Postcommunion of the feast of Christ the King: *"Qui sub Christi Regis vexillis militare gloriamur."*

31 Similar to the Collect of the feast of Pope St Pius V, May 5. For further examples see Knittel, "Lèpre du modernisme," 140, 182–88.

32 Collect of the feast of St Patrick, Bishop, Confessor, March 17.

33 Collect of the feast of St Augustine of Canterbury, Bishop, Confessor, May 28.

and happily [established] peace in the Church."[34] The Collect of the feast of St Peter Canisius, Confessor and Doctor (April 27), recalls not only that there are people of good will who "seek the truth" and who by his intercession "may joyfully find you, their God" (NOM), but also that there are those "erring" who should "return to the way of salvation." With St Robert Bellarmine, God not only "gave a bishop and doctor, who through his writings strengthened the Faith of the Church" (NOM), which is in any case the principal duty of each bishop and theologian. This Jesuit cardinal, born in 1542, was rather a "powerful defender of the Catholic Faith and of the Apostolic See against the heresies of the Protestant Reformers."[35] The Collect of the *Missale Romanum* (1962) thus reads:

> O God, who didst adorn blessed Robert Thy Bishop and Doctor with wondrous learning and virtue that he might lay bare the snares of error and maintain the rights of the Apostolic See: grant by his merits and intercession that we may grow in love of the truth, and that the hearts of the wayward may return to the unity of Thy Church.

This prayer does not lessen the charism of this saint, but rather increases it. It was precisely his astute refutation of the Protestant errors that made Cardinal Bellarmine the Catholic theological controversialist most feared by the Protestant Reformers, and to whose refutation several "*cathedrae anti-Bellarminianae*" were established. Furthermore, it is only the traditional prayer that speaks of the necessity of a return of heretics to the true religion of the Catholic Faith.[36] The classical missal opposes an abandon-

---

34   Collect of the feast of St Irenaeus of Lyon, June 28.

35   According to the introduction to the feast day (May 13) in A. Schott (ed.), *Das vollständige Römische Messbuch lat. u. dt.* (Freiburg i. Br.: Verlag Herder, 1958), 866. The new Schott Missal for the Weekdays II says differently (new: Sep. 17): "In 1576 he was called to the Roman College, where he held lectures on the distinctive teachings of both Christian confessions.... A reformer in the sense of the Council of Trent."

36   Cf. the traditional Good Friday Intercession: "Let us pray also for heretics and schismatics: that our Lord God would rescue them from all their errors, and recall them to their holy Mother, the Catholic and Apostolic Church." Cf. Kaschewsky, "Tendenzen," 335. For the Good Friday prayer for the Jews, cf. Barth, *Ist die traditionelle lateinische Messe antisemitisch?*, 74–101.

ment of the so-called ecumenism of return, the conviction of the Church of all ages that all confessions are in no way equally on the path to truth. The traditional orations recall in an uncomfortable way that in questions of faith there are not only various opinions, but also errors that must be overcome, or at least fought against. An abandonment of this battle would amount to a victory of relativism.[37]

THE SAINTS

The world of the saints, too, finds its place in the traditional rite in an unabbreviated form. The orations speak at least 200 times of the merits of the saints (*merita sanctorum*) who may help us and whom we may call upon in our prayers.[38] Many of the saints' miracles are mentioned only in the traditional orations. The great Jesuit missionary St Francis Xavier not only "won many peoples" (NOM) through his preaching, but also "by preaching and miracles... [joined] to [God's] Church the nations of the Indies."[39] St Nicholas, bishop of Myra, is not only invoked for his intercession (NOM), but God so adorned him "with countless miracles" that the Church may call upon "his merits and prayers."[40] Modern man's mentality is not the measure for liturgical prayer;[41] rather, the measure is the Church's traditional belief that, according to Christ's promise,

37 Cf. Ploeg, "'Neue' oder 'alte' Messe?," 476f.; Guillou, "Les oraisons," 62–65. It is striking that the NOM also omits a verse in the Tract of the Common of the Blessed Virgin: "*Gaude, Maria Virgo, cunctas haereses sola interemisti*—Rejoice, O Virgin Mary, thou alone hast destroyed all heresies." For this, cf. J. De Tonquédec, "Cunctas haereses sola interemisti," NRTh 76 (1954): 858–62; M. Fiedrowicz, "Überwinderin aller Häresien—Maria und die Liturgie in der überlieferten Form," *Dominus vobiscum* 8 (2014): 36–44.

38 Cf. the examples in Knittel, "Lèpre du modernisme," 136, 46–157, with reference to the omissions in the NOM. Cf. Ploeg, "'Neue' oder 'alte' Messe?," 477: "Everyone knows that Luther attacked the doctrine of the merit of good works. Now he has the posthumous success that the new liturgy is following in his footsteps."

39 Collect of the feast of St Francis Xavier, Confessor, December 3. Cf. Bianchi, *Liturgia*, 157–60.

40 Collect of the feast of St Nicholas, Bishop and Confessor, December 6. For further examples, see Guillou, "Les oraisons," 67–69.

41 Cf. Ploeg, "'Neue' oder 'alte' Messe?," 477: "That 'modern man' (who is that?) does not want to know about miracles only reveals his unbelief. The liturgy, however, should not pay any attention to the unbelief of the unbelievers, but should affirm the faith of the members of the Church."

His miracles will be present in the work of the saints (cf. Mk 16:17ff.). Without paying homage to a false historicity, the classical liturgy sees fit to value the "truth of legend."[42] Her trust in the witness of tradition is strong enough to preserve a place in the commemoration of saints for figures such as the confessor-bishop "Gregory the Wonderworker" (Thaumaturgus).[43] Apparitions of the saints are not beyond God's omnipotence, to which the traditional liturgy does not arbitrarily set limits. Thus on February 11, the Church observes not merely the "Memorial of the Immaculate Mother of God" (NOM), but instead celebrates "the apparition of the Blessed Virgin" at Lourdes,[44] as it first occurred on this day in that place in the year 1858.

Veneration of the saints in the traditional Catholic sense, taking in their merits, miracles, and apparitions, is only found thus unconstrained in the classical liturgy, which is a stranger to all rationalistic tendencies that would like to recognize the saints only for their exemplary function and seek to dismiss all that is purely supernatural.

THE LAST THINGS

Similarly in the realm of eschatology, the "last things"—the reality of the Last Judgment, punishment for one's sins, the possibility of eternal damnation—are expressed in the traditional liturgy in an unabbreviated manner. Its texts do not carelessly preach an optimism of salvation, but instead they call to mind uncomfortable truths of the Faith, which are not

---

42 Cf. W. Nigg, *Grosse Heilige* (Zurich: Artemis Verlag, [6]1958), 32: "There are legendary portrayals that describe the importance of a saint in an absolutely appropriate manner and sometimes, due to their inner truth, are far superior to all historical traditions. With regard to symbolic thinking, legends have the highest importance." Idem, *Die stille Kraft der Legende* (Freiburg i. Br.: Verlag Herder, 1982), 18: "Deism was already eager to deprive Christianity of miracles and the supernatural and to reduce it to a few leftovers acceptable for the intellect. The rejection of legends is a concession to the new positivism, which comes from the world of rationalism and knows nothing of the symbolic understanding of the legends. A religiosity without symbols, however, is heading for degeneration."

43 Cf. the introduction to his feast on November 17 in *The Roman Missal in Latin and English for Every Day*, ed. by an Irish Bishop (Dublin: M. H. Gill and Son, 1948), 1211. In the NOM, the feast is omitted.

44 Collect of the feast of the Apparition of the Immaculate Virgin Mary at Lourdes, February 11. In NOM, it is renamed "Memorial of Our Lady of Lourdes."

eliminated by no longer being mentioned.[45] The texts of the traditional funeral liturgy are entirely in accordance with the conviction of Western philosophy and theology that man possesses a spiritual and immortal soul[46] when they offer prayers for the soul (*anima*) of the departed that he may not fall into the powers of darkness, but that he be taken up by the holy angels and led into his heavenly home.[47]

The traditional teaching of the last things finds its most moving expression in the *Dies Irae* of the Mass for the Dead. This Sequence originated in the thirteenth century and was finally incorporated by Pope Pius V into the Roman liturgy, where it is sung for the Commemoration of All Souls as well as in the Masses for the Dead, such as on the day of burial. The text is a meditation on the personal meeting with the Judge of the World.[48] This Sequence is typical of the vastness of Catholicism, in that it does not shy away from seeing the genuinely Christian message even in the notions of pre-Christian times (*Teste David cum Sibylla*).[49] Contrary

---

45 Cf. Kaschewsky, "Tendenzen," 319.

46 Cf. Hoeres, *Der Aufstand gegen die Ewigkeit*, 81–93.

47 Thus the Collect, Secret, and Postcommunion of the Requiem Mass as well as the Absolution for the Dead and the prayers at the burial. Cf. J. Ratzinger, *Eschatology. Death and Eternal Life*, trans. by M. Waldstein / ed. by A. Nichols (Washington, DC: Catholic University of America Press, ²1988), 105: "The idea that to speak of the soul is unbiblical was accepted to such an extent that even the new Roman Missal suppressed the term *anima* in its liturgy for the dead. It also disappeared from the ritual for burial." Barth, "*Nichts soll dem Gottesdienst vorgezogen werden*," 40–44; Ploeg, "'Neue' oder 'alte' Messe?," 476.

48 Cf. H. T. Henry, "Dies Irae," *The Catholic Encyclopedia* IV (New York: Robert Appleton Company, 1908): 787f.; F. Rädle, "Dies irae": H. Becker / B. Einig / P.O. Ullrich (edd.), *Im Angesicht des Todes. Ein interdisziplinäres Kompendium* [Pietas Liturgica 3] (St Ottilien: Eos Verlag, 1987), 331–40, 332: "The text of the *Dies irae* is an exemplary expression of the intellectual powers of the Middle Ages. The powerful, almost archetypal biblical images of the cosmic end of the world, the death and judgment of the human race, the deeply experienced, comforting encounter of the individual with the gentle and merciful Jesus and the hope for the pledge of His salvation, and finally the liturgical action of the Church as an institution that intercedes and mediates salvation.... All these converge in a lively relationship with one another and ring out unforgettably from this sequence." Cf. A.M. Haas, "Dies irae, dies illa," IKaZ 38 (2009): 371–84; A. Stock, *Liturgie und Poesie. Zur Sprache des Gottesdienstes* (Kevelaer: Butzon & Bercker GmbH, 2010), 197–218; Gihr, *Die Sequenzen*, 234–306.

49 Cf. C. Schönborn, *From Death to Life: The Christian Journey*, trans. by Brian McNeil CRV (San Francisco: Ignatius Press, 1995), 183: "Here, too, the myths bear witness to a universal human experience, which is not cleared away in Christianity but is 'preserved' [in it]"; cf. ibid., 181f., where the convergence of the myths concerning the "dangers in transition" is emphasized.

to all rationalistic demands to obliterate mythological features in Christian prayers,[50] the classical liturgy is ever convinced that in Christianity, myth becomes truth[51] and thus even the pagans' Advent-like expectation may find a place in her prayers. *Et venit desideratus cunctis gentibus*, it states in the Prophecy of Haggai 2:8 (Vulg.): "And the desired of all the nations shall come." As Christ fulfills the "desire of nations," Christianity must not discard the expression of this desire as found in myths. It is a hallmark of the wisdom of the classical liturgy that it has never done this.[52]

THE SCHOOL OF PRAYER

The quoted orations illustrate how what is necessary above all is not changing the official prayer formulas in order to adapt them to the language and mentality of modern man, but on the contrary, letting people learn the language of the liturgy so that they may absorb its Christian mentality.[53] This is precisely what the classical liturgy exhibits in its language of prayer: "Each individual feast urges us to ask for its own particular grace, and with a delicate precision that leads the soul to the heart of the mystery being celebrated. We are brought to understand what is to be asked, how it is to be asked, and why it is to be asked."[54]

---

50   Thus, SC 93. According to Schönborn, *From Death to Life,* 183, this hymn is one that was sacrificed to a certainly too rationalistic liturgical reform. Similarly A. Gerhards, "Eschatologische Vorstellungen und Modelle in der Totenliturgie": idem (ed.), *Die grössere Hoffnung der Christen. Eschatologische Vorstellungen im Wandel* [Quaestiones disputatae 127] (Freiburg i. Br.: Verlag Herder, 1990), 147–58, 155; Barth, "*Nichts soll dem Gottesdienst vorgezogen werden,*" 44.

51   Cf. C. Schönborn, *Geheimnis der Menschwerdung* (Mainz: Matthias-Grünewald-Verlag, 1983), 11–20.

52   Cf. ibid., 18; H. Rahner, *Griechische Mythen in christlicher Deutung* (Basel: Verlag Herder, 1985).

53   Cf. Spaemann, "Liturgie — Ausdruck des Glaubens," 36–71, 64: "Those who demand that it (*sc.,* this language) should be such that modern man can immediately find himself in it without any further efforts demand the impossible. This postulate resembles another one, namely that the Church must give answers to the questions of contemporary man, without saying that perhaps she should first teach the right questions. When people wanted to know from Jesus what the just manner of distribution has to be in their hereditary problems, he declared himself to be incompetent. His teaching was, 'Seek first the kingdom of God.' That means, he did not let them find what they were looking for, but told them what to look for if they did not want to live in vain."

54   A Benedictine Monk [G. Calvet], *The Sacred Liturgy,* 87f.

The classical rite bears witness to the Catholic teachings of the Faith in their fullness. If particular aspects of the Faith completely disappear from the liturgy, or are strongly diminished in it, they are at risk of gradually disappearing from the religious awareness of the priests and the faithful. The traditional form of the Holy Mass is thus an important corrective that can counteract this loss of important truths of the Faith.

12

Epistle and Gospel

FORMATION OF THE LECTIONARY

The traditional Missal's lectionary was never a *creatio ex nihilo*, a completely new creation, but is rather the result of a much older liturgical tradition that has been continually developed, and is an expression of a millennium old order in the Roman Church.[1] The readings of the *editio typica* of 1962 are substantially identical[2] to those of the Missal of Trent (1570), which in turn incorporated the virtually unchanged lectionary of the *editio princeps*, the first printed edition of the *Missale Romanum* (1474). Its basis was the so-called *Comes* of Murbach, a Roman-Frankish book of pericopes, assembled at the end of the eighth century in Gaul and based on an older collection of readings dating back to the seventh century. By the mid-ninth century this lectionary had already substantially developed into the shape in which, through the Missal of the Roman Curia as well as subsequent missals of the thirteenth to fifteenth centuries, it finally found its place in the Tridentine Missal.[3] Thus, for more than 1,200 years, the Church read nearly the same pericopes over the course of the liturgical year. As this formed the memory of countless generations, there arose a kind

---

1 Cf. K. Gamber, "Further Critical Observations Concerning the New Order of the Mass and the New Order of Readings," idem, *Reform of the Roman Liturgy*, 63–75, especially 69–75; idem, "Die neue Lektionsordnung. Kritische Bemerkungen," UVK 4 (1974): 130–36; idem, *Fragen in die Zeit*, 91–93; idem, *Die Reform der römischen Liturgie. Vorgeschichte und Problematik* (Regensburg: Verlag Friedrich Pustet, ²1981), 42–45; P. Kwasniewski, "The Reform of the Lectionary," in A. Reid (ed.), *Liturgy in the Twenty-First Century: Contemporary Issues and Perspectives* (London / New York, NY: Bloomsbury T&T Clark, 2016), 287–320.

2 Some differences appear in Pius XII's reform of the liturgies from Palm Sunday through the Easter Vigil.

3 Cf. P. Sorci, "Il lezionario del Messale di Pio V," RivLi 95 (2008/1) [= Monografie di Rivista Liturgica: *Celebrare con il Messale di San Pio V*] 92–107, 92f.; Meyer, *Eucharistie*, 186 (bibliography), 192f.; C. Folsom, "Liturgical Books of the Roman Rite": A. Chupungco (ed.), *Handbook for Liturgical Studies* I. Introduction to the Liturgy (Collegeville, MN: The Liturgical Press, 1997), 245–314, 254–59.

of collective memory of the Church herself, which for over a millennium memorized, meditated on, and commented on the same texts at the same time. This consistency played a role in establishing Catholic identity, and the Church is indebted to it for her unity throughout the years.

Similarly to all of the Eastern Churches, the lectionary of the classical Roman rite comprises the cycle of a single year that follows the natural rhythms of time and thus perfectly corresponds to human nature. As the same readings recur at the same time year by year, they become a firm point of reference for the believer's spiritual life and can impress him more deeply and enduringly than could a sequence of readings changing over a multi-year cycle.[4] This memorability is also simplified by the generally brief pericopes of this missal, a characteristic of the austerity of the Roman rite.

Apart from the Ember days, whose practice by the early Christians included a greater number of readings (three on Wednesday, seven on Saturday), the Roman rite, in consensus with most of the Eastern liturgies, contains only two readings, i.e., the Epistle and the Gospel.[5] While on Sundays the first reading is generally taken from the letters of the Apostles, and is thus an "epistle" in the strict sense — during the Easter season sections of the Acts of the Apostles are included — Old Testament pericopes are found in the ferial Masses of Lent and particular feast days (e.g., Epiphany, the Assumption), as well as in votive Masses and Commons of the saints. The Old Testament is ever understood from a prophetic and typological perspective as the promise of and a prefiguration of the New Testament, which in turn illuminates the true meaning of the Old Testament prototypes.[6] As there are no designated Mass formularies for the weekdays outside of Lent and the octaves of Easter and Pentecost, there remains room for numerous feasts of the saints, votive Masses, or a repeated echo of the previous Sunday's Mass.

---

4 Cf. N.N., "Das 'alte' und das 'neue' Lektionar: ein Vergleich," UVK 39 (2009): 113–33, 128–30.

5 Ibid., 114f., 117, 125.

6 Cf. Jungmann, *Missarum sollemnia* I, 508f.; idem, *The Mass of the Roman Rite* I, 396; M. Festugière, *La Liturgie catholique*, 152, 160; C. Vagaggini, *Theological Dimensions of the Liturgy: A General Treatise on the Theology of the Liturgy*, trans. by L. J. Doyle and W. A. Jurgens (Collegeville, MN: Liturgical Press, 1976), 464–81.

SELECTION CRITERIA

What are the criteria that determine the selection of a particular pericope? The lectionary of the classical Missal does not aim at imparting to the faithful as comprehensive a knowledge of the Bible as possible, so that by means of a strictly rationally organized order of readings over a number of years they would hear from almost all of the books of Holy Scripture. The traditional lectionary is not primarily a systematic biblical instruction. Instead, it seeks above all to illuminate each celebrated liturgical mystery in light of Scripture and to bring the faithful to a deeper participation.[7] This lectionary enables, in a specific manner, a liturgical interpretation of numerous biblical texts, since frequently they were chosen so that the holy celebration might provide an exegesis adapted to the present, and become a realization (*hodie!*)[8] of the events of salvation that took place in the past.[9] A continuous biblical reading

7   Cf. N.N., "Das 'alte' und das 'neue' Lektionar," 120: "Rather, this lectionary seeks, in accordance with the logic of contemplation and the logic of love, to connect the various texts (readings, chants, prayers) with the spirit of the feast day, and to bring these texts into resonance among each other . . . in order to discover their numerous harmonies"; Festugière, *Liturgie*, 151: "The Church does not make her choice as a collector who compiles, but as an artist who composes. Sometimes the liturgy produces unsuspected harmonies by a simple combination of texts; sometimes it obtains striking effects by applying the texts to special circumstances of the ecclesiastical year or of human life. In both cases, a new beauty is added to that which the inspired pages had in their biblical context"; ibid., 124–26.

8   Cf. for example, the Collect of Easter Sunday: "*Deus, qui hodierna die per Unigenitum tuum aeternitatis nobis aditum, devicta morte, reserasti*" [O God, who on this day through Thine only-begotten Son hast overcome death and opened unto us the gate of everlasting life]. Similarly the Collect of the Ascension: "*Qui hodierna die Unigenitum tuum, Redemptorem nostrum, ad caelos ascendisse credimus*" [we who believe Thine only-begotten Son, our Redeemer, to have this day ascended into heaven].

9   Cf. A. Miller, "Schriftsinn und liturgischer Sinn," BenM 16 (1934): 407–13; A. Wintersig, "Methodisches zur Erklärung von Messformularen," JLW 4 (1924): 135–52, 139f.; Vagaggini, *Theological Dimensions of the Liturgy*, 481–86; D. Barsotti, *Christliches Mysterium und Wort Gottes*, trans. by L. Ebel (Einsiedeln: Benziger Verlag, 1957), 214–21, 214: "The liturgy of the Church interprets the Word of God through all its actions"; P. Parsch, *The Liturgy of the Mass*, trans. by H. E. Winstone (London / St Louis, MO: Herder, ³1961), 141: "The liturgy is not so much concerned with giving instruction in these pericopes as with pointing a mystical parallel; with showing us how Christ works in the Eucharist"; Dobszay, *Restoration*, 144: "The reform *misunderstood* the role of the Mass readings. In their rudimentary state they may have had a merely didactic function. In the classical Roman rite, however, the readings, and first of all, the Gospels, are clearly outlined images of the *mysteries*, remarkable passages that seize hold of people's attention. Therefore, not all passages are equally suitable to become Sunday's pericopes."

is by no means foreign to the traditional liturgy, though it does not have its place in the Mass, but rather in the Office, especially in Matins of the Divine Office or Breviary, where over the course of a year extensive passages are read, especially from the books of the Old Testament.[10] As the individual Mass formularies ordinarily possess fixed pericopes, thus not allowing the priest to choose between various readings, the celebrant's subjectivism is here limited. All individual preferences for biblical texts withdraw in the face of that which the Church has objectively prescribed.[11]

The time-honored lectionary of the Mass possesses a good intuition for the average powers of comprehension of the faithful, as it wisely limits the number of biblical texts, encourages memorability by yearly repetition, and favors understandability over completeness. Thus the traditional readings impressively bear witness to the doctrinal, pastoral, and catechetical wisdom of the Church.[12]

At the same time, however, the traditional lectionary withstands the temptation of eliminating excessively hard-sounding words from the biblical message for "pastoral" reasons[13] or replacing them with less offensive pericopes.[14] The 1570/1962 Missal does not contain any Scripture purged *"ad usum Delphini."* The Word of God remains a "sharp, two-edged sword" (Rev 1:16) and it is preached in season or out of season (cf. 2 Tm 4:2). Despite its limited number of pericopes, the time-honored lectionary guarantees the integrity of the proclaimed Word of God, to which nothing may be added, but also from which nothing may be taken away (cf. Rev 22:18f.).

---

10 Cf. N.N., "Das 'alte' und das 'neue' Lektionar," 120.

11 Cf. ibid., 123f.

12 Cf. Siffi, *La Messa di San Pio V*, 105.

13 Thus, for example, the persecution of the disciples (feast of St Stephen, Dec. 26); their hardships in the world (Third Sunday after Easter); the great affliction before the Second Coming of Christ (Last Sunday after Pentecost); the severity of judgment and the possibility of eternal damnation (Third Sunday after Epiphany); warning against false prophets (Seventh Sunday after Pentecost); the exhortation for an examination of conscience before Communion, so as to avoid eating and drinking judgment on oneself (Holy Thursday and Corpus Christi). See, for many more examples, P. Kwasniewski, "Not Just More Scripture, But Different Scripture": Foreword to M. Hazell, *Index Lectionum: A Comparative Table of Readings for the Ordinary and Extraordinary Forms of the Roman Rite* (s.l.: Lectionary Study Press, 2016), vii–xxix.

14 Cf. R. Kaschewsky, "'…auf dass der Tisch des Gotteswortes reicher bereitet werde,'" UVK 12 (1982): 111–15, 268–71.

13
Offertory

FORMATION

Although the Offertory prayers cannot boast the same venerable age as the Roman Canon, having only been included in their current form in the Papal Curia's Missal during the thirteenth century, they nevertheless constitute the homogeneous development of a very old prayer tradition. Since the fifth/sixth centuries there has existed an *oratio super oblata*, a prayer with which the priest finished placing the Eucharistic offerings upon the altar. In the oldest texts, the interpretation of the action as formulated in this prayer is imbued with notions of sacrifice.[1] Thus the gifts offered up to God (*dona, munera, oblatio, hostia*) and the sacrificial offering (*offerimus, immolamus*) are referred to, and their acceptance (*suscipe, respice, intende placatus*), the proper sacrificial disposition, or the fruit of the offered sacrifice is emphasized. In this way the *oratio super oblata* leads to the Eucharistic Prayer, as it already hints at a few of its notions, and it connects the offering of the faithful, often adapted to the liturgical mystery of a particular feast, with the sacrifice, which is completed in the Canon. As this prayer of offering was already associated with the interior sanctuary of the Canon, the original audible recitation was, under Eastern influence, replaced in Carolingian times (since the mid-eighth century) by a silent prayer, which received the name *secreta* (i.e., *secreta oratio*). Further silent prayers in great variety were added to this sequence since the eighth century and were connected with a

---

1   Thus, for example, First Sunday after Epiphany: "*Oblatum tibi ... sacrificium*"; Third Sunday after Epiphany: "*et ad sacrificium celebrandum ... sanctificet*"; Fourth Sunday after Epiphany: "*huius sacrificii munus oblatum*": Thurs. after Ash Wednesday: "*sacrificiis prae-sentibus.*" Cf. Jungmann, *Missarum sollemnia* II, 118; idem, *The Mass of the Roman Rite* II, 94f.; F.M. Quoëx, "Historical and Doctrinal Notes on the Offertory of the Roman Rite," *Theological and Historical Aspects of the Roman Missal* (CIEL UK, 2000), 53–75, 59–61; M. Righetti, *Manuale di storia liturgica* III, 268–71.

formal gesture of offering.[2] Insofar as this entire complex of Offertory prayers and rites has developed from the basis of the *oratio super oblata*, its liturgical function — the introduction to the mystery of the Eucharistic anaphora — is the key to the proper understanding of the entire Offertory.[3] Even though these prayers anticipate some of the notions in the Canon and even borrow from it individual formulas, these texts are in no way a superfluous duplication[4] or an unsuitable anticipation of the single sacrifice, but rather "endeavor to underline the one step taken during the entire oblation rite: the provisional offering of the material gifts."[5]

THE NOTION OF SACRIFICE

The Offertory can be considered as the preparation for the actual act of sacrifice (*hoc sacrificium tuo nomini praeparatum* [*Veni, Sanctificator*]). In the first part of the preparation, the material gifts of bread and wine, which have been set apart to be changed into Christ's sacred Body and Blood, are formally withdrawn from the realm of the profane, singled out, and dedicated to God.[6] Thus it is, as St Thomas Aquinas expressed, an "offering of

---

2 Cf. Quoëx, "Offertory of the Roman Rite," 61f.; P. Tirot, *Histoire des prières d'offertoire dans la liturgie romaine du VIIe au XVIe siècle* [BEL.S 34] (Rome: C.L.V.-Edizioni Liturgiche, 2007) [¹1985]. From this medieval variety, however, no arbitrary scope for design of the Offertory prayers can be derived for later eras, as G. Oury, *La Messe de S. Pie V à Paul VI* (Solesmes: Abbaye Saint-Pierre, 1975), 86, attempts to do: "Their reorganization does not touch the essence of the Mass."

3 Cf. Quoëx, "Offertory of the Roman Rite," 61, 64.

4 Cf. R. Dulac, "La bulle de saint Pie V promulgant le Missel romain restauré," *Itinéraires* 162 (1972): 13–47, 22: "To say that the offertory is a 'doublet' is not a liturgist's view, but a sacristan's. It is like saying that the left hand is a doublet of the right hand because you can hold a candlestick with one hand, or you can illuminate with a single candle."

5 Jungmann, *Missarum sollemnia* II, 124; idem, *The Mass of the Roman Rite* II, 99. Cf. A. Clark, "The Origin and Development of the Offertory Rite," EphLit 64 (1950): 309–44. Cf. J.-B. Bossuet, *Explication de quelques difficultés sur les prières de la Messe à un nouveau catholique* [Œuvres 4] (Paris: Librairie catholique Martin-Beaupré, 1868), 454: "The oblation of bread and wine that takes place in the Secret, and all the other prayers that precede the consecration, is only the beginning of the sacrifice."

6 Cf. Thomas Aquinas, *STh* III, 22,2, obj. 3 in *Summa Theologiae* vol. 50 (3a. 16–26): *The One Mediator*, trans. by C.E. O'Neill (Oxford: Blackfriars Publications [i.a.], 1965), 141: "Moreover, by the fact of being offered to God, the victim becomes consecrated to God."

matter to be consecrated" (*oblatio materiae consecrandae*).[7] By this act, the offered gifts are no longer of a purely profane nature, but instead the Church treats them with special reverence, even in cases where they do not reach the foreseen consecration.[8] St Thomas Aquinas expressly emphasizes the sacrificial character of this offering.[9] By means of the Offertory, the bread and wine become victims, being referred to as such in numerous prayers.

The Offertory is, to be sure, not an intrinsic component of the Eucharistic sacrifice, insofar as this is accomplished by the consecration alone. Nevertheless, it constitutes an integral and indispensable element of this sacrifice.[10] Thus St Thomas Aquinas saw the celebration of the mystery (*celebratio mysterii*) as a whole, encompassing the offering (*oblatio*), the consecration (*consecratio materiae oblatae*), and Communion (*perceptio*).[11] The Offertory constitutes the first phase of an extensive action, which has meaning only in its entirety. It expresses the objective of that action, that is, the sacrifice of the Mass, and at the same time the ultimate end, God's glorification, as well as the immediate end, man's salvation. The Offertory is also the adequate expression of the unity of the single sacrifice, insofar as man's sacrifice is included in Christ's sacrifice. The manifestation of this unity is here organically connected with the act of offering.[12]

Thus the Offertory represents a *locus theologicus* of the highest degree: its prayers and rites contain a theology of sacrifice. The offering (*Offerimus tibi*; *Suscipe, sancte Pater: ... quam ego indignus famulus tuus offero*; *Suscipe, sancta Trinitas: ... quam tibi offerimus*[13]) of a sacrifice (*Veni,*

---

7 Thomas Aquinas, *Sent.* IV, dist. 8, *expositio textus.* Cf. Quoëx, "Offertory of the Roman Rite," 66; Batiffol, *Leçons sur la messe*, 162–65.

8 Cf. *De defectibus circa Missam occurentibus* X,9.

9 Cf. Thomas Aquinas, *STh* III, 83,4, in *Summa Theologiae* vol. 59 (3a. 79–83): Holy Communion, trans. by Th. Gilby (Oxford: Blackfriars Publications [i.a.], 1975), 157: "*Offertur ut sacrificium.*"

10 Cf. M.L. Guérard des Lauriers, "L'offertoire de la Messe," *Itinéraires* 158 (1971): 29–69, 30.

11 Cf. Thomas Aquinas, *STh* III, 83,4, in *Summa Theologiae* vol. 59 (3a. 79–83): Holy Communion, 157: "So then, the people being instructed and prepared, the celebration of the mysteries is next proceeded to. This is both offered as a sacrifice and consecrated and received as a sacrament. So first the offertory, second, the consecration of the matter offered, third, the Communion."

12 Cf. Guérard des Lauriers, "L'offertoire," 46, 56.

13 Cf. P. Salmon, "Le *Suscipe Sancta Trinitas*," in *La Préparation de l'Eucharistie*, 217–27.

Sanctificator:... benedic hoc sacrificium) is unambiguously articulated. A clear distinction is made between the priest's act of sacrifice and that of the faithful (*Orate, fratres:... meum ac vestrum sacrificium*). This sacrifice is emphatically related to Christ's sacrifice (*ob memoriam passionis, resurrectionis, et ascensionis Domini nostri Jesu Christi*);[14] consequently, any independent offering by the Church is excluded. It is distinctly emphasized that not only Christ's death on the Cross but also His Resurrection and Ascension belong to the complete entirety of the sacrifice (*Suscipe, sancta Trinitas, hanc oblationem, quam tibi offerimus ob memoriam passionis, resurrectionis, et ascensionis Domini nostri Jesu Christi*), insofar as the surrender to God, in which the sacrifice consists, acquires its completion when Christ's sacrificed Body is glorified in the Resurrection and comes before the face of God for all time in the Ascension. The sign of the Cross made over the corporal with the paten and chalice before the offerings are placed upon it impressively emphasizes the reference to Christ's sacrifice on Golgotha.[15] The mixing of wine and water in the chalice recalls the blood and water that flowed from the side of Christ at the Crucifixion (cf. Jn 19:34). As the wine incorporates the water into itself, so has Christ taken upon Himself mankind and his sins and shed His blood for the people, who are symbolized by the water (cf. Rev 17:15),[16] in order that, as it states in the accompanying prayer, the wondrous original dignity of mankind may be renewed even more wonderfully (*humanae substantiae dignitatem mirabiliter condidisti et mirabilius reformasti*).[17] The addition of the water likewise demonstrates that during Mass not only Christ but the Church as

---

14 *Memoria* is here not understood as a simple remembrance, but rather as a realization (*réactualisation*) of Christ's sacrifice. Cf. Tirot, *Prières de l'offertoire*, 29.

15 Durandus, *Rationale divinorum officiorum*, IV,30,17 (CCM 140, 386): "*Disponit autem et collocat hostiam cum signo crucis, quia sicut Christi oblatio in cruce facta fuit, sic oblatio sacerdotis, que in illius memoriam fit, cum signo crucis fieri debet*" [He places and arranges the host with the sign of the Cross, because as the offering of Christ was done on the Cross, so should the offering of the priest, in remembrance of this action, be done with the sign of the Cross].

16 Cf. Innocent III, *De sacro Altaris Mysterio* 2,58 (PL 217, 833C-D / MSIL 15, 192); J. Kreps, "Le mélange d'eau et de vin," in *La Préparation de l'Eucharistie*, 197–207.

17 The prayer is a synthesis of Pope Leo the Great's Incarnation theology; cf. Kreps, "Le mélange," 204–207. On the omission of this section of the prayer in the MRom 1970, cf. L. Bianchi, "Wunderbar ist die Erschaffung, noch wunderbarer die Erlösung," *30 Tage* 17/3 (1999): 50–52; idem, *Liturgia*, 161–67.

well is offered up.[18] The recipient of the sacrifice is the triune God (*Suscipe, sancta Trinitas*), as He revealed Himself through the Incarnation. The offering (*offerimus*) aspiring upward (*ut in conspectu divinae maiestatis tuae . . . ascendat*) harmoniously joins with the request for sanctification of the gifts from above in the epiclesis (*Veni, Sanctificator*). At the same time the immediately preceding humble request for acceptance (*In spiritu humilitatis*) with its biblical echoes (Dan 3:39f.; Ps 50:19) emphasizes that the meaning of all exterior offerings lies in the *sacrificium invisibile*, in the personal surrender of one's heart and in the interior willingness to sacrifice: "The outwardly offered sacrifice is the sign of an inner, spiritual sacrifice through which the soul offers itself to God."[19] The *Suscipiat* that follows in answer to the *Orate fratres* conclusively emphasizes the twofold finality of the sacrifice of the Mass: the glorification of God as the ultimate end (*ad laudem et gloriam nominis sui*), and the sanctification of man and of the Church as the immediate end (*ad utilitatem quoque nostram totiusque Ecclesiae suae sanctae*).[20] For whom this sanctification is intended is specified in still other prayers. Beginning with the priest, who first offers the sacrifice for his own sins (cf. Heb 7:27), the circle enlarges during the prayer at the offering of the Host to include firstly those present, but also all believers in Christ, living and dead. The perspective is even more comprehensive at the offering of the chalice, which is offered "for our salvation, and for that of the whole world" (*pro nostra, et totius mundi salute*).

The offering up of the bread and wine is a symbol and expression of the priest's and people's sacrifice and their willingness to participate in Christ's sacrifice. The Offertory prayers show clearly that the Church's sacrifice is embedded in the Eucharistic sacrifice. In contrast to the sacramental sacrifice, which is completed by the consecration, this is a matter of a

---

18 Cyprian, *Epistula* 63,9.13 (CCL 3C, 401.406–8 / *The Letters of St Cyprian of Carthage*, vol. 3: Letters 55–66, trans. by G. W. Clarke, *Ancient Christian Writers* 46 [New York, NY / Mahwah, NJ: Paulist Press, 1986], 102f.105). The Council of Trent defended this practice against Luther's attacks; cf. sess. XXII, cap. 7 (DH 1748); can. 9 (DS 1759).

19 Thomas Aquinas, *STh* II–II, 85,2, in *Summa Theologiae* vol. 39 (2a2ae. 80–91): Religion and Worship, trans. by K. D. O'Rourke (Oxford: Blackfriars Publications [i.a.], 1964), 117.

20 The precise meaning of the terms only appears, however, provided these truths have been clearly expressed in the preceding Offertory prayers. Cf. Guérard des Lauriers, "L'offertoire," 55.

spiritual sacrifice. This act is indispensable should the faithful truly desire a share in Christ's sacrifice. Only by means of an actual participation in Christ's sacrifice will the twofold aim of the sacrifice of the Mass, God's glorification and man's sanctification, be achieved.[21] For this reason, such Offertory prayers and rites may be found in all liturgies without exception, in various forms though always expressive, be it right before the Eucharistic prayer, as in the Roman rite, or at the beginning of the Eucharistic celebration, as in the Orthodox *proskomide* or in the Gallican liturgy.[22] The assimilation, or the changing of the Church's sacrifice into Christ's sacrifice, is especially demonstrated in the closing prayers, which first (*In spiritu humilitatis*) refer to "our sacrifice" (*sacrificium nostrum*) and then "this sacrifice" (*hoc sacrificium*).[23] As the material gifts of bread and wine are already referred to during the Offertory as the "unspotted host" (*Suscipe, sancte Pater, hanc immaculatam hostiam*) and as the "chalice of salvation" (*Offerimus tibi, Domine, calicem salutaris*),[24] the Church is meditating in these prayers on that which the host and the contents of the chalice will soon become.[25] Thus it is a proleptic manner of speaking, which is also found elsewhere in the liturgy.[26] In her prayers, the Church anticipates that which takes place only at the consecration. Thus she uses the same expression (*immaculatam hostiam*) in the Offertory as after the consecration (*Unde et memores*).[27] The splendor of these material

---

21 Cf. Guérard des Lauriers, "L'offertoire," 32, 35.

22 Cf. G. Díaz Patri, "Unité de la foi et diversité liturgique": *Foi et liturgie* (CIEL, 2002), 141–87, 173–79.

23 Cf. Guérard des Lauriers, "L'offertoire," 54.

24 Reservations about these formulas were already discussed at the Council of Trent, but were not reflected in the statements of abuses (*abusus*). Cf. Guérard des Lauriers, "L'offertoire," 40–42; Quoëx, "Offertory of the Roman Rite," 65.

25 Cf. Tirot, *Prières de l'offertoire*, 77: "The liturgical prayer of the Church does not follow our Cartesian logic: it anticipates, it recalls, it goes, it comes, with a freedom which is that of the Spirit of God and of poetry. This is one of the reproaches that can be made to the recent liturgical reform: to have wanted to 'rationalize' the liturgical prayer in wishing to place there an 'order' that does not belong to its spirit, and thus to have deprived it of poetry. We are beginning to realize this and to miss the lyricism of the old liturgy."

26 Cf. Tirot, *Prières de l'offertoire*, 76, with examples from the *Missale Romanum* and Eastern liturgies.

27 Cf. Guérard des Lauriers, "L'offertoire," 56–64.

gifts' high purpose is already emphasized.[28] As the Church speaks thus of the offering of her own gifts from the very start, as if it were already Christ's perfect sacrifice, she confesses that only this sacrifice is pleasing to God, and it is only in connection with this sacrifice that she can offer herself to God.[29] The people's spiritual participation in the consecration is completed in an anticipated form during the Offertory prayers, in which the gaze is ever directed toward the coming sacramental offering.

The Offertory is the exact translation of the *lex credendi* into the *lex orandi*.[30] During the thirteenth century the Roman Curia had selected various prayer texts from older traditions — Frankish, Germanic, and Gallican (ninth/tenth centuries) — for this purpose,[31] in which the decisive factor for their selection and arrangement was the theological quality and expressiveness of the prayers.[32] The wording of these prayers wards off the misconception that the celebration of the Mass is simply a remembrance of the Last Supper, a meal to commemorate the death of Jesus, or merely an offering of thanks. In them is unambiguously expressed the momentous truth of the expiatory sacrificial character of the Mass (*sacrificium propitiatorium*), as it was not only dogmatically defined by the Council of Trent (DH 1753) but as it is already witnessed in the New Testament (Mt 26:29; Heb 9:12, 20–22) and by the early Church Fathers. The Offertory prayers clearly manifest that through the hands of the priest, the Church offers to God the Father His Son's sacrifice on Golgotha as her own sacrifice. Thus it is no wonder that these prayers constituted one of Luther's central points of attack and were omitted from Protestant services.[33] The fact that a liturgically separate part for

28 J. Bona, *Rerum liturgicarum libri II*, 2,9,3: *Opera omnia*, 338: "*Dicimus ergo, 'immaculatam hostiam' per relationem ad terminum substantiae panis et vini mox subrogandum.*"

29 Cf. Quoëx, "Offertory of the Roman Rite," 68, 70f.

30 Cf. Guérard des Lauriers, "L'offertoire," 46: The Offertory, as "the fruit of an elaboration that the Holy Spirit has aroused, guided and sanctioned . . . constitutes a sacred treasure which it would be a sacrilege to allow to be violated."

31 The *Orate fratres* already existed from the time of the eighth century.

32 Cf. Tirot, *Prières de l'offertoire*, 124; Quoëx, "Offertory of the Roman Rite," 62–64.

33 Cf. M. Luther, *Formula Missae et communionis* (WA 12, 207, 211). Cf. H.B. Meyer, *Luther und die Messe. Eine liturgiewissenschaftliche Untersuchung über das Verhältnis Luthers zum Messwesen des späten Mittelalters* [Konfessionskundliche und kontroverstheologische Studien 11] (Paderborn: Verlag Ferdinand Schöningh, 1965), 156–72; Brinktrine, *Messe*, 135:

preparing a sacrificial offering, placed variously before the consecration, organically developed not only in the Roman rite but also in all the other Western and Eastern rites demonstrates how indispensable it has always seemed to the Church to have prayers and ceremonies that emphatically manifest her understanding of the Eucharist as a sacrifice, further explaining the sacrificial theology contained in the Eucharistic prayer. The relatively young age of the Roman rite's Offertory prayers in no way justifies questioning their meaning and legitimacy.[34] They are the continuation and development of that which was contained in the old Roman liturgy's Secret (*oratio super oblata*) and the prayers of the Canon before the consecration (*Te igitur*; *Hanc igitur*; *Quam oblationem*).[35] Over the course of centuries, the more the Church has delved into the wealth of the sacrifice of the Mass entrusted to Her, the more her desire has increased to select certain jewels from this treasure and to contemplate them prayerfully, even before the beginning of the Eucharistic prayer.[36]

"A revolution in the field of liturgy, which the Church could never acknowledge."

34   Cf. Guérard des Lauriers, "L'offertoire," 68: "The Church could live 'previously' without what she gradually discovered and expressed afterwards, but now it is no longer possible for her to renounce it."

35   Cf. Brinktrine, *Messe*, 15.

36   Cf. Tirot, *Prières de l'offertoire*, 78: "It was therefore very useful that the Church, in the greater awareness that she was taking of the essentially sacrificial aspect of the Mass, insisted on this character in the prayers of the Offertory. The Council of Trent understood the opportunity against the heresy that denied it. It may be more urgent than ever to insist upon it."

14

The Roman Canon

HISTORY

The Roman Canon resembles the mysterious priest-king Melchisedech: "Without father, without mother, without genealogy, having neither beginning of days nor end of life" (Heb 7:3). The origin and earliest development of the *canon missae* remain mostly in darkness. Countless reconstruction attempts have been undertaken, but the early history of the Roman Canon remains hardly more than ruins of failed hypotheses.[1]

The fundamental core of the prayer is already observed by the end of the fourth century.[2] The Council of Trent spoke of various components, or phases of formation. It attributed the core components to Christ's own words of institution, regarded the original form as being handed down by the Apostles, and ascribed the final setting to the work of specific popes: "For it consists partly of the very words of the Lord, partly of the traditions of the Apostles, and also of pious regulations of holy pontiffs."[3]

The derivation of the Eucharistic prayer from apostolic tradition was repeatedly emphasized in late antiquity.[4] Pope Vigilius (537–555) spoke of the "text of even this Canon prayer that we have received by God's grace, handed down by the Apostles."[5] Like the Apostles' Creed (*symbolum apostolicum*), which truly reflects the apostolic preaching in its main contents,

---

1   Cf. J. A. Jungmann, *Missarum sollemnia* I, 64; idem, *The Mass of the Roman Rite* I, 50; Batiffol, *Leçons sur la messe*, 235; B. Botte, *Le Canon de la Messe Romaine. Edition critique, introduction et notes* [Textes et études liturgiques 2] (Louvain: Éditions de Abbaye du Mont César, 1935), 27; F. Cabrol, "Canon Romain," DACL 2/2 (1909): 1847–1905, 1900; B. D. Spinks, "The Roman canon missae": A. Gerhards / H. Brakmann / M. Klöckener (eds.), *Prex Eucharistica* III/1 (Fribourg/Switzerland: Academic Press, 2005), 129–43, 129.

2   On the various textual witnesses, cf. Cabrol, "Canon Romain," 1857–68.

3   Sess. XXII, cap. 4 (DH 1745). Cf. J. P. Theisen, "The Roman Canon and the Council of Trent," *Annuarium historiae conciliorum* 2 (1970): 284–302.

4   Cf. Schuster, *The Sacramentary*, vol. I, 312.

5   Vigilius, *Epistula* 1 *ad Profuturum Bracarensem episcopum* (PL 69, 18D).

though it was not determined by the apostles verbatim, the fundamental ideas and biblical assertions of the Roman Canon of the Mass can be considered as a compendium of apostolic teachings.

The possibility of the text having been originally composed in Greek and then translated into Latin during the course of the latinization of the Roman liturgy[6] is precluded on linguistic grounds.[7] That the available Greek prayer formulas provided some suggestions, though, is not unlikely. Thus a certain affinity to the Alexandrian tradition can be recognized, as found in the Egyptian anaphora of St Mark.[8] The formulation of the words of institution is an indication that the core of the Roman Canon possibly came from Latin-speaking North Africa,[9] as they largely follow the Old Latin translation of the Gospel of Matthew. This translation most likely originated in North Africa and contained in the words of consecration a conspicuous *enim*, which does not appear in the Vulgate (*hoc est enim corpus meum*; *hic est enim calix…*). In the course of the latinization of the liturgy during the fourth century, the prayer formula used by the North African Christians residing in Rome could have been entirely adopted for the celebration of the Mass and further developed.[10] Nevertheless, the title that Giovanni Pierluigi da Palestrina gave to one of his Masses, *Missa sine nomine*, also applies to this Eucharistic prayer.[11] The redactor of the Roman Eucharistic prayer remains unknown and nameless.[12]

---

6 Thus, for example, Th. Schnitzler, *Der Römische Meßkanon. In Betrachtung, Verkündigung und Gebet* (Freiburg i. Br.: Verlag Herder, 1968), 45f.

7 Cf. B. Botte, "Canon missae," RAC 2 (1954): 843f.

8 Cf. J.A. Jungmann, *Missarum sollemnia* I, 71; idem, *The Mass of the Roman Rite* I, 55; Spinks, "Roman canon," 133–35; Meyer, *Eucharistie*, 179; J. Schmitz, "Canon Romanus": A. Gerhards / H. Brakmann / M. Klöckener (eds.), *Prex Eucharistica* III/1 (Fribourg/Switzerland: Academic Press, 2005), 281–310, 282n9 (bibliography); R.A. Keifer, "The Unity of the Roman Canon: An Examination of its Unique Structure," *Studia Liturgica* 11 (1976): 39–58, 44–48.

9 Cf. Th. Klauser, *A Short History of the Western Liturgy* (London: Oxford University Press, 1969), 21; idem, "Der Übergang der römischen Kirche von der griechischen zur lateinischen Liturgiesprache": idem, *Gesammelte Arbeiten zur Liturgiegeschichte, Kirchengeschichte und Christlichen Archäologie*, ed. by E. Dassmann [JAC. E 3] (Münster: Aschendorff Verlag, 1974), 184–94, 191f.

10 Thus Spinks, "Roman canon," 134f.

11 Cf. Schnitzler, *Meßkanon*, 45.

12 Cf. Gregory I, *Epistula* 9,26 (CCL 140A, 587): "*precem quam scholasticus composuerat.*" According to Th. Schnitzler, *Die Messe in der Betrachtung* I (Freiburg i. Br.: Verlag Herder, ²1955), 54, we surmise a scholar familiar with ancient rhetoric, who revised the Canon

Over the course of centuries, in both East and West there developed a fixed schema for the Eucharistic prayer that contains particular elements (institution narrative, epiclesis, anamnesis, and request for acceptance) and certain expressions (*sursum corda, gratias agamus*). The basic form of the Roman Canon developed following this schema and containing such formulas, also with the use of particular expressions, sanctified by convention, from the Latin linguistic spirit.[13]

The term "canon" is a Semitic loanword (from *kanäh*, meaning measuring tube, balance beam, or guideline) and in a liturgical context is considered as the rule and measure of prayer.[14] Originally, this term was not synonymous with "unchangeable," just as the rule of faith, which was referred to in the same way (κανὼν πίστεως, *kanōn pisteōs*), was certainly determined in its core content, though still flexible in its wording. The Preface was also originally included as part of the Canon. Since the ninth century the *Te igitur* has been considered to be its beginning.[15]

St Ambrose offers an important point of reference for a more exact date. In his work *De sacramentis* (390/91) the core of the Roman Canon is present, with closely similar wording from *Quam oblationem* to *Supplices*.[16]

---

according to the laws of meter, rhythm, and *cursus*. According to Jungmann, *Missarum sollemnia* I, 73n27; idem, *The Mass of the Roman Rite* I, 56n27, however, this conclusion has hardly any bearing on the Canon. Similarly A. Heinz, "Papst Gregor der Große," 74, as well as R. Bellarmine, *Controversiarum de sacramento eucharistiae liber* VIII, 20 [*Opera* IV] (Paris: Vivès, 1873 [repr. Frankfurt a. M.: Minerva-Verlag, 1965]), 416.

13 Cf. Klauser, *A Short History of the Western Liturgy*, 20.

14 Cf. J. Bona, *Rerum liturgicarum libri II*, 2,11,1: *Opera omnia*, 343: "*Canon autem regula est, qua voce usa est Ecclesia, ut indicaret hanc esse regulam fixam et stabilem, qua novi Testamenti sacrificium celebrandum est*" [Now the Canon is a rule; the Church uses the term 'canon' to indicate that it is a fixed and stable rule by which the sacrifice of the new covenant is to be offered].

15 Cf. E. Lengeling, "Kanon," LThK² 5 (1960): 1284–86, 1285; J. Gassner, *The Canon of the Mass: Its History, Theology and Art* (Saint Louis, MO / London: Herder, 1950 [2nd impr.]), 50f., 116.

16 Cf. Ambrose, *De sacramentis* 4,21f.26f. (FC 3, 148.152 / Ambrose, *Theological and Dogmatic Works*, trans. by R. Deferrari, *The Fathers of the Church* 44 [Washington, DC: Catholic University of America Press, 1963], 304–6). A phrase from the *Supra quae* is quoted around 375 by Ambrosiaster, *Quaestiones veteris et novi testamenti* 109, 21 (CSEL 50, 268): "*sacerdos appellatus est excelsi Dei non summus, sicut nostri in oblatione praesumunt.*" Cf. G. Nicholls, "The History of the Prayers of the Roman Canon," *Theological and Historical Aspects of the Roman Missal* (CIEL UK, 2000), 29–52, 39–41; Jungmann, *Missarum sollemnia* I, 66; idem,

This is not, however, a precursor, but rather a parallel form of the Roman Eucharistic prayer created by Ambrose himself or another author, possibly also from a different Church, perhaps even adopted from the Roman Church,[17] whose "type and form we follow in all things."[18] Certainly, though, the sections of the Eucharistic prayer not mentioned by the Milanese bishop date back at least to the fifth/sixth century, according to the witness of contemporary sources.[19] The *Liber Pontificalis* explicitly noted and consciously kept account of single words, even of the most insignificant meaning, added by later popes (Alexander I, Sixtus I, Leo the Great, and Gregory the Great); these notes express the age and venerableness of the Roman Canon as well as the carefulness used in its design.[20] The actions of the popes and of other unknown persons are evocative of that figure described by Rainer Maria Rilke in a poem from his *Book of Hours*:

> We are all workmen: apprentice, journeyman, master,
> and we build thee, thou towering nave.
> And sometimes comes a grave wayfarer,
> who sends a thrill through our hundred souls,
> and trembling shows us a new skill.[21]

The Mass of the Roman Rite I, 51. On possible echoes by Bishop Zeno of Verona (362–372), cf. G. Jeanes, "Early Latin Parallels to the Roman Canon? Possible References to a Eucharistic Prayer in Zeno of Verona," JThS 37 (1986): 427–31.

17 Cf. J. Schmitz, *Gottesdienst im altchristlichen Mailand. Eine liturgiewissenschaftliche Untersuchung über Initiation und Messfeier während des Jahres zur Zeit des Bischofs Ambrosius († 397)* [Theoph. 25] (Cologne / Bonn: Peter Hanstein Verlag, 1975), 384–412; idem, "Einleitung": Ambrosius, *De sacramentis* [FC 3] (Freiburg i. Br.: Verlag Herder, 1990), 55; Spinks, "Roman canon," 131f.; J. Beumer, "Die ältesten Zeugnisse für die römische Eucharistiefeier bei Ambrosius von Mailand," ZKTh 95 (1973): 311–24.

18 Ambrose, *De sacramentis* 3,5 (FC 3, 121 / Ambrose, *Theological and Dogmatic Works*, 291).

19 Cf. Innocent I, *Epistula* 25 (PL 20, 553f.); Boniface I, *Epistula* 7 (PL 20, 767A); Celestine I, *Epistula* 23 (PL 50, 544C). Cf. Jungmann, *Missarum sollemnia* I, 69–71; idem, *The Mass of the Roman Rite* I, 53–55; Meyer, *Eucharistie*, 179; Botte, *Canon de la Messe*, 54f., 67–69; Spinks, "Roman canon," 136 (two-fold *Memento*, 6th century).

20 Cf. Bellarmine, *Controversiarum*, 418; I. Schuster, *The Sacramentary* vol. I, 312; A. Baumstark, "Das 'Problem' des Römischen Messkanons—Eine Retractatio auf geistesgeschichtlichem Hintergrund," EL 53 (1939): 204–43, 243. The individual contribution of the popes is admittedly often not precisely determined; cf. Gassner, *Canon*, 28.

21 R.M. Rilke, *Das Stunden-Buch* (Leipzig: Insel-Verlag, 1936), 20.

In a way similar to that modest and shy change in the building plans of the great church, only smaller modifications were made in the Roman Canon. Pope Gregory the Great (590–604) gave the Canon its final form; he rewrote the list of saints in the *Communicantes* and *Nobis quoque*, bringing the names into a symmetrical series, and in the *Hanc igitur*, where the celebrant mentioned the changing names and requests of the offerers, the pope formulated the request for peace (*diesque nostros in tua pace disponas*) and for salvation from eternal damnation as an all-encompassing reason for sacrifice.[22] The close connection between the Canon and the Our Father also dates back to this pope. Insofar as the text of the Canon in later times experienced only insignificant changes,[23] one can justly speak of the "Gregorian Canon" or "Gregorian rite," as well as the "Mass of St Gregory." From that time until the liturgical reform of Vatican II, the Eucharistic prayer remained untouched. In contrast to multiple liturgies of the East, the Roman *Canon missae* remained the single Eucharistic prayer in the West.[24] It is an impressive witness for the unity of the Roman Church, spanning time and space.[25]

Medieval theologians treated the Canon with great respect.[26] They

---

22 *Liber Pontificalis* 1, 66 (ed. by L. Duchesne, Paris: Éditions de Boccard, ²1955, 312). Cf. Heinz, "Gregor der Große," 74f.; Jungmann, *Missarum sollemnia* II, 226–232; idem, *The Mass of the Roman Rite* II, 180–85; Nicholls, "Prayers of the Roman Canon," 41–44.

23 J. Bona, *Rerum liturgicarum libri II*, 2,11,2: *Opera omnia*, 344: "*neminem ex Pontificibus post Gregorium Magnum quidpiam addidisse aut immutasse*"; quoted in Benedict XIV (olim Prosper Cardinal de Lambertinis), *De sacrosancto sacrificio missae* II, XII,12 (Mainz: Kirchheim-Verlag, 1879), 162. Cf. B. Botte, "Histoire des prières de l'ordinaire de la messe": B. Botte / C. Mohrmann (eds.), *L'ordinaire de la messe. Texte critique, traduction et études* [EtLi 2] (Paris: Les éditions du Cerf / Louvain: Éditions de Abbaye du Mont César, 1953), 15–27, 18–25; Schnitzler, *Meßkanon*, 48; Meyer, *Eucharistie*, 180.

24 Cf. Meyer, *Eucharistie*, 180.

25 Cf. Guillou, *Le livre de la messe*, 30: "This main prayer of the Canon has been meditated by so many saints, murmured by so many priests, that it cannot be compared to any other prayer. Keeping its original Latin form is the dazzling testimony of the necessary unity of the Roman Church in time and space. Its abandonment in practice would be an act of impiety."

26 Cf. Innocent III, *De sacro Altaris Mysterio* 4,1 (PL 217, 852D / MSIL 15, 244); Durandus, *Rationale divinorum officiorum* IV,36,1 (CCM 140, 418): "*Expositioni canonis hic vacare previdimus. Verumptamen quicquid exponendo conamur exprimere, vix ullius apparet esse momenti. Deficit namque lingua, sermo disparet, superatur ingenium, opprimitur intellectus*" [We have foreseen that there is now place for an explanation of the Canon; but whatever we try to express by explaining can hardly be of any significance, for the tongue falters, the words fail, the talent is overthrown, the intellect is overwhelmed].

did not seek to bring the text into unison with their own speculations by reshaping it. Rather they regarded the Canon as a fixed component of tradition and commented on it as a sacred text.[27] Among others, allegorical interpretations were disseminated, which primarily interpreted the course of the celebration of the Mass in its entirety as a symbolic representation of the mysteries of Christ—from the Incarnation to the Ascension—and especially related the individual parts of the Eucharistic prayer to the various phases of the Passion and Resurrection.[28]

The fact that the Canon remained unchanged for over 1,300 years is the clearest evidence for the reverence it always received, with a corresponding reluctance to lay a hand on such a holy inheritance.[29]

The Roman Canon was first explicitly attacked by Protestant reformers, who claimed the right to make profound changes to the liturgy based on their accusations of abuses in the Church. These changes did not leave even the innermost core of the sacrifice of the Mass unchanged. Luther described the Canon as "that mangled and abominable thing gathered from much filth and scum; . . . there the Mass began to be a sacrifice." According to Luther the Canon was idolatrous and the devil's concoction.[30] Later

---

27 Cf. Botte, "L'ordinaire," 27: "We should be grateful to the people of the Middle Ages for having preserved the Canon in its purity and for not having allowed their personal effusions or theological ideas to pass into it. One can imagine the complete mess we would have today if each generation had been permitted to remake the canon to the measure of their theological controversies or novel forms of piety. We can only hope for a continuing imitation of the good sense of these people, who had their own theological ideas but who understood that the Canon was not their playground. In their eyes, it was the expression of a venerable tradition, and they felt that it could not be touched without opening the door to every sort of abuse"; idem, *From Silence to Participation: An Insider's View of Liturgical Renewal* (Washington, D.C.: Pastoral Press, 1988), 80f., quoted in Reid, *Organic Development*, 193.

28 Cf. Spinks, "Roman canon," 139–41; C. Barthe, "The 'Mystical' Meaning of the Ceremonies," 179–97; C. Barthe / D. Millet-Gérard, Introduction: Guillaume Durand, *Le sens spirituel de la liturgie. Rational des Divins Offices.* Livre IV de la Messe (Geneva: Ad Solem Éditions, 2003), 7–65.

29 Cf. M. Davies, *Pope Paul's New Mass*, 328.

30 *Formula Missae et communionis* (WA 12, 207, 211 / trans.: http://www.righteousnessis-love.org/wp-content/uploads/2013/07/Martin-Luther-Works-of-Martin-Luther-Vol.-6.pdf). Cf. Meyer, *Luther und die Messe*, 250f.; W. Simon, *Die Messopfertheologie Martin Luthers. Voraussetzungen, Genese, Gestalt und Rezeption* [Spätmittelalter und Reformation. Texte und Untersuchungen, N. R. 22] (Tübingen: J.C.B. Mohr (Paul Siebeck), 2003).

reformers expressed themselves even more disparagingly.[31] All of these resentments and ranting tirades established the fact that the Roman Canon expressed the Catholic notion of sacrifice with total clarity. Consequently, Luther banished the entire Canon from divine worship and retained only the words of institution. In the Anglican *Book of Common Prayer* of 1549, the English reformer Thomas Cranmer replaced the Roman Eucharistic prayer with a new text of similar length that contained fragments of the old Canon but had lost the character of sacrifice and offering.[32] Against all efforts toward alienation, even the reformers' newly-made prayers not infrequently revealed a certain influence of the Roman Canon, as this was certainly the only Eucharistic prayer that the first generation of Protestants knew. Although each new prayer formula distanced itself even further from the original Canon, the actual ancestor remained ever recognizable.[33] "All who slander you depend only upon you!" — the words that the soul speaks to the Church in a poem by Gertrude von Le Fort[34] also apply to the Church's Eucharistic prayer. Already in antiquity an early Christian theologian expressed the heretic's want of creative power when he wrote of the schismatics: "Nor are they able to do anything new or anything else, except what they have long since learned from their own mother."[35]

After a few Catholic theological controversialists (Hieronymus Emser, Johann Eck) had defended the Roman Canon against the reformatory attacks,[36] the Council of Trent clarified the inerrancy of the Roman Eucharistic prayer:

---

31   Cf. H. Zwingli, *De Canone Missae Epicheiresis* (1523): *Huldreich Zwinglis sämtliche Werke* vol. 2 (Corpus Reformatorum 89) (Zurich: Theologischer Verlag, 1982 [repr. of Leipzig: Heinsius, 1908]), 552–608.

32   Cf. M. Davies, *Cranmer's Godly Order*, 195–209, 305–7.

33   Cf. Spinks, "Roman canon," 142f.

34   G. von Le Fort, *Hymnen an die Kirche*, 27.

35   Optatus of Milevis, *Contra Parmenianum* 1,11 (CSEL 26, 14 / Optatus, *Against the Donatists*, trans. and ed. by M. Edwards [Liverpool: Liverpool University Press, 1997], 11).

36   Cf. E. Iserloh, *Der Kampf um die Messe in den ersten Jahren der Auseinandersetzung mit Luther* [Katholisches Leben und Kämpfen 10] (Münster: Aschendorff Verlag, 1952); idem, *Die Eucharistie in der Darstellung des Johannes Eck: Ein Beitrag zur vortridentinischen Kontroverstheologie über das Meßopfer* [Reformationsgeschichtliche Studien und Texte 73/74] (Münster: Aschendorff Verlag, 1950).

Since it is fitting that holy things be administered in a holy manner, and of all things this sacrifice is the most holy, the Catholic Church, to the end that it might be worthily and reverently offered and received, instituted many centuries ago the holy Canon, which is so free from error (can. 6) that it contains nothing that does not savor in the highest degree of holiness and piety and raise up to God the minds of those who offer. For it consists partly of the very words of the Lord, partly of the traditions of the Apostles, and also of pious regulations of holy pontiffs.[37]

The actual reason (*enim*) for this inerrancy thus lies in the fact that the Roman Canon represents a legacy of sacred tradition. The Council sanctioned this teaching in its harshest manner as it threatened anyone who impugned the doctrinal and spiritual integrity of this prayer with excommunication: "If anyone says that the Canon of the Mass contains errors and therefore should be abolished: let him be anathema."[38] With the adherence to the Roman Canon, the Council of Trent had preserved the continuity of tradition in the Church, while paradoxically, the reformers' abandonment of that prayer disrupted the very continuity they sought with the primitive Church, as it constituted a break with the oldest prayer tradition of Christianity. The Anglican liturgical historian Gregory Dix accurately described the situation at the time as follows:

> The advantage of the Counter-Reformation was that it conserved the text of a liturgy which dated in substance from long before the medieval development. With this it preserved those primitive statements which indicated the true solution of the medieval difficulty, even though it was a long while before the post-Tridentine church made much use of them for the purpose. The protestants on the contrary discarded the whole text of the liturgy, and especially those elements in it which were a

---

37 Sess. XXII, cap. 4 (DH 1745). Cf. D.N. Power, "The Priestly Prayer. The Tridentine Theologians and the Roman Canon": G. Austin (ed.), *Fountain of Life*: In Memory of N.K. Rasmussen [O.P.] (Washington, DC: Pastoral Press, 1991), 131–64.

38 Sess. XXII, can. 6 (DH 1756).

genuine monument of that primitive Church they professed to restore. They introduced in its place forms which derived from and expressed the medieval tradition from which their own movement sprang.[39]

In the course of the liturgical reform, efforts to rewrite the Roman Canon or entirely remove it for ecumenical reasons met with opposition from Pope Paul VI. Instead, the creation of further Eucharistic prayers in addition to the old Canon was recommended.[40] If the Roman Canon could not lawfully be eliminated, it would be practically eliminated by the introduction of newer, shorter, and more theologically "neutral" Eucharistic prayers that accommodated "ecumenical correctness."[41]

THEOLOGY

In its theological depth, the Roman Canon is unsurpassable.[42] The Church's authentic teaching on the Eucharist finds expression in the Canon of the Mass, which makes manifest the Church's belief regarding the Eucharistic mystery.[43] The historical development of the Canon was an organic process in which the Church ever more deeply fathomed the legacy entrusted to her, gradually developing the implicit beliefs of early times and finally formulating them as explicit beliefs.[44] The Canon constitutes the origin and the core of the Eucharistic prayer. All

39 G. Dix, *The Shape of the Liturgy* (Glasgow: University Press, ²1954), 626. Cf. L. Capellatti, "Der römische Messkanon und das Konzil von Trient," *30 Giorni*, German edition No. 2/3 (2010): 51–55, 55 (= L. Bianchi, *Liturgia*, 171–81 [first appendix], 177).

40 Cf. A. Bugnini, *The Reform of the Liturgy*, 448–50.

41 Cf. May, *Die alte und neue Messe*, 37. For already similar criticism of comparable tendencies of the neo-Gallican liturgists, cf. Guéranger, *Institutions liturgiques* II, 183: "They diminished the dogma, they pruned from the worship all that seemed to them difficult to defend from the viewpoint of their adversaries. They wished not to shock, they wished even to satisfy, if it had been possible, the *reason* of the Protestants; they granted them victory in small measure, thus tacitly agreeing that the Reformation had certain [legitimate] grievances against the Church, which had allegedly sinned by exaggeration. A reckless tactic that success has never justified."

42 Cf. E. Guillou, *Le canon romain et la liturgie nouvelle* (Escurolles: Éditions "Fideliter," ²1990).

43 Cf. Gassner, *Canon*, 13–25.

44 Cf. Gassner, *Canon*, 14–16.

else is only an enrichment and unfolding of the Canon. The Ordinary of the Mass and the liturgical year developed over the course of time and placed themselves in concentric circles around the center of the Eucharist, which is formed by the Canon.

The Canon does not make the Eucharist into a sacrifice, but rather expresses the essence of the Eucharist as a sacrificial action. Even the first letter of the Canon, in the *Te igitur*, recalls the mystical *tau*, which in the Old Testament was written with sacrificial blood upon the foreheads of those whom God wished to be preserved (cf. Ezek 9:4,6), and which also represents the original form of the Cross, as the inscription on the Cross was specifically placed at the middle of the crossbeam (cf. Jn 19:19), so that from this the common form of the Cross later appeared. After decoration of the initial letters in the old sacramentaries became common, that T was treated as a cross and the figure of Christ was drawn on it. This representation was occasionally expanded to an entire Crucifixion scene, which, when later detached from the initial, became an independent image placed at the beginning of the Canon. Thus from its very beginning, the Roman Canon stands under the sign of the Cross.[45] In addition to the initial's symbolism of the Cross, the subsequent words of the *Te igitur* immediately denote the sacrifice (*sancta sacrificia*), which the Church offers (*offerimus*), praying for its graceful acceptance (*uti accepta habeas*) and beneficial effects (*pro Ecclesia*). As this determines the fundamental theme of the Eucharistic prayer, all further strophes revolve around this mystery of sacrifice, each from a different perspective. The prayers of the Canon reveal *what* is offered: a true sacrifice, consisting of Christ's Body and Blood (*Quam oblationem...*); *to whom* it is offered: the Father, against Whom we have sinned, Whose clemency and goodness we crave, to Whom we render all glory; *through whom* this sacrifice is offered: through Christ Himself (*per Jesum Christum*),[46]

---

45   Cf. Innocent III, *De sacro Altaris Mysterio* 3,2 (PL 217, 840f. / MSIL 15, 212); Guéranger, *The Traditional Latin Mass Explained*, 56–57; L. Eisenhofer, *Handbuch der Katholischen Liturgik* II (Freiburg i. Br.: Verlag Herder, 1933), 172.

46   The often-repeated closing formula *Per Christum Dominum nostrum* at the end of individual strophes of the Canon (*Communicantes*; *Hanc igitur*; *Supplices*; *Memento*; *Nobis quoque*), which were made optional in the MRom 1970, is not a break in the prayer, but rather

Who makes use of the priest (*nos servi tui*); *for whom* this sacrifice is offered: for many (*pro multis*), insofar as they constitute or are called to constitute the Catholic Church (*pro Ecclesia tua sancta catholica*) — for the Church on earth as well as for the Church Suffering (twofold *Memento*); *for what* the sacrifice is offered: for the forgiveness of sins and all concerns of the universal Church (*pro redemptione animarum, pro spe salutis et incolumitatis suae ... diesque nostras in tua pace disponas, atque ab aeterna damnatione nos eripi*). *What, to whom, through whom, for whom, for what*: all of these questions arising from the sacred action find their answer in the prayers that surround the sacrificial act of the consecration. The mystery completed on the altar is as suitably expressed as it is comprehensively construed.[47]

Thus the Canon consists of various prayers of offering, adoration, and intercession, which are directly connected to the consecration and clearly reveal that the institution narrative read during the Mass objectively actualizes the holy sacrifice; in no way does it seek to achieve only a remembrance of the Last Supper or possess a merely symbolic meaning.[48] This is also demonstrated typographically in missals — other than the NOM editions — that clearly set apart the words of consecration from the institution narrative by rendering them in all capital letters. This optical accentuation emphasizes that the consecration is completed by virtue of these words (*vi verborum*) and not merely an account of a past event.[49] When the priest has spoken the sequence of five prayers that precede and prepare for the consecration, he is sufficiently instructed to assess the objective reality and the full weight of these words.[50] Each prayer prevents him from reading or understanding the words of the Last Supper as a simple institution narrative (*recitative et historice tantum*). The

---

the Church's continual self-reflection that all of her prayers are only carried to God the Father through Christ, her mediator and High Priest.

47 Cf. R.-Th. Calmel, "Le déroulement du canon romain," *Itinéraires* 193 (1975): 100–7, 101.

48 Cf. R.-Th. Calmel, "Apologie pour le Canon romain. Deuxième section," *Itinéraires* 157 (1971): 36–54, 38.

49 Cf. Guillou, *Le canon*, 104; A. Ottaviani / A. Bacci, *The Ottaviani Intervention: Short Critical Study of the New Order of Mass*, trans. by A. Cekada, rev. and updated (West Chester, OH: Philothea Press, 2010), 55f.

50 Cf. Calmel, "Apologie," 44f.

previous prayers allow only for a sacramental, affirmative, and effective understanding of the words of institution that the priest speaks *in persona Christi*.[51] The latter is expressed also in the fact that the traditional rubrics of the Roman Canon call for a "reenacting" of Christ's actions through the celebrating priest. He not only reads aloud the words of institution, but copies Christ's gestures as they are described: at the moment of the *accepit panem/calicem* he takes the offerings in his hands, which were anointed by the blessing (*in sanctas et venerabiles manus suas*), lifts his eyes (*elevatis oculis*), gratefully (*gratias agens*) bows his head, makes a sign of the Cross at the *benedixit*, and in a humble attitude completes the transubstantiation, with his arms touching the altar, once more emphasizing the union with Christ.[52]

The *Unde et memores . . . offerimus* following the consecration already syntactically demonstrates that the remembrance is associated with and subordinated to the sacrifice: "calling to mind . . . we offer." The remaining prayers after the consecration — especially those that identify the Eucharist as the fulfillment of Old Testament prefigurations (Abel, Abraham, Melchisedech) and thus as a true sacrifice, but at the same time also describe it as an image of the heavenly liturgy of sacrifice (*supplices te rogamus*)[53] — again deepen this particular character of the holy action, in order to lead the entire sacrificial prayer into the closing doxology before the Father, through the Son, and in the Holy Ghost.

The request (*Supra quae*) that God may look upon the Church's offerings propitiously and serenely, as once He did upon the gifts of His just servant Abel, the sacrifice of our patriarch Abraham, and the holy gifts of His high priest Melchisedech, virtually contains a magnificent theology of history.[54] Primeval religion (Abel), Judaism (Abraham), and paganism (Melchisedech) are called to mind, all with their various sacrifices. From

---

51   Cf. R. Olazabal, "The Rites of the Consecration," *The Presence of Christ in the Eucharist* (CIEL UK, 2001), 133–53, 139–41.

52   Cf. ibid., 148f.; Folsom, "Gestures Accompanying the Words of Consecration."

53   Cf. Kreps, "La doxologie du Canon," in *Le Canon de la Messe*, 223–30.

54   Cf. J. Ratzinger, *Truth and Tolerance. Christian Belief and World Religions*, trans. by H. Taylor (San Francisco: Ignatius Press, 2004), 95–99; P. Massi, "Abele, Abramo e Melchisedech nel Canone," RivLi 53 (1966): 593–608.

a typological viewpoint,[55] three representative sacrificial figures of mankind are named, which prefigure, in different ways, the true sacrifice on the Cross: Abel, who offered to God the first-born of his flock and was killed though he was innocent; Abraham, who was prepared to sacrifice his only son Isaac; and finally Melchisedech, the King of Salem, priest of El Elyon — the "most high god," not just any god — who sacrificed bread and wine, the purest gifts of the earth. The Epistle to the Hebrews (5:6; 7:1–3) sees him as a representation of Christ's priesthood. The Church Fathers recognized in his sacrifice a symbol of the Eucharist.[56] By seeing the sacrifice of Christ thus prefigured, the Canon expresses the conviction that the traditional form of the sacrifice of the Mass is not merely the classical rite of the Roman church, but in addition represents the fulfillment of all religions.[57] These religions already contained within themselves a certain and related finality, and indicated the mystery of Christ in particular figures. The poet Gertrude von Le Fort rightly has the Church speak these words: "I was hidden in the temples of their gods, ... I was the desire of the ages."[58]

In the subsequent prayer (*Supplices te rogamus*), the heavenly view follows the historical view, the vertical perspective follows the horizontal perspective: "Command these offerings to be borne by the hands of Thy holy Angel to Thine altar on high." The angel, though sometimes interpreted differently,[59] stands for the unity of the earthly and heavenly liturgy. That there is a liturgy in heaven, and that it is the foundation and

---

55 Similarly the "Preface of the Most Blessed Sacrament" in the MRom 1962: "through Christ our Lord: Who, having abolished the empty shadows of animal victims, hath rendered acceptable for us in sacrifice His own Body and Blood: that in every place may be offered to Thy Name that clean oblation, which alone hath been pleasing to Thee." Cf. Barth, "*Nichts soll dem Gottesdienst vorgezogen werden*," 29–33.

56 Cf. G. R. Castellino, "Il Sacrificio di Melchisedec": A. Piolanti (ed.), *Eucaristia. Il mistero dell'altare nel pensiero e nella vita della chiesa* (Rome [i.a.]: Desclée de Brouwer, 1957), 11–22; H. Rusche, "Die Gestalt des Melchisedek," MThZ 6 (1955): 230–52; J. Daniélou, *The Bible and the Liturgy* (Notre Dame, IN: University of Notre Dame Press, 1956), 144–47.

57 Cf. Mosebach, *Heresy of Formlessness*, 8.

58 G. von Le Fort, *Hymnen an die Kirche*, 24.

59 Cf. B. Botte, "L'ange du sacrifice," in *Le Canon de la Messe*, 209–21; idem, "L'ange du sacrifice et l'épiclèse de la messe romaine," *Recherches de théologie ancienne et médiévale* 1 (1929): 285–308.

measure of the liturgy on earth, is emphatically recalled in this request by the Roman Canon, contrary to all of the neglect and suppression of this idea.[60] The Apocalypse describes this heavenly liturgy with thousands of angels, four mysterious winged beings and twenty-four ancients before the Throne of God.[61] In the center of the entire ceremony stands a Lamb, "as if it had been slain" (Rev 5:6). The once-accomplished sacrifice on Golgotha is timelessly present before the throne of God. The Liturgical Constitution states: "In the earthly liturgy we take part in a foretaste of that heavenly liturgy which is celebrated in the holy city of Jerusalem toward which we journey as pilgrims."[62] If the Roman Canon places the celebration of the Mass in this context and recalls that the liturgy already exists in heaven and all earthly celebration stands under its auspices ("You are come ... to the heavenly Jerusalem, and to the company of many thousands of angels," Heb 12:22), the measure and limits of all arbitrary reforming attempts are set. The Eucharistic celebration only seeks to be an echo, image, and icon of the heavenly liturgy. Thus the essential criterion for the liturgical form is that the heavenly liturgy be transparently visible through it.[63]

60 Cf. Gregory I, *Dialogi* 4,60,3 (SCh 265, 202); already quoted on p. 147, n21. Cf. E. Peterson, *The Angels and the Liturgy*, trans. by R. Walls (New York, NY: Herder and Herder, 1964); O. Heiming, "Der Engel in der Liturgie": Th. Bogler (ed.), *Die Engel in der Welt von heute* [LuM 21] (Maria Laach: Ars Liturgica Buch- und Kunstverlag, ²1960), 55–72, 60–66; Vagaggini, *Theological Dimensions of the Liturgy*, 347–50; K. Gamber, *Kult und Mysterium. Das Liturgieverständnis der frühen, ungeteilten Christenheit* [SPLi Beiheft 11] (Regensburg: Verlag Friedrich Pustet, 1983), 17–19, 56–62; idem, *Fragen in die Zeit*, 34–36, 44, 73; Gassner, *Canon*, 81–87.

61 Cf. J.-B. Bossuet, *Explication de quelques difficultés sur les prières de la Messe à un nouveau catholique* [*Œuvres* 5] (Paris: Librairie catholique Martin-Beaupré, 1868), 470: "This elevation that we desire — of our holy victim to the sublime altar of God — is here not asked in relation to Jesus Christ, who is already in the highest heaven, but rather in relation to us, and to the blessings we are to receive in elevating ourselves with Jesus Christ to this invisible altar."

62 Second Vatican Council, SC 8; cf. *Lumen Gentium* 50. Cf. A Benedictine Monk [G. Calvet], *The Sacred Liturgy*, 55: "Perhaps even in our days, as in the time of the primitive Church, the liturgy could still teach a materialistic world to look beyond its own leaden skies and to rediscover the savour of eternity."

63 Cf. Spaemann, "Bemerkungen eines Laien," 75–102, 82: "Anyone who knows the description of the liturgy of the Lamb in the Apocalypse will not seriously claim that the Novus Ordo, as it is actually celebrated, makes the unity of the heavenly and earthly liturgies just as vivid (*sc.*, as the old rite)."

The multiple requests for acceptance throughout the Canon,[64] which take up and expand on those of the Offertory, do not refer to the Son's sacrifice to the Father, which is ever accepted, but rather to the Church's sacrifice that she unites with that of Christ. Conscious of the insignificance of her gifts of bread and wine, but also from anxiety at not perfectly corresponding to the heart of her Bridegroom, the Church humbly asks the Father to accept graciously the expression of her own devotion.[65] The diversity of the other requests for the living and the dead is also an expression of a tender Catholicity of the praying Church, which embraces all people and concerns.[66] Thus each intention that originally had its place in the so-called "common prayer" (general intercessions) of the Church finds its fitting expression in the numerous intercessions of the Eucharistic prayer.

64   *Uti accepta habeas* (in the *Te igitur*); *Quam oblationem*; *Supra quae propitio ac sereno vultu respicere digneris et accepta habere*; *jube haec perferri . . . in sublime altare tuum* (in the *Supplices te rogamus*).

65   Cf. R.-Th. Calmel, "Le Canon romain," *Itinéraires* 146 (1970): 149–55, 153f.; idem, "Le Repas mystique," *Itinéraires* 146 (1970): 164–80, 175; idem, "Mahl und Opfer," UVK 1 (1970): 13–26, 21f.; I. Schuster, *The Sacramentary*, vol. I, 297: "As holy Scripture extols the faith of Abraham, Isaac, and Jacob, whose offerings typified and prefigured that of our altars, so we beseech the divine mercy to grant that our sacrifice — *sacrificium nostrum* — may be equally acceptable, seeing that the holy Eucharist is not only the sacrifice which the eternal High Priest offers of Himself, but according to the teaching of the Church is also the joint sacrifice of the priest, of the people present, of those who make offerings, of those for whom it is offered, etc. Since, then, in the holy Scriptures it belongs to the ministry of the holy angels to present to God the prayers and merits of the saints, we pray that they may perform the same office for the sacrifice which we offer upon our altars, so that it may abundantly bless all such as participate in it through Holy Communion. This is the true meaning of the *Supplices te rogamus*."

66   Cf. Calmel, "Repas mystique," 175f.; Abbé Maranget, "La Grande Prière d'Intercession," *Le Canon de la Messe*, 177–91, 191: "Thus, during the great Eucharistic prayer, the Roman liturgy assembles all the members of the militant, suffering, and triumphant Church in a very beautiful and logical group, as if to embrace them in the same oblation. The spiritual radiance of the Mass is as vast as that of Redemption. The Mass is the sacrifice of the whole human family. 'The Eucharistic intention,' writes Dom Cagin, 'is not impaired by the penetration of the deprecatory intentions that the diptychs, now associated with the anaphora (Canon), mingle with thanksgiving and pour, so to speak, into the inner core of the sacrifice, like the extra drop of water for the Saints and for the faithful, living and dead. By giving thus to the heart of the Canon an expression proper to the *adimpleo quae desunt passionum Christi* of the Apostle [I fill up those things that are wanting of the sufferings of Christ], does it not seem to express more fully the very real and living continuity, which is — by the union of the members and the Head — the unity of the sacrifice of Christ and his mystical body?'"

With the clarity of its terms, the richness of meaning of its statements, and the combination of its thoughts, the Roman Canon, both as a whole and in detail, most appropriately carries out the greatest mystery that Christ entrusted to the priests of His Church: the transubstantiation of bread and wine into the Body and Blood of the Lord. The Canon is the best preparation and encasing for this holy action, and its prayers most perfectly correspond to the mystery.[67]

WORDS OF CONSECRATION

After the Church surrounded the words of consecration with a series of prayers that manifest its objective sacrificial character, she placed the words themselves into their solemn arrangement in the institution narrative as in a precious shrine. It is the most comprehensive description of the events of the Last Supper, in which the accounts from the Evangelists and the Apostle Paul (1 Cor) are fused into a single unity and intensified with further passages from Scripture.[68] As the consecration text was able to be formulated without being directly bound to the letter of Scripture and following it word for word, it demonstrates first of all the priority of oral tradition over Scripture. The Church celebrated Holy Mass before the books of the New Testament existed. As the oral tradition—in this case, the liturgical practice of the Church—gradually condensed into written documents, the New Testament accounts of the Last Supper in turn later influenced the wording of the liturgy's consecration.

In contrast to the New Testament versions, the text of the Roman Canon is anxious to parallel (*simili modo*) and symmetrically arrange (*item*) as much as possible the formulations of the transubstantiation of bread and wine. In view of this tendency, it is striking that the formula for the consecration of the bread follows the version found in Matthew and Mark (*hoc*

---

67   Cf. Guillou, *Le livre de la Messe*, 29: The Roman Canon's "qualities of an always concrete majesty, deep humility, and adoring oblation make it a profound unity that brings together all of its prayers as the various elements of an admirable mosaic."

68   Cf. Olazabal, "The Rites of Consecration," 141–48; K. J. Merk, *Der Konsekrationstext der römischen Messe. Eine liturgiegeschichtliche Darstellung* (Rottenburg: Bader, 1915); P. Puniet, "La consécration. Sa place centrale dans le Canon de la Messe," in *Le Canon de la messe*, 193–208; G. Lucchesi, *Mysterium fidei. Il testo della consecrazione eucaristica nel Canone Romano* [Biblioteca Cardinale Gaetano Cicognani 4] (Naples: Auria, ²1960).

est enim corpus meum) and sets aside the addition contained in Luke and Paul (*quod pro vobis datur / tradetur*, Vulg.). Was it by the authority of St Peter that the Roman Canon retained the consecration formula to which his companion, the evangelist Mark, bore witness?[69] Moreover, the various biblical strands of tradition were compiled in the Canon text, that is, presented in a combined and unified manner (e.g., *tibi gratias agens* [Mt, Mk], *benedixit* [Lk, Paul]; *calix* [Lk, Paul] *sanguinis* [Mt, Mk]; *pro vobis* [Lk, Paul] *et pro multis* [Mt, Mk]). Finally, further Bible passages were introduced that related the institution of the Eucharist to the miracle of the multiplication of loaves (*elevatis oculis in caelum*, Mt 14:19), deepened it as being part of covenant theology (*aeterni testamenti*, Heb 13:20), and contemplated it in light of the Old Testament motif of the Good Shepherd (*praeclarum calicem*, Ps 22:5 Vulg.). Thus, as if from many pieces of a mosaic, the text of the Canon came into being, whose harmonious overall image no longer reveals the original variety of its ancestry.

The phrase *mysterium fidei* is itself mysterious in its significance. Probably borrowed from 1 Tm 3:9,[70] it was introduced into the chalice formula and received multiple explanations.[71] Medieval interpreters of the liturgy understood the word in the sense that the mystery completed in the Eucharist — the transubstantiation of bread and wine into the Body and Blood of Christ — could be understood only by means of subjective faith.[72] As

---

69   Cf. Guillou, *Le canon*, 105: "Saint Mark ... could not speak on such a fundamental matter otherwise than he (*sc.*, Peter) did; he saw and heard him celebrate the Eucharist. If only due to *Romanitas*, due to loyalty toward the first Shepherd of the Church. The simple '*Hoc est enim corpus meum*' preserves its ancient pedigree." According to E. C. Ratcliff, "The Institution Narrative of the Roman Canon Missae: Its Beginnings and Early Background," StPatr 2 (1957): 64–82, the text of the Canon follows Mt 26:26–28 to a large extent.

70   It states in 1 Tm 3:9 that the deacons ought to "[hold] the mystery of faith (*mysterium fidei*) in a pure conscience."

71   Cf. Jungmann, *Missarum sollemnia* II, 249–51; idem, *The Mass of the Roman Rite* II, 199–201; Gassner, *Canon*, 278–88; Oury, *La Messe*, 104–6; B. Capelle, "L'évolution du 'Qui pridie' de la messe romaine": idem, *Travaux liturgiques*, II, 276–86, 283f.

72   Cf. Florus of Lyon, *De actione missae* 62 (PL 119, 54); Durandus, *Rationale divinorum officiorum* IV,42,20 (CCL 140, 473); Dionysius Cartusianus, *Expositio Missae*, art. XXVIII, [*Opera omnia* 35] (Tournai: Typis Cartusiae S. M. de Pratis, 1908), 365: "*Quod enim sub forma vini sit sanguis Christi, secretum est valde, et omni intellectui creato incomprehensibile: imo, secundum Aegidium de Roma, angeli sancti hoc capere nequeunt. Hoc ergo sanguinis sacramentum est quoddam 'mysterium fidei,' et quasi objectum ipsius, quoniam fides versatur*

the *mysterium fidei* does not follow the words of consecration, but rather was inserted into them, the consecration itself is distinctly identified as a mystery of faith.[73] In the period in which this extension of the second consecration formula occurred (fourth/seventh century), the *mysterium fidei* would have been primarily a proclamation — originally perhaps completed by the deacon — of the soteriological significance of the chalice, which symbolically synthesizes the objective faith (*mysterium = sacramentum*), the order of salvation fully actualized in Christ, and the "mystery of godliness" (*mysterium pietatis*) described in 1 Tm 3:16.[74] In later times, this interjection bore witness to the Church's faith in the consecrational power of the words of Christ, which directly produce the transubstantiation themselves, and which do not cause the consecration only in union with an epiclesis, as some tendencies in Eastern theology maintain.[75]

Despite some enlargement of the institution narrative in the New Testament, the formulations of the Canon remain ever restrained, corresponding to the stylistic rules of the Roman liturgy, preserving the true mean between too little and too much. Thus the Roman text speaks of Christ's "holy and venerable hands," while other Western liturgies (Milan, Spain) do not mention this, whereas the Coptic liturgy adorns Christ's hands with a multitude of descriptions (*sanctas et immaculatas et incomprehensibiles et beatas et vivificas*).[76]

---

circa istud mysterium tamquam circa objectum: nam sola fide tenetur et creditur sub his sensibilibus formis contineri corpus et sanguinem Christi*" [That the blood of Christ is (present) under the form of the wine is a great mystery, incomprehensible for every created intellect: according to Giles of Rome, even the holy angels cannot conceive it. This sacrament of the blood is thus a "mystery of faith" and, so to speak, the object of it, because the faith is directed toward this mystery as toward its object: for by faith alone does one hold and believe that under these sensible forms are contained the body and the blood of Christ].

73 On the loss of this accentuation in the NOM, cf. Calmel, "Apologie," 21f.

74 Cf. Jungmann, *Missarum sollemnia* II, 251; idem, *The Mass of the Roman Rite* II, 200f.; Schnitzler, *Messe* II, 272: "An amazed exclamation about the richness of the chalice!"; Maertens, *Canon*, 80: "This blood is the sacrament that contains all the order of salvation offered to our faith"; Leo XIII, Encyclical Letter *Mirae caritatis* (ASS 34 [1902]: 641–54, 645 / J.J. Megivern [ed.], *Worship & Liturgy* [Wilmington, NC: Consortium Book, 1978], 6): "the mystery of the Eucharist, which is properly called the mystery of faith; for truly in this one mystery, by reason of its wonderful abundance and variety of miracles, is contained the whole supernatural order…"

75 Cf. Gassner, *Canon*, 287.

76 Cf. Capelle, "L'évolution," 278.

SIGNS OF THE CROSS

The sacrificial character of the Canon is emphasized also by the multiple signs of the Cross that accompany it in ornate arrangement, functioning as either effective blessings or symbolic illustrations. Before the consecration they possess a sanctifying function of preparing for the Eucharistic transubstantiation:[77] *benedicas haec* ✠ *dona, haec* ✠ *munera, haec* ✠ *sancta sacrificia* (*Te igitur*); *benedictam* ✠, *adscriptam* ✠, *ratam* ✠ (*Quam oblationem*); *benedixit* ✠ (*Qui pridie; Simili Modo*). Equally before and after the consecration they partly illustrate and intensify terms of blessing and sanctification — *sanctificas* ✠, *vivificas* ✠, *benedicis* ✠ (*Per quem haec omnia*) — and partly identify and distinguish particular words as being sacred: *corpus* ✠ *et sanguis* ✠ (*Quam oblationem*); *hostiam* ✠ *puram, hostiam* ✠ *sanctam, hostiam* ✠ *immaculatam, panem* ✠ *sanctum vitae aeternae et calicem* ✠ *salutis perpetuae* (*Unde et memores*); *sacrosanctum Filii tui* ✠ *corpus* ✠ *et sanguinem* ✠ (*Supplices te rogamus*).[78] The signs of the Cross witnessed since the eighth century were in part originally rhetorical pointing gestures that, according to ancient custom, accompanied the spoken word and were gradually stylized into a cross. The twenty-five signs of the Cross *in toto* thus continually refer to the sacrifice of the Cross:

> In celebrating Mass, the priest makes use of the sign of the cross to signify Christ's Passion which was ended on the cross. More briefly we may say that the consecration of this sacrament, the acceptance of this sacrifice, and its fruits, proceed from the power

77 Cf. Dionysius Cartusianus, *Expositio Missae*, art. XVIII, [*Opera omnia* 35] (Tournai: Typis Cartusiae S. M. de Pratis, 1908), 353: "*Si enim vestes et templum ac vasa ecclesiae benedicuntur ac sanctificantur ut sint apta instrumenta divini obsequii, quanto rationabilius est panem et vinum ante consecrationem benedici, ut sint apta materia transsubstantiationis supermirabilis atque divinae?*" [If the vestments and the building and the vessels of the church are blessed and sanctified in order to be apt instruments of the divine service, how much more reasonable is it to bless bread and wine before the consecration, so that they can be an apt matter for the most miraculous and divine transubstantiation?]

78 Cf. Brinktrine, *Messe*, 219–21; Jungmann, *Missarum sollemnia* II, 179–85; idem, *The Mass of the Roman Rite* II, 142–47; Schnitzler, *Messe* II, 121–23; R. Haungs, "Die Kreuzzeichen nach der Wandlung im römischen Messkanon," BenM 21 (1939): 249–61; Scheeben, *Über die Eucharistie und den Messkanon*, 121–28.

of Christ's cross, and accordingly, whenever mention is made of any of these, the priest uses the sign of the cross.[79]

The multiple signs of the Cross are always and everywhere signs of remembrance,[80] which refer to the Passion of Christ and identify the Mass as the realization of the sacrifice of the Cross. Moreover, the signs of the Cross before and after the consecration are also symbols of the blessing and grace that are contained in the Body and Blood of Christ and are to flow out over Christ's mystical body.[81] Especially after the consecration, the signs of the Cross emphasize the identity of the Eucharistic species with Christ's Body and Blood, offered up on the Cross.

STRUCTURE AND STYLE

With its repeated offerings and intercessions, as well as the twofold series of saints, the Canon appears at first glance to be nothing more than a loosely organized series of individual prayers, lacking that consistent main intention characteristic of the Eucharistic prayer of the *Traditio Apostolica* as well as the prayers of the Eastern Church, and similarly found in the *Exultet*.[82] Despite all the variety and segmentation, however, the text contains an inner unity.[83] It composes a song with many verses whose parallelism artistically fits around the words of consecration and reveals symmetrical architectonics.[84] The many interpolations before and after

79 Thomas Aquinas, *STh* III, 83,5 ad 3, in *Summa Theologiae* vol. 59 (3a. 79–83): Holy Communion, trans. by Th. Gilby (Oxford: Blackfriars Publications [i.a.], 1975), 169f.

80 Innocent III, *De sacro Altaris Mysterio* 5,2 (PL 217, 888 / MSIL 15, 344): "Signa (sc., spectant) ad historiam recolendam."

81 Cf. J.-B. Bossuet, *Explication de quelques difficultés sur les prières de la Messe à un nouveau catholique* [*Œuvres* 5] (Paris: Librairie catholique Martin-Beaupré, 1868), 473: "In Jesus Christ all His members are blessed, offered in this sacrifice, as one body with the Savior, so that the grace of the Head may be abundantly spread over them."

82 Cf. Jungmann, *Missarum sollemnia* II, 136; idem, *The Mass of the Roman Rite* II, 108; Spinks, "Roman canon," 130; Calmel, "Le canon," 151.

83 Cf. Keifer, "Unity of the Roman Canon," 53 (praise and participation in celestial glorification of the Father through Christ); Calmel, "Le canon," 152; idem, "Apologie," 38, 45 (notion of sacrifice).

84 Cf. Schnitzler, *Meßkanon*, 33–39; Meyer, *Eucharistie*, 179f.; Brinktrine, *Messe*, 191–95; Gassner, *Canon*, 43f., 259–62; critical of this, Jungmann, *Missarum sollemnia* II, 136n46 (not mentioned in the English edition); rings, or concentric circles, which lie around the center

the consecration only clarify the substance of this unity and consider its richness in many aspects and dimensions.[85]

The text is stylistically marked by the voluble, juridically exact manner of the ancient Roman language of prayer,[86] formed according to the rhetorical laws of meter, rhythm, and *cursus*,[87] influenced moreover by typical usages for referring to the majesty of the emperor in Roman imperial language (*Te igitur clementissime*).[88] The author of the Canon quoted by Ambrose was familiar with legal terminology and the pagan Roman style of prayer, as seen in various and abundant expressions.[89] It was a time during which the pagan Roman aristocracy, in view of the growth of Christianity, recollected their own past and sought to revitalize their literary and sacred inheritance. Thus the Canon may be considered as a Christian counterpart to this. Its abandonment of verbatim Bible passages and the conscious imitation of pagan sacred language were at this time an attempt to convey the classical Roman legacy to Christianity, and to facilitate the conversion of pagans. Insofar as these tendencies can also be recognized in various works of St Ambrose, the bishop of Milan's involvement with the formulation of the Eucharistic prayer is not precluded.[90]

In comparison to the Ambrosian text, the Roman Canon exhibits an even stronger stylization in this sense.[91] Alongside the quest for linguistic elegance, the accumulation of almost synonymous terms is characteristic (*supplices rogamus ac petimus*; *haec dona, haec munera, haec sancta sacrificia illibata*; *quam pacificare, custodire, adunare, et regere digneris*). This volubility of juridical precision was a feature of pagan prayer and an expression of

---

point of the Consecration: cf. Gassner, *Canon*, 44.

85   Calmel, "Le canon," 151f.

86   Cf. Keifer, "Unity," 45 (bibliography); Baumstark, "Antik-römischer Gebetsstil im Messkanon."

87   Cf. Schnitzler, *Meßkanon*, 39.

88   Cf. Spinks, "Roman canon," 136 (bibliography); Keifer, "Unity," 45.

89   M. Zelzer, "Liturgisches Gebet nach dem Zeugnis des Ambrosius": *La preghiera nel tardo antico dalle origini ad Agostino*. XXVII Incontro di Studiosi dell'Antichità Cristiana, Roma, 7–9 maggio 1998 [Studia ephemeridis Augustinianum 66] (Rome: Inst. Patristicum Augustinianum, 1999), 309–15, 313.

90   Cf. Zelzer, *Gebet*, 314f.

91   Cf. C. Mohrmann, "Quelques observations sur l'évolution stilistique du Canon de la Messe romaine," *Études sur le latin* III, 227–44, 234; eadem, "Le latin langue de la Chrétienté occidentale," *Études sur le latin* I, 51–81, esp. 76–81.

the *gravitas romana* as well as of meticulousness of cultic activity, which, in dealing with the divine powers, was concerned to formulate requests correctly, precisely, and unambiguously.[92]

In contrast to this stylistic dependence on pagan prayer tradition, the vocabulary of the Roman Canon remains deeply Christian and markedly biblical.[93] Only a few exceptions exist where terms of pagan sacrifice found their way into the Christian Eucharistic prayer (i.e., *purus* in the *Unde et memores*). Only later, when paganism was finally overcome and no longer presented a threat to Christianity, did certain terms of ancient religious discourse find acceptance into liturgical Latin (*ara, templum, oraculum, sacerdos*). Thus the Roman Canon is a good example of the Christian "use" (χρῆσις, *chrēsis*) of pagan culture. While on the one hand the Canon demonstrates an understanding of Christian prayer and was able to use ancient artistic forms, on the other hand it refused to surrender to an imprudent acceptance of pagan terms, which in this decisive phase would have distorted or obscured the identity and distinctiveness of the Christian Faith.

The classical Canon created a synthesis of *Romanitas* and *Christianitas*:

> Without abandoning what the first Christian centuries had created in the isolation of the primitive communities, the fourth and fifth centuries achieved a convergence between the two worlds of Christianity and antiquity. This convergence in no way means a thinning of Christian culture. It rather enriched and deepened it as it added to the inheritance of the first Christian centuries precious human values. The so-called Gelasian Canon (Roman Canon) gives to us, in its solemn verbosity and occasionally juridical manner, a gem that expresses the bond between *Romanitas* and *Christianitas*, which for centuries past has remained one of the characteristic features of the Roman liturgy.[94]

92 Cf. Mohrmann, *Liturgical Latin*, 78; eadem, "Quelques observations," 239n39.

93 Cf. Mohrmann, *Liturgical Latin*, 80; eadem, "Quelques observations," 240f. Th. Maertens, *Pour une meilleure intelligence du canon de la messe* [ParLi 42] (Bruges: Apostolat liturgique Abbaye de Saint-André, 1959), 109, emphasizes that the vocabulary is a doctrinal source of the utmost importance.

94 Mohrmann, *Liturgical Latin*, 81.

THE SILENT CANON

The silent praying of the Canon is among the peculiarities of the classical rite.[95] This practice did not exist from the beginning, but was rather the result of a longer process in which the original audible recital of the Eucharistic prayer was abandoned in favor of a quiet delivery. In Eastern regions, starting in the fourth century, parts of the Eucharistic anaphora were prayed with a quiet voice, or even silently. In the West this development was introduced only later. Thus there were transitional forms such as the recited tone or speaking in a low voice. After individual churches observed the practice of a silent Canon at various times, this custom was employed in the Frankish domain around the year 800 and then during the early ninth century prevailed throughout Europe.[96] Against the reformatory demands for a loud proclamation of the Eucharistic prayer, the Council of Trent emphatically defended the existing practice of praying the Canon with a low voice (*submissa voce*): "If anyone says that the rite of the Roman Church prescribing that part of the Canon and the words of consecration be recited in a low voice must be condemned . . . let him be anathema."[97] The rubrics of the *Missale Romanum* of 1570 for the first time define the exact delivery, explaining in the instructions that *secreto* means loud enough for the celebrant to hear his own voice without being heard by those standing around him.[98]

As the Church practiced the silent Canon for 1,200 years, as already described, there were certainly serious reasons for it. These reasons were by no means only of a practical nature, such as efforts for brevity or consideration of the faithful who no longer understood the sacred language.

---

95 On the origin and reason for the silence of the Canon, cf. C. Lewis, *The Silent Recitation of the Canon of the Mass* (Bay Saint-Louis, MS: Divine Word Missionaries, 1962); B. Deneke, "Schweigen vor Gott. Gedanken zur Kanonstille," *Umkehr* 3 (1994): 20–27; J. A. Jungmann, "*Praefatio* und stiller Kanon": idem, *Gewordene Liturgie. Studien und Durchblicke* (Innsbruck / Leipzig: Rauch, 1941), 87–119; W.-M. de Saint-Jean, *Silence sacré et intériorité*, 75–89; idem, "Silence et intériorité dans la liturgie," *Liturgie et sacré* (CIEL, 2003), 273–350, 335–43; E. de Moreau, "Récitation du canon de la messe à voix basse. Étude historique," NRTh 51 (1924): 65–94; Schnitzler, *Messe* II, 273–76; Kwasniewski, *Noble Beauty*, 71–75, 202–3, 235–55.

96 Cf. Jungmann, *Missarum sollemnia* II, 131; idem, *The Mass of the Roman Rite* II, 104; idem, "*Praefatio*," 108; Spinks, "Roman canon," 137f.

97 Sess. XXII, can. 9 (DH 1759). Cf. J. P. Theisen, "The Roman Canon and the Council of Trent," 294–301.

98 Cf. *Rubricae generales missalis* XVI,2.

Rather, they were reasons of a symbolic nature, which had their origin especially in Eastern notions of mystery, and after first influencing the Gallican liturgy, which was marked by Oriental influences, they also influenced the approach to the Roman Canon in the second half of the tenth century.

Dum medium silentium tenerent omnia..., reads the antiphon to the Magnificat of the Sunday within the octave of Christmas: "While all things were in quiet silence, and the night was in the midst of her course, Thine almighty Word, O Lord, leapt down from heaven from Thy royal throne." The great mysteries of salvation happened quietly, surrounded by silence. The Incarnation and birth of the Son of God, His death and resurrection took place in the realm of silence. As a realization of those events of salvation, it is appropriate for the liturgy to veil the mystery with the shroud of silence, "to honor the inexpressible with humble silence."[99]

The Eastern Church had already begun withdrawing the holy action from view by means of an iconostasis. This was by no means foreign to the Western Church, as the curtains of the baldacchino altars show (already witnessed around 800).[100] The veiling of the mystery on the visual level corresponds to the silence on the auditory level. The silent praying of the Canon is, as it were, an iconostasis that surrounds the consecration and the actualization of the sacrifice of the Cross, and it is precisely through that silence that the mystery may be sensed. The holy silence is proper for indicating and bringing to mind the profundity, inscrutability, and inexpressibility of the mysteries that take place on the altar.

Already the earliest explanations of the Mass that refer to the silence of the Canon around the year 800 associate this with the mysterious character of the holy action:

---

99   Ps.-Dionysius the Areopagite, *De divinis nominibus* 1,3 (PTS 33, 111).

100   Cf. K. Gamber, *Heilige Zeiten — heiliger Raum* (Regensburg: Verlag Friedrich Pustet, 1989), 64f.; idem, *Zum Herrn hin*, 12–14; idem, *Kult und Mysterium*, 28–30. J. Braun, *Der christliche Altar in seiner geschichtlichen Entwicklung* II (Munich: Alte Meister Guenther Koch & Co., 1924), 167–71, emphasized that in Europe the curtains primarily served only as decoration, and not as mantles. Only later interpreters of the liturgy (i.a. Durandus, *Rationale* I,3,35 [CCM 140, 46]) pointed out the latter function.

> After a great silence has been kept all around, the priest now begins to consecrate the host.... The consecration of the Body and Blood of the Lord is, from my point of view, always carried out in silence because the Holy Ghost, remaining in them, produces the same effect of the sacraments in a hidden way, which is why it is also called in Greek *mysterium*, as it contains a mysterious and hidden arrangement.[101]

The silence of the Canon thus primarily serves to raise up and to protect the mystery.[102] Already the Church Father Basil of Caesarea recognized in the fourth century the connection between silence and mystery, when he wrote that "the awful dignity of the mysteries is best preserved by silence."[103]

The wording that the priest "silently enters into the Canon" (*tacito intrat in canonem*),[104] originally signifying only the introduction of the officiant at a particular place, was already interpreted by the medieval liturgical commentators since the twelfth century as a comparison between the Canon and a sanctuary, whose threshold the priest passes over at that moment. Again, an image from the Old Testament is here suggested in the actions of the Mass. In the Temple in Jerusalem there was a tabernacle (with an altar of burnt offerings, table of show-bread,

---

101 *Quotiens contra se* 1,4,11; cf. *De antiquis ecclesiae ritibus*, ed. E. Martène (Antwerp: de la Bry ²1736 [repr. Hildesheim: Verlag Georg Olms, 1967]), I, 456.

102 Cf. Innocent III, *De sacro Altaris mysterio* 3,1 (PL 217, 840 / MSIL 15, 212): "*Ne sacrosancta verba vilescerent, dum omnes paene per usum ipsa scientes, in plateis et vicis, aliisque locis incongruis decantarent, decrevit Ecclesia, ut haec obsecratio quae secreta censetur, a sacerdotibus secrete dicatur*" [Lest the sacrosanct words should become vile when all people know them almost by heart through hearing, and sing them in the streets and places and in other inappropriate locations, the Church has decided that this prayer, which is regarded as secret, is said by the priests secretly]. Cf. A. Franz, *Die Messe im deutschen Mittelalter* (Bonn: Nova & Vetera, 2003 [repr. of Freiburg i. Br.: Verlag Herder, 1902]), 624f., 627f.

103 Basil of Caesarea, *De Spiritu sancto* 66 (FC 12, 276 / Basil of Caesarea, *The Treatise* De Spiritu Sancto, *the Nine Homilies on the Hexaemeron and the Letters of Saint Basil the Great, Archbishop of Caesarea*, ed. by Ph. Schaff / trans. by B. Jackson, *A Select Library of the Nicene and Post-Nicene Fathers of the Christian Church*, 2nd series, 8 [Oxford: James Parker / New York: The Christian Literature Company, 1895; repr. Grand Rapids, MI: Wm. B. Eerdmans Publishing Co., 1978], 42).

104 *Ordo Romanus* V, 58 (Andrieu II, 221): "*Surgit solus pontifex et tacito intrat in canonem.*" Cf. Jungmann, "*Praefatio*," 101–4.

and seven-armed candlestick), into which only the officiating priest was allowed to enter, and, separated from that by a curtain, the Holy of Holies (with the Ark of the Covenant), into which only the High Priest could enter once during the year (cf. Heb 9:7).[105] The Canon of the Mass was also considered to be a sanctuary that the priest alone could enter. The holy silence corresponds to the sanctity of this innermost space, which remains closed to the people. The Catholic priest thus enters into the Holy of Holies in the manner of the Old Testament High Priest, in order to stand before the face of God in this other-worldly space on behalf of the people. It was not least of all this special position of the priest, as expressed in quietly spoken prayers befitting him alone, that provoked the protest of the reformers and prompted Luther to describe such silent prayer as the work of the devil.[106] The fathers of the Council of Trent, however, were well aware of the closeness of the bond between dogma and liturgical form. By defending the silent Canon, they simultaneously confirmed the special position of the priest, which was clearly expressed by the manner of prayer. He partakes in Christ's mediation and is thus essentially separated from all the other faithful.[107] When the priest silently prays the Canon while turned toward the altar, it is the most fitting expression that here a priest, "taken from among men and [having been] ordained for men in the things that appertain to God" (Heb 5:1), enters into the innermost sanctuary in order to allow the mystery of the sacrifice of the Cross to be realized. The present congregation can contribute nothing to the execution of this act of sacrifice. The silent prayer of the Canon thus distinguishes this as a specifically priestly action and is able to shape and deepen the ecclesiastical appreciation of the ordained priesthood.[108]

---

105 Cf. Gamber, *Heilige Zeiten*, 64f.

106 Cf. M. Luther, *Ein Sermon von dem neuen Testament, das ist von der heiligen Messe* (WA 6, 362). Cf. Meyer, *Luther und die Messe*, 255f.; Franz, *Messe*, 635.

107 Cf. Thomas Aquinas, *STh* III, 83,4 ad 6, in *Summa Theologiae* vol. 59 (3a. 79–83): Holy Communion, 163: "Other words which the priest alone recites belong to his proper office; that he might offer up gifts and sacrifices for the people. Some he says aloud, such as the prayer common to him and the people; others are for him alone, such as the offertory and consecration, consequently they are said in a low voice."

108 Cf. Deneke, "Schweigen," 23–25.

For the celebrant himself, the silent Canon is of inestimable value:

> While the congregation sings, he must fulfill his own duties
> in complete silence, without communicative confirmation by
> the faithful, and thus he stands entirely alone at the forefront
> of God's people, *in persona Christi*, before God's majesty. This
> awareness — under the condition of a worthy and devout comple-
> tion — forms his conscience and moreover gives to him an inner
> freedom for an entirely personal union with Christ, Who gives
> Himself up in the sacrifice.[109]

At the same time, the silent Canon also offers just such a freedom to
the common faithful. The inaudible Eucharistic prayer prevents them from
being contented with merely listening, remaining passive in the face of
exterior audibility and supposed intelligibility.[110] The silent completion of
the rite rather demands a more intense interior involvement in order to
unite oneself with the holy action. A further personal freedom is granted to
the believer for his participation — a freedom that fully respects his dignity
and maturity as a baptized person and does not in the least regulate the
form of his participation:

> While the audible and vernacular recitation of the Eucharistic
> prayer generally restricts those attending Mass to a determined
> manner of participation, when it is in silence, the holiest focal
> point of the Mass becomes a room with many doors. The entrances

---

109   J. Nebel, "Die 'ordentliche' und die 'ausserordentliche' Form," 196n26.

110   Cf. M. Gurtner, *Reflexionen zur Theologie der Liturgie. Liturgie als Vorwegnahme
des Himmels auf Erden* (Aadorf: Benedetto-Verlag, 2009), 97f.: "When the entire Canon is
recited aloud by the priest, the personal prayer, the personal contact with God, is nipped
in the bud. You listen more or less attentively, but you do not really pray. If the Mass is
recited aloud, the proportion of the individual degenerates into a pure 'listening to the
Mass.' This was often a heavy charge against the 'old' Mass: one 'does' nothing, one does
not really participate, one only hears it. But this accusation is much more likely to apply to
a Mass recited out loud, because it does not allow the individual to penetrate actively into
the praying event. The fact that it is outwardly silent does not mean that the believers do
nothing; it is rather a requirement for being able to do the right thing at all."

to the mystery include everything from reading along in their missals to silent contemplation, which constitutes the proper and highest form of participation.[111]

Even the ancient philosopher Aristotle wrote in the first chapter of his *Metaphysics*: "We prefer seeing to everything else."[112] Plato had likewise connected the ascent to perfection with looking: "A man finds it truly worthwhile to live, while he contemplates essential beauty."[113] If contemplation can be defined as "loving awareness" and as "beholding the beloved,"[114] then the silent Canon facilitates exactly this contemplative encounter with Christ. The following depiction impressively describes the possibilities of observation that the silent Canon enables:

> The faithful hear nothing more of the Canon of the Mass after the Sanctus, and they are relegated completely to looking. Image after image is offered to them: it is almost an iconostasis offered to their eyes. Image after image reveals to them what the priest does at the altar, what Christ accomplishes through him. But all of the images are drawn into the mysterious background of mystical silence before God, to Whom the most sublime sacrifice is offered.[115]

Thus it becomes possible for the faithful to grasp what is essential in an intuitive manner and to learn contemplative prayer. The silence does not conceal the liturgical word, but envelops its outer form in order to lead to a better participation in its inner content. Silence enables inner hearing to approach the mystery.

---

111 Deneke, "Schweigen," 26.
112 Aristotle, *Metaphysics* 980a.
113 Plato, *Symposium* 211d–12a.
114 Cf. Pieper, *Happiness and Contemplation*, 72.
115 J. Pascher, *Eucharistia. Gestalt und Vollzug* (Münster / Freiburg i. Br.: Aschendorff Verlag [i.a.], ²1953), 211.

SUMMARY

As the Council of Trent emphasized, there is nothing contained in the Roman Canon "that does not savor in the highest degree of holiness and piety and raise up to God the minds of those who offer" (DH 1745). By reason of this effect, the Canon possesses the character of a sacramental.[116] Just as the sacramentals in general, through the intercession of the Church, produce spiritual effects and are ordered to the sacraments while surrounding them with solemnity, preparing for them, and contributing to the safeguarding of the sacramental grace, so too the Roman Canon can graciously dispose the priest and the faithful for worthily celebrating the Eucharistic sacrifice and receiving the sacrament. The content and progression of the prayers, the accompanying gestures — signs of the Cross, bows, genuflections, kissing the altar — and, not least of all, the silence surrounding the Canon strengthen faith in the Eucharistic Real Presence and in the reality of the sacrifice, lead to a humble and grateful adoration of the mystery, and renew, purify, and intensify the intention and devotion of the celebrant.[117]

---

116   Cf. Gassner, *Canon*, 10: "The Canon is not merely doctrine and instruction, but it is a sacramental, and the greatest sacramental."

117   Cf. Gassner, *Canon*, 26–34; Folsom, "Gestures Accompanying the Words of Consecration."

15
Lex orandi—lex credendi

TRUE REFLECTION OF THE TRADITIONAL TEACHINGS OF THE CHURCH

An impressive witness of the way in which the encounter with the classical liturgy imparts an understanding of the essence of the Church comes from Paul Claudel. As already mentioned, after his sudden conversion he became acquainted with the Catholic faith not through the reading of religious writings, but rather while participating in the spectacle of the liturgy in the cathedral of Notre Dame in Paris. He writes:

> It is as if someone I know held his theology course all alone at the end of the dreary nave of Notre Dame for six or seven years....
> With my face pressed against the choir screen, both hands clasped to the rood screen, I observed the Church in her life and in this way understood everything.[1]

The liturgy is thus often described as the noblest organ of the ordinary magisterium of the Church.[2] Pope Pius XI wrote in his encyclical *Quas Primas* (1925):

> For people are instructed in the truths of faith, and brought to appreciate the inner joys of religion far more effectually, by the annual celebration of our sacred mysteries than by any official pronouncement of the teaching of the Church. Such pronouncements usually reach only a few and the more learned among the faithful; feasts reach them all; the former speak but once, the latter

---

1 P. Claudel, *Der Strom. Ausgewählte Prosa* (Frankfurt a. M.: Ullstein Verlag, 1955), 179 (from: *L'épée et le miroir*, Paris: Éditions Gallimard, 1939).
2 Cf. Festugière, *La Liturgie catholique*, 121.

speak every year—in fact, forever. The Church's teaching affects the mind primarily; her feasts affect both mind and heart, and have a salutary effect upon the whole of man's nature.[3]

In a private audience the same pope explained: "The liturgy is a very great thing. It is the most important organ of the ordinary magisterium of the Church.... The liturgy is not the teaching of this or that person, but rather the teaching of the Church."[4] Pope Pius XII described the liturgy as "a faithful reflection of traditional doctrine believed by the Christian people through the course of ages."[5] Likewise he emphasized: "The entire liturgy, therefore, has the Catholic faith for its content, inasmuch as it bears public witness to the faith of the Church."[6]

---

3 Pius XI, *Quas Primas* (AAS 17:603 / Seasoltz, *Documentation*, 42): "*In populo rebus fidei imbuendo per easque ad interiora vitae gaudia evehendo, longe plus habent efficacitatis animae sacrorum mysteriorum celebritates quam quaelibet vel gravissima ecclesiastici magisterii documenta. Siquidem haec in pauciores eruditioresque viros semel, illae quotannis atque perpetuo, ut ita dicamus, loquuntur; haec mentes potissimum, illae et mentes et animos, hominem scilicet totum, salubriter afficiunt.*" On the special "pedagogy" of the liturgy, cf. B. Capelle, "L'intellectualité religieuse du croyant et la messe": idem, *Travaux liturgiques* I, 140–51, 146f.; M. Righetti, *Manuale di storia liturgica* I: Introduzione generale (Milan: Àncora Editrice, 1950), 27f.; Vagaggini, *Theological Dimensions of the Liturgy*, 512–18.

4 "Résumé textuel de l'audience accordée le 12 décembre 1935 à Dom B. Capelle," QLP 21 (1936): 134. Cf. A. Bugnini, *Documenta pontificia ad instaurationem liturgiae spectantia (1903–1953)* [BEL.P 6] (Rome: C.L.V.-Edizioni Liturgiche, 1953), 70f. Cf. Y.M.-J. Congar, *La foi et la théologie* [Le mystère chrétien. Théologie dogmatique 1] (Tournai: Desclée de Brouwer, 1962), 146f.: "The sovereign value of the liturgy does not consist in an arsenal of arguments, but is due to the fact that it is the 'teaching of the Church.' It incorporates and translates as much as possible the Catholic understanding of all things. Even when it reflects a reaction against heresy, the liturgy expresses the faith of the Church in a particularly positive, interior, and total way; it always implements the whole Christian mystery. It goes beyond simple instruction and incorporates all the educative sap of the Church's motherhood. It is the educational environment of the meaning of God, of the meaning of man, of the deepest and most total meaning of the religious relationship in Jesus Christ, which is the core of Revelation. Through it, one enters into its intelligence in a concrete, living way, by its very practice." Cf. Vagaggini, *Theological Dimensions of the Liturgy*, 512–29.

5 Pius XII, Encyclical Letter *Ad Coeli Reginam* (AAS 46 [1954]: 631 / http://w2.vatican.va/content/pius-xii/en/encyclicals/documents/hf_p-xii_enc_11101954_ad-caeli-reginam.html): "*Sacra vero liturgia, quae doctrinae a maioribus traditae et a christiano populo creditae est veluti fidele speculum.*"

6 Pius XII, *Mediator Dei* (AAS 39:540 / Seasoltz, *Documentation*, 121).

Truly, the liturgy of the traditional Roman rite contains, reveals, and teaches the Catholic faith in all its richness and abundance. The Benedictine Bernard Capelle, Abbot of Mont César, wrote:

> Above all it is in the liturgy that the Church teaches and confesses her entire Christianity. Oh, when one thinks of the intellectual shortcomings of mankind, as soon as he seeks to deepen religious truth; when one once compiles the disturbing record of his errors and confusions in questions of the faith; when one observes around himself what selfish narrow-mindedness, what pettiness, what superficiality, and what bourgeois banality incessantly seek to take the place of Jesus Christ's inestimable message in his soul, then the heart is immediately filled with an unspeakable gratitude toward the Church, who tirelessly proclaims in all purity and in all plenitude the teaching of light and mercy to all of her children each week, sublimely when she speaks of God, gently and compassionately when she turns toward the simple sinners that we are.[7]

THE LITURGY AS LOCUS THEOLOGICUS

In the interaction of prayers, readings, chants, rites, ceremonies, and rubrics, all the central mysteries of the faith find their comprehensive expression, which not only clearly bears witness to dogmatic truths, but at the same time clothes them with a beautiful form of poetry and art, bringing them closer to human nature.

Especially for Christology and the doctrine of the Trinity, for ecclesiology and Eucharistic dogma,[8] the classical liturgy forms a valuable

---

7   B. Capelle, "Le vrai visage de la liturgie": idem, *Travaux liturgiques* I, 33–43, 35 (English trans. based on the author's German trans.); cf. idem, "L'intellectualité religieuse," ibid., 150; D. v. Hildebrand, *Liturgy and Personality*, 115: "In the fulfillment of the Liturgy, which (more than anything else) breathes the classical spirit, man is placed in the truth; he achieves the true, valid relation to God and the world, and by this he becomes free from all bogging-down in the dead-ends of useless thoughts and illusory problems, free from one-sidedness, extravagance, self-deception, repression, and artificial evasions; he does not live in a world of subjective illusions."

8   Cf. F. Clément, "The Christology of the Roman Missal," *Theological and Historical Aspects of the Roman Missal* (CIEL UK, 2000), 17–28; M. Drew, "The Doctrine of the Holy Trinity

locus theologicus that shows how the Church's faith is made manifest in her prayers.[9]

In the prayers, again and again the Trinity—the core dogma of the faith—is called upon and worshiped: in the *Suscipe, sancta Trinitas* of the Offertory, in the *Placeat tibi, sancta Trinitas* before the final blessing, in the Preface of the Holy Trinity used in all common Sundays of the liturgical year, in the priest's second prayer of preparation for Holy Communion (*Domine Jesu Christe, Fili Dei vivi, qui ex voluntate Patris, cooperante Spiritu sancto...*), in the doxologies of the prayers at the foot of the altar, Introit, and *Lavabo*, and finally in the Trinitarian closing formula of the prayer at the commingling of the water and wine, of the *Libera nos* after the Our Father, as well as after the Collect, Secret, and Postcommunion.[10]

With regard to the mystery of the Eucharist, the belief in the Real Presence is powerfully demonstrated, especially in the numerous gestures of reverence. The sacrificial character of the Mass is likewise expressed in diverse ways, such as in the Offertory, Preface of the Most Blessed Sacrament, Roman Canon, orientation of celebration, and the closing priestly prayer *Placeat tibi*. Clearly recognizable is the Church's belief, already verifiable since the earliest witnesses of the second century, that here is offered a sacrifice of praise, thanksgiving, impetation, and reparation for those present and absent, living and deceased.[11] Especially the aspect of

---

in the Traditional Roman Missal," ibid., 109–26; M. Schmitz, "Aspects of the Ecclesiology of the *Missale Romanum*," ibid., 181–95; B. Valuet, "The Dogma of the Eucharist in the Roman Missal," ibid., 201–32; A. Santograssi, "La liturgie romaine, la foi et l'oecuménisme": *Foi et liturgie* (CIEL, 2002), 329–67; A. Wintersig, "Die Selbstdarstellung der Kirche in ihrer Liturgie," *Mysterium. Gesammelte Arbeiten Laacher Mönche* (Münster: Aschendorff Verlag, 1926), 79–104.

9 Cf. J. Schumacher, "Die Liturgie als 'locus theologicus,'" FKTh 18 (2002): 161–85; idem, "La liturgie comme 'lieu théologique'": *Foi et liturgie* (CIEL, 2002), 49–79; M. Cappuyns, "Liturgie et théologie," *Le vrai visage de la liturgie* [Cours et conférences des semaines liturgiques XIV] (Louvain: Éditions de Abbaye du Mont César, 1938), 175–209; M.J. Weber, "La liturgie est 'la didascalie de l'Église' (Pie XI). A. Par son enseignement dogmatique," ibid., 89–114; M. Vieujean, "La liturgie est 'la didascalie de l'Église' (Pie XI). B. Par sa doctrine spirituelle," ibid., 115–31; I. Berthier, *Tractatus de locis theologicis* (Turin: Typographia Pontificia, 1900), 424–40.

10 A critical comparison with the MRom 1970 by May, *Die alte und die neue Messe*, 66.

11 Cf. J. Pohle, "Mass, Sacrifice of the," *The Catholic Encyclopedia* VIII (New York: Robert Appleton Company, 1910): 253f.; K. Gamber, "Die heilige Messe ein Opfer—seit wann?," idem, *Fragen in die Zeit*, 48–52; K.S. Frank, "Zum Opferverständnis in der Alten Kirche—ein Diskussionsbeitrag": K. Lehmann / E. Schlink (eds.), *Das Opfer Jesu Christi und seine Gegenwart in der*

the propitiatory sacrifice (*effectus propitiatorius*), as the Council of Trent finally and dogmatically defined it against the reformatory challenges (DH 1743; 1753), is clearly expressed in the classical Missal (*Suscipe, sancta Trinitas* in the Offertory, *Memento* of the Living and the Dead in the Canon, and *Placeat tibi* before the final blessing). Historically considered, the belief in the sacrificial character of Christ's death ever stands in tight correspondence with the proper understanding of the sacrificial character of the Mass; emphasis on the latter simultaneously defends the reality of the sacrifice of the Cross.[12]

The special position that the priest occupies during the enactment of the Mass, insofar as he acts *in persona Christi* by virtue of his ordination and is thus essentially distinct from the common priesthood of all believers,[13] is also clearly manifested in the classical rite of the Mass and preserved from leveling. The admission of guilt (*Confiteor*) and the most immediate prayer of preparation for Holy Communion (*Domine, non sum dignus*), not

---

Kirche. Klärungen zum Opfercharakter des Herrenmahles [Dialog der Kirchen 3] (Freiburg i. Br.: Verlag Herder, 1983), 40–50; H. Moll, "Die Lehre von der Eucharistie als Opfer in den beiden ersten christlichen Jahrhunderten": G. Stumpf (ed.), *Eucharistie — Quelle und Höhepunkt des ganzen christlichen Lebens* [14. Theologische Sommerakademie Diessen 2006 des IK Augsburg] (Landsberg: Initiativkreis Kath. Laien und Priester in der Diözese Augsburg, 2006), 57–70; H. Moll, *Die Lehre von der Eucharistie als Opfer. Eine dogmengeschichtliche Untersuchung vom Neuen Testament bis Irenäus von Lyon* [Theoph. 26] (Cologne / Bonn: Peter Hanstein Verlag, 1975); J. Betz, "Die Prosphora in der patristischen Theologie": B. Neunheuser (ed.), *Opfer Christi und Opfer der Kirche — Die Lehre vom Messopfer als Mysteriengedächtnis in der Theologie der Gegenwart* (Düsseldorf: Patmos-Verlag, 1960), 99–116; J. A. Jungmann, "Oblatio und Sacrificium in der Geschichte des Eucharistieverständnisses," ZKTh 92 (1970): 342–50.

12   Cf. R. Spaemann, "Ist ein opferloses Christentum möglich?": *Altar und Opfer*. Die Vorträge des dritten internationalen Kolloquiums: Geschichtliche, kanonische und theologische Arbeiten über die römisch-katholische Liturgie [CIEL: Poissy, Oktober 1997] (Korntal: Laienvereinigung für den Klassischen Römischen Ritus in der Katholischen Kirche, 1998), 8–16, 13: "The Council [of Trent] defined that the Holy Mass, as a reenactment of the sacrifice of the Cross, is a real and true sacrifice. It defined it against Luther, who saw in the sacrifice of the Mass a threat to the belief in the singularity and uniqueness of the sacrifice of Christ. In fact, we see today that the sacrifice of the Mass is the real bastion of this belief. Only since the sacrificial character of the Mass has been called into question or thrust into the background within the Catholic Church, too, do we now find a growing number of theologians denying that the death of Christ was a sacrifice."

13   *Ministerial and Common Priesthood in the Eucharistic Celebration*. The Proceedings of the Fourth International Colloquium of Historical, Canonical and Theological Studies on the Roman Catholic Liturgy [Poissy, October 7–9, 1998] (London: CIEL UK, 1999).

spoken together by the priest and people but rather one after the other; the numerous prayers executed silently by the priest alone; the orientation of celebration emphasizing the priest's intermediary function; the differentiation between those who are ordained and those who are non-ordained in their manner of participation in the sacrifice of the Mass (*Orate, fratres, ut meum ac vestrum sacrificium*; *Hanc igitur oblationem servitutis nostrae, sed et cunctae familiae tuae*; *Unde et memores, Domine, nos servi tui, sed et plebs tua sancta*); the gestures during the consecration that copy Christ's actions and make the eternal High Priest recognizable in the figure of the celebrant; and finally the *Placeat tibi*, in which the priest himself, one last time, brings to mind the merit and importance of the sacrifice of the Mass he has offered — all of these things emphatically demonstrate the specific nature of his priesthood and oppose a reduction of the ordained officiant to a mere superintendent of the congregation.[14] Many phrases, even in the Roman Canon itself, demonstrate that the faithful are in no way excluded from participating in the liturgy and that the classical rite cannot be regarded as a merely clerical liturgy (*Memento, Domine, . . . et omnium circumstantium, pro quibus tibi offerimus, vel qui tibi offerunt*; *sed et cunctae familiae tuae*).

The hierarchical structure of Holy Orders, furthermore, not only appears in the texts,[15] but also in the ceremonial form of the classical liturgy. The "Mass with people" (*Missa cum populo*) in the parish is not the norm; the norm is the Papal Mass and Pontifical High Mass. All other ways of celebrating the Mass are thus derivative and reduced forms of that celebration in its complete form, so that many rituals become intelligible only in view of their descent from the richly embellished Pontifical High Mass. Thus even a "private Mass" ultimately bears the mark of the ideal form of the Catholic liturgy and preserves at least rudimentary elements of that model. In this way the unbroken continuity of the traditional rite is demonstrated, since through all historical developments it never relinquished its dependence on its origins.

---

14 Cf. K. Gamber, "Der Priester als Liturge," idem, *Fragen in die Zeit*, 163–67. A critical comparison with the MRom 1970 by May, *Die alte und die neue Messe*, 70.

15 Cf. Schmitz, "Aspects of the Ecclesiology of the *Missale Romanum*," 189–92.

The words of the Epistle to the Hebrews apply to each celebration of the liturgy: "But you are come to Mount Sion and to the city of the living God, the heavenly Jerusalem, and to the company of many thousands of angels, and to the church of the firstborn who are written in the heavens... and to the spirits of the just made perfect" (Heb 12:22f.).[16] The classical rite of the Mass repeatedly envisions this community of angels and saints by naming, venerating, and calling upon individual saints as intercessors, especially the Blessed Virgin. One sees this at the beginning of the *Asperges* prayer (... *mittere digneris sanctum Angelum tuum de caelis*), in the admission of guilt (*Confiteor Deo omnipotenti, beatae Mariae semper Virgini, beato Michaeli Archangelo, beato Joanni Baptistae, sanctis Apostolis Petro et Paulo, omnibus Sanctis*, and likewise in the second part of the prayer), at the kissing of the altar (*per merita Sanctorum tuorum, quorum reliquiae hic sunt, et omnium Sanctorum*), at the blessing of the incense (*per intercessionem beati Michaeli archangeli ... et omnium electorum suorum*), at the Offertory (*in honorem beatae Mariae semper Virginis, et beati Joannis Baptistae, et sanctorum Apostolorum Petri et Pauli, et istorum et omnium Santorum*), in the Canon (*Communicantes; Nobis quoque*), and after the Our Father in the *Libera nos* (*intercedente beata et gloriosa semper Virgine Dei Genetrice Maria, cum beatis Apostolis tuis Petro et Paulo atque Andrea, et omnibus Sanctis*).[17] In particular, the two series of saints' names, which appear in the Roman Canon before and after the consecration, present in their hierarchical arrangement (Apostles, first successors of Peter, bishops, priests, deacons, and laity) and variety (men and women, all professions and ages) an impressive image of the Church triumphant, with which the Church on earth reverentially understands herself to be in communion (*Communicantes et memoriam venerantes*).[18]

---

16   On the connection between the earthly and heavenly liturgy, cf. Gamber, *Kult und Mysterium*, 17–19, 56–62; idem, *Fragen in die Zeit*, 34–36, 44, 73; Peterson, *The Angels and the Liturgy*.

17   A critical comparison with the MRom 1970 by May, *Die alte und die neue Messe*, 68.

18   Cf. V.L. Kennedy, *The Saints of the Canon of the Mass* [Studi di antichità cristiana 14] (Vatican City: Pontificio istituto di archeologia cristiana, ²1963); E. Hosp, *Die Heiligen im Canon Missae* (Graz: Verlags-Buchhandlung Styria, 1926); D. Joly, *La messe expliquée aux fidèles* (Étampes: Éditions Clovis, ²1998), 378: "In the *Communicantes* and the *Nobis quoque peccatoribus* ... , the basic idea is faith and trust in the communion of saints: we are

This perspective, this view of the *Ecclesia triumphans*, strikingly calls to mind that the Church is always greater than those assembled in that moment for divine worship and that the true majority in the Church always possesses a diachronic character. The *sanctorale* of the *Missale Romanum* (1962) also establishes a strong presence of the saints over the course of the liturgical year, as feasts of many saints are included only in the traditional calendar,[19] and commemoration days of other saints are not degraded to a *memoria ad libitum*, thus being left to personal decision,[20] but rather occupy an obligatory place in the liturgical remembrance of the Church. The traditional liturgy admits of no *damnatio memoriae*. How little the veneration of the saints distracts the faithful's view from Christ and therefore requires a liturgical reduction is impressively demonstrated in a report from the mid-second century, when the Church of Smyrna announced the death of her bishop Polycarp in a letter: "For we worship Him (i.e., Christ) as the Son of God, while we love the martyrs as disciples and imitators of the Lord, for their unconquerable affection for their own King and Teacher."[21]

---

in communion with them, we honor their memory; we trust in their merits and prayers; we expect from their intercession the help of divine protection; we hope to be associated with them in the blessed life. All men redeemed by Jesus Christ form His kingdom. Whether they have already reached the end of their struggle, are still struggling on earth, or are expiating their faults in purgatory, there exists between the citizens of this unique city that is the Church an active commerce, an exchange of gifts and benefactions. The actions, the sufferings, the merits, the satisfactions, all the fruits of grace, are a common treasure everyone draws from and everyone contributes to."

19 Thus, e.g., Apollonia (Feb. 9), Gregory the Wonderworker (Nov. 17), as well as — no longer in the general Roman calendar, but only in the German calendar — Barbara, Christopher, Valentine, Catherine of Alexandria [until 2002, when she was reintroduced into the general calendar], and many others. *In toto*, over 300 saints were removed from the general calendar. Cf. P. Siffi, *La Messa di san Pio V* (Genoa / Milan: Marietti, 2007), 121f. E. Peterson, *Theologische Traktate* (Munich: Kösel-Verlag, 1951), 175 cautioned against the consequences of oblivion: "The bourgeoisification of Protestantism . . . is only the necessary consequence of the Protestant rejection of the cult of martyrs and saints."

20 Thus, e.g., the feast of the great Pope Pius V, who codified the so-called Tridentine Missal, in the MRom 1970. Cf. Ploeg, "'Neue' oder 'alte' Messe?," 478.

21 *Martyrium Polycarpi* 17,3 (A. Lindemann / H. Paulsen, *Die Apostolischen Väter* [Tübingen: J.C.B. Mohr / Paul Siebeck, 1992], 278–80 / *The Apostolic Fathers*, trans. by F.X. Glimm, J.M.F. Marique / G.G. Walsh, *The Fathers of the Church* 1 [New York, NY: Christian Heritage, Inc., 1946], 160).

THE MOST IMPORTANT
INSTRUMENT OF TRADITION

The traditional rite of the Mass proves itself to be a clear and complete testimony of the central truths of the Faith, a demonstration of the true Faith, so that the rule of prayer (*lex orandi*) at the same time presents an authentic rule of faith (*lex credendi*).[22] Not a single core element of the *depositum fidei* is concealed, diminished, or ambivalently formulated.[23] Unambiguous and unabbreviated, the traditional form of the Mass manifests that which the Church believes, has ever believed, and ever will believe. Accordingly, this liturgy is referred to as "tradition in its most powerful and solemn form,"[24] and as "the most important instrument of tradition."[25]

The celebration of the liturgy in its traditional form thus constitutes an effective counterweight for all levelings, reductions, dilutions, and banal-izations of the Faith. Many who are unfamiliar with the classical liturgy and are acquainted only with the re-created form believe that what they

---

22 Comparisons with the NOM in Barth, "*Nichts soll dem Gottesdienst vorgezogen werden,*" 18f., 37; May, *Die alte und neue Messe,* 72f.; C. Barthe, *La messe à l'endroit: un nouveau mouvement liturgique* (Paris: Éditions de l'Homme nouveau, 2010), 88; Siffi, *Messa di San Pio V,* 66f.

23 Cf. Pius VI's Constitution *Auctorem Fidei* (1794) and his criticism, referring to analogous cases, of the Synod of Pistoia (1786), which refrained from using the term "transubstantiation" (DH 2629): "29. The doctrine of the synod ..., inasmuch as, by this imprudent and suspicious omission, the knowledge of an article pertaining to the faith is removed as well as an expression consecrated by the Church to safeguard her profession of faith against heresies; and insofar as it is intended to lead to its oblivion as if it were a matter of a merely scholastic question: <is> pernicious, derogatory to the exposition of Catholic truth regarding the dogma of transubstantiation, <and> favorable to heretics."

24 Guéranger, *Institutions liturgiques* I, 3: "Liturgy is the tradition itself in its highest degree of power and solemnity." Critical of the new liturgical creations of the 17th/18th centuries, idem, *Institutions liturgiques* II, Paris: Sociéte générale de librairie catholique, ²1880, 239: "Until then, it was thought that the liturgy was the Tradition, and just as we do not handle the Tradition as we want, we do not handle liturgy either at will ..." Cf. C. Johnson, *Prosper Guéranger (1805–1875): A Liturgical Theologian. An Introduction to His Liturgical Writings and Work* [Studia Anselmiana 89 / Analecta liturgica 9] (Rome: Pontificio Ateneo Sant'Anselmo, 1984), 310–21; E. Guillou, "Dom Guéranger, docteur de la liturgie," *Itinéraires* 197/198 (1975): 69–106, 86–90.

25 J.-B. Bossuet, *Instruction sur les états d'oraison VI* [*Œuvres* 5] (Paris: Librairie catholique Martin-Beaupré, 1868), 464: "The main instrument of the Church's Tradition is contained in her prayers." Quoted in P. Guéranger, *Institutions liturgiques* IV (Paris [i.a.]: Sociéte générale de librairie catholique, ²1885), 342; further quotations from other authors ibid., 341–53. Cf. Congar, *Tradition & Traditions,* 427–35; *Catechism of the Catholic Church* (1993), No. 1124.

see and hear there is the entirety of the Faith. Scarcely anyone senses that central passages have been removed from biblical pericopes. Scarcely anyone notices if the Church's orations no longer expressly attack error, no longer pray for the return of those who have strayed, no longer give the heavenly clear priority over the earthly, make the saints into mere examples of morality, conceal the gravity of sin, and identify the Eucharist as only a meal. Scarcely anyone even knows what prayers the Church said over the course of centuries in place of the current "preparation of the gifts," and how these prayers demonstrated the Church's understanding of the Mass as a sacrifice, offered through the hands of the priest for the living and the dead.

The Church Father St Basil of Caesarea, during the mid-fourth century, described the serious dogmatic disputes of his time and related how certain members of the Church had broken with tradition, abandoning the traditional beliefs:

> The doctrines of the Fathers are despised; the traditions of the Apostles are set at nought; crafty inventions are introduced in the churches; ... the wisdom of the world (cf. 1 Cor 1:20) takes first place, the glory of the cross having been thrust aside. The shepherds are driven out, and in their places fierce wolves are brought in, who tear asunder the flock of Christ (cf. Acts 20:29). The houses of prayer are destitute of those who assembled there; the deserts, full of lamenting people. The older men grieve, comparing the former state with the present; the young are more to be pitied, being unaware of their deprivation.[26]

When one applies this description to the present, it captures the startling actuality—above all, its final sentence! Indeed, the number of those who are completely unaware that there once existed another "form" of the liturgy, and who know only the re-created form of the Mass, has irresistibly increased. The multitude of those who believe that the form of divine

---

26   Basil of Caesarea, *Epistula* 90,2 (Collection des Universités de France, 195f. / St Basil, *Letters*, vol. I: 1–185, trans. by A.C. Way, *The Fathers of the Church* 13 [Washington, DC: Catholic University of America Press, 1951], 199f.).

worship familiar to them contains substantially all that the Church believes and has always believed is continually increasing. On the contrary, whoever also becomes familiar with the traditional form of the Roman rite of the Mass will, over the course of the liturgical year, discover many feasts and many saints whose existence was formerly unknown to him, which he will not want to do without from that point on; he will hear countless words of which he perhaps knows nothing at all, which are also contained in the Bible and belong to the entire message of the Gospel; above all, he will experience—not only directly through the texts, but also owing to the entire form of the rite itself—that the Mass is much more than and altogether different from a mere remembrance meal, but that it is rather a sacrifice, the realization of the sacrifice of the Cross upon the Church's altar, celebrated by the angels in heaven and mankind on earth.

That the liturgical richness of the Church is much more comprehensive and far greater than that which the "ordinary form" (*forma ordinaria*) of the Roman rite is capable of manifesting has been repeatedly stressed in recent years. The expanded opportunities to celebrate the traditional rite of the Mass expressly seek to open up anew the treasures of tradition to *all* the faithful: "In a special way, it is a matter of making available to all the faithful the liturgical riches of the Church, and to do it in a way that those who have not yet seen them may discover these treasures of the Church's liturgical heritage."[27] The instruction *Universae Ecclesiae* fully

---

27 A. Card. Cañizares, "Préface de l'édition espagnole": N. Bux, *La réforme de Benoît XVI. La Liturgie entre innovation et tradition* [Annexe 2] (Perpignan: Édition Tempora, 2009), 199. K. Koch, "Zwei Formen des einen römischen Messritus. Liturgietheologische Hinführung zum Motu Proprio von Papst Benedikt XVI," IKaZ 36 (2007): 422–30, 423: "Pope Benedict is convinced that with the Roman liturgy that has evolved over the centuries, as found in the Roman Missal of 1962, the Church has been given a liturgical treasure that must not be lost, but should be preserved even for the future of the Catholic Church." D. Card. Castrillón Hoyos, "Wir müssen den Schatz ergreifen" (press conference and lecture given in London, June 14, 2008), *Rundbrief Pro Missa Tridentina* 35 (2009): 11–15, 12: "He (*sc.*, the pope) offers us this wealth, and it is very important for the new generation to know the past of the Church. This kind of worship is so noble and so beautiful—the greatest theologians have expressed our faith in it. The worship, the music, the architecture, the paintings—these elements form a whole of the highest value. The Holy Father wants to provide these means to all believers, not just to the few groups who ask for it, but so that all members in the Catholic Church know this way of celebrating the Eucharist."

explains the purposes of the motu proprio *Summorum Pontificum* in this sense: "The motu proprio... has the aim of giving to *all* the faithful the Roman liturgy in the *usus antiquior*, considered as a precious treasure to be preserved."[28] The appropriation of this liturgical heritage will be successful in the long term only if the traditional rite of the Mass as *lex orandi* is at the same time able to have a lasting influence on the *lex credendi* and is in turn thoroughly supported by it.[29]

Protecting the precious treasure of the traditional liturgy belongs to the preservation of the *depositum fidei*. The Apostle Paul admonished his student: "O Timothy, keep that which is committed to thy trust" (1 Tm 6:20). In timeless fashion, the early Christian priest and monk, St Vincent of Lérins, interpreted this apostolic instruction as applying to the preservation of the deposit of the faith and at the same time to the dimension of worship: "The Timothy of today is either, speaking generally, the Universal Church, or, in particular, the whole body of ecclesiastical superiors who ought to have for themselves and to administer to the people an integral knowledge of divine worship."[30] The traditional Mass is the expression, formed over centuries, of this unspoiled knowledge of divine worship, as well as its tried and true guarantor.

28 Pontifical Commission *Ecclesia Dei*, Instruction *Universae Ecclesiae* (May 13, 2011), No. 8a: "*Ipsae Litterae intendunt: a) Liturgiam Romanam in Antiquiori Usu, prout thesaurum servandum, omnibus largire* (recte: *largiri*) *fidelibus.*" On the correct translation of *largiri* as "giving" instead of the weaker "offering," which is found also in the official English version, cf. H.-L. Barth, "Eine Mahnung an die Bischöfe. Zur römischen Instruktion zur Feier der alten Messe," KU 14/6 (2011): 26–40, 27f.

29 M. Schneider, lecture given at the Philosophical-Theological Academy Brixen (Bressanone), March 16, 2009, 9: "Behind the 'old Mass' is not only a ceremony, but also a specific image of God and a specific understanding of faith and theology, as well as a definite understanding of art and religious practice (fasting, sobriety, confession, etc.). For the old Mass to enjoy a future in the parishes in times to come, it is necessary to introduce the faithful into its theology and the broad horizon in which it stands." Quoted in Conrad, "Ein Ritus in zwei Formen?," 256.

30 Vincent of Lérins, *Commonitorium* 22,2 (CCL 64, 176f. / Vincent of Lérins, *Commonitories*, 307f.): "*Quis est hodie Timotheus, nisi vel generaliter universa ecclesia vel specialiter totum corpus praepositorum, qui integram divini cultus scientiam habere vel ipsi debent vel aliis infundere?*"

Quotations from works or articles written in foreign languages are usually translated into English by the author, unless otherwise indicated.

List of Abbreviations

GENERAL ABBREVIATIONS

art.	articulus (= article)
cap.	caput (= chapter)
comm.	commentated
i.a.	inter alios / alia (= among others / other things)
MRom	Missale Romanum
n.	note (usually a footnote)
NOM	Novus Ordo Missae
prep.	prepared
s.a.	sine anno (= without year of publication, i.e., year of publication not indicated)
s.l.	sine loco (= without place of publication, i.e., place of publication not indicated)
s.n.	sine nomine (= without name)
s.p.	sine pagina (= without page, i.e., page not indicated)
SCR	Sacred Congregation of Rites

BIBLIOGRAPHICAL ABBREVIATIONS

AAS	Acta Apostolicae Sedis
BEL.P	Bibliotheca 'Ephemerides liturgicae'. Sectio practica
BEL.S	Bibliotheca 'Ephemerides liturgicae'. Subsidia
BenM	Benediktinische Monatsschrift
CCL	Corpus Christianorum, Series Latina
CCM	Corpus Christianorum, Continuatio Mediaevalis
CIC	Codex Iuris Canonici
CIEL	Centre International des Études Liturgiques
COD	Conciliorum Oecumenicorum Decreta
CSEL	Corpus scriptorum ecclesiasticorum latinorum
CT	Concilium Tridentinum
DACL	Dictionnaire d'archéologie chrétienne et de liturgie
DDC	Dictionnaire de Droit Canonique

DH	Enchiridion symbolorum, definitionum et declarationum de rebus fidei et morum: A Compendium of Creeds, Definitions, and Declarations on matters of faith and morals (Denzinger/Hünermann/Fastiggi/Nash; 43rd ed., San Francisco: Ignatius Press, 2012). The translations from the Council of Trent have sometimes been emended in light of *The Canons and Decrees of the Council of Trent*, trans. Rev. H. J. Schroeder, OP (Rockford, IL: TAN Books, 1978).
DS	Enchiridion symbolorum definitionum et declarationum de rebus fidei et morum (Denzinger/Schönmetzer)
EtLi	Études liturgiques
EL	Ephemerides Liturgicae
FC	Fontes Christiani
FKTh	Forum Katholische Theologie
GdK	Gottesdienst der Kirche. Handbuch der Liturgiewissenschaft
IKaZ	Internationale Katholische Zeitschrift
JAC.E	Jahrbuch für Antike und Christentum — Ergänzungsband
JLW	Jahrbuch für Liturgiewissenschaft
LJ	Liturgisches Jahrbuch
LO	Lex orandi
LQF	Liturgiegeschichtliche Quellen und Forschungen
LuM	Liturgie und Mönchtum
MD	La Maison-Dieu
MSIL	Monumenta Studia Instrumenta Liturgica
MThZ	Münchener Theologische Zeitschrift
NRTh	Nouvelle revue théologique
ParLi	Paroisse et liturgie
PG	Patrologia Graeca (Migne)
PL	Patrologia Latina (Migne)
PTS	Patristische Texte und Studien
QLP	Questions liturgiques et paroissiales
RAC	Reallexikon für Antike und Christentum
RBen	Revue bénédictine de critique, d'histoire et de littérature religieuses
RevSR	Revue des sciences religieuses
RivAC	Rivista di archeologia cristiana
RivLi	Rivista Liturgica
SC	Sacrosanctum Concilium
SCh	Sources Chrétiennes
SpicFri	Spicilegium Friburgense
SPLi	Studia patristica et liturgica
SSL	Spicilegium sacrum Lovaniense

List of Abbreviations

StPatr	Studia Patristica
Theoph.	Theophaneia
ThGl	Theologie und Glaube
UVK	Una Voce Korrespondenz
WA	Weimarer Ausgabe (D. Martin Luthers Werke)
ZKTh	Zeitschrift für Katholische Theologie

BIBLIOGRAPHY

EDITIONS

Missale Romanum. Editio princeps (1570). Edizione anastatica, Introduzione e Appendice a cura di M. Sodi / A.M. Triacca (Monumenta Liturgica Concilii Tridentini 2), Vatican City: Libreria Editrice Vaticana, 1998.

Missale Romanum anno 1962 promulgatum, reimpressio, introductione aucta, ed. by C. Johnson / A. Ward (Bibliotheca Ephemerides Liturgicae. Subsidia, Instrumenta Liturgica Quarreriensia, supplementa 2), Rome: C.L.V.-Edizioni Liturgiche, 1994.

Missale Romanum ex decreto SS. Concilii Tridentini restitutum Summorum Pontificum cura recognitum, editio typica 1962, Ratisbonae: Sumptis et Typis Friderici Pustet, 1962 (editio tertia iuxta typicam 1964).

Missale Romanum 1962, New York, NY: Benziger Brothers, 1962.

Missale Romanum ex decreto SS. Concilii Tridentini restitutum Summorum Pontificum cura recognitum, Vatican City: Libreria Editrice Vaticana, 2010.

Missale Romanum ex decreto SS. Concilii Tridentini restitutum. Summorum Pontificum cura recognitum. Editio iuxta typicam, Thalwil / Nördlingen: Priesterbruderschaft St Petrus, 2013.

LITURGICAL DOCUMENTS OF THE HOLY SEE

Megivern, J.J. (ed.), *Worship & Liturgy* (Official Catholic Teachings), Wilmington, NC: Consortium Book, 1978.

International Commission on English in the Liturgy (prep. by G. Fontaine, ed. and trans. by Th. C. O'Brien). A Joint Commission of Catholic Bishops' Conferences, *Documents on the Liturgy 1963–1979: Conciliar, Papal, and Curial Texts,* Collegeville, MN: Liturgical Press, 1982.

Seasoltz, R. Kevin (ed.), *The New Liturgy: A Documentation, 1903 to 1965,* New York, NY: Herder and Herder, 1966.

THE ROMAN RITE IN GENERAL

Aigrain, R. (ed.), *Liturgia. Encyclopédie populaire des connaissances liturgiques,* Paris: Bloud et Gay, 1930.

A Benedictine Monk (= G. Calvet OSB), *The Sacred Liturgy,* London: Saint Austin Press, 1999.

Braun, J., *Liturgisches Handlexikon,* Regensburg: Verlag J. Kösel & Verlag Friedrich Pustet, ²1924.

— idem, *Liturgia Romana: Eine Darstellung des römischen Ritus in lexikalischer Gestalt,* Hannover: Giesel, 1937.

Cassingena-Trévedy, F., *La liturgie: Art et métier*. Préface de Mgr R. Le Gall, Geneva: Ad Solem Éditions, 2007.

Eisenhofer, L., *Handbuch der katholischen Liturgik*, 2 vols. (I: Allgemeine Liturgik; II: Spezielle Liturgik), Freiburg i. Br.: Verlag Herder, ²1941/1942.

Gitton, M., *Initiation à la liturgie romaine*. Préface du Cardinal J. Ratzinger, Geneva: Ad Solem Éditions, 2003.

King, A.A., *Liturgy of the Roman Church*, London / New York / Toronto: Longmans & Green, 1957.

Kwasniewski, P., *Noble Beauty, Transcendent Holiness: Why the Modern Age Needs the Mass of Ages*. Foreword by M. Mosebach, Kettering, OH: Angelico Press, 2017.

Lang, U.M. (ed.), *The Genius of the Roman Rite: Historical, Theological, and Pastoral Perspectives on Catholic Liturgy* (Proceedings of the 11th international colloquium of CIEL, held in Merton College, Oxford from September 13 to 16, 2006), Chicago / Mundelein, IL: Hillenbrand Books, 2010.

Lechner, J. / Eisenhofer, L., *The Liturgy of the Roman Rite* (trans. by A.J. and E.F. Peeler from the 6th ed.; ed. by H.E. Winstone), Freiburg / London: Herder and Herder, 1961.

Le Vavasseur, L.-M. / Haegy, J.-A., *Manuel de liturgie et cérémonial selon le rite romain*, 17ᵉ éd. réfondue, corrigée et mise à jour par le P. Louis Stercky, 2 vols., Paris: Librairie Lecoffre J. Gabalda, 1940.

Mercier, G., *La liturgie, culte de l'église: Sa nature, son excellence, ses principes fondamentaux, ses éléments constitutifs. Le rôle des autres formes de dévotion*, Mulhouse: Éditions Salvator, 1961.

Mosebach, M., *The Heresy of Formlessness: The Roman Liturgy and Its Enemy*, revised and expanded ed., Brooklyn: Angelico Press, 2018.

Radó, P., *Enchiridion Liturgicum complectens theologiae sacramentalis et dogmata et leges iuxta novum codicem rubricarum*, 2 vols., Freiburg i. Br.: Verlag Herder, 1961.

Schmidt, H.A.P., *Introductio in liturgiam occidentalem*, Rome: Herder, 1960.

Shaw, J. (ed.), *The Case for Liturgical Restoration*, Brooklyn, NY: Angelico Press, 2019.

Sodi, M. / Toniolo, A. / Bruylants, P. (eds.), *Liturgia Tridentina. Fontes Indices Concordantia 1568–1962* (Monumenta liturgica piana 5), Vatican City: Libreria Editrice Vaticana, 2010.

Tamburini, S., *Il fascino della Liturgia Tradizionale*, Verona: Fede & cultura, 2009.

Thalhofer, V., *Handbuch der katholischen Liturgik*, 2 vols., Freiburg i. Br.: Verlag Herder, 1883–1890, ²1912.

HISTORY

Amiot, F., *History of the Mass*, trans. by L.C. Sheppard (Faith and Fact Books. Star Books 109), London: Burns & Oates, ²1966.

Batiffol, P., *Leçons sur la messe*, Paris: Librairie Lecoffre J. Gabalda, ⁹1941.

Bibliography

Botte, B., "Histoire des prières de l'ordinaire de la messe": B. Botte / C. Mohrmann (eds.), *L'ordinaire de la messe. Texte critique, traduction et études* (EtLi 2), Paris: Les éditions du Cerf / Louvain: Éditions de Abbaye du Mont César, 1953, 15–27.

Cabrol, F., *The Mass of the Western Rites*, trans. by C.M. Antony, London: Sands, 1934.

Crouan, D., *Histoire du missel romain*, Paris: Éditions Pierre Téqui, 1988.

Davies, M., *A Short History of the Roman Mass*, Charlotte, NC: TAN Books, 1997.

Denis-Boulet, N.M. / Boulet, R., *Eucharistie ou la messe dans ses variétés: Son histoire et ses origines*, Paris: Letouzey et Ane, 1953.

Fortescue, A., *The Mass: A Study of the Roman Liturgy*, London: Longmans, Green and Co., ⁵1953 (repr. Fitzwilliam, NH: Loreto, 2005).

Jungmann, J.A., *Missarum Sollemnia: Eine genetische Erklärung der römischen Messe*, 2 vols., Freiburg i. Br.: Verlag Herder, ⁵1962.

— idem, *The Mass of the Roman Rite: Its Origins and Development (Missarum Sollemnia)*, trans. by F.A. Brunner C.Ss.R., 2 vols., New York, NY: Benziger, 1951 (repr. Notre Dame, IN: Christian Classics, 2012).

King, A.A., *Liturgy of the Roman Church*, London / New York / Toronto: Longmans & Green, 1957.

Un moine de Fontgombault, *Une histoire de la messe. Introduite par deux conférences du cardinal Joseph Ratzinger à Fontgombault* (La Nef. Hors-série no 25 novembre 2009), Feucherolles: La Nef, 2009.

O'Brien, J., *History of the Mass and Its Ceremonies in the Eastern and Western Church*, New York: The Catholic Publication Society Co., ¹⁵1879.

Puniet, J. de, *The Mass: Its Origin and History*, trans. by the Benedictines of Stanbrook, London: Burns Oates & Washbourne Ltd., 1931.

Reid, Alcuin (ed.), *A Bitter Trial. Evelyn Waugh and John Carmel Cardinal Heenan on the Liturgical Changes*, rev. ed., San Francisco: Ignatius Press, 2011.

— idem, *The Organic Development of the Liturgy: The Principles of Liturgical Reform and Their Relation to the Twentieth-Century Liturgical Movement Prior to the Second Vatican Council*, San Francisco: Ignatius Press, 2005.

Righetti, M., *Manuale di storia liturgica* III. *L'eucaristia. Sacrificio (messa) e sacramento*, Milan: Àncora Editrice, ²1956.

Schuster, I., *The Sacramentary (Liber Sacramentorum): Historical and Liturgical Notes on the Roman Missal*, trans. by A. Levelis-Marke, 5 vols., London: Burns & Oates, 1924–1930.

EXPLANATIONS OF THE MASS
AND *MISSALE ROMANUM*

Barthe, C., *La messe. Une forêt de symboles. Commentaire allégorique ou mystique de la messe romaine traditionnelle avec indications historiques et rituelles*, Versailles: Via romana, 2011.

A Benedictine Monk (i.e. Gerard Calvet OSB), *Discovering the Mass*, trans. by J.P. Pilon, London: Saint Austin Press, 1999.

Brinktrine, J., *Die heilige Messe in ihrem Werden und Wesen*, ed. and introduced by P. Hofmann, Augsburg: Dominus Verlag, ⁵2015 (repr. of 3ᵗʰ ed. 1950).

Cassingena-Trévedy, F., *Te igitur. Le missel de saint Pie V. Herméneutique et déontologie d'un attachement*, Geneva: Ad Solem Éditions, 2007.

Chivré, B.-M. de, *The Mass of Saint Pius V: Spiritual and Theological Commentaries*, Winona: STAS Editions, 2010.

Croegaert, A., *Les rites et prières du saint sacrifice de la Messe. Plans pour sermons et leçons*, 3 vols. (I: La messe de catéchumènes; II: La messe des fidèles depuis l'offertoire jusqu'à la secrète; III: La messe des fidèles depuis la préface jusqu'à la fin), Malines: s.n., 1953/1954.

— idem, *The Mass: A Liturgical Commentary*, abridged trans. by J. Holland Smith, 2 vols. (I: The Mass of the Catechumens; II: The Mass of the Faithful), Westminster, MD: The Newman Press, 1958/1959.

Dunney, J.A., *The Mass*, Kansas City, MO: Angelus Press, 2007 (New York, NY: The MacMillan Company, 1924).

Gaudron, M., *Die Messe aller Zeiten. Ritus und Theologie des Meßopfers*, Altötting: Sarto-Verlag, 2006.

Gihr, N., *The Holy Sacrifice of the Mass: Dogmatically, Liturgically and Ascetically Explained* (trans. from the 6th German ed.), St Louis, MO / London: Herder, 1949 (New York, NY: CreateSpace Independent Publishing Platform, 2015).

Guéranger, (Dom) P., *Explanation of the Prayers and Ceremonies of Holy Mass*, trans. by L. Shepherd, published as *The Traditional Latin Mass Explained*. Foreword by P. Kwasniewski. Brooklyn: Angelico Press, 2017.

Jackson, J.W., *Nothing Superfluous: An Explanation of the Symbolism of the Rite of St Gregory the Great*, Lincoln, NB: Redbrush, 2016.

Joly, D., *La messe expliquée aux fidèles*, Étampes: Éditions Clovis, ²1998.

Lebbe, B., *The Mass: A Historical Commentary*, Dublin: Brown and Nolan, 1948.

Le Brun, P., *Explication de la messe* (LO 9), Paris: Les éditions du Cerf, 1949.

Lefebvre, M., *The Mass of All Time: The Hidden Treasure*, Kansas City, MO: Angelus Press, 2007.

Le livre de la Messe. Mysterium fidei. Le texte de la Messe de saint Pie V. Présenté par Mgr Marcel Lefebvre. Commenté par Dom Guillou. Accompagné des images du Saint Sacrifice et des prières du Propre, Paris: Société de production littéraire, 1975.

Moorman, G.J. / Schmitz, R.M., *The Latin Mass Explained: Everything Needed to Understand and Appreciate the Traditional Latin Mass*, Rockford, IL: TAN Books, 2007.

N.N., *Introibo ad altare Dei: La Messe commentée*, Fontgombault: Association Petrus a Stella, 1992.

Parsch, P., *The Liturgy of the Mass* (trans. and adapted by H.E. Winstone. Introduction by C. Howell), London / St Louis, MO: Herder, ³1961.

Bibliography

Pinsk, J. / Perl, C.J., *Das Hochamt. Sinn und Gestalt der Hohen Messe*, Salzburg / Leipzig: Verlag Friedrich Pustet, 1938.

Ramm, M., *Zum Altare Gottes will ich treten: Die Messe in ihren Riten erklärt*, Thalwil: Haus Maria Königin [i.a.], ⁵2011.

Theological and Historical Aspects of the Roman Missal: The Proceedings of the Fifth International Colloquium of Historical, Canonical and Theological Studies on the Roman Catholic Liturgy (Versailles Novembre 1999), Kingston & Surbiton: CIEL UK, 2000.

THE EUCHARIST IN GENERAL

Barth, H.-L., *Die Messe der Kirche: Opfer — Priestertum — Realpräsenz*, Tremsbüttel: Una Voce Edition, 2016.

Brillant, M. (ed.), *Eucharistia. Encyclopédie populaire sur l'eucharistie*, Paris: Bloud et Gay, 1941 (¹1934).

Corblet, J., *Histoire dogmatique, liturgique et archéologique du sacrament de l'eucharistie*, 2 vols., Paris / Bruxelles / Genève: Société Générale de Librairie Catholique, ²1885/86 (¹1881/1882).

Hedley, J.C., *The Holy Eucharist*, London / New York: Longmans, Green, 1911 (¹1907).

Jourdain, Z.-C., *La Sainte Eucharistie: Somme de théologie et de prédication eucharistiques*, 4 vols. (I: Théologie eucharistique. De l'eucharistie comme sacrement; II: Théologie eucharistique. De l'eucharistie comme sacrifice; III: Culte et dévotion. Du culte liturgique rendu par l'Église au très saint sacrement; IV: Culte et dévotion. Dévotion envers la Sainte Eucharistie objet et pratique), Paris: Hippolyte Walzer, Libraire-Éditeur, 1897–1901.

Piolanti, A. (ed.), *Eucaristia: Il mistero dell'altare nel pensiero e nella vita della chiesa*, Rome / Paris / Tournai / New York, NY: Desclée de Brouwer, 1957.

— idem, *Il Mistero Eucaristico*, Vatican City: Libreria Editrice Vaticana, ⁴1996.

THE RUBRICS

Bukovec, P., «*Rubricarum Instructum*»: Die Rubrikenreform Papst Johannes' XXIII. im Vorfeld des Konzils: S. Heid (ed.), *Operation am lebenden Objekt. Roms Liturgiereformen von Trient bis zum Vaticanum II*, Berlin: be.bra-wissenschaft-verlag, 2014, 185–98.

Bourbon, A., *Introduction aux cérémonies romaines ou notions sur le matériel, le personnel et les actions liturgiques, le chant, la musique et la sonnerie*, Luçon: Impr. de F. Bideaux, 1864.

Bouvry, G.F.J., *Expositio Rubricarum Breviarii, Missalis et Ritualis Romani. Cum adnotationibus de origine, ratione ac sensu mystico rubricarum, caeremoniarum et festorum in IV partes distributa*, 2 vols. (I, p. 1: De rubricis in genere; I, p. 2: Expositio rubricarum tam generalium, quam specialium breviarii Romani; II, p. 3: De missali Romano; II, p. 4: De rituali Romano), Paris: Éditions Casterman, 1857/59.

Fortescue, A. / O'Connell, J.B. / Reid, A., *The Ceremonies of the Roman Rite Described*. Revised and updated in the light of Pope Benedict XVI's *Summorum Pontificum*, London / New York, NY: Continuum International Publishing Group, [15]2009 (London: Burns, Oates and Washbourne, [1]1917).

Gasparri, P., *Tractatus canonicus de Sanctissima Eucharistia*, 2 vols., Paris / Lyon: Delhomme et Briguet, 1897.

Hartmann, Ph. / Kley, J., *Repertorium Rituum: Zusammenstellung der rituellen Vorschriften für die bischöflichen und priesterlichen Funktionen*, Paderborn: Verlag Ferdinand Schöningh, [14]1940.

Kieffer, G., *Rubrizistik oder Ritus des katholischen Gottesdienstes nach den Regeln der heiligen römischen Kirche*, Paderborn: Verlag Ferdinand Schöningh, [9]1947.

Lane, J., *Notes on Some Ceremonies of the Roman Rite*, 2 vols., Dublin: Burns, Oates & Washbourne, [4]1948 / [3]1953.

McManus, F.R., *Handbook for the New Rubrics*, London: Geoffrey Chapman, 1961.

Müller, J.B. / Frei, E., *Riten- und Rubrikenbuch: Für Priester und Kandidaten des Priestertums*, Freiburg / Basel / Wien: Verlag Herder, [24]1961.

Murphy, P.L., *The New Rubrics of the Roman Breviary and Missal*: Translation and Commentary, Sydney: Catholic Press Newspaper Co., 1960.

Mutel, A.Ph.M. / Freeman, P., *Les normes du rite romain en sa forme extraordinaire*: La Messe et l'Office. Code des rubriques du bienheureux Jean XXIII. Textes extraits du Missel et du Bréviaire romains avec introduction et traduction, Perpignan: Adoremus, 2008.

O'Connell, J.B., *The Celebration of Mass. A Study of the Rubrics of the Roman Missal* (Revised Throughout in Accordance with the New General Rubrics of the *Codex Rubricarum* [1960] and the Typical Edition of the Roman Missal [1962]), Milwaukee, WI: Bruce, [4]1964; repr. Boonville, NY: Preserving Christian Publications.

— idem, *Simplifying the Rubrics of the Roman Breviary and Missal: Text of the Decree "Cum Nostra" (23rd March, 1955)*, with an English version and a commentary, London: Burns & Oates, 1955.

— idem, *The Rubrics of the Roman Breviary and Missal: The General Decree "Novum Rubricarum" of S.C.R., 26 July 1960*. With an English translation, London: Burns & Oates, 1960.

Sacra Congregatio Rituum, "Decretum generale, quo novus rubricarum Breviarii ac Missalis Romani codex promulgatur": AAS 52 (1960) 596–740.

Sacra Congregatio Rituum, *Rubricae Breviarii et Missalis Romani et documenta adnexa, cum indice analytico*, Vatican City: Typis Polyglottis Vaticanis, 1960.

Trimeloni, L., *Compendio di Liturgia pratica*. Terza edizione aggiornata e ampliata a cura di P. Siffi. Prefazione di S.E. il Card. Dario Castrillón Hoyos, Milan: Marietti, [3]2007 (repr. 2010; [2]1963, [1]1958).

Bibliography

LITURGICAL YEAR

Denis-Boulet, N.M., *The Christian Calendar*, trans. by P.J. Hepburne-Scott, London: Burns & Oates, 1960.

Guéranger, Dom P., *The Liturgical Year*, trans. by L. Shepherd, 11 vols., Dublin: Duffy, [1]1868–1901 (repr. 15 vols., Fitzwilliam, NH: Loreto Publications, 2013).

Hanon de Louvet, R., *En marge du Missel Romain: Commentaire historico-liturgique du Propre du Temps*. Préface de M. le Chanoine P. Halflants, Wetteren: Jules de Meesters et Fils, 1929.

Kellner, K.A.H., *Heortologie oder die geschichtliche Entwicklung des Kirchenjahres und der Heiligenfeste von den ältesten Zeiten bis zur Gegenwart*, Freiburg i. Br.: Verlag Herder, [3]1911.

Kramp, J., *Messliturgie und Gottesreich. Darlegung und Erklärung der kirchlichen Messformulare* (Ecclesia orans VI–VIII), Freiburg i. Br.: Verlag Herder, [5-9]1922/23.

Lefebvre, G., *Méditations liturgiques illustrées*: Le Sanctoral, 2 vols., Bruges: Apostolat liturgique Abbaye de Saint-André / Paris: Société liturgique, 1932.

— idem, *Méditations liturgiques illustrées*: Le Temporal, 2 vols., Bruges: Apostolat liturgique Abbaye de Saint-André / Paris: Société liturgique, 1942.

Loehr, Ae., *The Mass Through the Year*, trans. by L.T. Hale, 2 vols., London: Longmans, Green / Westminster, MD: Newman Press, 1958–1959.

Milcarek, P., "Memory, Presence and Contemplation — The Feasts of our Lord in the Traditional Roman Missal": *The Presence of Christ in the Eucharist*. The Proceedings of the Sixth International Colloquium of Historical, Canonical and Theological Studies on the Roman Catholic Liturgy (Versailles November 2000), Kingston & Surbiton: CIEL UK, 2001, 55–70.

Nilles, N., *Kalendarium manuale utriusque ecclesiae orientalis et occidentalis*, 2 vols. (I: Immobilia totius anni festa; II: Mobilia totius anni festa), Innsbruck: Typis et sumptibus Feliciani Rauch (K. Pustet), 1896/97.

Parsch, P., *The Church's Year of Grace*, trans. by W.G. Heidt, 5 vols., Collegeville, MN: Liturgical Press, 1953–1959 (2nd ed. 1962–1967).

Pascher, J., *Das liturgische Jahr*, Munich: Hueber, 1963.

Pinsk, J., *Gedanken zum Herrenjahr*, Mainz: Matthias-Grünewald-Verlag, 1963.

Stricker, S., "Das Heilige Jahr der Kirche": Abtei Maria Laach (ed.), *Die betende Kirche*, Berlin: St Augustinus-Verlag, [2]1927, 257–401.

— idem, "Das Kirchenjahr": *Mysterium. Gesammelte Arbeiten Laacher Mönche*, Münster: Aschendorff Verlag, 1926, 63–78.

Tyciak, J., *Jahreskranz der Güte Gottes: Das Jahr der Kirche*, Mainz: Matthias-Grünewald-Verlag, 1953.

ORIENTATION OF PRAYER

Davies, M., "Gemeinsam zum Herrn hin gewandt!": UVK 34 (2004) 326–41.

Fournée, J., "Missa versus Deum": UVK 9 (1979) 17–27, 85–96.

Gamber, K., *Zum Herrn hin! Fragen um Kirchenbau und Gebet nach Osten* (SPLi Beiheft 18), Regensburg: Verlag Friedrich Pustet, 1987.

— idem, "Celebrating the Mass *Versus Populum*: Liturgical and Sociological Aspects": idem, *The Reform of the Roman Liturgy: Its Problems and Background*, trans. by K.D. Grimm, San Juan Capistrano, CA / Harrison, NY: Una Voce Press [i.a.], 1993, 77–89.

— idem, "Celebration 'Turned Towards the People'": idem, *The Modern Rite. Collected Essays on the Reform of the Liturgy*, trans. by H. Taylor, Farnborough: Saint Michael's Abbey Press, 2002, 25–34.

Heid, S., "Gebetshaltung und Ostung in frühchristlicher Zeit": RivAC 82 (2006 [publ. 2007]) 347–404.

— idem, "Haltung und Richtung. Grundformen christlichen Betens": IKaZ 38 (2009) 611–19.

— idem, "Tisch oder Altar? Hypothesen der Wissenschaft mit weitreichenden Folgen": idem (ed.), *Operation am lebenden Objekt. Roms Liturgiereformen von Trient bis zum Vaticanum II*, Berlin: be.bra-wissenschaft-verlag, 2014, 351–74.

Lang, U.M., *Turning Towards the Lord: Orientation in Liturgical Prayer*, San Francisco: Ignatius Press, 2004.

Levatois, M., *La messe à l'envers: L'espace liturgique en débat: Essai*, Paris: Éditions Jacqueline Chambon, 2009.

— idem, *L'espace du sacré: Géographie intérieure du culte catholique*, Paris: Éditions de l'homme Nouveau, 2012.

Reinecke, M., "L'orientation de l'autel: histoire et théologie": *La Liturgie, Trésor de l'Église*. Actes du premier colloque d'études historiques, théologiques et canoniques sur le rite catholique romain (Notre-Dame-du-Laus Octobre 1995), Paris: CIEL, 1996, 187–217.

SACRED LANGUAGE

Barth, H.-L. (ed.), *Latein — Sprache der katholischen Kirche und des christlichen Abendlandes*, Jaidhof: Rex-Regum-Verlag, 2000.

Crouan, D., *La Messe en latin et en grégorien*, Paris: Éditions Pierre Téqui, 2006.

Doerner, A., *Sentire cum Ecclesia! Ein dringender Aufruf und Weckruf an Priester*, Mönchengladbach: Kühlen, 1941, 325–53.

— idem, "Die lateinische Kultsprache und die Gegner der Kirche": UVK 18 (1988) 216–37.

Gomez Gane, Y., « *Pretiosus Thesaurus* »: *La lingua latina nella Chiesa oggi*, Vatican City: Libreria Editrice Vaticana, 2009.

Lang, U.M., "Historische Stationen zur Frage der lateinischen Liturgiesprache": S. Heid (ed.), *Operation am lebenden Objekt. Roms Liturgiereformen von Trient bis zum Vaticanum II*, Berlin: be.bra-wissenschaft-verlag, 2014, 221–37.

— idem, *The Voice of the Church at Prayer: Reflections on Liturgy and Language*, San Francisco: Ignatius Press, 2012.

Lécureux, B., *Le Latin, langue de l'Église* (Nouv. éd. revue), Paris: Éditions Pierre Téqui, 1998.

— eadem, "Latein die Sakralsprache der römischen Kirche": UVK 31 (2001) 259–84.

Bibliography

Lentner, L., "Das geschichtliche Phänomen der Kultsprache": Th. Bogler (ed.), *Sakrale Sprache und kultischer Gesang. Gesammelte Aufsätze* (LuM 37), Maria Laach: Ars Liturgica Buch- und Kunstverlag, 1965, 37–61.

Manz, G., *Ausdrucksformen der lateinischen Liturgiesprache bis ins elfte Jahrhundert* (Texte und Arbeiten. Abteilung 1, Beiträge zur Ergründung des älteren lateinischen christlichen Schrifttums und Gottesdienstes, Beiheft 1), Beuron: Beuroner Kunstverlag, 1941.

Mohrmann, C., *Liturgical Latin: Its Origins and Character. Three Lectures*, Washington, DC: Catholic Univ. of America Press, 1957 (repr. London: Burns & Oates, 1959).

— eadem, "Notes sur le latin liturgique": eadem, *Études sur le latin des Chrétiens* II: Latin chrétien et médiéval, Rome: Edizioni di Storia e Letteratura, 1961, 93–107.

— eadem, "Die Rolle des Lateins in der Kirche des Westens": *Theologische Revue* 52 (1956) 1–18.

— eadem, "Sakralsprache und Umgangssprache": eadem, *Études sur le latin des Chrétiens* IV: Latin chrétien et latin médiéval, Rome: Edizioni di Storia e Letteratura, 1977, 161–74.

Schönberger, A., "Eine *apologia pro latinitate* aus Meisterhand": UVK 33 (2003) 294–318.

Viain, D., "Les langues liturgiques": *La Messe en question: autour du problème de la réforme liturgique, de la liturgie traditionnelle et réformée, le combat pour la messe*. Actes du Vᵉ congrès théologique de Sì Sì No No, Paris, 12–13–14 avril 2002, Versailles: Courrier de Rome, 2002, 339–80.

GREGORIAN CHANT

Apel, W., *Gregorian Chant*, London: Burns & Oates, 1958 (repr. Bloomington, IN: Indiana University Press, 1990).

Baron, L., *L'expression du chant grégorien. Commentaire liturgique et musical des messes des dimanches et des principales fêtes de l'année.* Lettre-préface de A. Le Guennant, 3 vols. (I–II: Le Temporal; III: Le Sanctoral), Plouharnel / Morbihan: Abbaye Sainte-Anne de Kergonan, 1947/1948/1950.

Charlier, H. and A., *Le chant grégorien*, Bouère: Éditions Dominique Martin Morin, ²1991.

Crouan, D., *La Messe en latin et en grégorien*, Paris: Éditions Pierre Téqui, 2006.

Ebel, B., "Der heilige Gesang der Kirche": Abtei Maria Laach (ed.), *Die betende Kirche. Ein liturgisches Volksbuch*, Berlin: St Augustinus-Verlag, ²1927, 403–21.

Gire, Y., *L'année grégorienne. Commentaire des chants du propre de la messe des dimanches et fêtes.* Préface par Dom Hervé Courau, Bouère: DMM, 2000.

Gröbler, B.K., *Einführung in den Gregorianischen Choral*, Jena: Verlag IKS Garamond, ²2005.

Hiley, D., *Gregorian Chant*, Cambridge: Cambridge Univ. Press, 2009.

Hodes, K., *Der Gregorianische Choral. Eine Einführung*, Langwaden: Bernardus-Verlag, ³1990 (Aachen: Patrimonium-Verlag, ⁵2012).

Hourlier, J., *Reflections on the Spirituality of Gregorian Chant* (New ed. / rev. and trans. by G. Casprini and R. Edmonson), Orleans, MA: Paraclete Press, 1995.

Pierik, M., *The Spirit of Gregorian Chant*, Boston, MA: B. Humphries, 1939 (repr. Whitefish, MO: Kessinger Publishing, 2010).

Pohl, R. (ed.), *Enchiridion Musicae Sacrae. Musica sacra in den Zeugnissen des Glaubens und der Kirche*, Aachen: Einhard, 2010.

Sandhofe, H.P., "Was ist Gregorianik?": UVK 29 (1999) 291–301.

Saulnier, D., *Gregorian Chant: A Guide to the History and Liturgy*, trans. by M. Berry, Brewster, MA: Paraclete Press, 2009.

Schönberger, A., "Der gregorianische Choral": UVK 20 (1990) 250–55.

Schola Saint Grégoire (ed.), *Saint Grégoire-le-Grand. Chant grégorien. Art et prière de l'Église. Historique de la Schola*. Préface du Cardinal Paul Poupard, Paris: Éditions Pierre Téqui, 2004.

Treacy, S., "Gregorian Chant": A. Reid (ed.), *T & T Clark Companion to Liturgy: The Western Catholic Tradition*, London / Oxford / New York, NY / New Delhi / Sydney: Bloomsbury T&T Clark, 2016, 239–57.

— eadem, *A Plain and Easy Introduction to Gregorian Chant*, Charles Town, WV: CanticaNOVA Publ., 2007.

Wagner, P., *Einführung in die gregorianischen Melodien. Ein Handbuch der Choralwissenschaft*, 3 vols. (I: Ursprung und Entwicklung der liturgischen Gesangsformen bis zum Ausgange des Mittelalters; II: Neumenkunde. Paläographie des liturgischen Gesanges; III: Gregorianische Formenlehre. Eine choralische Stilkunde), Leipzig: Breitkopf & Härtel, ³1911 (vol. I), ²1912 (vol. II), 1921 (vol. III) (repr. Hildesheim [i.a.]: Verlag Georg Olms [i.a.], 1962 and 1970).

RITUALITY AND SACRALITY

Lang, U.M., *Signs of the Holy One: Liturgy, Ritual and Expression of the Sacred*, San Francisco: Ignatius Press, 2015.

Liturgy and the Sacred. Proceedings of the Eighth International Colloquium of Historical, Canonical and Theological Studies on the Roman Catholic Liturgy (Versailles November 2002), London: CIEL UK, 2003.

THEOLOGY OF THE *MISSALE ROMANUM*
Orations

Bianchi, L., "A Survey of the Theology, History, Terminology, and Syntax in the Prayers of the Roman Missal," *Theological and Historical Aspects of the Roman Missal*, CIEL UK, 2000, 127–64.

Brou, L., *Les oraisons des dimanches après la Pentecôte: Commentaire liturgique* (ParLi 38), Bruges: Abbaye de Saint-Andre, 1959.

— idem, *Les oraisons dominicales: De l'Avent à la Trinité* (ParLi 50), Bruges: Abbaye de Saint-Andre, 1960.

Bibliography

Bruylants, P., *Les Oraisons du Missel Romain: Texte et Histoire*, 2 vols. (I: Tabulae synopticae fontium Missalis Romani. Indices; II: Orationum textus et usus juxta fontes) (EtLi 1), Louvain: Centre de documentation et d'information liturgiques, Abbaye du Mont César, 1952 (repr. 1965).

Capelle, B., "Commentaire des collectes dominicales du missel romain": idem, *Travaux liturgiques de doctrine et d'histoire I. Doctrine*, Louvain: Centre Liturgique, Abbaye du Mont César, 1955, 199–266.

Cappuyns, M., "La portée religieuse des 'Collectes'": *La Préparation de l'Eucharistie. De l'introït à l'offertoire* (Cours et conférences des semaines liturgiques VI), Louvain: Éditions de Abbaye du Mont César / Bruges: Desclée de Brouwer, 1928, 93–103.

Cekada, A., *Work of Human Hands: A Theological Critique of the Mass of Paul VI*, West Chester, OH: Philothea Press, 2010, 219–45.

Ellebracht, M.P., *Remarks on the Vocabulary of the Ancient Orations in the* Missale Romanum (Latinitas Christianorum primaeva 18), Nijmegen / Utrecht: Dekker & van de Vegt, ²1966.

Haessly, M.G., *Rhetoric in the Sunday Collects of the Roman Missal*: with introduction, text, commentary, and translation, Diss. Ursuline College for Women, Cleveland, OH / St Louis, MO: The Manufacturers Printery, 1938.

Martindale, C.C., *The Prayers of the Missal: The Text of the Prayers with a Devotional Commentary*, 2 vols. [I: The Sunday Collects; II: The Offertory Prayers and Post-Communions], New York, NY: Sheed & Ward, 1937–1938.

Olewinski, D.J., "Défense et propagation de la foi dans le missel tridentin": *Foi et liturgie*. Actes du septième colloque d'études historiques, théologiques et canoniques sur le rite romain. Préface de Mgr George Pell (Versailles Novembre 2001), Versailles: CIEL, 2002, 369–450.

Pflieger, A., *Liturgicae orationis concordantia verbalia*. Pars prima. Missale Romanum, Rome: Herder, 1964.

Pristas, L., *Collects of the Roman Missals: A Comparative Study of the Sundays in Proper Seasons Before and After the Second Vatican Council* (T&T Clark Studies in Fundamental Liturgy), London: Bloomsbury, 2013.

— eadem, "Theological Reflections that Guided the Redaction of the Roman Missal (1970)": *The Thomist* 67 (2003) 157–95.

Readings

Baudot, J., *The Lectionary, Its Sources and History* I-II, trans. and adapted by A. Cator, London: Catholic Truth Society / St Louis, MO: B. Herder, 1910.

Beissel, S., *Entstehung der Perikopen des römischen Meßbuches. Zur Geschichte der Evangelienbücher in der ersten Hälfte des Mittelalters* (Stimmen aus Maria Laach. Ergänzungsheft 96), Freiburg i. Br.: Verlag Herder, 1907 (repr. Rome: Herder, 1967).

Fortescue, A., "Gospel in the Liturgy": *The Catholic Encyclopedia* VI, New York, NY, 1909, 659–63.

Gamber, K., "Further Critical Observations Concerning the New Order of the Mass and the New Order of Readings": idem, *The Reform of the Roman Liturgy: Its Problems and Background*, San Juan Capistrano, CA: Una Voce Press [i.a.], 1993, 63–75, especially 69–75.

Godu, G., "Epîtres": DACL 5/1 (1922) 245–344.

— idem, "Évangiles": DACL 5/1 (1922) 852–923.

Kwasniewski, P., "The Reform of the Lectionary": A. Reid (ed.), *Liturgy in the Twenty-First Century: Contemporary Issues and Perspectives*, London / New York, NY: Bloomsbury T&T Clark, 2016, 287–320.

— idem, "Not Just More Scripture, But Different Scripture": Foreword to M.P. Hazell, *Index Lectionum: A Comparative Table of Readings for the Ordinary and Extraordinary Forms of the Roman Rite* (Lectionary Study Aids 1), s.l.: Lectionary Study Press, 2016, vii–xxix.

Ranke, E., *Das kirchliche Perikopensystem aus den ältesten Urkunden der römischen Liturgie dargelegt und erläutert. Ein Versuch*, Berlin: Reimer, 1847.

Sorci, P., "Il lezionario del Messale di Pio V": RivLi 95 (2008/1) [= Monografie di Rivista Liturgica: Celebrare con il Messale di San Pio V] 92–107.

N.N., "Das 'alte' und das 'neue' Lektionar: ein Vergleich": UVK 39 (2009) 113–33.

Offertory

Cekada, A., *Work of Human Hands: A Theological Critique of the Mass of Paul VI*, West Chester, OH: Philothea Press, 2010, 275–304.

Clark, A., "The Origin and Development of the Offertory Rite": EphLit 64 (1950) 309–44.

Coppens, J., "Les prières de l'offertoire et le rite de l'offrande": *La Préparation de l'Eucharistie. De l'introït à l'offertoire* (Cours et conférences des semaines liturgiques VI), Louvain: Éditions de Abbaye du Mont César / Bruges: Desclée de Brouwer, 1928, 185–96.

Fortescue, A., "Offertory": *The Catholic Encyclopedia* XI, New York, NY, 1911, 217–19.

Guérard des Lauriers, M.-L., "L'offertoire de la Messe": *Itinéraires* 158 (1971) 29–69.

Hauke, M., "Das Offertorium als Herausforderung liturgischer Reformen in der Geschichte": S. Heid (ed.), *Operation am lebenden Objekt. Roms Liturgiereformen von Trient bis zum Vaticanum II*, Berlin: be.bra-wissenschaft-verlag, 2014, 317–49.

Quoëx, F., "Historical and Doctrinal Notes on the Offertory of the Roman Rite": *Theological and Historical Aspects of the Roman Missal: The Proceedings of the Fifth International Colloquium of Historical, Canonical and Theological Studies on the Roman Catholic Liturgy* (Versailles 1999), Kingston & Surbiton: CIEL UK, 2000, 53–75.

Schönberger, A., "Das Offertorium": UVK 3 (1973) 103–12.

Tirot, P., *Histoire des prières d'offertoire dans la liturgie romaine du VIIe au XVIe siècle* (BEL.S 34), Rome: C.L.V.-Edizioni Liturgiche, 1985 (repr. 2007).

Bibliography

The Roman Canon

Le Canon de la Messe. De la préface à la communion (Cours et conférences des semaines liturgiques VII), Louvain: Éditions de Abbaye du Mont César / Bruges: Desclée de Brouwer et Cie, 1929, 135–208.

Botte, B., *Le Canon de la Messe Romaine. Edition critique, introduction et notes* (Textes et études liturgiques 2), Louvain: Éditions de Abbaye du Mont César, 1935 (repr. Louvain 1962).

Cabrol, F., "Canon Romain": DACL 2/2 (1925) 1847–1905.

Calmel, R.-Th., *Si tu savais le don de Dieu . . . I: La Messe* (Collection Veillez et Priez), Paris: Nouvelles Éditions Latines, 2007.

— idem, "Le Canon romain": *Itinéraires* 146 (1970) 149–55.

— idem, "Le Repas mystique": *Itinéraires* 146 (1970) 164–80.

— idem, "Apologie pour le Canon romain". *Itinéraires* 157 (1971) 19–35.

— idem, "Deuxième section: Maintenir le Canon romain": *Itinéraires* 157 (1971) 36–54.

— idem, "Le déroulement du Canon romain": *Itinéraires* 193 (1975) 100–7.

— idem, "Mahl und Opfer": UVK 1 (1970) 13–26.

Capelle, B., "L'évolution du *Qui pridie* de la messe romaine": idem, *Travaux liturgiques de doctrine et d'histoire*. Vol. II: Histoire, part 1: La messe, Louvain: Centre Liturgique, Abbaye du Mont César, 1962, 276–86 (first published: Recherches de théologie ancienne et médiévale 22 [1955] 5–16).

Fortescue, A., "Canon of the Mass": *The Catholic Encyclopedia* III, New York, NY, 1908, 255–67.

Gassner, J., *The Canon of the Mass: Its History, Theology and Art*, St Louis, MO / London: Herder, 1950 [2nd impr.].

Guillou, É., *Le canon romain et la liturgie nouvelle*, Escurolles: Éditions « Fideliter », 1989 (Escurolles: Éditions « Fideliter », ²1990).

Hasselberg-Weyandt, W., "Der Römische Kanon": FKTh 28 (2012) 266–82.

Jungmann, J.A., *The Eucharistic Prayer: A Study of the* Canon Missae, trans. by R.L. Batley, London: Challoner Publications, 1956.

Maertens, Th., *Pour une meilleure intelligence du canon de la messe* (ParLi 42), Bruges: Apostolat liturgique Abbaye de Saint-André, 1959.

Nicholls, G., "The History of the Prayers of the Roman Canon": *Theological and Historical Aspects of the Roman Missal*: The Proceedings of the Fifth International Colloquium of Historical, Canonical and Theological Studies on the Roman Catholic Liturgy (Versailles 1999), Kingston & Surbiton: CIEL UK, 2000, 29–52.

Scheeben, M.J., *Über die Eucharistie und den Messkanon. Zwei Aufsätze des Kölner Theologen aus den Jahren 1862 und 1866*, ed. and comm. by M. Stickelbroeck (Schriften der Philosophisch-Theologischen Hochschule Sankt Pölten 2), Regensburg: Verlag Friedrich Pustet, 2011, 50–128.

Schmitz, J., "Canon Romanus": A. Gerhards / H. Brakmann / M. Klöckener (eds.), *Prex Eucharistica* III: Studia, part 1: Ecclesia Antiqua et Occidentalis (SpicFri 42), Fribourg/ Switzerland: Academic Press, 2005, 281–310.

Schnitzler, Th., *The Mass in Meditation*, trans. by R. Kraus, vol. I, St Louis, MO: Herder, 1959.

— idem, *Der Römische Meßkanon in Betrachtung, Verkündigung und Gebet*, Freiburg i. Br.: Verlag Herder, 1968.

Sirot, P.-M., "Durch den Schleier hindurch Erklärung des Römischen Kanons": UVK 15 (1985) 217–32, 277–94, 331–49; UVK 16 (1986) 3–19.

— idem, *Par delà le voile. Illustration du canon romain* (Collection "Spiritualité, Doctrine, Expériences" 8), Paris: Eds. du Cédre, 1973.

Spinks, B.D., "The Roman *canon missae*": A. Gerhards / H. Brakmann / M. Klöckener (eds.), *Prex Eucharistica* III: Studia, part 1: Ecclesia Antiqua et Occidentalis (SpicFri 42), Fribourg/Switzerland: Academic Press, 2005, 129–43.

Williamson, H.R., *The Great Prayer: Concerning the Canon of the Mass*, London: Collins 1955 (repr. Herefordshire: Gracewing, 2009).

Spirituality

Bacuez, L., *Du divin Sacrifice et du prêtre qui célèbre* (3ᵉ ed. rev. et aug.), Paris: A & R. Roger et F. Chemoviz, 1904.

Chaignon, P., *The Sacrifice of the Mass Worthily Celebrated*, trans. by the most Rev. Louis de Goesbriand. With a preface and meditation aids by Dom Bede Babo, OSB, New York: Benziger Brothers, 1951 (repr. s.l.: Os Justi Press, 2018).

Dionysius Cartusianus, *Expositio Missae* (*Opera omnia* 35), Tournai: Typis Cartusiae S.M. de Pratis, 1908.

Wilhelm Durandus, *Rationale divinorum officiorum Der geistliche Sinn der göttlichen Liturgie*, Prolog und Buch IV (deutsch), eingeleitet u. übersetzt v. C. Barthold, Mülheim/ Mosel: Carthusianus Verlag, 2012.

Hildebrand, D. v., *Liturgy and Personality*, s.l.: The Hildebrand Project, 2016.

Olier, J.-J., *L'esprit des cérémonies de la messe. Explication des cérémonies de la grand'messe de paroisse selon l'usage romain*, Perpignan: Édition Tempora, 2009 (first ed. 1657).

Schnitzler, Th., *The Mass in Meditation*, trans. by R. Kraus, 2 vols., St Louis, MO: Herder, 1959–60.

Zundel, M., *The Splendour of the Liturgy*, trans. by E. Watkin, London: Catholic Book Club, 1939 (repr. New York, NY: Sheed & Ward, 1944).

Art

Hoppenot, J., *La Messe dans l'histoire et dans l'art, dans l'âme des saints et dans notre vie*, Lille / Paris: Société Saint-Augustin [i.a.], 1906.

Tea, E., "L'Eucaristia nell'arte": A. Piolanti (ed.), *Eucaristia. Il mistero dell'altare nel pensiero e nella vita della chiesa*, Rome / Paris / Tournai / New York, NY: Desclée de Brouwer, 1957, 1191–1204.

Vloberg, M., *L'eucharistie dans l'art, ouvrage orné de 202 héliogravures, couvertures et hors-texte, enluminures de R. Lanz*, 2 vols., Grenoble / Paris: B. Arthaud, 1946.

Bibliography

Summorum Pontificum

Aillet, M., *The Old Mass and the New: Explaining the Motu Proprio* Summorum Pontificum *of Pope Benedict XVI*, trans. by H. Taylor, foreword by Bishop D. Rey, San Francisco: Ignatius Press, 2010.

Barth, H.-L., *Hermeneutik der Kontinuität oder des Bruchs? Aspekte der Theologie Papst Benedikts XVI.*, Bobingen: Sarto-Verlag, 2012, 58–104.

Benedictus PP. XVI / Benedict XVI (pope), "Litterae Apostolicae Motu proprio datae Summorum Pontificum": AAS 99 (2007) 777–81.

— idem, "Epistula ad Episcopos Catholicos Ecclesiae Ritus Romani Epistola ad Episcopos ad producendas Litteras Apostolicas motu proprio datas, de Usu Liturgiae Romanae Instaurationi anni 1970 praecedentis" / "Letter of His Holiness Benedict XVI to the Bishops on the occasion of the publication of the Apostolic Letter 'Motu Proprio data' *Summorum Pontificum* on the use of the Roman liturgy prior to the reform of 1970 (July 7, 2007)": AAS 99 (2007) 795–99.

Graulich, M. (ed.), *Zehn Jahre Summorum Pontificum. Versöhnung mit der Vergangenheit Weg in die Zukunft*, Regensburg: Verlag Friedrich Pustet, 2017.

Kwasniewski, P.A., *Resurgent in the Midst of Crisis: Sacred Liturgy, the Traditional Latin Mass, and Renewal in the Church*, foreword by J. Robinson, Kettering, OH: Angelico Press, 2014.

May, G., "Die Instruktion 'Universae Ecclesiae' der Päpstlichen Kommission 'Ecclesia Dei'": UVK 41 (2011) 233–44.

Mosebach, M., "Das alte römische Meßbuch zwischen Verlust und Wiederentdeckung": UVK 40 (2010) 9–20.

— idem, "Zurück zur Form. Das Schicksal des Ritus ist das Schicksal der Kirche": UVK 47 (2017) 206–14.

Pontificia Commissio Ecclesia Dei, "Instructio 'Universae Ecclesiae', ad exsesequendas exsequendas Litteras Apostolicas Summorum Pontificum a S. S. Benedicto PP. XVI Motu Proprio datas / Instruction on the application of the Apostolic Letter *Summorum Pontificum* of His Holiness Benedict XVI given Motu Proprio": AAS 103 (2011) 413–20.

Rehak, M., *Der außerordentliche Gebrauch der alten Form des Römischen Ritus. Kirchenrechtliche Skizzen zum Motu Proprio* Summorum Pontificum *vom 07.07. 2007* (MThS.K 64), St Ottilien: Eos Verlag, 2009.

Rothe, W.F., *Liturgische Versöhnung. Ein kirchenrechtlicher Kommentar zum Motu proprio "Summorum Pontificum" für Studium und Praxis*. Mit einem Vorwort des Vize-Präsidenten der Päpstlichen Kommission "Ecclesia Dei," Augsburg: Dominus-Verlag, 2009.

Siffi, P., *La Messa di San Pio V. Osservazioni sul rito tridentino in risposta ai critici del Motu Proprio* (I rombi, nuova serie 51), Genoa / Milan: Marietti, 2007.

Stegherr, M., *Die Renaissance der katholischen Tradition. Die Reform der Reform Benedikts XVI. und die Gemeinschaften der Tradition*. Mit einem Vorwort von A. Wollbold, Heimbach/Eifel: Patrimonium-Verlag, 2015, 311–435.

Weishaupt, G., *Päpstliche Weichenstellungen. Das Motu Proprio Summorum Pontificum Papst Benedikts XVI. und der Begleitbrief an die Bischöfe. Ein kirchenrechtlicher Kommentar und Überlegungen zu einer "Reform der Reform,"* Bonn: Verlag für Kultur und Wissenschaft, 2010.

Woods, Th.E., *Sacred Then and Sacred Now: The Return of the Old Latin Mass*, Fort Collins, CO: Roman Catholic Books, 2008.

INDICES

The Biblical quotations are from the *Douay-Rheims Bible*, Fitzwilliam, NH: Loreto, 2007, which bases its numbering on the Vulgate. The Missal quotations are taken from *The Daily Missal and Liturgical Manual*, London: Baronius Press, 2011.

Index of Persons

Index of Subjects

Indices

Jerusalem, 15, 62, 97, 132, 141, 144, 287

Jerusalem, heavenly, 138, 189, 222, 236, 276, 299

Judgment, 137n25, 247, 248n48, 254n13

Judica me, 40, 53, 76

Kingship of Christ, 100, 132n12, 239, 243

Kyrie, 9, 15, 62, 83–85

Last Blessing, 32, 38n94, 123

Last Gospel, 30, 40, 46n7, 53, 64, 86, 123–25, 206, 209n45

Last Supper, 4, 104, 143–44, 153, 208, 211n50, 261, 273, 278

Latin, 39, 153–78, 185, 284

Latinization, 156–58, 264

Lectionary, 38, 237, 251–54

Lent (*Quadragesima*), 86, 100, 121, 128–29, 131, 134, 136–37, 240n5, 241

Lex orandi, 36n83, 211, 261, 293–304

Literature (sacred, profane), 49, 62n29, 175

Locus theologicus, 184, 198, 257, 295–300

Low Mass, 10, 49n16, 69–72, 88n33, 89, 125, 205n38, 228

Martyrs, 18, 48, 85, 89, 103, 105, 130, 300

Meal, 4–5, 59, 143–44, 149, 150n32, 261, 302–3

Mediator Dei, encyclical letter, 59n21, 71n10, 73n17, 142n7, 159n27, 161, 167n51, 172n68, n70, 186n126, 204n33, 210, 225, 226n98, n99, 228n104, 230n119, 294n6

Memento, 103–4, 105n86, 266n19, 273, 297–98

Merits, 103, 105, 245–47, 277n65, 300n18

Middle Ages, 17–20, 24, 28, 59, 63, 105–6, 129n5, 132, 147, 160, 169, 177, 211, 268

Milan, 15, 17, 22, 33–34, 280

Missal (Roman), xiii, 24, 26, 38–41, 194–95, 197, 236

Missale Romanum (1570), 14, 27–41, 44, 52, 55n10, 61, 71, 198, 216n63, 236–37, 251, 254

Missale Romanum (1962), 13, 40–41, 43, 52, 54, 61n24, 71, 100, 251, 254, 303n27

Minister/acolyte, 10, 64, 69–72, 74–75, 78–79, 83, 95, 113–14, 117, 125, 129, 205–6

Monasticism, 21, 28, 59, 62

Mysterium (Mystery of Faith), 152, 154, 159, 162, 164–65, 257, 279n70, 280, 279–80, 286–87

Mystery of the feast, 83, 88, 91, 99, 133, 255

Mythology, 248n49, 249

Neo-Gallican Liturgy, 34, 55, 271n41

Nobis quoque peccatoribus, 79, 103, 105, 108, 299n18

Notion of sacrifice, 7, 256–62, 269

Oblation, 94, 98, 256n5

Octave, 40, 92n47, 122, 128, 130n7, 132–33,

Offerimus tibi, 255, 257–60, 272, 274

Offertory, 19, 21, 31, 33, 46n7, 53, 94–96, 119, 174, 183, 207, 210n46, 255–62, 277, 296

Oration, 15, 43, 87–89, 164n42, 236, 239–50, 302

Ordo Romanus primus, 14, 18, 20, 54, 69

Pall, 71, 95, 105n87, 217

Participatio actuosa, 87n27, 165, 186, 225–31

Particles, 112, 113n111, 114n114, 117–18, 216–17, 230n116

Paten, 71, 95, 105n87, 108–9, 112–14, 117–18, 204, 209, 216, 258

Pater Noster, 43, 71n10, 107–8, 199

Pax, see Greeting/kiss of peace

People, 9, 26, 59, 61n23, 72, 73n16, 74n20, 75, 77–80, 93, 98, 104n84, 106–7, 121–23, 141–43, 146–49, 151n38, 166–67, 172, 224n92, 225, 249, 288, 293–94

Pericope, 43, 251–54

Per quem haec omnia, 105, 209n45, 281

Pistoia, Synod of, 56, 171–72, 301n23

Placeat tibi, 122–23, 296–8

329

About the Author

MICHAEL FIEDROWICZ, born in Berlin in 1957, is a Roman-Catholic priest of the archdiocese of Berlin. He studied Theology, Philosophy, Latin Philology, and Patristics at Berlin, Paderborn, and Rome universities. Since 2001 he has been Professor of History of the Early Church, Patrology, and Christian Archeology at the Theological Faculty of Trier. His many works include *Apology in Early Christianity*, *Theology of the Church Fathers*, *Handbook of Patristics*, and *Ecclesia militans*.

CPSIA information can be obtained
at www.ICGtesting.com
Printed in the USA
BVHW041608150323
660505BV00005B/467/J

9 781621 385240